AN ECONOMIC HISTORY
OF SCOTLAND
1100–1939

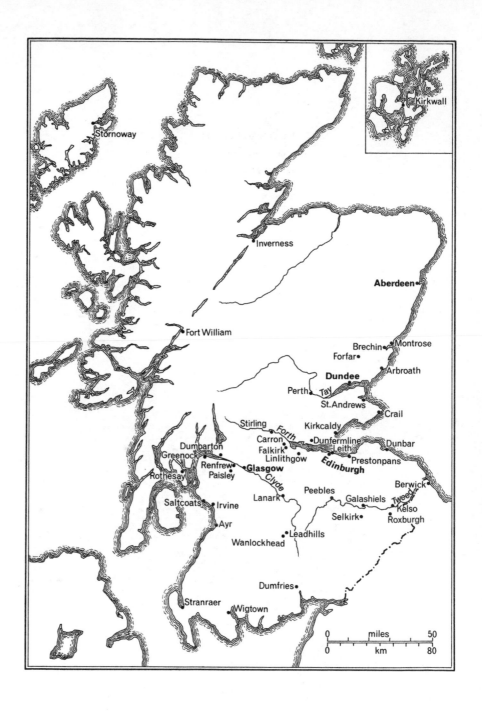

Stornoway

Kirkwall

Inverness

Aberdeen

Fort William

Brechin • Montrose
Forfar •
Dundee • Arbroath
Perth • Tay
St.Andrews
Crail

Stirling • Kirkcaldy
Forth • Dunfermline • Dunbar
Dumbarton Carron • Leith
Greenock Falkirk • Prestonpans
Renfrew • Linlithgow **Edinburgh**
Rothesay Paisley **Glasgow**
Clyde
Saltcoats • Lanark Peebles Berwick
Irvine Galashiels Tweed
Ayr Selkirk • Kelso
Roxburgh
Leadhills
Wanlockhead

Dumfries •

Stranraer Wigtown

miles
0 ⊢⊢⊢⊢⊢⊢ 50
0 ⊢⊢⊢⊢⊢⊢ 80
km

An
ECONOMIC HISTORY
of
SCOTLAND
1100–1939

S. G. E. Lythe
and J. Butt

BLACKIE
Glasgow & London

Published by Blackie and Son Limited
Bishopbriggs, Glasgow G64 2NZ
5 Fitzhardinge Street
London W1H 0DL

ISBN 0 216 90065 4

Printed by Thomson Litho Ltd., East Kilbride, Scotland

Preface

In Scotland down to World War II the promotion of economic history in general was largely bereft of institutional support. In the universities the discipline was represented—at best—by a single lecturer, operating in the somewhat nebulous area between History and Political Economy and contributing optional classes at a relatively elementary level. In the schools it was unknown. It is hardly surprising, therefore, that the major pre-1939 contributions came either from academics holding posts in bigger departments or from scholarly enthusiasts outside the universities. But they were so rare that the works by Professor Scott, Professor Hamilton, Dr Grant and Mr Marwick were virtually the only reasonably modern books directly bearing on the economic history of Scotland.

By contrast the subject has been arousing increasing interest within Scotland in the past generation. The evidences abound on every hand: the establishment of university professorships and full-scale departments, the changing balance of the articles in the *Scottish Historical Review* and in the publications of the Scottish History Society, the growing abundance of relevant archival material both in the Scottish Record Office and in local collections, the interest—both public and academic—in the relics of the economic past, and the appearance of Economic History in the school curriculum leading to examinations at the Ordinary and Higher grade. Given this vastly increased institutional and public support, it would have been disgraceful if the output of academic research and publication had not responded. The references and suggestions for further reading relating to each chapter in this book will give some indication of the literature now available for the more advanced student and general reader.

But it would be idle to pretend that gaps do not remain, or that, at many points, we have written with any real hope of being definitive. Rather would we like to think that we have given a reasonably accurate introduction to our subject in the present state of knowledge, and where we are conscious of ignorance we have not tried to disguise it.

As far as possible we have eschewed jargon for the sake of clarity—sometimes, it might be argued, at the cost of economy in language. We would like to think that our colleagues in universities and schools will forgive our temerity in making under-qualified generalisations about matters of daunting controversy. Our excuses are the narrow compass set by the length of this book and our desire to stimulate interest in our subject. Because our treatment of it is broadly thematic, we have often been concerned with showing how economic historians think rather than with trying to load the book with a comprehensive factual treatment of every possible topic.

A division at 1707 happened to coincide with our individual areas of interest and has certain merits even in the study of economic affairs, but because neither the strengths nor the weaknesses of post-Union Scotland can be understood without reference to earlier times we hope that the book is sufficiently cohesive to justify the time-span we have included in it.

We are grateful for help to our colleagues in the Department of History in the University of Strathclyde, in particular to Dr T. M. Devine who shares in the teaching of the subject and who read the typescript and made a number of helpful suggestions. The typing and—we regret to admit—often the retyping of the manuscript was undertaken cheerfully (or so we hope) by Mrs Buchanan, Mrs Thrippleton, Miss Hewitt and Miss Kelly.

University of Strathclyde   S.G.E.L.
1975   J.B.

Contents

Preface   *page* v

PART ONE: BEFORE THE UNION

I	The State of the Population before 1707	3
II	The Land and Land Utilisation	15
III	The Burghs	27
IV	Industry before 1707	39
V	Fishing and Overseas Trade	52
VI	The State and Economic Life	70

PART TWO: SINCE THE UNION

VII	Population and Economic Growth 1707–1871	87
VIII	Agriculture and Economic Growth 1707–1871	108
IX	Commerce and Credit 1707–1871	136
X	The Rise of Industry 1707–1871	161
XI	Scotland in the International Economy 1870–1939	201

Appendices	243
Further Reading, Notes and References	257
Index	287

List of Tables

1 Estimates of the population of Scotland *c.* 1100–*c.* 1600 *page* 4
2 The ten most populous counties 1755   88
3 Urban populations *c.* 1755   88
4 The ten most populous counties 1871   94
5 Percentage regional distribution of population 1755–1871   95
6 Percentage of population in different age-groups 1755–
     1871   106
7 Percentage of population in different occupations 1871   106
8 Prices allowed for cattle in lieu of rent 1729–49   112
9 Livestock numbers 1814–68   114
10 Arable crop acreages in Fife 1800   120
11 Cereal crop acreages 1814–68   123
12 Exports of grain from Scotland 1707–52   128
13 Spirits exported to England 1780–1820   129
14 Quantities of malt charged for duty 1810–40   131
15 Tobacco imports and re-exports 1755–75   147
16 Distribution, depositors and deposits of savings banks
      1839   157
17 Denomination of savings and average deposits 1839   158
18 Capital of Scottish savings banks 1845–70   158
19 Insurance valuations for Scottish businesses 1790–1800   173
20 Sizes of cotton-spinning firms according to insurance
      valuations *c.* 1795   174
21 Distribution of cotton firms *c.* 1795   187
22 The Scottish iron industry: output and capacity 1780–
      1840   192
23 Furnaces and output 1840–70   194
24 Capital raised by Scottish railway companies 1825–70   196

25	Cereal prices 1870–1939	*page* 206
26	Acreage of crops and grasses 1870–1939	207
27	Arable crop acreages 1870–1939	207
28	Livestock numbers 1870–1939	208
29	An index of agricultural prices 1927–39	213
30	Gross output of British agriculture 1908–39	214
31	Gross valuation of Scottish output 1907–35	215
32	Scottish steel production 1885–1900	215
33	Major categories of production by value and employment 1907	217
34	Shipbuilding output and Scottish share of UK output 1882–1938	219
35	Housebuilding in Scotland 1929–39	225
36	Number of shops in Aberdeen 1861–1938	228
37	Trade through Scottish ports 1900–38	231
38	Number of bank branches in Scotland 1870–1939	234
39	Estimates of British capital abroad 1870–1914	235
40	Estimates of Scottish foreign investment 1870–1914	236
41	Returns on investments in selected American land and cattle companies	238

List of Abbreviations

Except where obvious, the only abbreviations used throughout are the following:

BPP	:	British Parliamentary Papers
Cmd	:	Command Paper
EcHR	:	Economic History Review
GCA	:	Glasgow City Archives
OSA	:	Old Statistical Account
NSA	:	New Statistical Account
SGM	:	Scottish Geographical Magazine
SHR	:	Scottish Historical Review
SJPE	:	Scottish Journal of Political Economy
SRO		Scottish Record Office
TSA	:	Third Statistical Account

PART 1

BEFORE THE UNION

CHAPTER I

The State of the Population before 1707

IT IS hard to conceive of any topic in Scottish economic history about which greater uncertainty prevails. Apart from such local and specialised counts as the number of burgesses attending a town meeting, the number of men mobilised for a Border foray, or the number of baptisms recorded in a single town in an isolated period, virtually no early statistics of direct demographic value have survived. Historians have therefore been thrown back on more or less justifiable deductions from often fragmentary indirect evidence, yet even on this tenuous basis some have indulged in considerable flights of speculation. The secondary literature is, indeed, peppered with relatively categorical assertions. We read, for example, that: in c. 1300 the population was 400,000, give or take 50,000;[1] in the fifteenth century it was probably not more than a quarter of a million;[2] 'in the sixteenth century it numbered about 700,000';[3] and 'in 1550 it was between five and six hundred thousand, a figure not much greater than it had been in the time before Robert the Bruce' but that the country was then (i.e. 1550) 'on the eve of a population explosion'.[4] Finally, it is possible to find estimates for c. 1700 ranging from 800,000 to a million and a quarter.[5]

Ingenious exercises, undertaken by the late Lord Cooper and by Professor J. C. Russell, have attempted to relate the population of Scotland to those of England and Wales respectively on the assumption that the arithmetical ratios remained more or less constant over long periods.[6] For what such calculations are worth they provide the figures for Scotland given in Table 1.

3

Though, in the absence of any firm basis, there must be wide margins of possible error, such estimates may nevertheless be of some value in indicating the order of magnitude of the people whose fortunes we shall be describing, and there can at least be no doubt that, subject to periodic ups and downs, the population as a whole grew very considerably in the centuries covered by the first part of this book.

Table 1 : *Estimates of the population of Scotland c. 1100—c. 1600*

Period	Cooper	Russell
Late 11th century	250,000	275,000
Early 14th century		550,000
Late 14th century	400,000 (? +)	
Mid-16th century		690,000
Late 16th century	800,000	

In the present state of knowledge of medieval Scotland we cannot be any more precise about geographical distribution. It is easy to say that the ratio between Highlands and Lowlands was less unbalanced than it is today, but even if we acknowledge the evidence of deserted settlements in the glens it is difficult to see how the Highlands could ever have supported a population of any great absolute density. Furthermore, if taxable capacity bore any relationship to size of population—admittedly a debatable assumption—then the evidence of medieval diocesan valuations points to the conclusion that the mass of the population lay across the centre of the country, up into Moray and along the broad straths and glens. At all events such worthwhile regional studies as have been undertaken tend to support the rational view that by the late Middle Ages population was relatively heavy in areas with a high food producing capacity. It is likely, for example, that by the early sixteenth century Ayrshire had something like 50,000 people, indeed it has been suggested that this represented about the maximum the old agrarian system could sustain, and that thereafter the rate of growth fell off.[7] All the indications are that by the twelfth century south-east Scotland had a type of relatively close rural settlement—nucleated village with parochial status and sometimes with outlying settlements—for which there is no parallel in the Highland areas proper.

Further north the evidences are tenuous in the extreme. The normal nuclei—churches, monasteries, castles—around which more humble dwellings might cluster, were widely spaced. Certainly there was some infiltration from the south, for even if the story of the subjugation of Moray and the planting of Anglicised settlers is half legend, there can be no doubt that by the thirteenth century there had been substantial movement of 'Southerns' into Moray, the proprietors had Norman or Saxon names, and Celtic tenure had disappeared.[8] Penetration was not confined to the mainland. The planting of Lowlanders in the outer isles, a familiar story by 1600, had antecedents, for it has been reckoned that by then a quarter of the population of Shetland already had surnames suggesting main-land origin and there were certainly many Lowlanders in Orkney by the mid-fifteenth century.[9] Such evidence as exists, therefore, indi-cates at least some mobility of population and, contrary to the pattern of the eighteenth and nineteenth centuries, it looks as if the dominant trend had been northward from the Lowlands.

Undoubtedly, however, the most significant change in the geo-graphical distribution of the population of medieval Scotland arose from the rise of towns. Perspectives again are, however, essential, for important as they were in the administration and economic life of the nation, it is clear that even leading Scottish towns of the thirteenth century might have a population of less than a thousand. In 1291 about eighty burgesses were listed at Berwick-on-Tweed and about seventy at Perth. If we add families, apprentices and servants and possibly some craftsmen, it is unlikely that the totals can have been more than 500–600. Fifty years later, if Froissart can be trusted, Edinburgh was 'less of a town than Tournai', containing fewer than 400 houses. With time, town populations certainly increased. In 1426 there were 110 burghal tenures in Selkirk; in 1477 Stirling had 120 burgesses and, in 1550, some 400 adult males; in 1517 Arbroath had about 200 hearths (suggesting a total of about 1000 persons); in 1408 and 1451 Aberdeen tax rolls contained about 350 family heads (a population of say 2000); at a weapon showing at Lanark in 1581 154 fencible men (aged sixteen to sixty) turned out and this tallies pretty closely with the assembly which had elected the provost ten years earlier when the forty-five absentees were described as 'the third pairt of the town'.[10] By any available test it is plain that, by the 1500s, Edinburgh, Dundee, Aberdeen and Perth had emerged as the biggest towns. Estimates of Edinburgh's population in the days of John Knox have ranged from 9,000 to 30,000, but the firm evidence (for example the numbers of fencible men) would suggest a figure towards the lower end of the range. If relative shares in national taxation are any guide, then contemporary Dundee was half as big, and therefore had possibly 5,000 inhabitants, Aberdeen possibly 4,000, and Perth possibly 3,000. Circumstantial evidence points to vigorous town growth in the later sixteenth century, and the 7,031 which Kennedy assigned to Aberdeen for 1592 in his *Annals of Aberdeen* is probably a true reflection at least of the trend.

Thereafter both size and distribution become a little more definable. We have tolerably safe evidence that in 1624, when it was destroyed by fire, Dunfermline had 287 families, giving a population rather greater than Paisley's, which, in 1634, is said to have been about 1,150. Three separate counts at Dumbarton, spanning 1627 to 1651, agree on round about 150 heads of families and therefore a resident population of below 1,000. Whereas in Knox's time the top eight towns had all lain east of Stirling, by 1604 Glasgow had risen to fifth, and by 1695 to second place, paying in 1695 almost half as much tax as Edinburgh which then housed at least 30,000 people. The population history of Glasgow has been subject to a wealth of statistical speculation on which modern research casts justifiable doubts, but it looks as if, by the 1690s, Glasgow had risen to 14,000–15,000, ranking high among the leading towns of the British Isles.[11]

It is significant that the adjustments in the geographical balance had never involved any considerable growth in a strictly inland burgh. Clearly, exposure to assault had retarded the growth of Border towns, but places such as Cupar, Forfar and Brechin, all exercising wide administrative and ecclesiastical functions in the Middle Ages, similarly failed to attract population growth. It looks as if, down to the transport revolution of the eighteenth century, easy access to navigable water was an essential prerequisite of vigorous burgh development.

In town and country alike, the rate of population growth had been subject to a variety of pressures among which—because of the human propensity to report calamities—the adverse are the easier to identify. Pending detailed research we are almost wholly ignorant of such basic demographic data as birthrates, normal expectancy of life, and the like. Contemporary writers were, however, unanimous about the high birth rate.[12] Thus, according to Aeneas Sylvius (later Pope Pius II) in the fifteenth century, the women were comely and pleasing and not distinguished for their chastity. L. von Wedel, a century later, observed that they 'have children without number', an achievement which, according to a loyal Scottish commentator (Sir Thomas Craig in his *De Unione Tractatus* of 1603) was based on a healthy diet of home-grown food.

However fecund the people may have been, there can be no doubt that population growth was restrained by 'Malthusian' checks— notably war, famine and plague. 'The Scots are not industrious,' wrote Don Pedro de Ayala in 1498, 'and the people are poor. They spend all their time in wars, and when there is no war they fight with one another.' Though there is palpable exaggeration in Sir Thomas Craig's estimate of 200,000 slain 'in consequence of the wicked conflict to which Edward I provoked Scotland', the murderous invasions and punitive reprisals, from the Battle of the Standard in 1138 via Flodden and the 'rough Wooing' to the battles of the Civil Wars, must have taken a heavy toll of the young menfolk of the nation. Similarly domestic feuds—themselves bespattered with blood—were suppressed only by further slaughter. Even after 1600, when a measure of respectable government was established over the Lowlands, a massacre of the Colquhouns at Glenfruin (1603) and the subsequent deliberate harrying of the Macgregor clan could still take place on the adjacent Highland fringe.

The sword and the axe cut down fighting men. Famine and pestilence, 'twoo buddes of the sam tre' as Henryson called them, were no respecters of sex or age. Contemporary statements of mortality have about the same statistical reliability as the 10,000 daffodils which the poet Wordsworth saw 'at a glance'; it is almost inconceivable, for example, that Calderwood's estimate of 20,000 dead in Edinburgh in the mid-1580s can be more than a measure of the impression which remained in his mind long after the event. Similarly as grain markets were, at best, regional, the word 'famine' does not necessarily imply starvation on a national scale, but certainly both pest and regional food shortage came often, and, in the towns at least, some-times hit very hard. Apart from direct evidence of famine in 1258 and indirect in 1300–1, the record is blank until the arrival of the Great Pestilence (later ages called it the 'Black Death') in 1349–50. Its ravaging of England in 1349 had been attributed by Scotsmen as Divine intervention on their behalf, so much so that they planned an invasion which turned into a hasty return home when the troops assembled near Selkirk were themselves affected by plague. The relatively low temperatures and the wide open spaces of Scotland would not seem to provide an environment conducive to colonisation by the house-rat and its fleas which transmitted this bubonic plague. Nevertheless the Scottish chroniclers, John of Fordun and Andrew of Wyntoun, writing within the memory of men who had survived the plague, both report that about a third of the population perished, Fordun adding that the main sufferers were 'the meaner sort and common people'. The most recent writers[13] on the Black Death tend to the view that Fordun and Wyntoun may have exaggerated; cer-tainly this was a familiar occupational weakness of medieval chroniclers. Nevertheless even if the third should be a quarter or even a fifth it still represents a huge swathe across the rank and file of the population, and if we add the further mortality from sporadic recurrences down to c. 1400 it is at least possible that by then the population had fallen significantly below the level of the early decades of the century.

In general, however, the first half of the fifteenth century was healthier. Where pestilence is recorded, as at Dumfries in 1439 and St Andrews in 1442 it seems to have been localised. Much of the country was affected in 1450 and again in 1498–1500, and the 'gret hungyr' of 1482 seems to have been widespread, but the plague out-breaks in 1455, 1475 and 1493 were apparently restricted to the Edinburgh area. So on balance it seems that despite the blood-letting from invasions, Border forays, family feuds and the like, the basic conditions in the fifteenth century were such as to support a recovery of population from the setback of 1349–1400. By contrast the sixteenth century seems—at first sight at least—to have witnessed nearly unbroken series of natural calamities. The expansion of over-seas trade reduced the immunity from European contagion, and it is significant that time and time again the east-coast ports took vigorous quarantine action against ships and cargoes coming from Europe. Similarly if population had expanded it must have pressed harder against the domestic food producing capacity of the country and so aggravated the risks of famine where crops were diminished by weather or hostile armies. There remains, nevertheless, the possibility of the false impression created by the frequency of recorded evidences, for by the sixteenth century burgh authorities, the privy council and eventually the Convention of Royal Burghs, were increasingly active in both elementary public health and market regulation.

On the basis of this further evidence we can roughly chart the broad fluctuations in social well-being for the sixteenth century. Outbreaks of plague seem to have been local until 1529–31 when what seems to have been bubonic plague affected the country from the Forth to the Moray Firth. Then followed another phase of purely local alarms and outbreaks, with, from 1550 to 1564, apparently complete freedom from any abnormal mortality despite some severe winters and food shortages in 1563. A plague of serious dimensions, accompanied by dearth, hit Edinburgh in 1568, resulting, according to one authority, in 2,500 deaths[14] and certainly producing both a very complete set of anti-plague regulations and Scotland's first treatise on the subject—Gilbert Skeyne's *Ane Breve Description of the Pest*.

Apart from food shortage in the early 1570s and a few local plague scares, conditions seem to have been reasonably good until the mid-1580s which experienced the onset of both scourges. The plagues of 1584–5 were among the worst ever experienced in the Forth-Tay area, arriving at West Wemyss, spreading to Perth (where, according to that town's *Chronicle*, 1,427 died), thence down the coast to Dysart and Kirkcaldy and, by early 1585, to Edinburgh. Simultaneously food began to run short and by 1587 the severity of the shortage is reflected in the enormous effort exerted by Scotsmen to secure grain in the Baltic ports, a situation which was to be repeated ten years later. Though food shortage may have been widespread, the visitations of the plague had, in general, been largely confined to the Forth-Tay area so that not only the inland districts but also Aberdeen had enjoyed relative immunity. After about 1600 (when Scotland's domestic conditions encouraged greater internal movement of people and goods), the incidence seems to have been more widespread.

Thus—to quote typical evidences—in 1601 there was plague as far north as Glenelg and those who could fled to the 'farr Highlands' in search of 'purer aire';[15] simultaneously there was something which seems like typhus in Glasgow; in 1604 the burgh of Lanark was taking precautions; in 1606 Ayr and Stirling were 'almaiste overthrown with the seiknes'; at Dundee in 1607

> Promiscuous funerals crowded, old and young;
> All round were grief and signs of horrid death,[16]

as the town was stricken by typhus; at Perth a remarkable display of 'blue fyre' (Northern Lights?) presaged the pest and in 1608–9 some 200 died there. Then, apart from severe grain shortage in 1623 and a relatively minor outbreak of plague in Edinburgh in 1624, life seems to have been easier until 1635 when food shortage and plague came together, the latter apparently affecting mainly the south-east and the Borders. The Borders feature again in outbreaks in 1644 which introduced another phase of widespread and intense hardship. Evidences of infection can be collected from almost every Scottish town north to Aberdeen, west to Glasgow and south to Peebles. It was, says a recent medical historian, 'one of the worst and most extensive invasions of bubonic plague that Scotland ever experienced',[17] and it was not wholly abated until 1648. It coincided with seasons of weather-damaged crops and resulted in a wave of mortality which, in the eyes of some contemporaries, was Divine punishment for the nation's disloyal schisms. If we add to plague and scarcity the pillaging by often badly-disciplined armies, we reach the inevitable conclusion that the Scotland of the Civil Wars was an unhealthy place.

In the event this was the last of the medieval plagues in Scotland. A variety of urban preventative methods—quarantine, disinfection, lime-washing, perhaps rat-poison—seems to have saved Scotland from the English Great Plague of 1665–6. It is true, however, that smallpox, often fatal to young children, was increasing in incidence. First recorded in Aberdeen in 1610 it reached epidemic proportions in 1641 and 1672 when some 800 deaths were reported in Glasgow alone. But the final killing time of the seventeenth century came not from epidemic but from genuine famine, when, from 1695 to 1699, every harvest but one was seriously deficient. Contemporary opinion put the resulting mortality at anything from a fifth to a third of the population, and we may assume that in badly hit areas this kind of fraction so reflects the grim truth that there must have been an absolute decline in population.

An unavoidable conclusion is that, apart altogether from the mortality resulting from war and domestic violence, and apart from the significant volume of emigration, the growth of population had been held in check by natural calamities which, at times had assumed massive dimensions. The Black Death stands out in stark relief as the first of which we have reasonably safe evidence. Towards the end of our period, the twenty or twenty-five years from the mid-1580s to the early 1600s, the 1640s and again the 1690s each saw abnormal mortality on a scale severe enough as radically to modify the normal demographic evolution and, in a broad way, to maintain some rough balance between the old unimproved agricultural system and the demands made upon it.

The extent to which, by the seventeenth century, emigration had become a safety valve for excessive population pressure can be deduced from the classic studies by Insh and others on Scottish colonial schemes and overseas ventures. In fact, apart from new openings in Northern Ireland and the Americas, the pattern was long established and the channels firmly cut. Fully to exploit their intellectual capacity, the young men of a country on the outer periphery of the European medieval world naturally moved towards the centre to the south and south-east. So long as relations with England allowed, some went to Oxford and, partly for their benefit, a Scottish family endowed Balliol College in the late thirteenth century. Even in periods of strained relationships Scots still went to English universities—from 1357 to 1393 some ninety safe conducts were issued by the English for this purpose[18]—but the trend was now firmly towards France. It has been estimated that in the later fourteenth century well over half of all Scottish students on the Continent were in Paris, where, even at this period, the Scots College was assuming a hazy identity. Inevitably, with the Reformation, part of the stream was diverted to Protestant universities of the Low Countries and of England, but even then Paris remained a favoured centre. Some returned, either immediately or after a gap, to enrich the cultural life of Scotland: Elphinstone and Boece to establish King's College at

Aberdeen in 1495; Kinloch to become Court Physician to James VI, but many were lost for significant periods or for good, and their loss must be regarded as a form of brain drain from a nation that needed all the brains it could command.

Scotland's long history as a supplier of mercenary soldiers reflects a complex of tensions and deficiencies in the society. Throughout the later Middle Ages, Islesmen, especially Macdonalds, were drawn by poverty or clan conflict to hire themselves as soldiers to Irish chiefs; similarly the close diplomatic alliance with France was cemented, at least from the time of Joan of Arc, by the presence of Scottish troops under the French flag; relatively quickly they were formally organised as the Scots Guard, of which Scott wrote in *Quentin Durward*; and many settled in France with often gallicised names so that 'Gowrie' became 'Gohory'. Numerically the French contingents were probably inferior to those which, in the sixteenth and seventeenth centuries, fought in Northern Europe, notably in the armies of Gustavus Adolphus (who is alleged to have had 10,000 Scots) and later still in the Low Countries and Russia.[19]

The toll of emigration contains yet another recurring item: the Scots trader. From at least the fifteenth century there is abundant evidence of Scotsmen within a wide spectrum of trading occupations scattered throughout the whole of Western Europe from Scandinavia to the Bay of Biscay and east as far as the Vistula. Some were clearly temporary residents, factors and the like, but many were clearly permanent, forming, as in Danzig, a distinct alien community, or, as in Dieppe and Rouen, becoming assimilated with the native population. The Scottish burgh records often pinpoint their departure by the issue of birth briefs to men 'travelland be way of merchandise to the Kingdome of Poill';[20] travellers in foreign parts, notably the Scotsman Lithgow in the 1630s, claimed to have met thousands of Scottish pedlars and merchants in the interior of Europe; the literature of sixteenth century Scandinavia is full of references to the 'Skotter', a term which, in that century at least, seems to have signified nationality.[21] Some flourished, some became beggars (if indeed they were ever anything else), some eventually returned to Scotland.

We are left with the conclusion that, even before 1600, Scotland had been subject to a not inconsiderable drain on the intellectually and physically superior sectors of her manpower. No doubt there were compensations arising from the establishment of economic and cultural contacts abroad, and no doubt emigration relieved pressure on limited resources at home, but here our immediate concern is with demography and with yet another element on the debit side of the population balance sheet. And after about 1600 the rate of outflow almost certainly increased as wider areas of opportunity were opened within the British Isles and the Americas. A stronger flow to England —sometimes for educational, sometimes for economic reasons—can be traced back certainly to the mid-sixteenth century when both nations had become Protestant. The Union of the Crowns in 1603 and the subsequent easing of legal discrimination, whilst not precipitating the southward flood of ravening beggars which English critics had threatened, certainly encouraged migration and well-to-do travellers on the Great North Road dipped in their purses for the support of the 'sundrie necessitors Scottish pepile' they encountered on the roadside. Emigration to Northern Ireland, on the other hand, appears as a major feature in Scottish demographic history for the first time shortly after 1600 when, as part of the final elimination of the native Irish landowning families, parts of the country were offered for plantation by Protestant Scots. By 1613 the traveller Fynes Moryson found 'all the North [of Ireland] possessed by colonies of English, but especially of Scots'. The process continued intermittently through the seventeenth century: by the middle years it was reckoned that about 50,000 Scots were in Ulster, by 1691 twice as many, and still more went in the famine years later in that decade. Irvine was one of the main points of departure, and when Brereton was there in 1636 they told him that on some days as many as 300 had sailed on a single tide and that in two years more than 10,000 had gone, some of them from as far north as Inverness. There can be no doubt that emigration on that scale by a generation already reduced by the plagues of the 1580s and early 1600s, must have had a material effect on the size and composition of the people of Scotland in the decades before the Civil Wars.

By comparison, seventeenth-century voluntary emigration to the Americas was relatively small. A variety of motives prompted several minor attempts to establish national colonies in the New World. The numbers directly involved in the Nova Scotia venture of the

1620s and in the Darien Scheme of the 1690s were small; both ended as Scottish graveyards rather than Scottish colonies. Between the two, especially in phases of religious persecution in Scotland, significant numbers of emigrants ventured to New Jersey (two ship-loads from Aberdeen and Montrose in 1684 with 290 settlers) and to South Carolina.

To those recognisable groups must be added those who went as individuals or perhaps in handfuls for service in the English or Dutch colonies, and to them again must be added those who were kidnapped as forced labourers. In fact the toll of voluntary emigrants across the Atlantic is almost certainly exceeded by that of involuntary. Transportation of socially or politically undesirables, talked about freely by James VI, became regular policy from 1648 when Cromwell began transporting his Scottish prisoners of war to the plantations in North America and the West Indies. Thenceforth, to the end of the seventeenth century, periodic shipments of Covenanters, criminals, paupers, 'lusty Susies', gipsies and various other categories of 'dissolute and loose persons' continued to cross the Atlantic in num-bers large enough to influence the demographic pattern in the homeland.

CHAPTER II

The Land and Land Utilisation

THE years between 1057, when Malcolm Canmore became king by conquest, and 1286, when Alexander III died by tragic accident, constitute the most formative period in the rural history of Scotland down to the eighteenth century. The process of political unification was already advanced by 1057, but the population was heterogeneous in racial origin, legal systems were essentially regional and land tenures were based on local tradition. Towns, in any worthwhile sense of the word, did not exist, much potentially arable land was covered with forest or occupied by bog, stock were at hazard from wolves and thieves, and apart from the simple craft which might ply the rivers and coastal waters, organised transport was unknown.

In two centuries, and especially in the reign of David I (1124–53), this primitive land was exposed to surges of external influence so that, up to and in some areas into the Highland zone, what had been essentially a Celtic-Irish society became conspicuously Anglo-Norman. The transformation was accomplished by the importing of men, of institutions and of concepts, free to develop within a relatively stable political environment and supported by a relatively effective royal administration. The Scottish royal house married Anglo-Norman brides, its young men were familiar with the English court, it brought to Scotland a small host of Anglo-Norman followers, some of them feudal landowners in England, to whom it gave extensive landowning rights in Scotland. The Borders ceased to be a significant social frontier, and feudal tenure—for that was the consequence of the process—spread north as a reality to Moray and, perhaps mainly

15

as an influence on concepts of landowning and succession, had some influence within the Highland zone. But though, as Dr Grant writes, 'the feudal system may be truly said to have been woven into the social fabric of Scotland', Scotland never became a typically feudal nation, and certainly the standardisation of rural life in the 'manorial system' has no exact counterpart in Scotland.[1]

Under the cover of generally firm royal rule and with relative freedom from invasion—a happy state which lasted until the 1290s—feudal landowning with its abundance of English and French experience seemed to provide a blueprint for a stable rural economy. In fact relationships within it changed relatively quickly. Whereas, in the twelfth century, references to *nativi* or *bondi*, in effect slaves, are common, by the next century the extreme servile state was dying out and by the 1360s, possibly with the shortage of labour after a spate of wars and plagues, it was rare in the extreme. But if the toilers of the soil passed imperceptibly into free men, even only as humble as cottars, they were—with a few exceptions—never able to acquire any supportable claim to security of tenure. Scotland never produced anything like the copy-hold tenure of England or the family group landholding of Wales, and this insecurity was to impede technical progress in Scottish agriculture down to the eighteenth century.

Primarily, the Anglicised baron of the twelfth century was concerned about the collection of revenues and the fulfilment of services by the tenants. There is no direct proof that he was an agricultural innovator. That rôle, for medieval rural Scotland, has popularly been attributed to the monks. With the great abbeys of the Borders—Coldingham, Kelso, Melrose and the rest—up to Coupar Angus and Beauly, twelfth-century Scotland acquired a chain of initially alien cultural centres, located mainly in rural areas, inhabited—because many were Cistercian—by men pledged to the virtues of isolation and manual toil. The numbers in full monastic orders were smaller than the surviving ruins might suggest: Paisley in 1300 had twenty-five; Crossraguel in 1405 had only ten and possibly never more than twelve; Melrose in the late fifteenth century had seventeen, but they had cosmopolitan connections, great influence and great wealth.[2] By monastic endowment, kings and nobles took out an insurance against hell-fire: by 1265 Kelso alone enjoyed a major part of the revenues of thirty-seven parishes, and taking the land as a whole it is likely that about one-half of the revenues of all parish churches were appropriated by monasteries or other high ecclesiastical institutions. In a sense, therefore, the revenues which the abbeys deployed, arose, in part anyhow, from the impoverishment of other sectors of the community, but if they served as 'growth points' then the benefit may in the end have outweighed the cost. An admittedly critical authority has concluded that 'in the twelfth century it [monasticism] did more than anything else to bring Scotland into line with general European civilisation' and that 'on the whole it was a beneficient squirearchy'.[3] We know that the monks were responsible for clearing and draining land and establishing orchards and granges, but they are best known as sheep farmers. The list of wool producers compiled in about 1300 from Flemish sources by Francesco Pegolotti includes details for Newbattle, Melrose, Balmerino, Coupar Angus, Kinloss, Dunfermline, Dundrennan and Glenluce with passing reference to seven other Scottish monastic houses. From this and other contemporary sources we know that Melrose, with flocks numbering 12,000, had a wool output comparable to that of the great Yorkshire houses of Rievaulx and Jervaulx, and that in terms of quality Coupar Angus and the abbeys of south-west Scotland ranked high among all British producers.[4]

In Western Europe generally the fourteenth century was a period of tensions and changes in rural society. In Scotland the high hopes engendered under the Alexanders were blighted by the Wars of Independence and by the onset of periodic plagues from c. 1350. Foreign invasion and occupation, dramatic changes in the fortunes of great landowning families, frequent confiscation of land, an impecunious treasury and the demands of a 'war economy', strained the resources of a country poor in natural endowment and weakened by loss of life. Such financial records as survive from the first half of the fourteenth century show sharp falls in the revenues of both lay and church properties; but a merit of a simple rural economy is its recuperative capacity: the soil cannot be destroyed, stock can be driven to the safety of the hills, cottar houses of turf and thatch are easily rebuilt. Nevertheless, as in any period of political anarchy, the Wars of Independence, together with their aftermath of royal weakness, strengthened the hands of any baronial landowners shrewd or lucky enough to survive, many of whom secured grants of 'regality' which gave them virtually sovereign powers within their territories. Similarly lesser men grouped themselves under the shelter of, preferably, a powerful kinsman. The bargaining power of lesser men was based, especially after the Black Death, upon their scarcity: 'henceforth', writes Professor Smout, 'the lords would be only too anxious to get tenants on their estates even if it meant granting every man his personal freedom.'[5]

Accordingly from about the fourteenth century new forms of tenure slowly spread. There are indirect earlier traces of 'kindly tenure', a vague concept which embodied some element of right to succession to a tenancy and which seems to have prevailed mainly in the Scottish West and on the estates of the Diocese of Glasgow. A few instances of leases up to four years have been noted for the late fourteenth century, and certainly from about 1400 the Scots Parliament tried to provide some legislative protection for tenants, though here—as in most matters—we must distinguish carefully between the intention of the Act and its execution. A third development in tenure is illustrated by a reference to the alienation of property 'forever' by the monks of Cambuskenneth in 1380. This was the perpetual hereditary tenure now almost universally known in Scotland as 'feuing'. It began for fiscal reasons when needy superiors preferred a substantial down-payment (the 'grassum') followed by an annual revenue rather than the miscellany of dues and services normal under the other tenures, and by the middle of the fifteenth century the kings also began to avail themselves of this means of securing a stable money income. All these developments must be kept in rigid perspective: we must not assume that secure conditions of tenure swept the country, for as late as the sixteenth century informed observers were still listing insecurity as a major drag on Scottish agricultural improvement. They were, nevertheless, indicators both of fluidity and of responsiveness to conditions induced by political and economic pressures.

Major developments, from the arrival of the Anglo-Norman barons onwards to the Reformation, eventually created a social distinction between the Scotland south of the Highland Line and the geographical Highlands. No such distinction was clearly visible down to the Wars of Independence; indeed, for this early period, there is an arguable case that the major differences lay respectively south and north of the Forth. Especially in the lower areas of the south-east the common pattern was the relatively large concentrated settlement with its arable holdings in scattered rigs throughout the adjacent open fields : in short a north of England type of farming community. North of the Forth both settlements and arable lands were generally more dispersed and the very terminology of land units reflected a different culture, especially the use of the word 'davoch' the exact meaning of which is still open to debate. In the present state of knowledge of Scottish agrarian history, certainly down to 1700, every general-isation must be tempered by the reminder that there were innumer-able variations.

But obviously when cultivating tenants are poor, capital equipment was likely to be provided along with the holding by the owner. In Scotland, where evidences of this practice exist from Kelso in 1290 to the Highlands in almost any period, it was known as 'stuht' or 'steelbow' tenure, and the proprietor's contribution commonly consisted of the livestock. Though there is no positive evidence before c. 1300, the 'infield-outfield' system evolved throughout the country, a division of land whereby the 'infield' was continuously tilled whilst elsewhere a patch of pasture was broken up for tillage (the outfield) and then abandoned in favour of another when the natural properties of the soil were exhausted. Though the pattern changed with time, the arable farm was originally related to the capacity of the plough and its team of oxen. A ploughteam of eight (the property, say, of four tenants) would therefore tend to determine the size of the mini-mum rural community, namely, about four cottages which would constitute the typical farm town of much of the Lowlands or the clachan of the Highlands. Some element of joint tenure was common, and the subdivision of the arable units facilitated redistribution at short or longer intervals according to local practice. The very existence of joint tenure encouraged the establishment of some sort of intermediary between tenants and superior. The characteristic Scottish response was the 'tacksman' system whereby one individual, often a kinsman of the superior, became responsible for the collection of rents and all other charges incidental to tenure, and though there are early examples, it seems as if the system expanded most rapidly in the sixteenth and seventeenth centuries when these payments were often at least partly commuted from goods and labour to cash. In short, the motives—like those which encouraged feuing—may have been primarily fiscal, and in a sense the two developments could be regarded as alternative devices in the landowner's battle to keep pace with rising prices and a changing pattern of domestic life.

Lest it be thought that a common pattern might have emerged regionally with the passing of time it is instructive to summarise some evidences of diversity and continuing flux within a single estate as illustrated in the rental book of Coupar Abbey which spans the period 1443 to 1538.[6] Some of the Abbey's smaller tenancies consisted entirely of infield; elsewhere, in less fertile areas, the ratio could be as high as four acres of outfield to one of infield. Probably under pressure of labour shortage, the granges, once a kind of demesne land farmed by the monks, had, by the 1450s, been divided and sublet, but on no discernibly consistent basis. Cottars might be sub-tenants of husbandmen or they might be direct tenants of the Abbey. By the late fifteenth century at least, joint tenure was breaking down: on one Coupar estate tenants in 1473 were given the option of land either in runrig or in separate holdings and on other estates longer leases were becoming fairly common. Nevertheless, though there is widely scattered evidence of continued attempts to follow the example of the early monastic pioneers in the reclamation of land, the long-term contribution to grain production was limited by the primitive husbandry. Thus, in a dispute about the rents of Drygrange on the estates of Melrose Abbey it was reported that 'land reducit furth of wood and forest' and originally productive, had, by 'continual use and occupation' come to 'silk infertilitie and unplentioisnes' that it was not worth the rent.[7] Plainly the land in general was under-utilised. Outfield cultivation represented a kind of flexible perimeter which no doubt responded in a vague way to demand, but primitive implements and techniques—coupled with all the other ills to which the tenant was heir—prevented any real consolidation of spatial expansion.

If the spatial extension of arable or intensive pastoral farming is the obverse of the coin, the clearing of waste or forest is its reverse. In his monumental *History of Scottish Forestry* M. L. Anderson took the view that the clearing of forests between about 1200 and about 1400 was more rapid than ever before or since and that there was no significant reversal of the trend until the seventeenth century.

Thus Ettrick Forest, covering some three hundred square miles and administered by the early kings as a deer forest was, under James IV, increasingly used for sheep runs and let on terms similar to those prevailing on estates elsewhere in the country.

How much of the country, at any time before 1700, could be properly classed as woodland is difficult even to estimate, not least because of the imprecision of the wood 'forest' as used in early records. Whilst some element of boscage was an essential component, the major emphasis seemed often to lie primarily on animal life and hunting rights and the administration of forest laws. Classical writers —Pliny and Ptolemy—had hearsay accounts of a huge 'Caledonian Forest' somewhere in Perthshire, but nobody ever said he had seen it with his own eyes. Contemporary accounts of woodland by reliable observers often suggest wide regional variations: Major, for example, in 1521 could write of 'great woods' round the lower slopes of mountains, and Taylor in 1618 believed that the Earldom of Mar had enough great trees to supply the navy with masts for forty years, yet Moryson's assertion that there were no woods in Fife is supported by the dependence of the east-coast ports on imported timber. We know that the woodlands, in the Borders and elsewhere, had suffered from deliberate clearance and that natural re-afforestation had been thwarted by heavy grazing, especially by goats, but there seems reasonably clear evidence for the view that extensive wooded areas existed and simply awaited the arrival of enterprise and transport for their exploitation. Thus towards the end of the sixteenth century Inverness merchants did a steady business in timber from Glengarry and Glenmoriston and logs were floated down Loch Ness. A century later Samuel Pepys thought he was onto a good scheme for 'fetching timber and deals from Scotland ... which, while London is building, will yield good money', and Phineas Pett (nephew of an official at the naval base at Chatham) lived at Inverness for two years in further-ance of this enterprise.[8] Some ten years later Alexander Robertson of Struan built sawmills on Loch Rannoch and dispatched some 176,000 deals southwards by water, many of them incidentally stolen en route.[9] Success stimulates enterprise, and in broadly the same period landowners such as William, Earl of Gowrie, his kinsman Duncan Campbell of Glenorchy ('Black Duncan of the Cowl') and the Earls of Lauderdale and Strathmore, buying fir seed, rearing and planting trees, inaugurated a policy of scientific afforestation which is one of the rare signs of improvement in the rural economy of pre-1707 Scotland.

Scotland's ability to maintain even her low standards of living depended to a high degree down to 1707 on her ability to export the products of animals, domesticated and wild. All the early writers agreed that whatever else the nation may have lacked it was 'richt proffitabill in store of bestiall'. A break-down of Scotland's exports at any period before the eighteenth century proves that this was no idle boast: in 1614, for example, skins and hides represented well over a quarter of the total value of the country's export trade. As we have seen, stock farming on an extensive scale was a feature of medieval monastic economy. Both its extent and its exposure to hostile forces can be illustrated from items in the English wardens' reports to Henry VIII of the spoil taken in their forays of July–November 1544; 10,386 nolt (i.e. horned cattle); 12,492 sheep; 1,296 nags and geldings, and Hertford's invasion of 1545 still lay ahead.[10] Further afield small sheep (somewhat akin to the modern Soay breed), black cattle, horses and goats were reported by the writers of the early sixteenth century. Donald Munro, for example, in 1549, gave a glowing account of the intensity of land utilisation generally in the Western Isles, and according to Boece in 1527 the land teemed not only with flock and fowl but even with 'dogges' of such 'marvellus wit' that would have turned any modern police-dog handler green with envy.

In fact the extent of stock farming before the eighteenth century age of improvements must be assessed with caution. There is no evidence, before that period, that the Highlands proper had more than a few small flocks of small sheep, so that, in 1603 for example, the entire clip of the Campbell flock at Balloch weighed only six stones.[11] A little wool or coarse plaiding might be sent south, but on the whole the Highlanders found a use for all the wool they could shear or glean. What with human predators, the killing of lambs by wolves and eagles, and the competition of goats for hill pastures, the Highlands were no easy environment for sheep. Restriction was further imposed by the nature of the sheep themselves—'delicate little beasts' Dr Grant calls them—which needed careful tending and housing, and by the use of ewes' milk for human consumption to the detriment of the lambs. On the other hand the pastures of the mild western fringe and the straths, supplemented by the summer sheilings on the hills, lent themselves to cattle rearing, and it is plain that cattle were as much the backbone of the Highland rural economy as an integral component of the culture. The great festival of Beltane was concerned equally with cattle and men. Sent south either via Inverness or along the natural routes which later became the drove roads, or providing the hides for sale to merchants from Perth or Dundee, the cattle went a long way towards paying for the imports which enabled the clan leaders to keep in some sort of rapport with the standards of Western European culture. The pig made some impact in the towns where he was treated as a public nuisance, but he never penetrated rural economy to any significant extent, 'swyne flesh' being, according to Bishop Lesley, 'a food in which our countrie peple has lytle plesure'. Goat skins, on the other hand, appear with such regularity among Scottish exports as to support the presumption that the goat must have been widespread and, in remoter areas, probably semi-feral. So far as one can judge, horses were the only domesticated animals subject to any sort of systematic breeding. For virtually any period between the thirteenth century, when the Abbey of Melrose acquired a stock of brood mares from Patrick, Earl of Dunbar, and the seventeenth, when a stallion from the royal stud was sent (in return for eagles) to the Laird of Glenorchy, we have evidence of the relative sophistication of horse-breeding. The economy could scarcely have functioned without the pack-horse, and the scale of breeding is reflected in Edward's passing reference to the 'thousands of unbroken horses' which fed on the Grampian slopes in North Angus in 1678.[12]

Arrayed against the pastoral farmer was a formidable inventory of contenders: the wolf, the fox, the wild cat, the eagle, the martin, the badger; and of ruminants—notably the deer—which competed for his scarce grazings. Organised hunts, notably the 'tinchel' in which herds of deer were coralled in a closing ring of beaters and dogs,[13] the introduction of firearms and the absence of a close season, are thought to have made inroads on the deer population though the late seventeenth century accounts, such as John Ochterlony's description of Angus in about 1682, refer regularly to venison as a main item of diet. Popular detestation, backed by Acts of Parliament and the insistence on many Highland estates that tenants hold suitable weapons, eventually reduced the menace of the wolf. On a map of about 1300 in the Bodleian Library, the western parts of Sutherland bear the ominous caption *hic habundant lupi;* two centuries later Boece wrote that wolves were 'richt noisum to the bestiall in all pairtis of Scotland', and the Inverness burgh records of the same period show that in winter the wolf would approach human habitations. But the economic balance is not easy to strike, for against the depredations by wild life must be set the flesh, skins, eggs and feathers which contributed to the nation's diet and trade.

As the basic human occupation, agriculture was naturally a matter of concern to the government. If Acts could have produced oats, Scotland would have been a well fed land. From 1366, when legislation sought to prevent damage to crops by horsemen, to 1685 when Parliament passed the Act which was later to simplify the process of enclosure, the volumes of Scottish Acts abound in well-intentioned legislation dealing with matters such as the planting of trees, the destruction of pests, the protection of plough-oxen and of lambs, the safety of corn-stacks and the security of feuars of land.[14] Unfortunately, in Scotland, there was always a formidable gap between the law and its enforcement, and any realistic account of rural Scotland in medieval and early modern times must make doleful reading. It is arguable that, over the centuries, the pressure to produce enough grain for seed, to meet rent payment in victual and to sustain the food requirements of a rising population, led to exhaustion of infield and to growing cultivation of marginal land. Mr Symon, for example, believes that as a result crop yields probably fell to an appreciable degree from the thirteenth to the sixteenth century.[15] It is tolerably clear, too, that as the use of money became more general and as landowners became subject to the pressures of rising prices, more widespread rack-renting added to the tribulations to which the tiller of the land was subject. The Lord Lovat of the 1620s, whose chronicler recorded that 'if a gentleman's son could seek to raise a tenant he would flatly deny him', was exceptional for his benevolence.

Upward pressure on rents and grassums, however unwelcome to the tenant, can be regarded as the first crude groping towards the more rationalised technique of estate management which charac-

terised the later eighteenth century. We can speak with some
assurance of positive management on monastic estates down almost
to the eve of the Reformation, but on lay estates the evidences are
relatively scarce before the seventeenth century which produced some
notable examples. At Baldoon (near Wigtown) Sir David Dunbar
had 'neer two hundred milch kine' and, by elementary selective
breeding, produced bullocks to send south for fattening in Norfolk.
Both his successor and Sir George Campbell of Cessnock (Ayrshire)
got leave to import breeding stock from Ireland. In Breadalbane,
150 miles north, the Duncan Campbell of the early 1600s could well
claim to be the first Highland 'improver', returning from his travels
in France and Flanders with ideas about forestry, horse-breeding,
perhaps even irrigation and certainly rules of husbandry, which were
adopted on his lands in the first half of the seventeenth century.[16]
And as the century drew on, literate Scotsmen were at least made
aware of the deficiencies in their rural economy. In 1670 two
Edinburgh doctors established near Holyrood a plot forty feet square
to cultivate medicinal herbs. Within five years a much bigger area
was acquired and in due course it became a botanic garden with a
marked impact on Scottish horticulture. Then in 1683 John Reid, in
his book *The Scots Gard'ner*, advocated the potato which was already
being grown experimentally by the Edinburgh doctors. At the very
end of the century two books—Donaldson's *Husbandry Anatomized*
and Lord Belhaven's *Countrey-man's Rudiments* pointed in no uncer-
tain terms to the technical weaknesses of Scottish agriculture and
preached the virtues of current English innovations, liming, fallow,
root crops and the like.

How far the typical laird or tenant-farmer responded is still uncer-
tain. Apart from the famine years of the 1690s the general food
position of post-Restoration Scotland as reflected both in literary
record and in the level of prices was plainly happier than in any
sustained earlier period for which adequate records survive. As we
shall see in Chapter V, not only were imports generally low but often
there was a surplus for export and, by the last generation of the
seventeenth century, official opinion was discouraging imports and
positively encouraging exports. One possible explanation was a
marked improvement in internal marketing facilities—almost 250
non-burghal markets were authorised between 1660 and 1707—

which made for smoother distribution of internal supplies.[17] There are evidences from the early 1600s of the increasing use of lime in the Lothians and Ayrshire whereby the naturally sour outfield soil could be brought to higher productivity, and events such as the draining of Loch Semple (Renfrewshire) 'to render it susceptible to all improvements of agriculture' suggest some extension of the cultivated acreage. But it seems improbable that many lairds or tenants had the capital or the will for any extensive land improvement, and the generally low level of grain prices from the 1650s to the early 1690s did nothing to encourage them.[18] Improvement in productivity was almost certainly a local phenomenon, and if there was in fact a rise in overall production between c. 1660 and 1707 it is tolerably clear that it must have been attained in general by the use of traditional techniques on an extended area of cultivation.

CHAPTER III

The Burghs

ONLY ONE industry left any significant imprint on the Scottish countryside of pre-1700. In times beyond the reach of documentary record, rural Scotland, especially in the North-east and beyond, had seen the evolution of successive types of stone or stone and timber erections, culminating in the broch which represents the peak of the prehistoric builders' achievement. Current archaeological research seems to indicate that some at least of these early works were again occupied, perhaps spasmodically, in the Middle Ages. But in terms of scale and craftmanship even the broch at Mousa or the Celtic Christian round towers at Brechin and Abernethy pale before the splendour and volume of both lay and ecclesiastical building produced by the twelfth and thirteenth centuries. This was the outward and visible sign of the opening of Scotland's frontiers to the flood-tide of Anglo-Norman culture. Masons from the south came to build or supervise the building of motte and bailey castles, the symbols of proprietorial strength, of monasteries and abbeys, of parish churches and of cathedrals including that of St Magnus at Kirkwall in the Norse earldom of Orkney. The cathedral church of St Andrews, in its heyday 391 feet long, was a massive erection by any European standards; between 1240 and 1249 no fewer than 140 parish churches were consecrated within the diocese which it dominated; its ruins, like those at Elgin or Crossraguel or Jedburgh, reflect, even after seven centuries, something of the scale of Scottish medieval building.

With the Wars of Independence the Anglo-Norman cultural link was cut. Diversion of effort to war, invasion and destruction,

27

followed, after 1350, by shortage of labour, are not unexpectedly reflected in a relatively barren period which, except for some private castle building, persisted until about the close of the fourteenth century. Then, perhaps in a kind of reaction against monasticism, wealthy patrons turned to the building and endowment of a chain of collegiate churches of which perhaps Roslin (Midlothian) is the finest example. If, to these, we add examples of contemporary castles and palace building—Linlithgow (begun in 1374 and extended in 1427), Ravenscraig (1460)—we are led to support recent conclusions that traditional opinion about fifteenth century Scotland has been over-coloured by the record of sensational and often bloody events.[1] Its output of new buildings, its wealth of native literature from James I himself to Dunbar, its newly erected universities, all suggest that when the English were occupied at home with the Wars of the Roses, the upper crust of Scottish society could sustain a high level both of affluence and of cultural awareness.

By the Reformation the moral obligations to support ecclesiastical building had ceased to lie on the conscience of the Scots laity. In the towns wealthy laymen (such as George Heriot in Edinburgh) might found schools or hospitals, but in the countryside the notable new building of the late sixteenth and seventeenth centuries was the baronial castle, becoming, as the years passed, less of a fortress and more of a dwelling house, incorporating some features which may fairly be called 'Renaissance' and yet sufficiently distinctive in style as to warrant the label 'Scottish Baronial'. Many of the masterpieces survive: Craigievar, Fyvie, Glamis, Earlshall; of others, as Edzell, Caerlaverock and Earl Patrick's Palace at Kirkwall, sufficient remains to substantiate the thesis that they were the products of an affluent aristocracy sufficiently cultured to employ craftsmen of genius.[2]

But over the long period the most conspicuous result of building lay in the emergence of towns. The historians of Celtic Scotland have evidence of some sort of town life before the eleventh century, but the modern concept of a burgh with some element of self-government and some sense of identity dates from the time of David I. Thereafter the balance between rural and urban life changed only slowly. By the 1500s the burghs were, collectively, reckoned capable of bearing one-sixth of national taxation, but it seems likely that even in the 1600s not more than one person in ten lived in conditions which, either legally or socially, could be classed as urban.

The creation and early growth of burghs reflected a fusion of economic and administrative factors in varying proportions. As they were part of a wider urban development affecting most of west Europe, the Scottish burghs were based on foreign (generally English) models and were, at least in part, occupied by immigrants among whom English or perhaps Flemish was the common speech. Whilst it seems obvious that, in the more stable and affluent conditions established by David I and his successors, urban growth would have come as a natural socio-economic response, it is nevertheless clear that this growth was a positive object of royal policy. Many early burghs were based on a royal castle, the headquarters of the royal official, the sheriff. 'The new burgh', wrote Croft Dickinson, 'was an economic counterpart of the new castle',[3] and by a natural association it tended to become the favoured economic focus of the whole region within the sheriff's jurisdiction. Hence, because the spread of urban life was associated with the extension of royal authority, the location of old Scottish burghs was often determined initially by strategic considerations and, as Professor Smout points out, it is obvious that the Highlands and the west coast north of the Clyde were regarded as so far beyond the pale as to be unfit for burghal settlement.[4]

The Anglo-Norman feudalism which, as we have seen, dominated all Lowland Scotland, was conceived primarily in terms of the relationships within a rural society. A burgh was a thing apart with unique needs: the right to bequeath and inherit property, the right of local jurisdiction, the right to collect local dues, and so forth. Hence it was of the very essence of a burgh that it possessed a legal title placing it outside the reach of feudal jurisdiction, and, as such a title could be granted only by the king or by someone under his authority, the erection of burghs (in the legal sense) can be traced by the granting of charters by the crown or by great barons and churchmen. A rough count indicates that, between 1120 and 1400, seventy-four charters were granted, of which forty-five were direct from the crown and hence constitute the foundation documents of royal burghs. Some changed in status; some, notably Roxburgh and Berwick, fell temporarily or permanently into the hands of the English; most, as we saw in Chapter I, were small in population, but nevertheless their growth had provided southern and eastern Scotland with a string of focal points in which trade and manufacturing were subject to formal organisation and through which external economic contacts could be canalised and regulated.

By the fourteenth century some important changes were afoot. The privileges introduced in the charter—the monopoly of trade, the holding of a market and the like—had not originally been accompanied by either administration or fiscal independence. Gradually, however, the crown had developed the practice of farming the collection of dues within the burgh to a third party, and this inevitably raised the possibility of the burgh itself acting as farmer. Hence from 1319, when Aberdeen secured its feu-ferme charter, one burgh after another moved along this route to something approaching fiscal autonomy. The growing financial demands within and upon the burghs and above all perhaps the contribution required of them towards the ransom of David II in the late 1350s, tended to raise the status and influence of the merchants who were, in general, the wealthier members of the burgh communities. Hitherto craftsmen and merchants were on an equal footing, so that, for example, craftsmen were often selected as burgh officials, but after *c.* 1350 there are abundant evidences of sharp differentiation on the grounds of occupational status. The concept of collective action by the merchants was not new, for from the previous century more and more burghs had acquired a merchant guild, its regulations generally upon the model of the statutes drawn up for the merchant guild of Berwick from 1249 onwards, and from this base the merchants in a typical Scottish burgh developed a feeling of group consciousness and acquired a grip on local government which was, by *c.* 1550, so complete that the presence of craftsmen on the council could be regarded by outsiders as the mark of an inferior burgh. This tendency was strengthened by legislation, notably the Act of 1469 which made burgh councils virtually self-perpetuating but which also required each craft to select one member to represent its interests. A few crafts already had some sort of organisation, but by and large the development of the incorporated craft as a feature of Scottish urban life dates from about the 1470s, and the timing suggests that craft incorporation was essentially a process of self-defence within merchant-ridden communities. A hundred years later the tide was beginning to turn. A more liberal Act of Parliament of 1556 removed some of the legal obstacles, but though henceforth new 'sets' (or constitutions) for burghs followed this lead, the craftsmen in Stirling in 1612 still resorted to public demonstrations and the raising of their 'Blue Blanket' flag to protest against a levy imposed by the council on grain brought into the town. And even when craftsmen secured a voice on councils, the merchants remained the social aristocracy, dominant in public office, in education and in church and, by their affluence, the torch bearers of cultural advancement in urban life. Their consciousness of class and their resolve to monopolise trading remained intact. As late as 1650, for example, the Stirling merchant guild was still enforcing an old decree that none of its members should 'cum to the kirk with gray cloakes of countrey cloathe', and in 1696 its attempt to prevent a glover from selling other wares was, on appeal, upheld by the Court of Session.[5]

Inevitably the possession of privileges led to conflict over territorial bounds: Dumbarton and Glasgow were at odds for centuries over the control of Clyde commerce, just as Perth and Dundee squabbled over that of the Tay. But equally because the burghs formed a distinct stratum and because merchants had interests in common it was natural that some mechanism for collective burghal action should become a feature of Scottish economic and social life. At a very early stage the burghs of Berwick, Edinburgh, Roxburgh and Stirling (after the English invasions Linlithgow and Lanark replacing Berwick and Roxburgh) acquired a distinctive status as 'The Four Burghs', and from the late 1200s to c. 1500 the Court of the Four Burghs intervened in inter-burgh disputes, regulated weights and measures and so on. But by the latter date vitality in burgh growth lay clearly on the east coast where Leith (Edinburgh's outport), Dundee and Aberdeen dominated foreign trade and where the chain of Fife ports from St Andrews round to Kirkcaldy was on the threshold of a phase of remarkable trading activity. The old body, therefore, could no longer fairly claim to speak on mercantile matters, and by the 1480s there were moves to create what, within sixty years, had become the Convention of Royal Burghs.

Not all burghs, as we have seen, were direct royal creations, and, in general, as time passed, the tendency was for a relatively greater growth of burghs of barony. Of the nineteen new royal burghs which were erected between 1560 and 1660, only one was a new creation;

the others, which included Glasgow, were all promotions of existing burghs, twelve ecclesiastical and six baronial. In the same period 125 burghs of barony were erected (though fifty of them were little more than 'ghost' or parchment burghs) and this trend continued strongly down to 1707. But even if, numerically, the royal burghs lost ground, they had acquired an exclusive monopoly of foreign trade in the staple goods which put them in a category apart. Whether this was the true intent of a general charter of 1364 is open to doubt,[6] but certainly this was the gloss that later generations put upon it, and it was not seriously modified until 1672–98 when, as the outcome of intensive bargaining by the burghs and a spate of Acts of Parliament, the non-royal burghs were admitted to legal participation in sea-borne commerce.

It is not surprising that hitherto the central concern of the Convention of Royal Burghs had been the conduct of overseas trade. 'Until the later part of the seventeenth century,' its historian wrote, 'no trade of any importance was carried on except under the auspices and control of the convention, whether organised, as was the trade with the Low countries, or carried on by individual members.'[7] This organised sector, as we shall see in Chapter V, focussed on the Scottish Staple in the Low Countries, and though there were instances of royal intervention the routine oversight of the Staple was very much within the province of the Convention. In domestic affairs the Convention determined the share of each burgh in national taxation, settled disputes between them, acted as a mouthpiece and offered advice to the Crown—sometimes when not invited. It was founded on no charter or statute, yet it became something like an economic parliament, providing a forum for debate and voting in a land where decisions were all too often reached by other and less rational processes.

The relationship between town and country had both negative and positive aspects. The monopoly of trade and of organised industry, which extended throughout the sheriffdom of which the royal burgh was the centre, had been responsible for the absence of nucleated villages over much of the country and of rural fairs and markets down to the late seventeenth century, and may well have limited the range of rural craft industries.[8] On the other hand urban residence was by no means incompatible with agricultural interests. Even where the

town was walled—and generally the wall was little more than the
outer fence of the burgesses' gardens—open countryside was within
ten minutes walk of the tolbooth, and, in the early burghs at least,
farming seems to have been regarded as a normal burgess activity.
Thus a twelfth century Ayr charter provided that with his toft every
burgess should have six acres of land, and, in the extreme case of a
small burgh of barony, trade and industry might be little more than a
'superstructure' erected on a more solid base of 'small scale agriculture and pastoral farming'.[9] Even in the greater burghs, and as late as
the sixteenth and seventeenth centuries, merchants' accounts can include items about the purchase of 'muk' and other agricultural
necessaries. And for a prosperous townsman the step from farming
to country landowning was short and easy. Sometimes the way was
paved by loans to local lairds or by marriage to their daughters,
sometimes it was a matter of simple purchase.

Town life presents both a social challenge and a social opportunity.
The need for disciplined life increases broadly in direct correlation
to the concentration of population, but concentrated wealth can supply the means for alleviating social tensions and for creating harmonious living. Once the burghs had freed themselves from
immediate control by royal nominees, the *praepositi* or *ballivi*, administration and justice within their bounds became the concern of
the Head Court, theoretically a meeting of all the burgesses, from
which in the larger burghs there emerged in time a smaller body
(the 'dousson' in fourteenth century Edinburgh), but which could
persist intact in the smaller places to the seventeenth century. Day
to day running was the concern of the provost and bailies, elected
annually, and constituting a burgh court with a complex pattern of
administrative and judicial functions. Few records survive before the
sixteenth century of the detailed working of either burgh courts or—
in places where there was a merchant guild—guild courts, and
consequently the picture which emerges may not perfectly reflect the
earlier centuries. What we see is town government by a narrow clique,
closely related by marriage and mercantile interest; fussily interfering
in everyday life; pioneering, or at least freely accepting, the move
from the Old Church to the Reformed Kirk; jealously guarding its
economic and social standing; by no means innocent of graft; not
always competent to enforce even its own 'acts' and 'statutes'.

But in passing judgement we must bear in mind that the financial resources of the burgh were limited. In general terms its regular revenues derived from four sources: rent of land, fines ('unlaws') in the burgh court, the petty customs (as distinct from the great customs on staple goods which went direct to the Crown) and miscellaneous items such as tolls on bridges, fees for the use of burial cloth and so on. From these the burgh had to meet the feu to the Crown as defined in its feu-ferme charter, but any surplus formed the basis of the common good which was at the disposal of the local authority. For exceptional outlays, whether local or to meet a special national levy such as a royal marriage or an armed expedition, the burgesses were subject to a stent, a form of local tax often the source of such keen resentment that in the 1660s Kirkcaldy had to summon military assistance. Borrowing seems to have become increasingly prevalent: in 1613, for example, Ayr owed £1,100 to Adam Ritchie at an interest rate of ten per cent;[10] by the 1690s Perth and Dundee both claimed to be applying something of the order of one-half of their free revenues to the service of debts; and in 1687 Kirkcaldy owed the equivalent of £2,000 sterling.

Where, as for Ayr, scholarly research has been undertaken into the use made by burghs of their free funds, a comparison of the pre-Reformation and post-Reformation periods indicates that expenditure on common works fell from about thirty per cent of the total to about twenty per cent; religion and education between them occupied about forty per cent in both periods; the cost of legal actions, expenses of commissioners and so forth rose from twelve or thirteen per cent to about twenty per cent; and the cost of hospitality similarly rose from about five per cent to about ten per cent. Common works embraced the physical properties of the burgh ranging from footpaths to the clock in the tolbooth, the latter requiring the professional services of a keeper who, at Banff in the early 1600s, was liable to a twenty-five per cent reduction from his salary if the clock 'happin to be ane quarter hour out of temper'. The constant maintenance of almost all common works suggests a low standard of construction though the ports had the specially difficult problem of storm damage to harbour and foreshore.

The financial outlay of the burgh on education, on religion, on welfare and on legal and similar charges raises the broader issue of

how far the entrenched merchant interests aspired to anything which
can fairly be called 'social justice'. Had they, in other words, any
sense of communal good, or did they behave, as James VI asserted,
as if the 'whole common weale' were 'ordayned for making them up'?
In the vital matter of education the burgh school is recognisable by
the fifteenth century: in 1464 at Peebles the burgh was appointing a
master, by the early 1500s this kind of lay burghal support was
common, and by the eve of the Reformation the Council at Dundee
was in open conflict with the Abbot of Lindores about the appointment of a schoolmaster. With the Reformation, though in 1567 the
new kirk secured the right to test the religious orthodoxy of teachers,
education in the burgh became more unequivocally a council
responsibility, and its chief concern thenceforth was to ensure the
fees 'to be payit be ilk bairn' went to the teacher of the school
which it officially recognised and supported. The evidences of newly
created burgh schools after the Reformation are few and far between,
and the educational system inherited by seventeenth century
Scotland fell pitifully short of that envisaged in *The First Book of
Discipline*. Occasionally the local body went beyond the minimum
of providing a schoolmaster's salary and maintaining his premises:
the Edinburgh council minutes reflect a genuine care for education;
Edinburgh University originated from the anxiety of the Council to
have a 'towns college', and occasionally elsewhere a council or guild
would provide board and clothes for a lad at university, but there
is not much sign of any widespread enthusiasm for education and,
apart from the classic exception of George Heriot in Edinburgh,
private merchants do not seem to have been much more open-
handed. On the credit side it must be recorded that some places
had sizeable schools—there were 300 at Perth Grammar School in
1587—and the curriculum, firmly grounded in grammar, following,
indeed sometimes still employing, the text of the fourth century
Aelius Donatus, produced in each generation a sprinkling of men of
high literary talent and a hard core of literate merchants and master
craftsmen.[11]

An even more acid test of the social conscience of the controlling
groups is provided by their handling of the process of pauperism.
Whether pauperism in fact became more widespread in the sixteenth
century is a matter of debate: certainly we hear more about it in

contemporary literature. The pre-Reformation religious houses had done something to alleviate it, and it seems reasonable to suppose that for Protestant Scotland the problem was aggravated by rising prices, crop failures and pestilence. In response a series of Acts of Parliament from 1579 onwards created a complicated administrative structure in which the kirk sessions acted as the practical instrument of poor relief and which provided powers to levy a local rate for the purpose.[12] A compulsory levy involved such a tricky business of assessment that when Dundee tried it in 1637 the two nominated 'stentors' went to sea to avoid the 'weightiness of the matter'.[13] In an outburst of zeal for cleaning up the town ready for the General Assembly, Glasgow in 1638 authorised a special levy[14] and a few kirk sessions seem to have collected goods for poor relief on some sort of rough assessment, but by and large relief continued to rely on voluntary contributions with each parish tending its own poor and displaying a vigorous hostility to vagrants from elsewhere. In short this was another area in which day-to-day practice bore only accidental resemblance to the intentions either of Knox or of the lawmakers.

To be fair to the townsmen, however, it must be remembered that the guild bodies normally made independent provision for their own sick and widows. Furthermore, they inherited and increased private endowment of hospitals and the like for the accommodation of at least a minority of the poor. Finally, perhaps because it seemed a good advertisement of godliness, they were remarkably open-handed in donating public funds to other towns which had suffered from fire or similar calamity or, further afield, for the relief of Christians captured by Moslem pirates, for 'poor Greeks, professoures of the word' or—despite their religion—for shipwrecked Spaniards who were cast ashore from the wrecked Armada.

In any event a wise public authority is more concerned about the prevention of pauperism. If, as seems reasonable to suppose, pauperism stemmed in part from scarcity and rising prices, then we should look critically at burghal control of prices and of markets generally for evidence of the workings of a social policy. Market regulations were, ostensibly at any rate, designed to secure discipline, to prevent undercover dealing and to restrain anything which smacked of 'cornering' or creating a monopoly. At times councils themselves bought whole consignments of goods for resale to burgesses, but normally their activity was limited to oversight and prosecution of those who, for example, failed to expose their wares on the open market or sold inferior products. But whilst no individual might establish a monopoly, the council (or the court of the merchant guild) insisted on retaining the collective monopoly of its own traders. The admission of strangers and those who were not freemen of the burgh to its commercial activities was always restricted. The Argyll Gait or Argyll Street, in later times a familiar feature of the Scottish town, was in the Middle Ages an approach road outside the town proper, marking the place where stranger traders must rest their bales and await the condescension of the burgesses. Later they entered the town but to trade only under prescribed conditions. Indeed, in strict law, non-freemen were excluded from full trading rights until the Burgh Trading Act of 1846.

It has been said that the burgess in the time of Queen Mary was more concerned about prices than about religion,[15] and if entries in the burgh records are any guide the fixing of prices was a major method of market control for most of the sixteenth century and, in some places at least, down to the Civil Wars. It will be noted that this was a period of generally rising prices throughout Western Europe, and it is tempting to think that the aim of the Scottish burghs was the protection of the middle-class consumer, especially as the schedule was normally limited to goods which entered pretty directly into his cost of living: wheat, malt, bread, ale, wine, tallow and candles. Ventures beyond this list—shoes at Inverness, 'wyld mete and tame foullis' at Edinburgh, 'tartane' cloth at Aberdeen—raised difficulties of definition and are relatively uncommon, and oats, the diet of the poorer people, were rarely included. For reasons which we have examined already, the quantity of grain was liable to fluctuate widely from harvest to harvest and, by a process long familiar to agricultural economists, its open market price would tend to fluctuate even more widely. To ensure continuity of supplies of grain, burghs must of necessity have offered something like the open market price and therefore in their grain-bread price structure they started from a more or less externally determined point. As grain, according to an analysis of baking costs published in 1638, represented about three-quarters of the final cost of the loaf, it would be reasonable to expect that bread prices would be highly sensitive to the price of grain. And this is exactly what the Dundee bakers claimed in a dispute with their burgh council which dragged on from 1561 into the 1580s, at the height of which the bakers threatened to go on strike.[16] The outcome there, and later in Edinburgh, was the promulgation of a fairly sophisticated table showing the permitted price of bread in relation to the current price of wheat. A further case study of price fixing in Stirling[17] between 1600 and 1625 throws up the interesting conclusion that whilst the price of wheat fluctuated from £6 to £12 a boll, the weight of the twelve penny loaf neither rose above 16 oz. nor fell below 12 oz. All in all it looks as if the effect of burghal price fixing— at least for wheat, bread, ale and candles—was to keep the cost to the public more stable than the prices of the respective raw materials. The bakers' and brewers' and candlemakers' grumbles in years of high raw material prices must be set against their silence in years when supplies were plentiful.

On paper at least the burghs actively intervened in those facets of economic life which most closely touched the pockets of the well-to-do burghers. The constant reiteration of many of their regulations makes one suspect that enforcement was not conspicuously successful. In general too, the bailies seem to have been much less zealous in the prosecution of economic offenders than in pursuing moral delinquents, assisting the kirk session in enforcing church attendance and, after about 1590, in joining in the periodic witch-hunts.

CHAPTER IV

Industry before 1707

I t is arguable that the branches of building—some facets of which were discussed in the previous chapter—collectively represented over the centuries the greatest single industry and certainly the only major 'capital goods' industry. Yet down to modern times its techniques remained almost static and its fluctuations in output were a consequence rather than a cause of wider trends within Scottish society. In short, whilst in no way underestimating the scale of the building trades, it is to other areas of industry that we must look for signs of dynamism and positive influence.

The emergence of extractive industries can mark a phase in evolution from a purely rural economy. Because of the geological structure, coal outcropped at numerous places around the Forth and in Fife, and there is reason to suppose that systematic outcrop working began under the direction of the monks at Newbattle.[1] Coal was obtained by the English forces during the Wars of Independence at places as far afield as Glasgow and Edinburgh, some of it for the use of their farriers.[2] Aeneas Sylvius who spent a sunless winter in Scotland in 1435 commented on the marvellous black stones with which the poor warmed themselves, whilst Hector Boece, a century later, recorded coal in Fife of 'sa intollerable heit . . . that they resolve and meltis irne', a fair indication of its use by smiths. These are reasonable indications of at least small scale extraction in the central belt before 1540, and it is at least likely that this relatively early use of coal was associated with the lack of local timber for charcoal.[3]

For the middle decades of the sixteenth century there are abundant

39

references to coal production, ranging from the traveller's account of Estienne Perlin in 1552 to the lets negotiated by burghs, and a modern authority has estimated that annual output about 1540 was of the order of 40,000 tons.[4] Exports were already causing some alarm, and an Act of 1563, banning the export of 'great coal', triggered off an argument which was still raging in the 1590s. But the industry was on the eve of great expansion, promoted by politically influential landowners and based on the application of new mining techniques in coastal areas where waterborne transport—either coastal or overseas—provided a cheap outlet which, until the later seventeenth century, was relatively free from foreign import restrictions. Professor Nef's estimated output for the 1680s—almost half a million tons—may be too high, but by any test this was a growth industry. By the standards of the sixteenth century there was still great scope for expanded output from outcrops and shallow seams, but deep mining was already coming with all its problems of drainage, ventilation, haulage and labour, and working had already extended north to the isolated Jurassic deposit at Brora. The capital—considerable by earlier standards—came mainly from landed proprietor families such as Elcho, Elphinstone, Dundas, Bruce, Hamilton, Wemyss and Cunninghame. The standard was set by Sir George Bruce of Carnock who, under a lease of 1575, reopened an old Cistercian coal-working at Culross.[5] His mine, an 'unfellowed and unmatchable worke' according to the Water-Poet John Taylor, had two entries, the one on the land, the other from an artificial island built up in the Forth; many of its workings were below the river bed, and, to counteract flooding, Bruce had a horse-drawn chain pump by which thirty-six buckets brought water to the surface. Clearly this involved both capital and technical ability of a high order, and some at least of the labour force was imported from England.

But though skilled technicians might be secured by attractive wages, the mass of the labour force—the 'hewers' and the 'bearers' who carried the coal to the pit-head in buckets—presented a different problem. In the seventeenth century these men and women 'suffered a degradation without parallel in the history of labour in Scotland'.[6] By Acts of 1606 and 1641, reinforced by legal decisions, first the underground and then the surface workers were liable to find themselves condemned to a lifetime of serfdom at the mine or the salt work. Vagrants and criminals might be similarly condemned and the practice of 'arling'—whereby a collier was bribed to agree that his newly-born child become a collier—coupled with the social isolation of the mining communities, meant that colliery serfdom tended to become hereditary. How rigorously the Acts were enforced is open to some doubt, but it seems certain that by the later seventeenth century the great bulk of the Scottish coal-mining labour force operated under conditions approximating to serfdom.

So the undoubted economic stimulus which came from the rapid expansion was bought by human degradation. But there can be no two opinions about the force of the stimulus, considered either in terms of the rôle of coal in Scotland's exports or in terms of its widening employment as an industrial fuel. Because it occurred freely in coastal areas its first major industrial use was in salt production. Surviving place-names, from The Pans (near Crail) to West Pans and Prestonpans on the Forth and across the country to Saltcoats in Ayrshire, symbolise the widespread distribution. Its antiquity is attested by the grants of salt-pans or salt-making rights to the monasteries, and by the existence, as early as 1286, of the office of Master of the Royal Saltworks. The simple process of boiling salt water in pans could be practised wherever fuel was available. The limitations on growth arose in part from the competition of imported salt which was held to be superior for curing fish, in part from the lack of organisation and capital, and in part from the restricted supply of coal at any point more than a few miles from an outcrop. The expansion of the later sixteenth and seventeenth centuries is therefore, not surprisingly, closely linked with mining, and the landowning entrepreneurs were common to both industries.

Such a group could ensure privileges, so that, for example, their operatives became subject to the same legal servility as the colliers, the strict sabbatarianism of the Synod of Fife was modified in favour of some Sunday work at salt-pans, and in 1667 the Kirkcaldy Council resolved that salters remain exempt from tax 'as they have always been'. It was only when landowning capital moved in that the technique and scale of production could be stepped up to the point where a single iron evaporating pan in the 1630s could measure eighteen feet by nine and where 'innumerable' pans could be visited along the coasts of East Fife and the Firth of Forth.[7] Saltcoats offers a splendid case study. Salt-making there, as a peasant industry, had at the most a record of fitful success until the 1680s when Robert Cunninghame built a number of large pans in association with his own coal-pits and, following the example of the east coast proprietors, built a harbour for his export trade. In some centres at least the operative salt-makers were paid in kind by a share of the salt which, in turn, they sold to cadgers who retailed it to inland consumers.

Iron-making, which will feature prominently in later chapters, has at best a shadowy history before the eighteenth century. The archaeologists are revealing more Iron Age and medieval bloomeries: more than twenty have recently been reported in Perthshire,[8] and, in due course, the famous inventory compiled by W. I. Macadam in the 1880s will have to be revised.[9] These early bloomeries, using either bog-iron or ore from outcrops, and relying often on skilful siting to ensure a natural draught, were in general so ephemeral that it is abuse of language to speak of a medieval Scottish iron industry and probably Froissart was at least half right when, about 1390, he wrote of Scotland that 'it is almost impossible to get iron to make horseshoes, or leather for harness: everything comes ready made from Flanders'.[10] By the sixteenth century the blast furnace was coming into use in the more advanced industrial countries. Its demands, in terms of charcoal, aroused official alarm when in the very early 1600s there was talk of introducing these new 'irne mylnis' to the Highlands, and it was only an influential magnate who could get exemption from the laws against the felling of trees for iron founding. At Letterewe (in Wester Ross) Sir George Hay (later to be Lord Chancellor of Scotland) established what must be regarded as the prototype of Scottish iron furnaces for the whole period from c. 1600 to the establishment of Carron. By comparison with some of the classic sites—Bonawe or Furnace—the location does not seem to have been ideal for easy access for the ore imported from Ulverston (Lancashire), but against that it was a good collecting point for charcoal burnt in the woods around Loch Maree. Hay settled a colony of English furnacemen to get the works going, and, down at least to 1621 produced iron enjoying a high reputation among Scottish smiths.

By contrast, the winning of lead in Scotland had a long and continuous history and gave some support to Scottish exports. Lead was known to exist at several places: there was working at Glenorchy (Argyll) in 1424; in 1527, according to Boece, Lochaber was 'full of minis, sic as irne and leid'; and Donald Munro in 1549 reported workings in Islay and Lismore.[11] But for practical purposes Scottish lead-mining meant the small knot of settlements between Crawford and Sanquhar—notably Leadhills and Wanlockhead. Probably known to the Romans, the lead-bearing seams were certainly worked again by the thirteenth century, when, for example, in 1264 the king paid for the carriage of seven cart-loads of lead from Crawfordmuir to Rutherglen. Similarly occasional references prove at least spasmodic production, but there is no indication of continuous expansion until the mid-sixteenth century when output was high enough to support very substantial exports. A second boost came when the mines passed under the control of Sir John Hope. 'Having,' wrote Sir Robert Douglas, 'in 1638, acquired by marriage, the property of the valuable mines of Leadhills, he applied to the attainment of skill in mineralogy; and his endeavours were attended with so great success, that he brought the art of mining to a degree of perfection unknown before that time in Scotland.'[12] He died in 1661 appropriately perhaps of the 'Flanders sickness' which he had contracted whilst selling lead in Holland. Certainly Hope's own *Diary* supports this opinion of his consuming interest in mineralogy and shows also his anxiety to persuade English workmen to join his Scottish enterprises.[13] Under this impetus lead-mining in the late seventeenth century spread to nearby Wanlockhead (where there had long been some mining for gold) and there was a revival in Islay.

But these dull minerals, coal, iron and lead, excited the imagination less than the glitter of gold and silver. It is unfair to suggest that obsession about precious metals was unique to the mercantilists: at all ages people have lusted for them, and in a country such as Scotland where the provision of an adequate coinage was always a major problem the lusting had a valid economic backing. With some consistency, though with limited success, the Scottish rulers sought to augment their precious metal resources by imposing bans on the export of coins and, from James V to James VI by active encouragement to prospectors in Scotland. Though hopes of an El Dorado were raised in many districts, the real focus again was the bleak upland around Leadhills. Gold—probably alluvial—was found in the time of James IV, and from 1526 to the early 1600s a succession of prospectors—Germans, French, Flemings, English and Scots—were licensed to seek. The story was told by one of them, Stephen Atkinson, author of the *Discoverie and Historie of the Gold Mynes in Scotland* and right-hand man of Bevis Bulmer, the last of the line of English prospectors. For a time—perhaps the second and third quarters of the sixteenth century—200–300 operatives produced enough gold to make the bonnet-pieces of James V's coinage and to enrich the Scottish Regalia, but Crawfordmuir was no Witwatersrand, and eventually the laird's daughter's wedding ring absorbed the output. Silver was commonly associated in nature with lead, and it seems likely that down to the sixteenth century the anxiety to produce silver resulted in the lead being destroyed during the process of cupellation whereby the two metals are separated.[14] Though, by the later part of that century, cargoes of Spanish colonial silver were reaching Europe, James VI and his prospectors pressed ahead in the search for more Scottish silver and had at least a limited measure of success with the chance discovery of silver at Hilderstone (Linlithgow—now remembered as 'Silvermine') where, by 1608, over sixty miners were employed and which, by the middle of the seventeenth century, had become part of the mining empire of Sir John Hope.

Nature equipped Scotland tolerably well for the making of glass, but apart from a single reference to production at Falkland in 1506–7 there is no evidence of an active glass industry until about 1610 when Sir George Hay, whose ironworks at Letterewe we have already noted, got a licence to set up a glassworks at Wemyss. The site was good, close to supplies of sand, kelp (for alkali) and coal, and in easy reach of Leith; Hay employed Italian craftsmen (some of whom deserted their English employers in his favour), and within a short time his glass was competing actively in England with that produced by the monopolist Robert Mansell. In the event Mansell won, for in 1627 Hay sold the works to Thomas Robertson, a London merchant acting as intermediary for Mansell, and by 1631 production at Wemyss ceased. Later attempts at revival were apparently abortive,[15] but in the second half of the seventeenth century Scotland's determination to industrialise was not so easily frustrated. John Ray reported of Prestonpans that 'I saw glass being produced there in August 1661', and from 1664 (and perhaps earlier) there was glass-making at Leith employing, by 1700, about 120 skilled blowers.

It will be observed that the industrial developments we have so far considered were, by their nature, largely rural in location, promoted often by landowners, and at least potentially capitalistic in structure. Whilst the relative amounts of surviving evidence may be somewhat misleading, it seems nevertheless a safe deduction that this group of industries experienced their main growth in the sixteenth and seventeenth centuries when, certainly, they were the subject of an unprecedented amount of official attention and when they reflect, in however pale a way, the 'industrial revolution' which Professor Nef has detected in Western Europe generally between c. 1540 and c. 1640. In terms of man- or woman-hours none of them would at any time compare with the textile industries. Using locally produced or easily transportable raw material, simple and durable equipment, offering employment to both sexes and almost all ages, virtually immune both from the economies of scale and of continuous production, textile manufacture was a natural Scottish industrial growth in either an urban or a rural setting.

The wool cloth industry, the traditional backbone of Scottish textiles before the Union of Parliaments, always displayed a rough pattern of specialisation. Country cloth, which for convenience can be grouped as 'plaiding', made from local wool, provided the clothing for the mass of the population and supported the export trade. Over the centuries it was almost certainly the most valuable single branch of manufacturing industry in Scotland, and though practised everywhere it seems to have displayed relatively heavy concentration in Angus, the Mearns and Aberdeenshire. Evidences, from the wool prices of c. 1300 which we noted in Chapter II to the opinion of Boece in 1527 that 'it has nae compair in Albion', suggest that this was a region of fine quality wool, and the references to waulk mills in the records of the Abbey of Coupar Angus indicate that the water-driven fulling mill (which had spread rapidly in England in the thirteenth century) was used as an adjunct to at least some parts of the rural cloth industry.

Town-made cloth, on the other hand, was 'made' in the sense that it was more completely finished by shearing and dyeing. The early history is frankly puzzling, for as W. C. Dickinson pointed out,[16] the earliest burgh charters often place great emphasis on cloth making and yet by the fourteenth century the status of the urban cloth-makers was clearly inferior to the urban merchants, and, even when they acquired some sort of standing, the numerical strength of the weaver and allied crafts was never very great. It is tempting to suggest that, as in England, cloth making in the thirteenth century tended to move out to the countryside to local wool, cheap labour and abundant water, and that the townsman found it more profitable to trade in cloth rather than to make it. Nevertheless town-made cloth, the concern of a least three crafts—weavers, dyers and waulkers— supplemented by knitted hose, represented the 'better end' of the trade and, save those rich enough to buy imported fabric, the typical burgess and his family spent their waking hours enclosed within it.

But 'not for hundreds of years, and only after a long struggle, was Scotland to achieve any success as a maker of woollen fabrics'.[17] This industry provides a unique case study of the attempts of official Scotland—crown, Convention of Royal Burghs, Parliament—to foster success in both the quantitative and qualitative sense. Attempts to increase quantity of production inevitably conflicted with the interests of merchants engaged in the export of raw wool, but nevertheless the history of continuous attempts to keep Scottish wool within Scotland dates from debates in the Convention of Royal Burghs in the 1570s. Moved, so it was said, by compassion for the poor and unemployed among the Scottish cloth-makers, Parliament responded in 1581 by an Act banning exports of wool, and though there was some exemption by licence and no doubt some evasion, it looks as if the volume of exports fell significantly in the thirty years during which the ban persisted. In broadly the same period the first serious attempts were made to raise quality and diversify production so that Scotland was to have first hand experience— however limited—of the making of 'New Draperies' which the English had already learned from the Flemish. Wisely the Scots went to the source, and from the 1580s there were a few Flemings in Scotland endeavouring, in the face of pig-headed craft guild resistance, to demonstrate the making of new fabrics. Progress was negligible, but around 1600 another attempt was made, strengthened this time by a temporary ban on the import of English wool cloth

and by the intervention of James VI who had been appraised of 'the
grite abuses and imperfectionances of the claith maid ordinarly
within this realm'. In the years immediately following, recruiting
agents were sent to the Low Countries but though small groups of
Flemish workers were established in Edinburgh, Ayr, Perth and
Dundee, the old story was repeated and by 1609 the small unhappy
remnant had clustered together in the Canongate in Edinburgh.

As the Scottish domestic market could unquestionably have sustained a small progressive wool cloth industry we are led to the
conclusion that the responsibility for failure lay partly in the quality
of Scottish wool but chiefly in the conservatism of the burgesses and
the rigidity of burghal organisation. The King and his advisers,
altogether more enlightened and flexible, made one more major
attempt by the creation in 1623 of the Standing Commission on
Manufactures. This arose indirectly from debates and memoranda
(notably a report by Sir William Seyton) on the best use of Scotland's
native raw materials, notably her wool of which, according to Seyton,
there had been a notable rise in production since 1603. The Commission, a remarkably modern type of body, was empowered to
handle the whole gamut of problems involved in industrial expansion:
choice of industries, location, regulation, technical skill needed and
so forth, and had James VI lived another ten years it might have
effected a real breakthrough.[18]

Legislative encouragement was resumed in the 1640s with the
exemption of fine imported wool from duties and with the exemption
of certain operatives from military service, reinforced, after the
Restoration, by fresh bans on the export of Scottish wool and by
restrictions of the import of foreign cloths. To encourage the import
and accumulation of capital and to promote better organisation two
Acts of 1661 and 1681 offered considerable fiscal inducements to
the promoters of new industrial enterprises, simplified the establishment of joint-stock companies and offered privileges to immigrants
with skill or capital.[19] This was full-blooded mercantilism: never
before had industrial entrepreneurs in Scotland been offered so much
protection and privilege. The response in the wool cloth industry
came mainly from a small group of companies of which (because its
records survive) that founded in 1681 at Newmills (now Amisfield)
at Haddington is the best known. Promoted mainly by the local

landowner, Sir James Stanfield, and the Edinburgh merchant Robert Blackwood, it brought trained weavers from Yorkshire and South-west England, and as the Privy Council had recently resolved to provide uniforms to 'distinguish sojers from other skulking and vagrant persons', the new company made active attempts to secure the valuable government contracts. The outcome immediately pin-pointed the basic weakness of the Scottish cloth industry as a whole: its costs were too high, and especially in the years just after the Revolution when the Acts against the importation of cloth and the export of wool were not enforced, Newmills was in low water. With more vigorous application of the protective acts after 1701 it picked up, but it seems to have made no attempt to adjust to the changed conditions after 1707 and was wound up in 1713. In fact it had been only one of a whole chain of enterprises for the making of wool fabrics promoted in the later decades of the seventeenth century, mainly under the influence of the legislation of 1661 and 1681. Almost certainly the biggest was the Woollen Manufactory of Glasgow, promoted in 1699 by a group of ten which included a distiller and the Principal of the University. Promising to make a vast range of 'damasks, half silks, drogets, capitations ... and other stuffs' for summer and winter apparel, its payroll of no fewer than 1,400 operatives suggests that it must have been organising existing domestic production, and for all its high promises it fades from the record after 1704.[20]

In short the wool cloth industry was not conspicuously healthy even before 1707. Indeed if we are looking for a genuine 'growth' sector in Scottish textiles our search is more likely to end with linen. It had always rested on two foundations: the flax to which the arable farmer devoted one or two of his precious infield rigs and the flax which shippers brought home from the Baltic, and in consequence it was always widespread and catered in part for immediate domestic demand. Though, in the nature of things, the imported flax and such yarn or cloth as was marketed passed through the hands of town-based merchants, the production itself was largely rural and, because of the paucity of rural records, its scale and distribution cannot even be estimated. What is certain is that, by the sixteenth century, the working of flax and hemp had become, by Scottish standards, a substantial industry, producing a range of fabrics from the 'good domicks for table and bed' of Dunfermline down to the twill, harden, cordage and sailcloth which constituted its bread and butter. By 1689, in the words of Thomas Morer, it had become 'the most noted and beneficial manufacture of the kingdom'. In so far as concentrations can be identified they were in the regions around the Tay and the Clyde, both of which had local mercantile facilities for the growing export trade in both fabrics and yarn.

The more sophisticated secondary industries developed slowly and were, in general, still weak in 1700. The provenance of the surviving pieces of medieval Scottish gold and silver ware is highly doubtful: perhaps some of the medieval brooches were the work of *ceardan* or travelling tinkers and one of the magnificent maces of the University of St Andrews (pre-1461) has been described as 'manifestly Scottish',[21] but there is no evidence of the goldsmiths as a separate organised craft before the fifteenth century and it is not until the early part of the sixteenth century that Scottish origin can be firmly attributed to a significant range of pieces. The Royal Crown of Scotland was certainly refashioned for James V by John Mosman just as nearly thirty years earlier John Currour had made one for Queen Margaret, and as the sixteenth century went on, Scottish gold- and silversmiths came into their own with the development of standing mazers—'the most beautiful objects ever produced by the goldsmiths of this or any other country'.[22] And after the iconoclasm of zealous Reformers, the Church—prodded by an Act of 1617—began replacing communion plate whilst well-to-do laymen commissioned silver mounts for the traditional quaich. However detrimental the Union of Crowns may have been to other facets of Scottish culture it did not hamper the evolution of gold and silver work which, both technically and aesthetically, was reaching its peak a hundred years later.

In more utilitarian fields the industrial history of Scotland is a story of attempts by Crown and legislature—broadly from 1600 onwards—to stimulate domestic production with a view to cutting down imports. The favoured instruments were first the monopoly or patent and then, after *c*. 1660, the company. Thus the history of soap-making begins with a patent of monopoly to Nathaniel Udward in 1619 for the erection of a soap-work in Leith coupled with an attempt to ban imports, and continues via fresh patents to the establishment of the Glasgow Soaperie in 1667. Sugar-refining, possibly tried before 1660, became a firmly rooted industry with the establishment in 1667 of the first of what quickly became a group of Glasgow sugar houses with an important by-product described in an Act of 1695 as 'a drug rather than a liquour'. The growth of paper-making depended primarily on the demands of the printers, and though a press was established in Edinburgh in 1508 only about 308 items were printed in Scotland before 1600 and Scottish publishing did not assume major proportions until the late seventeenth century. It is hardly surprising, therefore, that a paper-making licence granted in 1590 seems to have been abortive and 'it was not till the year 1675 that . . . paper-works were actually founded'[23] at Dalry on the Water of Leith.

When we survey the industrial experiments of the late seventeenth century, from textiles to bell-founding and from soap to pins and needles, we may imagine that the dawn was breaking. Or was it a false dawn? The development rested on a rational involvement of merchant capital, most of it Scottish, which was not afraid or ashamed to import skilled labour from England and Holland. But the weaknesses were manifold. All the evidence suggests high-cost production and a domestic market too small for real economies of scale. In other words the whole fabric depended upon protection and privilege.

As a link with overseas trade—the subject of the next chapter—it is appropriate to look briefly at the provision of ships and at the tenuous evidences before 1707 of a Scottish shipbuilding 'industry'. So far as we can judge the great bulk of Scottish sea-borne traffic was conducted in Scottish-owned ships. But they were small. An examination of the shipping frequenting the Baltic from c. 1500 to c. 1650 shows that the capacity of the average Scottish ship was only about one-third of that of the average Dutchman, and it is likely that the old enclosed Scottish harbours were incapable of coping with these bigger vessels belonging to Dutch or Hanse ports. Furthermore, except perhaps at Leith, there is no evidence of anything which can be called a permanent or Scottish shipyard, so that elsewhere the building of a ship involved the erection of temporary stocks on a suitable waterside site. Such sporadic building can be traced throughout the centuries: in c. 1249 a vessel was built at Inverness for the Earl of St Pol and Blois; in the fifteenth century Bishop Kennedy

of St Andrews built 'a great barge'; as part of his naval policy
James IV brought shipwrights from France, and his *Great Michael*,
launched in 1511 at Newhaven, was a monster by any contemporary
standard; the *Bonacord* was built at Aberdeen in 1606 of wood
floated down the Dee, and in 1643 Captain George Scott took
carpenters to Inverness and there built a 'ship of prodigious bignes'[24]
using wood from the Lovat forests in Glen Moriston. More important
in the aggregate, and certainly more continuous, was the ship repair
work which went on in most ports whereby shipwrights retained and
handed on their skill. In any event the few known instances of
building in Scotland pale before the recurring evidences of purchases
overseas, especially from Holland and Norway, not only of ships but
also of rigging. Certainly by the seventeenth century the Dutch were
the most efficient and cheapest shipbuilders in Europe, and nobody
could compete with the Baltic suppliers of cordage. So late as 1698,
when at long last a rope-work had been established in Glasgow, the
shipowners on the east coast resisted a proposed ban on imports on the
grounds that it was cheaper to fetch rope from the Continent than to
buy Scottish-made. As later history shows, the ensuing compromise—
a duty of 50s. per cwt. on imports—was a silver spoon in the mouth
of the infant industry.

CHAPTER V

Fishing and Overseas Trade

HOWEVER unflattering the early writers may have been on most aspects of the Scottish economy, they were unanimous about her rich endowment in fish. Pedro de Ayala, at the end of the fifteenth century, speaks of *piscinata Scotia*; Lesley, a little later, said of Lochaber that the lochs and rivers 'swormand sa plenteouslie' with salmon and other fish that they could be taken without any piscatorial skill; Major thought that the abundance of fish was Divine compensation for the lack of sunshine; and Hitchcock, in 1580, described how herring rose in shoals 'out of the deepes on both sides of Scotlande'. Throughout the country the then unpolluted inland waters provided a vital reinforcement to grain and flesh in the domestic dietary and, from the thirteenth century at least, provided also salmon for curing and export. This salmon traffic passed especially through Aberdeen, though Montrose, Dundee and Leith also feature, and it is significant that even in the fourteenth and fifteenth centuries, when relations with England were far from harmonious, there is still a string of references to the export of Scottish salmon to London.[1] In the process of time merchants employed increasingly sophisticated methods in their dealings with the salmon-river proprietors, making down-payments in advance for the catch. Thus in the early 1600s Lord Lovat agreed to such a 'forehand Block' with Duncan Forbes of Inverness and John Yeoman of Dundee, and as the market price thereafter rose sharply he suffered 'vast losse' by his dealing with these 'cunning fellows'.[2]

If the export figures for 1614 can be taken as typical, salmon

represented almost one-third of the total value of fish exported from
Scotland. The remainder was almost all herring, and though Parliament had legislated for the protection of salmon from the time of
James I onwards there can be no doubt that the herring fisheries
became increasingly prominent in the minds of Scotland's merchants
and legislators. Though there had been a substantial Scottish herring
fishery before 1400 it seemed to assume such proportions from
c. 1450 when, for example, Loch Fyne had become a recognised
ground, that one might be tempted to accept the old tradition of the
westward migration of the herring from the approaches to the Baltic.
Similarly an Act of Parliament of 1493, which optimistically in-
structed the burghs to acquire fishing boats and tackle so that Scotsmen should no longer miss the 'greit innumerable ryches' of the sea,
may point to the same conclusion. Furthermore though Dutchmen
had for centuries sent an occasional boat to Scottish waters, their
major interest seems to date from about 1500 and assumed such
proportions that, by the 1530s, there was all but open war between
them and native fishermen.

The history of the Scottish herring fishing from c. 1500 to 1707 is,
in fact, an account of attempts to meet the challenge provided by
the technical efficiency and organisational skill of the Dutch. It was
necessary, first of all, to ensure that the activities of Lowland
fishermen were not thwarted by the parochialism of Highland coastal
lairds. Dr Grant has said that anxiety to ensure the smooth operation
of the herring fisheries was the chief economic motive in James VI's
subjugation of the Western Highlands and Isles.[3] Secondly, if the
western fisheries were to be developed, it was necessary to establish
bases in an area which, as we have seen, was conspicuously short
of burghs. In the reign of James VI burghs of barony were authorised
at Gordonsburgh (Fort William), Campbeltown and Stornoway
where the proprietor, the Earl of Seaforth, introduced a few Dutchmen to pioneer the development of a locally-based fishery. Parliament
and the Convention of Royal Burghs provided a substantial corpus
of regulations for discipline in the fleets, for standardisation and
control of packing, for improved methods of curing red herring, and
for restricting the facilities available to foreign fishermen.

But the industry remained fragmented, bedevilled by local and
often conflicting interests, and, above all, short of capital. To remedy

these defects an Anglo-Scottish Commission produced a grandiose project for a Society of the Fishery of Great Britain with semi-autonomous regional subsidiaries[4] which, it was hoped, would go a long way towards reconciling local vested interests. A start was made in 1632 with 'the Association of the Lord Treasurer and others for the Fishing', based on Lewis and with a nominal capital of £11,750. Seven years later, by which time the Earl Marshal had replaced the Lord Treasurer as chief promoter, only £2,280 had been paid up and the company was over £4,000 in debt. The depredations of Dunkirk privateers, coupled with the hostility of the Islemen and lack of support from the Scottish courts, had extinguished what faint hope there ever was, and thirty years elapsed before anything comparable was attempted. Then, in 1670, The Royal Company for the Fishery of Scotland eventually took shape with the sole right of fishing off the coasts of Scotland and Greenland. Apart from its attempts to collect dues on exported herring there is little evidence of its activities and it was formally dissolved in 1690.

Over roughly the same period a Glasgow company fought a losing battle to maintain a Greenland whale fishery, but in general the Scottish fisheries remained in the hands of a multitude of small boat owners operating within a ten or fifteen mile belt of Scottish coastal water. The aggregate scale must not, however, be understated. In 1587, we are told there 'arivit in the red of Aberdeen ouitt of lochbruin [Loch Broom] of Scottish schipis, ane hundred sailis',[5] and the Glasgow historians speak of 'nine hundred boats' in the Clyde herring fishery in the early seventeenth century.[6] Amateurish it may have been by Dutch standards, but by Scottish standards it was a major economic undertaking.

Similarly by Dutch standards, Scottish overseas trade was never above the feather-weight class and was, in a sense, largely peripheral to the main stream of the country's economy. But small as it was, overseas trade fulfilled a number of vital functions. For those who could afford to buy, it provided some compensations for the climate and technical limitations of Scotland by the supply of exotic wines, fruits and manufactures. It brought into the country a range of industrial raw materials—flax, dyestuffs, iron, potash, salt—which, by 1600 at least, were helping to create miniature growth points in the economy. At moments of acute food shortage the expertise of the

traders was urgently required to secure emergency supplies of grain
from abroad. Some elements in the economy—the production of skins
and hides at any time, the herring fisheries, the production of coal
in the seventeenth century—could never have attained their size on
purely domestic demand and have something of the character of
'export industries'.

Except for the creation of a small transatlantic connection, Scottish
overseas traders in 1700 were following furrows cut centuries before,
though there had been significant changes in the relative importance
of the different routes and the introduction of some new commodities.
Almost certainly the biggest secular fluctuations were in the English
trade. The evidences down to about 1300—tenuous though they may
be—demonstrate reasonably regular seaborne links with Lynn,
Yarmouth, Dunwich and Southampton using Berwick as the
principal Scottish emporium,[7] and we must always presume the
existence of some overland traffic across the Borders. By either
method the trader avoided the hazards of wide sea crossing. How
far the long phase of political hostility after c. 1300 demolished this
fabric of commerce cannot be precisely stated. In a classic study of
English overseas trade in the fifteenth century[8] almost the only
references to Scotsmen relate to their piratical activities for which
indeed they had a European reputation. Yet whenever relations with
England eased, by truce or simply exhaustion, attempts were made
to re-establish trade, and a surprisingly large number of safe-conducts
(many of them for ships) were issued by the English in favour of
Scotsmen in the middle decades of the fifteenth century and the
pattern was repeated a hundred years later after the 'Rough Wooing'.[9]
Furthermore an examination of the activities of German merchants
in Boston, Ipswich and elsewhere in the early 1300s has shown that,
by 'various strategems', it was possible to maintain trade with
Scotland even in the face of official English prohibitions.[10]

There is, however, no firm evidence of any permanent revival until
after 1560 when diplomatic relations eased and when the two nations
had the common bond of Protestantism. Apart from the Dundee
Shipping Lists from 1581 onwards we have no series of Scottish port
records before the seventeenth century, but the English port books
which have been sampled for this purpose prove that from the 1580s
onwards there were regular Scottish exports to England of salt, fish

(notably 'Haberdine fish' and herring), coal (especially of the *charbon d'Ecosse* to London), skins and hides, wool when the Privy Council allowed it or when it was smuggled, sometimes grain, linen cloth and yarn, and knitted hose. In return England sent a great range of manufactured goods from beer to bibles and from bowstrings to tobacco pipes.[11] Already by 1600 England was competing with the Low Countries as Scotland's source of the more advanced manufactures.

Clearly the revival of this trade pre-dated the Union of the Crowns, and down to *c.* 1640 Anglo-Scottish relationships remained generally conducive to its growth. But after the chaos of the Civil Wars and the experience of the shot-gun common market of 1654–60 the atmosphere changed as both nations turned to the fashionable protectionist policies. So, according to the author of *Britannia Languens* (1680), until an Act passed some five years earlier 'intituled *Trade Incouraged* (by which the Importation of Scotch Cattle was stopt) England did furnish Scotland with wrought Wire of all sorts, Haberdashers Ware... Upholsterers Ware... Cutlers Ware... and Shop-sellers Ware', but since the Act the Scots either make these things themselves or buy them from 'other Foreigners'. Nevertheless, though paucity of statistics and the extent of smuggling preclude any definitive statement, it is likely that by 1700 the English was the most valuable single branch of Scotland's external trade.[12] On the export side two features predominated. As early as 1662 over 18,000 Scotch cattle left their imprint on the streets of Carlisle, and though there were great annual variations (resulting in part from English bans), there were years towards the end of the century when 60,000 head followed the Carlisle route alone. The second was the vast quantity of linen cloth and yarn, by value at the end of the century sometimes as much as one-half of all Scotland's recorded exports to England. In return, manufactures continued to constitute the biggest group, but increasingly tobacco and sugar assumed almost equal prominence and, when famine struck Scotland in the 1690s, England was a main supplier of grain.

Though, through the centuries, there are occasional references to trade with Drogheda and other Irish ports, various factors combined to restrict the scale of traffic with Ireland. At times the attitude of England had been positively hostile to its growth. Down to the seventeenth century the most active of Scotland's seaports lay on the coast most remote from Ireland. But more fundamental was the fact that, at least until about 1600, neither country was in any real economic sense complementary to the other. Thereafter the prospects must have seemed brighter. The final establishment of English rule in Ireland (under Elizabeth) coincided with an improvement in Anglo-Scottish relations; the plantation of Ulster forged a set of family links with Scotland; the growth of the west-coast ports— Ayr, Irvine and Glasgow—provided better equipped bases for trade; the growth of Scottish coal-mining offered a commodity generally lacking in Ireland. Certainly throughout the seventeenth century there is evidence of much toing and froing, mainly in small boats which could run well up the river mouths (a not inconsiderable factor in smuggling), and there are some years, for example 1695–6, when Irish arrivals feature prominently at Glasgow. The composition of the trade was summarised by Fynes Moryson in 1613 as fish, coal and whisky to Ireland and, in return, yarn, hides and silver. On the export side it is clear that coal grew in importance as the century went on: in 1683 a total of 1,864 tons was recorded and in 1700 4,471 tons, already enough to provide a powerful stimulus to the Scottish mine-owners around Irvine and to constitute a threat to those of the Whitehaven district who had traditionally monopolised the Irish market. Though sometimes frustrated by official bans there was a substantial return trade in live animals, notably horses and cattle, the latter, one suspects, mainly lean animals for fattening in south-west Scotland in readiness for the English market. Certainly, too, in the 1690s, Irish arable farming was strong enough to send grain to famine-stricken Scotland.

This purchase of grain from Ireland (and, as we have seen, from England) reflected a significant change in the traditional pattern of Scotland's relations with the Baltic. Though disrupted sometimes by wars within the Baltic, this ancient connection had never suffered from any lasting hostility against Scotland, and, as we saw in Chapter I, Scottish settlers and factors were accepted in the South Baltic towns. Here, from Lubeck and Hamburg in the west, to Danzig and Königsberg in the east, commerce rapidly grew in scale and sophistication under the aegis of the Hanse League (founded in 1241), providing an outlet for a great hinterland with a wealth of natural products. A letter of 1297 from William Wallace to the burgesses of Lubeck and Hamburg implies an existing Scottish mercantile link,[13] and recent research on the Hanse has revealed regular fourteenth-century links between Edinburgh and Bremen and the presence of Hanse factors and merchants in Leith, Dunbar, Glasgow and Aberdeen.[14] The fifteenth century opened badly when, as reprisal against the depredations of Scottish pirates, the Hanse threatened, and from 1415 to 1436 enforced, a ban on Scottish ships in their ports, but recovery came easily, and by the later part of the century contacts were substantial. In 1474–6, for example, twenty-four Scottish ships are recorded at Danzig[15] and in 1485, when there was a shortage of Biscay salt, the Danzig merchant Caspar Weinreich was offering Scottish salt at a highly competitive price.[16]

With the sixteenth century the pattern becomes increasingly clear because of the availability of records of ships and cargoes passing through the Sound.[17] The first deduction is that between 1497 and 1547 an annual average of twenty-eight Scottish ships entered and returned, and at that stage their Baltic port of call was almost entirely within the Hanse group. The indications that, even then, the eastern Baltic was the main single focus, are confirmed after 1557 when the Sound Register becomes more detailed and even more clearly after 1580 when the evidence of the few surviving Scottish port books can be introduced. Thus, of twenty-nine ships arriving at Dundee from the Baltic between 1580 and 1589, twenty-one were from Danzig, and of the 122 Baltic arrivals listed at Leith from 1636 to 1644, ninety-six were from Danzig and Königsberg. One other major change in the geographical pattern of Scottish trade within the Baltic becomes apparent in the late sixteenth century. Though there were older Scottish links with Sweden's west-coast ports, trade with Stockholm did not begin until *c.* 1560 but by the 1580s had become both a regular and valuable branch.[18]

A trade which could involve a voyage of six weeks, the payment of tolls at the Sound, the hazards of piracy and shipwreck, and—if delayed—the possibility of a winter in the ice, was clearly the result of great attractions. Though precise computation is impossible, it is tolerably clear that the attractions did not include a trade balance favourable to Scotland. Though the Baltic ports fed a large market for Scottish salt, cloth, fish, skins and hides, and sometimes coal, the market was competitive and certainly in the longer period seems to have involved some drain of coin and precious metals from Scotland. But to a remarkable extent the growth of manufacturing in Scotland hinged upon the availability of Baltic raw materials. Imports of flax and hemp largely from Danzig and considerable in almost every year covered by the Sound records from 1562 onwards, were exceptionally high in the 1630s and 1640s and again in the 1670s. Pitch and tar, potash, copper, wax and tallow, sawn timber, and ships rigging and tackle further illustrate the essential 'utility' nature of the imports. The strengthening of the link with Stockholm made available high quality charcoal-smelted iron, either as 'osmund' (pig) or 'gaid iron' (malleable) and by the closing decades of the seventeenth century about one-sixth of the iron exports from the Baltic was carried in Scottish vessels. And though originally most of these imports were—naturally—to eastern Scottish ports, by the later seventeenth century a rapidly growing part was following the long and hazardous voyage round to the Clyde.

Even if Scotland's industry could have survived without Baltic raw materials it is nearly certain that Scotsmen would have starved without Baltic grain, especially rye. The volume of shipping engaged in the trade displays most remarkable annual fluctuations. Thus whilst the annual average number of Scottish vessels involved in the later sixteenth century might be of the order of forty, this average would include peak years such as 1587 when 124 Scottish ships sailed to the Baltic, eighty of them in ballast. The simple fact was that Danzig and Königsberg, linked by waterways with a vast rural hinterland, were the emergency granary of Europe, and, down to about 1640, a crop shortage in Scotland is immediately reflected in the number of ships sailing for the Baltic. Thereafter the pattern changed. Except in 1679 and 1684 grain imports from Danzig were slight and—most significant of all—were minimal during the famine years of the 1690s.

Scottish connections with Norway, racial and dynastic, were commemorated in ballad and legend, but the commerce had a realistic base. Norwegian timber, transported to the coasts over frozen ground and—by the late sixteenth century at least—cut by water driven saws, was more accessible to the merchant of Leith or Dundee than the assorted trunks halfway up a remote Highland hillside. The cargo was easily handled on open decks, the commercial techniques were simple, and the 'hamebringing' of timber was held by official Scotland to justify exemption from bans even on the export of grain and certainly after *c.* 1660 a fair amount of Scottish grain was being sent to Norway to pay for timber. Of the scale of the trade little is known before the sixteenth century, but by the 1580s between spring and late autumn it was involving about one-third of the shipping of a major port such as Dundee. Increasing urban building, coupled with the demands of shipwrights, coopers and carpenters, maintained it at a high level through the seventeenth century when an increasing amount of Norwegian timber was imported direct to the Clyde.

But though it occupied so much ship space, the Norwegian trade was never, in terms of value, the most important element in Scotland's external economy. Without doubt the elements most cherished by Scotsmen were those arms of trade which thrust south-east and south to the Low Countries and France. The reason is simple. Scotland needed a point of commercial contact both with more advanced industrial communities and with markets for exotic produce. When, by about 1300, relations with England deteriorated, Scotsmen turned naturally to even better sources on the opposite shore of the North Sea. By 1313 the English were already protesting to Flanders about the facilities given to Scottish traders but the Flemish even then were taking a stand on open trading, and by 1347 the first tentative move was made for the establishment of a Scottish Staple at Middleburgh. In the event it took 200 hundred years for the final establishment of the Staple which, in spite of the counter claims of Middleburgh, Antwerp and Bruges, was finally fixed at Campveere.[19] The Staple—a part commercial, part social centre—was unique in Scottish commercial history. It provided an organised base for Scottish traders in the midst of Europe's most advanced mercantile area and greatest general emporium. With the Reformation and the creation of a Calvinist link, Scotland's main focus of interest was on that part of the Low Countries which became Holland, but with the seventeenth century the official concentration on a Staple port began to disintegrate. After the Restoration, it has been said, the Staple in the Low Countries was an anachronism[20] and by the end of the century—apart from a few from Aberdeen—most Scottish vessels were going to Rotterdam rather than to Veere.

No simple generalisation can do justice to the range of Scottish imports from the Low Countries: the couplet in *The Libel of English Policie* (written *c.* 1430) about half the ships being full of cart-wheels and wheelbarrows is palpably nonsense. From sources such as the Ledger of Andrew Haliburton, the Scottish factor at Middleburgh in the 1490s, and from the much more extensive Dutch records,[21] it is plain that in the late Middle Ages the Low Countries were Scotland's main suppliers of spices, of small manufactures ranging from stationery to weapons and from household fitments to soap, and of fruits and onions; that they were at least a leading source of dyestuffs and textiles; that they could serve as entrepôt for wine and grain; and that they were able to provide servicing functions from the re-gilding of a clock face to the dyeing of linen. Cargoes to Scotland were almost always mixed, consisting sometimes of such a miscellany of small lots that one is forced to assume that they were virtually individual orders. It is plain also that a Scottish factor there would carry out a mixture of assignments: arranging, for example, for the transmission of money to Rome to 'expedite' the issue of a dispensation, or sending a messenger on to Venice on behalf of the Duke of Ross.

The return trade was relatively simple. Certainly odds and ends of Scottish wares appear, such as the two bales of Scottish cloth sent by Francesco Datini from Bruges to Majorca in 1396, but the medieval backbone consisted of skins and hides, and wool and fish. Then, about the 1480s, 'steinkolen' begins to appear in the Dutch records, a fore-warning of a new and growing Scottish export. The location of the main coal and salt producing area—around the Forth—facilitated the trade, and the Dutch could offer payment in sound currency. The allegation in the 1620s that whilst coal was virtually unobtainable in Angus scores of Dutch ships were being laden in the Forth is borne out by the Veere records which show, in some years, as many as fifty arrivals of colliers from Scotland. Similarly there is no reason to doubt Brereton's report in the 1630s that 'the greatest part' of the salt made between Musselburgh and Stirling went to Holland. There was a local demand in Holland for both salt and coal for fish-curing, brewing and the like, but there are indications also of re-export within the multilateral trade network of which the Dutch were masters.

Because, after 1603, Scotland could no longer have an independent foreign policy, her relationship with Holland was jeopardised by the Dutch wars of Cromwell and Charles II. The equally ancient association with France was similarly in peril, partly because the *raison d'être* for the Auld Alliance had evaporated after 1560, but more specifically because of the protectionist policy of Colbert from the 1660s and of the open hostility to France under William III. It is significant that the special commercial privileges of Scotsmen in France, which had been widened in 1534 and reached their maximum in 1558, were withering perceptibly in the early seventeenth century, and after 1663 no amount of protest would induce Louis XIV to exempt the Scots from a special levy on foreign ships in French harbours.[22]

Geographically the trade with France involved two main regions with different attractions. From at least the early fifteenth century Scotsmen were being accepted as burgesses in Dieppe where, though for a time they had their own chapel in the Church of St James served by a 'soi-disant prêtre écossais', they tended to become absorbed in the native population.[23] This northern region—to Scottish traders particularly Dieppe and Rouen—drew on a hinterland of rich agriculture, of advanced industrial technology and of internationally famous fairs. In consequence the commercial attractions were basically similar to those of the Low Countries, and the composition of trade was not greatly different. Thus James IV, with commendable gallantry, presented Lady Catherine Gordon with a gown of 'tawny Rouen cloth'; George Buchanan, more appropriately, had a gown of 'Paryse black'; in 1531 there was a craze in Scotland for Rouen hats; when Millar set up his printing press in 1507 he used characters from Rouen; regularly Scotland bought woad and other dyestuffs and, sometimes, grain.

The attraction of the other major French market is amply demonstrated by the regularity with which Scottish seamen were prepared to face yet a further 500 miles of stormy and often English-ridden waters to reach it. For centuries the Biscay ports, outstandingly La Rochelle and Bordeaux, were, to Scotsmen, synonymous with salt and wine. 'The English, Scots and Scandinavians', wrote Jean Bodin in 1568, 'buy our wines, saffron, and plums, but above all our salt', and, he explained further, they often came in ships ballasted with sand and paid for the salt in cash. Production in the coastal salines was simple and, because of the warm summers, no artificial means of evaporation was involved, but besides being relatively cheap this Biscay salt had a high reputation especially for fish-curing. Virtually no records survive for any period before the early 1400s; those for the fifteenth century, though broken and incomplete, prove at least the existence of the trade; and by 1563–4 it was such that eleven shiploads of salt left La Rochelle for Scotland.[24] By the late sixteenth century, when La Rochelle became a major stronghold of French Protestantism, fellow-feeling reinforced commercial interest, and salt imports occupied a substantial part of Scotland's shipping during the autumn of each year. Rising Scottish salt output, coupled with the effects of both civil war in France and Anglo-French hostility, reduced the importance of Biscay salt at least to the east coast, but it remained of importance to the fish-curers of the Clyde area who— apart from Saltcoats—had few local sources of supply.

By the seventeenth century, it has been said, the drinking of French wine in Scotland was 'a sign of almost ostentatious civility'.[25] Certainly, in spite of pious protests from Privy Council and churchmen, it was conducted on a grand scale. A reasonable estimate would be that, around 1610–20, French wine was legally entering Dundee at a rate of 50,000 gallons a year, Aberdeen at perhaps 20,000 and Leith at perhaps a quarter of a million.[26] How much more came in illegally nobody can say, for smuggling was always possible and often easy. Though the direct link with Bordeaux went back at least to the mid-thirteenth century, it is clear that, down to the late fifteenth century, part of Scotland's wine came indirectly, via the Low Countries, north France or even England. But by the reign of Queen Mary, Council Minutes (for example at Dundee) spoke of the time 'when the Bordeaux ships come in' as a regular and no doubt welcome annual event. The bulk of the cargo consisted always of casks of claret-type wine, accompanied sometimes by a few casks of vinegar; some brandy (there is a reference in 1569 but the brandy trade grew up mainly a century later); a few packs of woad; a few barrels of dried plums.

This was a high-value branch of Scotland's import trade, and the indications are, that at least to the mid-seventeenth century, it was offset by direct commodity exports. By any pre-1700 European standards France had a great population, still mainly Roman Catholic, located largely inland, and consequently presenting a major market for fish. The French commercial historians give priority to Scottish salmon, but, in bulk, salmon was clearly exceeded by herring. And though the French could export the finer cloths, their working population offered a market for Scottish linen and wool, and their craftsmen were willing to make up the hides and skins which Scottish merchants could send them.

Beyond Biscay lay the great potential market of Iberia, never much exploited by Scotsmen. Clearly the length of the voyage was itself a disincentive, and after 1560 the official attitude of the Kirk was hostile. Spaniards as such were still accepted as fellow humans: thus the burgh of Ayr spent £6 on food, lodging and footwear for a party of 'pure Spainyardis' who came ashore from the wreck of the Armada,[27] but four years later the ministers in Edinburgh secured a ban on commercial trips to Spain until merchants could go without fear of the Inquisition.[28] So Scottish trade with Spain remained, at best, a minor extension of that with the Biscay coast of France, and it was only towards the end of the seventeenth century, when the French trade was dislocated by war, that sailings from Spain with wine and salt became a regular occurrence. And beyond Gibraltar the record is hazy, although certainly Scotsmen had some familiarity with the Mediterranean world. Thus Alexander I had an Arabian horse and Turkish armour and there is a story of the building of a Crusader ship at Inverness in 1249.[29] By the 1500s subscriptions were being solicited for the relief of Scottish mariners held captive by the Algerian pirates or by the 'Turks', and certainly some Scottish vessels entered the Mediterranean, mainly, so it would seem, under charter to foreign shippers. Both seamen and ships may have added to Scotland's overseas earnings, but direct trade between Scotland and points beyond Gibraltar was negligible.

Obsession with domestic problems combined with shortage of capital to bar Scotland from any immediate participation in the widening commercial opportunities which stemmed from the discovery of the sea route to the Far East and of the continent of America. When by the early 1600s, she was somewhat better equipped, most of the accessible territories had been pre-empted by monopolistic imperial powers whilst Scotland had lost her diplomatic independence. There are tenuous evidences of Scottish probes into the Newfoundland trade,[30] but the major effort of the early seventeenth century, the attempted settlement of Nova Scotia, foundered on the rocks of French opposition and English indifference. Substantial success had to await the emergence in Glasgow of a group of merchants with the resolution and the resources to circumvent the political obstacles.

The origins of this development—in effect the beginning of Glasgow's colonial trade—are obscure. When Tucker visited Glasgow in 1655 in connection with his survey of revenues he was told that Glasgow traders had 'adventured as farre as the Barbadoes'[31] but because of the long periods involved (and hence the slow turn-over of capital) they had given up the enterprise. The reference may have been to the voyage of the Glasgow owned *Antelope* which, in 1647, had arrived back at the Clyde with 20,000 lb. of tobacco from Martinique. At the time of Tucker's visit the English colonies were, legally, being opened to Scotsmen, but by the time that Scotland had begun to recover from the devastation of the wars the free-trade phase had ended and by the English Navigation Act of 1660 Scotsmen fell under the same exclusion as Dutchmen and other trade rivals. And yet, by the early 1680s, an annual average of seven ships were making the return trip between the Clyde and the New World.[32] Though, for lack of surviving records, there is no means of assessing its extent in the 1690s, it is clear that, in the face of seemingly heavy odds, a significant Glasgow-controlled colonial trade had been created before the Union of 1707. It reflected the calculated resolve of Glasgow to enlarge its commercial horizon.

Hitherto its rôle had been basically regional: importing wine for the local markets, sending boat-loads of coal to Ireland, as an emporium for the West supplying drapery goods to the Macleods at Dunvegan, but inhibited always by Dumbarton's claim to the right of controlling shipping in the deep-water channels of the lower Clyde. As more distant trading required larger vessels—and by the mid-seventeenth century Glasgow merchants were buying 200-tonners—the process of expansion hinged on the physical development of port facilities which the town began in 1662 by building a quay at the Broomielaw and then, much more ambitiously in 1668, by acquiring a site for the deep-water harbourage of Port Glasgow. The commercial drive and capital came notably from a company of 107 merchants founded in 1668 to trade with the American and West Indian colonies,[33] headed by Walter Gibson whose versatility stretched from malt-making to transporting captive Covenanters. We know that occasionally the English Navigation Laws were relaxed in favour of Scotsmen, but when they were operative the Scottish Privy Council made no attempt to co-operate with the English against infringements,[34] and it seems that the Glasgow men's transatlantic activity was in plain breach of the laws to which their king had assented. As Professor Smout has said, 'the sharpest thorns in the flesh of the English officials were Glasgow merchants like Provost Walter Gibson, who sailed his vessels home disguised as English ships and imported Nevis sugar straight home to the refineries on the Clyde'.[35]

It is ironic that the great national transatlantic project, the 'Darien Scheme', which was legally above-board, ended in utter disaster. As established by statute in 1695, the Company of Scotland trading to Africa and the Indies was conceived as a commercial undertaking. It conformed to the current economic ambitions of the Scottish Parliament, and, because of its possibilities as a rival to the English East India Company, it attracted a short-lived surge of support in London. Under the influence of William Paterson (who had mercantile experience in the West Indies) its directors resolved to establish a colony and trading base on the Isthmus of Panama where, from 1698 to 1701, its agents and settlers fought a losing battle against unhealthy climate, jealousy, incompetence, Spanish hostility and English non-co-operation. Apart from the stores taken out and a little trading (in 1701) on the African coast, it played no direct material part in the commercial history of Scotland. But the financial and psychological consequences were deep. Frozen out of London and Hamburg by the opposition of English vested interests, the directors had to rely in effect on Scottish capital in a period when, because of crop failures and overseas trade difficulties, the Scottish economy was hard pressed. Their calls on stockholders yielded £153,631, about a quarter of the total originally estimated as necessary. And whilst it is true that after 1707 the shareholders were not ungenerously compensated, the fact remains that in the critical years leading up to the Union when Scotland was desperately short of liquid capital most Scotsmen held England to blame for the £153,631 rotting in the humid heat at Darien.

The pattern of Scotland's external trade is relatively clear. To some extent the wares of that trade—certainly imports—never moved far beyond the point of entry. It is, for example, a tolerably safe proposition that Edinburgh, Perth, Aberdeen, Dundee and, as time went on, Glasgow, contained a very substantial fraction of the market for wines, imported cloth, timber and dyestuffs. But it is equally evident, from household accounts and the like, that wines were conveyed far inland and it is self-evident that though such bulk exports as coal and salt were produced near the point of export, others, such as skins and hides, originated often in the heart of the Highlands.

Yet our knowledge of both the physical equipment of inland transport and of the commercial mechanism involved is deplorably slight. The *via regia* was a grandiose label for a beaten track, distinguished more by the theoretical protection of the king's peace than by the quality of its surface. Before 1617 no serious attempt was made to provide the means for highway maintenance, and it seems that the Act of that year, which enabled the Justices of the Peace to mobilise labour and carts and to raise money locally, was largely disregarded. Maps of the seventeenth century, especially Greene's *New Map of Scotland* (1679) show a pattern of tracks, intensive, as one might expect, in the eastern counties south of the Tay, but extending north via Aberdeen and on to Dunnet Head. A distinguished scholar has said of the reign of Charles I that there was 'considerable traffic on the coast road up from England' and that 'roads ran through the Lothians and Fife and up to Dundee and Aberdeen'[36] and there was certainly an old cart-way for mineral traffic from Leadhills via Biggar to the Forth. We know little, however, of the quality of the tracks or how far they were used by wheeled vehicles. From the time of Queen Mary a few wealthy people had owned coaches, perhaps prestige symbols, but even in towns their use must have been limited by the narrow wynds. A Warrant to the magistrates of Lanarkshire in 1671 speaks of the road from Blackburn to Kirk O' Shotts as 'a sufficient way . . . for coaches and carts', and seven years later William Home of Edinburgh was seeking a patent for a stage coach service to Glasgow. But contemporary observers such as Morer specifically denied that stage coaches were employed, and there is no firm evidence of a professional coach-builder in Scotland in the 1690s. If in fact there was an increase in inland trade it seems that its long distance component must still have depended mainly on the pack horse.

The record of bridge-building is only slightly more substantial. Locally bridges were often erected by monastic houses: Kelso built one over the Ettrick in the reign of Alexander II and the *Rentale Dunkeldense*[37] contains the detailed accounts of the building of a stone bridge over the Tay there in the time of the poet-bishop Gavin Douglas. The first Clyde bridge at Glasgow—though probably of wood—is commonly attributed to Bishop Rae who died in 1367, and that over the Dee at Aberdeen was one of the benefactions of the great Bishop Elphinstone (died 1514). Yet even with national financial assistance it was impossible to maintain a bridge at such a key strategic centre as Perth. After a series of considerable patchings in the late 1500s, it was finally resolved to replace the old medieval bridge there by a new stone structure designed by John Mylne, the King's Master Mason, and financed by contributions from all over the country. Finished in 1617 it fell in 1621, the result either of a 'mighty spate', or, as some thought, of Divine retribution for the episcopalian iniquities in the Five Articles of Perth. Whatever the cause, 150 years elapsed before it was replaced. The crossing of the Clyde just south of Lanark, an almost equally vital link, was provided from the fifteenth century by a ferry furnished originally by the chaplain of St Katherine's altar in St Nicholas Chapel at Lanark. From time to time the burgesses of Lanark pled for assistance to build a bridge but only in 1695, when the ferry had been wrecked by floods, did they get a positive decision.[38]

In short, overland transport, relying mainly on the pack horse, the sledge or the droving of animals, was even in the seventeenth century a slow and inefficient business. The constant attention—both in building and repair—to harbours simply emphasises the fact that the commercial life of Scotland depended primarily on water transport. Coastal or river boats could reach virtually every major concentration of population, and whilst the evidences are fragmentary there are indications of a very considerable amount of shipment from one port to another. In part this reflected simply the transport of locally-produced commodities such as salt or coal for local consumption else-where, but equally clearly it could form part of a more complex process of redistribution of imports or of gathering of exports. Thus, to quote typical cases from the seventeenth century *Aberdeen Shore Work Accounts*, the arrival in 1624 of wheat and wine from Dundee and timber from Leith would imply that domestic entrepôt activities existed and that Leith in particular served a very extensive hinterland. But landward penetration remained costly, restricted and sometimes hazardous. In short there was no real prospect of any general dispersion of economic growth without a substantial improvement in overland transport facilities, and of this, down at least to the eighteenth century, there is hardly any sign.

CHAPTER VI

The State and Economic Life

OUR examination of the main aspects of the economy of Scotland down to 1707 can lead only to the conclusion that it remained a relatively retarded member of Western European society. The Reformation apart, none of the great surges of European ideas had made any deep impact: feudalism had been halted by the Highland Line and had largely petered out in the political chaos of the fourteenth century; monasticism had come and gone; the 'Age of Discoveries' had resulted in two transatlantic graveyards; the Renaissance had influenced only limited aspects of life; and the new science of Galileo, though striking some responsive chords, was as yet producing little practical effect. The reasons are to be sought in part in the facts of geography: the natural endowment of Scotland—the relative scarcity of arable land, the harsh climate—and in her peripheral location. But geography cannot provide the whole explanation. Economic and social progress depend upon the existence of certain elements of infrastructure: a political system adequate to ensure reasonable security for person and property both within the country and on legitimate business abroad; to provide such basic tools of economic life as safe communications, a stable currency and the institutions of law and of learning; either to encourage its people to display initiative or itself to give a lead. The purpose of this chapter is to enquire how far government in Scotland fulfilled these elementary requirements.

The word 'government' needs examination in this context. Scotland had some form of parliamentary body from the reign of

Alexander III, and the twelve published volumes of Acts of the Parliament of Scotland seem to reflect a substantial amount of positive governmental activity. But like most ancient Scottish institutions, Parliament (properly 'The Estates') was a unique body. Even in its later and relatively effective days, it consisted of blocks of commissioners representing sectional interests; except for a brief period after 1640 and again after 1689, it had no independent powers of initiating legislation but was almost wholly the tool of the Crown; it met only briefly and irregularly, and, worst of all, it had no control over the execution of its statutes. The second limb of central government, the Privy Council, emerged from the group of magnates and officers who constituted the king's council of the twelfth century. Under a strong monarch it was a valuable device for keeping powerful barons usefully employed in the service of the state: under a weak king (or during a minority) it became a warring ground of baronial factions. It was never a purely executive body: its 'Acts' (such as that of 1625 revoking all grants of land made by the Crown since 1542) had both the appearance and the force of law, and as the Council included the executive officers of state, enforcement was at least probable. Two further bodies, whilst representing sectional groups, cannot be excluded, for both were capable of action affecting the public weal. The first—the Convention of Royal Burghs—we have already considered in Chapter III as a kind of burghal economic parliament. The other—the General Assembly of the Kirk—emerged after the Reformation as the keeper of the conscience of the nation and, especially in the 1640s, clearly entertained notions of a theocratic state.

Yet we must offer the suggestion that these were simply the trappings of government. What mattered in the final analysis was whether, somewhere in Scotland there was a man or a small group who could exercise decisive rule, for Scotland was governed by men, not by institutions. Approached thus, it comes as no surprise to find that the 'Golden Age' when much of Scotland entered into full communion with Anglo-Norman culture was a period of long and generally strong reigns—Malcolm Canmore for thirty-five years, Alexander I for seventeen, David I for twenty-nine, William the Lion for forty-nine, Alexander II for thirty-five and Alexander III for thirty-seven. The death of the child-queen Margaret in 1290 left the

succession open to dispute and thus paved the way for English intervention, and in spite of the triumph of Robert Bruce and his reign
to 1329, the stage had been set for a long drama of battle for power
in Scotland. 'From Robert Bruce to James VI' wrote one of Scotland's
classic historians, 'we reckon ten princes; and seven of these were
called to the throne while they were minors, and almost infants.'[1]
Defied in the West by the Lords of the Isles who exercised a *de facto*
independence, challenged in the South by the Douglases, ineffective
over much of the Highlands, committed by the Auld Alliance to
hostility to England, the youthful kings had little chance of providing
lasting conditions of stability and order. Certainly the Stewart
dynasty achieved remarkable continuity and yielded periods of
promise, notably the reign of James IV who, as Professor Mackie has
said 'gave to the Scottish realm an effective power which made it a
"new monarchy"; his reign was the expression of his own personality
and its achievements were largely due to his own vigour and his own
ability.'[2] After Flodden the good work was resumed by James V, but
like his father he could not, or would not, avoid re-opening the
breach with England which, if history showed anything, was fatal to
Scotland's material progress. For all his faults, and they were many,
James VI sought and achieved security both for the nation and for
himself. He came to the throne in 1567 and died—in his bed—in
1625. Scotland had never known such continuity of rule.

The failure over the centuries to ensure uniform administration of
law and order—the fundamental requirement for economic progress
—was not for any lack of attempts. As we have seen in Chapter II,
the feudal structure of the twelfth and thirteenth centuries involved
both the delegation of judicial and administrative authority to the
barons and the extension of more direct crown administration
through the agency of the sheriff, and by the end of the thirteenth
century some thirty sheriffdoms were in being. With the Wars of
Independence and the troubles of the fourteenth century this feudal
structure disintegrated so that, even in the central belt, there were
long periods when the word of the nearest baron meant more than
the king's writ. Establishment of royal authority was most elusive on
the margins of the kingdom. The virtually independent rule of the
Lord of the Isles, though seriously challenged in 1429, survived until
1493, and even then the West was anything but obedient to the Crown.

Another century was to pass before, by the somewhat dubious tactics of the Band of Icolmkill [Iona], the western chiefs were subdued. In the far north, another piece of sharp practice by James III secured Orkney and Shetland to the Scottish Crown, but again the local magnate was 'subject' in no more than name until Earl Patrick was brought to trial and, with his heir, executed in Edinburgh in 1615. To the south, the Borders, because of their exposure to English intrigue, were a running sore. From 1515 to 1602 alone, no fewer than eighty-seven judicial or armed expeditions were mounted in attempts to establish order, involving at times fencible men from as far north as Forfar. Again there was no solution after 1603 when James VI could deploy both Scottish and English forces in simultaneous assault.

The complement of good government is good justice. The twelfth-century kings attempted to provide criminal jurisdiction through the office of Justiciar, supplemented by their own Council which could convene as a court of justice. Parliament, when it emerged as a recognisable institution, had judicial functions—and an increasingly defined rôle in civil actions, and it was on this foundation that James I began the establishment of a more regular 'central' court sitting in Edinburgh. At first unprofessional in personnel and limited in scope, it was reorganised by James IV and by the 1530s became the professional College of Justice. And gradually a corpus of national law was created, starting from a mass of local customary laws, fed in the twelfth and thirteenth centuries by borrowings from England, refreshed in the sixteenth by the 'reception' of Roman Law and reduced to order for the first time by Stair and Mackenzie in the late seventeenth. In law, as in justice and administration, localism in Scotland was a long time a-dying.

Attempts by Scottish 'governments' both to supply the tools for the economy and to evolve an economic policy have to be set and assessed within this context of monarchical and institutional weakness. Once the economy began to move beyond the elementary barter stage, it required a medium of exchange, and in Scotland, as in most of Western Europe, the making of coins was an attribute of monarchy. By contrast, however, with some countries, the demand in Scotland was relatively small, partly because over much of the rural sector, payments (for example of rents) often continued to be made at least partly in kind until the seventeenth and eighteenth centuries, and partly because traders were accustomed to using any coin that came to hand, irrespective of its nationality. The Renfrew coin hoard,[3] containing only 153 Scottish coins (all 1249–1329) out of a total of 674, though possibly untypical in its high English component, nevertheless illustrates the prevalence of foreign coins in fourteenth-century Scotland. Later evidences, from merchants' accounts and the like, suggest that in the next two centuries continental coins (especially Scandinavian, French and Iberian) had come into daily use in mercantile circles and by the later sixteenth century their value in terms of Scottish currency was periodically fixed by Parliament or Privy Council.

The general opinion of numismatists is that Scotland had no regular domestic coinage before the silver pennies of David I, struck at Berwick and Roxburgh. Under Alexander III silver was minted more widely, and the first gold—the noble—came under David II. But already, by the 1360s, the Scottish silver coinage was moving on the downward slope of depreciation. To give coins greater durability, coiners in both England and Scotland had always infused a small amount of alloy. Even so in the coinages of the twelfth and thirteenth centuries a pound (lb.) of silver had yielded only 252 pennies. David II squeezed another hundred from each pound; with Robert II (c. 1390) the pound yielded over 500, and then in the next century James II and James III cast prudence so far to the winds that by 1483 the pound of silver was being made into 1,680 pence. At that level, depreciation had already brought the Scottish currency to a point where a Scottish coin was reckoned as worth only about a quarter of the English equivalent, and worse was to come with renewed depreciation in the sixteenth century until, by 1603, the £ Scots was worth only one-twelfth of the £ English, and this ratio then remained constant until the two coinages were merged after 1707.

Debasement could provide a temporary palliative to the chronic shortage of circulating money, and certainly the provision of coins with low purchasing power was socially desirable. But especially in periods when it was being actively and officially applied—for example in the second half of both the fifteenth and sixteenth centuries—it not only had an unsettling effect on commercial relations but contributed materially to the rise in commodity prices within Scotland. Behind it lay two related causes. Scotland suffered from a chronic inability to produce or to earn an adequate supply of precious metals but, nevertheless, was confronted with rising public expenditure and relatively inflexible public revenue. In other words the problem of the coinage and the apparently wilful ineptitude of rulers in handling it cannot be divorced from the more general issue of public finance.

The medieval kings had limited but well-recognised regular sources of income[4] based in part on the obligations of feudal tenants-in-chief and royal burghs, in part on fines and in part on the great custom levied on the export of wool, skins and other staple wares. These could be supplemented by exceptional levies—or 'aids'—for a variety of objects from the ransom of a king, the marriage of his son, the dispatching of an embassy to a foreign country, to defence or armed expeditions or, sometimes, to a local enterprise such as building the Tay Bridge at Perth in 1578. From time to time, as in 1556 when Mary of Guise was faced with a huge deficit inherited from her predecessors, there were proposals for a perpetual general tax, but in the event there was no significant permanent change in the sources of revenue until 1644 when the first general excise duties were levied. From time to time the Crown had such uncovenanted windfalls as the forfeiture of the Douglas estates in the fifteenth century; the feuing of Crown lands, which we discussed in Chapter I, had a strongly fiscal motive; the tightening up of justice and administration contributed—through fines—to the revenues of an effective ruler such as James V; and in the decades before the Reformation, the Roman Church was willing to bid for the continued loyalty of Scotland by making substantial contributions to the national treasury.

The scales, however, were increasingly tipped by rising expenditure. Uncovenanted gains were offset by such uncovenanted losses as the ransom paid between 1357 and 1377 for the release of David II from English captivity and by the growing cost of internal and external defence. In the fifteenth century, when the survival of any Scottish monarch depended increasingly upon his ability to deploy forces superior to those of unruly barons, artillery became as much a practical necessity as a symbol of prestige. English cannon were fired in Scotland in the early 1300s, but, apart from a stray reference in 1340, the history of Scottish artillery dates from the fifteenth century with weapons of various names but alike in their high cost, unpredictable behaviour and heavy demands in terms of manpower and draught beasts. But though there were failures—the rebel Earl of Angus could gloat over the inability of James V to reduce Tantallon in 1528—this new weapon powerfully reinforced the traditional method of forcing surrender by blockade. Similarly by the time of James IV and V the Crown was spending money on the foundation of a Scottish navy of purpose-built vessels. Mons Meg, which could reputedly throw a shot nearly two miles, was paralleled at sea by the *Great Michael* of 1511, 240 feet long with a crew of 300 sailors and 120 gunners. The changing techniques of warfare were creating demands which the traditional feudal levies could not satisfy: the need for trained gunners and for garrison troops who would not expect to go home when their forty days' service was expired. Furthermore the more sophisticated way of life associated with the Renaissance was penetrating the Scottish Court by the time of James III and found a willing exponent in the person of James IV. James V was more successful than his predecessors, or indeed than most of his successors, in maintaining a high level of expenditure and yet building up a not inconsiderable hoard of private treasure. The more efficient financial administration by officials such as Robert Barton was paying dividends in increased regular revenue, but his main asset was the pressure he could bring to bear on the Church even to the extent of providing benefices for his illegitimate sons. Whether, if foreign relations had flowed smoothly, his policies would have continued successfully is an open question, for by the mid-sixteenth century Scotland was falling victim to the great upward surge of prices which bedevilled national finances in every state of Western Europe for the next hundred years.

'No sixteenth century ruler after James V,' Mrs Mitchison has written, 'had strength to do more than live from hand to mouth, and none of them had enough grasp of elementary economics to do even this in an intelligent way.'[5] The precariously placed rulers of the mid-sixteenth century were unlikely to risk their position by imposing taxation adequate to wipe out the deficits which each inherited from his predecessor. For most—notably perhaps the Regent Morton— currency depreciation offered a tempting short-term solution. It is true that from the 1560s the Crown's regular revenues were supplemented by its share of the old Church incomes, and as the reign of James VI proceeded more use was made of *ad hoc* taxations, income from customs was substantially improved by the inclusion of duties on certain imports in 1597 and by more efficient collection, money was raised from the sale of monopolies and tithes, whilst in 1596 the appointment of the 'Octavians'—a sort of financial 'Brains Trust'—though soon frustrated, was a promising device for regulating expenditure and was later revived by Charles I. It remains clear, however, that down to the seventeenth century the central government of Scotland was run on a frayed and badly-knotted shoe-string.

By the closing years of James VI, and even more after the 1640s, taxation became an increasingly regular occurrence and bore on a wider spectrum of the population. It may be true that money was a less potent factor in Scotland than in England in the process of stirring up opposition to the government of Charles I, but, both by his demands on the lay occupants of pre-1560 Church properties and by the increasing regularity of taxation of rents (after 1621 for all practical purposes an annual event) Charles alienated many who might otherwise have tolerated his ecclesiastical policies. But though Scotsmen were becoming accustomed to paying a fairer price for government, it was only with Civil Wars and the heavy hand of the Commonwealth that the demands of the rulers began to bite deeply. During the fighting, which went on intermittently until 1651, the depressed economy was exposed both to *ad hoc* levies to support armies or, locally, as penalties for backing the wrong side, and to the new excise duty of 1644. Originally imposed as a temporary device—until, according to the then Dundee member, 'parliament shall find out ane better way to provide money'—the excise was highly unpopular in that it bore directly on malt and a range of consumer goods, but, like most allegedly 'temporary' imposts, it stuck. Indeed, under the Commonwealth, Scotsmen paid heavily in taxes for the firm government they received and for the employment provided in the building and servicing of garrison establishments. A contemporary described, for example, how the Cromwellian troops at Inverness 'not only civilised but enriched this place', but one suspects that the 'sighs and teeres, pale faces and embraces,'[6] which marked the final disbandment of the garrison in 1662 portray the reactions of the girls rather than those of their tax-paying fathers.

Because late seventeenth-century Scotland was, by force of circumstances, involved in increasingly expensive wars, she followed English experiments both in devising new heads of revenue and in reorganising tax collection. The vote to Charles II by the Scottish Parliament of an annual sum of almost half a million pounds (Scots) confirmed the earlier trend towards annual taxation, and, again following earlier patterns, the major element in taxation—the 'cess'—was largely based on property values. As the county areas had no appropriate mechanism for valuation the principal heritors were nominated as 'commissioners of supply' and remained, under this title, the backbone of rural administration until the end of the nineteenth century.

The record so far is not very impressive. But that is not to say that the nation's lawmakers lacked notions of broad economic strategy. In so far as we can generalise, it seems that down at least to the late sixteenth century, the overall objective was the attainment of domestic plenty by regulations to ensure the free movement of goods to domestic markets and by restriction of exports. Legislation from 1449 onwards, reinforced by a mass of burghal edicts, sought to prevent the forestalling of goods, especially of food; an Act of 1452 required farmers to thresh their stacks before 31 May; whenever domestic harvests fell short, Parliament or Privy Council banned the export of grain; down to 1597 customs were levied only on exports, and a complicated code of regulations aimed at forcing overseas traders to bring back precious metal in at least part return for the goods they sold abroad.

The general intention of this medieval legislation—it would perhaps be rash to call it 'policy'—stands in such sharp contrast to that of the late seventeenth century that we may at least speculate on the possibility of a deliberate swing to a 'mercantilist' attitude. Certainly by the middle years of James VI's reign there are clear signs of experiments in more positive *étatism*. The introduction of import duties in 1597, though motivated by fiscal considerations, marked the beginning of a protectionist industrial policy which blossomed after the Restoration. Bans on the export of wool reinforced the active encouragement to new industries which we noted in Chapter IV. By the 1670s the dominant concern for food consumer-interests was giving place to discouragement of food imports and, by the 1690s, to encouragement of exports. Similarly attempts to provide the tools of the economy, from the beginnings of a royal postal service after 1603 to the creation of the Bank of Scotland in 1696, illustrate the kind of positive state action which characterised classical mercantilism. True enough, the roads of post-Restoration Scotland were still paved mainly with good intentions, but there had been no fewer than four statutes about highways since 1617. Nobody could accuse Parliament of not trying.

But what basically determined the pattern of the Scottish economy was not economic legislation as such. Over the centuries Scotland took major decisions, none of them initially for solely economic reasons, yet each fraught with the possibility of enormous economic consequences. Of these decisions the Alliance with France, the break with Rome, the Union of the Crowns and the Union of Parliaments, stand out with such prominence as to demand examination. Though alliance with France can be traced back to 1173 when William the Lion made common cause with Louis VII and though the last two Alexanders took French brides, the Auld Alliance as a permanent feature in Scotland's international relations begins with the Wars of Independence as a response to Edward III's ambitions to dominate Scotland. Renewed from time to time by formal agreement, it attained its final phase of close intimacy in the two decades before 1560 when Scotland was well on the road towards becoming an outlying French province. The counter argument, of course, is that but for the Alliance Scotland might well have become an English province, conceivably another Ireland, and it is impossible to weigh the actual cost (in men and resources) of supporting the French against the possible cost of resisting occupying forces. There can be no doubt that, through the Alliance, France attracted direct Scottish trade. For the obvious reasons of ease of access and common language there was always a natural tendency to trade with England; as we saw in Chapter V, this was resumed whenever diplomatic relations allowed, and given a different political history it is conceivable that Scotland would have come to rely on English entrepôt facilities to sustain much of her traffic to and from those European areas whose products were complementary to her own. For the composition of French imports to Scotland is, in itself, nothing to do with the Alliance. Scotland needed wines and dyestuffs and salt: she would have sought them whatever the international relations might have been, and we might argue that the favourable terms on which her traders operated in France was only partial recompense for the hazards which faced them in the English Channel and the North Sea. Socially and culturally, the balance is easier to strike. If Scotland were to overcome the domestic barriers to enlightenment, she needed a direct link with the outer world, and particularly with the world of the Renaissance. The Alliance provided that link.

The link was not readily broken, but it suffered irreparable damage from the two major events of 1560, the treaty with England and the legislation which cut Scotland adrift from Rome. By any standards the Acts of the Parliament of August 1560 which abrogated papal authority and forbade the Mass were positive statecraft with immense implications for both the internal and the external policies of the nation. But as an economic change, involving the secularisation of Church property, the Scottish Reformation had begun long before 1560. Thirty years earlier, the papacy, alarmed lest English heretical doctrines took root in Scotland, made important concessions to James V. A series of negotiations from 1532 to 1541 resulted in the payment by the Church of a lump sum of £72,000, ostensibly to finance the new College of Justice, and an extension of the period during which the Crown could make nominations to vacant prelacies. Despite the enormous wealth of the Church—some have reckoned its regular income at ten times that of the Crown—the new exactions sharply accelerated the process of feuing of Church lands as a means of raising ready money.[7] But even more important was the increasing exploitation of the right of royal patronage which, in effect, had been clinched by James III in the early 1470s. Thenceforth, according to W. L. Mathieson, 'down to the Reformation...the wealth of the Church was at the mercy of the King and of all who could obtain his favour.'[8] Thenceforth, indeed, more and more Church lands were held *in commendam*—theoretically 'in trust'—by laymen. 'By open flattery', wrote Major in 1521, 'the sons of our worthless nobility get the governance of covenants *in commendam* . . . and out of them fill their own pockets.'[9] Urban resentment against the apparent idleness of the cloistered orders remained, but for king, nobility and lairds there was no economic need to break with Rome: they were doing very well out of the Church already.

Though the legal act of Reformation can be pin-pointed, the implementation, even at the mundane level of finance and property, was to occupy and annoy Scotsmen for the next two generations. What had, by Scottish standards, been a very wealthy Old Church gave place to a very poor New Kirk. Against the income of the unreformed Church just before 1560, estimated at £400,000 (Scots), it is instructive to compare the 300 merks (£200 Scots) a year which made Knox the most highly-paid minister in the Reformed Kirk.[10] The settlement of 1562 whereby two-thirds of the revenues of the Old Church was to remain with the existing beneficiaries, and the other one-third was to be divided between Crown and New Kirk is indicative of the relatively small immediate impact of the Reformation on the distribution of wealth as compared with the parallel process in England. By no means were all monastic buildings immediately abandoned— it is possible that there was still a monk at Crossraguel in 1611[11]— and though some former Church lands were converted into hereditary temporal holdings in 1587, James VI was too aware of conflicting interests to accept any radical plan for wholesale restoration or transfer. Indeed the whole problem of both properties and teinds remained fluid until the early years of Charles I, when—in effect— the existing owners of Old Church lands were offered a permanent title and a machinery was set up for the handling of teinds and the fixing of stipends which endured relatively unchanged until 1925.[12]

But if the Reformation had only minor direct material effects, may it not be that its major effect came indirectly through the contribution of the Kirk to changes in outlook and attitude? The light-hearted attitude, typified by James V, succumbed by the seventeenth century to a deadly serious régime which sought—seemingly with limited success—to enforce a rigid code of moral conduct and a godly way of life. Professor Smout, whose analysis of the social impact of the Reformed Church should be consulted,[13] concludes that in the end (that is by the eighteenth century) Scottish Presbyterianism had bred a seriousness of purpose which, given the right conditions, could become a national economic asset, and through general education— a main plank of the reformers in the 1560s which was nearing achievement at least in the Lowlands by the later seventeenth century—the seriousness of purpose was increasingly informed and articulate.

The broad thesis, expounded originally by Max Weber,[14] that

Calvinism can be equated with economic individualism and made for economic growth, hardly fits the facts as we know them for Calvinist Scotland.[15] Neither in the local records of burghs and kirk sessions, nor in the preaching and writing of the Scottish divines, is there any consistent support for the view that the merchants of 1600 were any less free from group control than those of 1500 or that material prosperity had in any way become equated with godliness. It would, indeed, be easier to support the thesis that, by its interference, the Kirk was a hindrance rather than an encouragement.

Though the events of 1560 made logically for an erosion of the Auld Alliance and a closer link with England, the Union of the Crowns of 1603 was in no sense an inevitable consequence. Basically it was accomplished to satisfy the political convenience of England. James went south with the obsequious backing of his Scottish Parliament and fortified by the arguments of Sir Thomas Craig whose *De Unione Regnorum Tractatus* became a classic exposition of the case for union. How far it represented the views of Scotsmen generally is impossible to judge. To James the common Crown was but the starting point for a more complete unification of the two sections. By use of prerogative powers he brought the two currencies into a state of uniformity, symbolised by the issue of the gold 'Unit' and the use of the motto *'quae Deus coniuxit nemo separet'*; by similar powers he so diminished the customs duties that, for three or four years after the Union, there was virtual free trade between the two countries;[16] by a collusive action in the English courts he ensured that the *post-nati* (i.e. those born after 1603) should not suffer alien disabilities on moving from the one country to another. But to become a permanent reality, economic union required Acts of the two Parliaments, and though the Scots could have been cajoled into agreement, the debates in London produced a flood of invective and abuse which not even James himself could staunch. It is in fact a highly instructive exposition of current English views on Scotsmen, who were regarded either as pernicious blood-suckers or as low-wage blacklegs. At all events the plan for economic union was shelved, to be revived and enforced by the Cromwellians in effect from 1652, formally from 1654, to 1660. Nevertheless it is broadly true that the common Crown and the political stability that went with it made for closer social links with England, and in spite of the reimposition

of customs duties it looks as if the revival of Anglo-Scots trade—
visible before 1603—continued down to the Civil War.

The Union of 1603 was, for most Scotsmen, something remote
and beyond their control; the Union of 1654 was imposed; by
contrast the Union of 1707 was accepted by a majority vote of the
Scottish Parliament after a widespread debate extending over several
years. Though prefaced by a phase of acute political tension and
active maneouvre, and though decided in a political institution, the
extent of economic motivation and of economic consequences put
1707 in a class quite different from 1603 and 1654.[17] We have sought
throughout this Chapter for evidences of 'positive' economic policy
in Scotland. After the Restoration, and particularly when Parliament
acquired greater freedom after 1689, Scotland was actively launched
on a 'mercantilist'-type policy, fostering her own industries and
seeking to expand overseas trade. But because of the conditions of
the Union of 1603 she was embroiled in England's foreign disputes,
but could neither—in compensation—count on either diplomatic or
armed support for Scots enterprises overseas nor could she legally
engage in English plantation trade. But in spite of these handicaps,
the Scottish economy had shown considerable growth, at any rate
down to the 1680s, and despite the customs barriers (revived after
1660) trade with England in linen and black cattle had become such
a main prop of her commercial structure that, whenever there was
a threat of economic recession, Scotsmen began talking about a
common market with England. An increasing note of bitterness
entered the debate in the 1690s as Scotland entered the lean years
of famine and suffered the Darien disaster, the latter a blow to
pockets and prestige, and conclusive proof of the impotence of
Scottish enterprise abroad under the conditions of the Regal Union.

That this union was unsatisfactory was the one point of common
consent in the Parliament which met in 1703. Its first Acts, in 1703
and 1704, dealing with a range of matters from 'War and Peace' to
the export of wool, represented a challenge which the English could
not ignore and which precipitated the threat of economic reprisals
including a ban on the valuable traffic in cattle and linen cloth. The
debates which proceeded in an atmosphere heavy with tension and
in the setting of a depressed economy revealed a deep split of Scottish
opinion with a modicum of economic reason and a mass of rhetoric

on either side. Though so much of the volume of pamphlets published between 1702 and 1705 was concerned with economic issues and with the desperate need to improve the trade balance and the general commercial health of the nation, there was no agreement on the appropriate political solution. Defoe, with much Scottish backing, argued— to use the title of one of his tracts—the *Advantages of Scotland by an Incorporate Union with England*; Andrew Fletcher, the two Blacks and a strong supporting group, argued that the remedy lay in a greater degree of independence, possibly within a federal framework. How far the final vote in the Scottish Parliament in the deep midwinter of 1706–7, with three out of every five in favour of the Treaty of Union, reflected either the force of economic argument or the play of economic self-interest has not, perhaps cannot, be defined.[18] But if the vote had gone the other way, succeeding chapters of this book would have told a very different story.

PART 2

SINCE THE UNION

THE Treaty of Union was unlikely immediately to disturb the trends in the Scottish economy which have been described in Part 1. However, Scotland's absorption within the English protective system buttressed by the Corn Laws and the Navigation Acts could not but be beneficial to agriculture and trade in the long term. Even though the gains from the Union of 1707 were slow in coming, the expansion of the cattle trade, the linen industry and the tobacco trade occurred more rapidly than would have been possible if England's Parliament had remained hostile. The equalisation of duties between the countries meant, in practice, an increase in most Scottish excise and customs charges. Since part of the revenue raised in Scotland would be used to service the English National Debt incurred before 1707, the Treaty provided for compensation. The costs of administration within Scotland were to be paid from 'The Equivalent', a sum of £398,085 10s. representing the calculated revenue yield then current; 'An Arising Equivalent', consisting of any increase in revenue achieved by 1714, was to be paid and used for a variety of specifically Scottish projects including compensation to investors in the Darien Scheme. Economic and social policy henceforth was largely determined at Westminster and was increasingly British rather Scottish in its objectives. For that reason it has not been extensively treated here.

CHAPTER VII

Population and Economic Growth
1707–1871

UNTIL the census of 1801 firm evidence on the number of people in Scotland is lacking. However, much qualitative information suggests that at the time of the Union the population had declined compared with that of the most prosperous period of the seventeenth century. Certainly, it is clear that the 'Seven Ill Years' from 1693 to 1700, with the particularly severe harvest failures in 1695, 1696, 1697 and 1698, provide a classic example of the Malthusian effect of continuous famine on population growth.[1] Thus, a figure of about a million seems reasonable for the total population of Scotland in 1707.[2]

There was slight but perceptible growth over the next half-century, if Alexander Webster's *Account of the Number of People in Scotland* is to be accepted.[3] He reckoned the population about 1755 at 1,265,380, and allowing for difficulties of computation, this was probably not too inaccurate.[4] The distribution of the population in the ten most populous counties at that time is shown in Table 2.

Significantly, five of the first six were in the east, and five of these ten might be considered as part of the Highlands. North of the Tay lived fifty-one per cent of the population; the central belt (defined as the counties of Ayr, Renfrew, Lanark including Glasgow, Dunbarton, Stirling, Clackmannan, Fife, the city of Dundee and the Lothians including Edinburgh) contained another thirty-seven per cent; the remaining eleven per cent were scattered over the more southerly counties from Berwick to Wigtown.[5]

Essentially, the population was ruralised—one town, Edinburgh

Table 2 : *The ten most populous counties 1755*

County	Population
Perth	120,116
Aberdeen	116,168
Midlothian	90,412
Lanark	81,726
Fife	81,570
Angus	68,883
Argyll	66,286
Inverness	59,563
Ayr	59,009
Ross and Cromarty	48,084

with Leith, had more than 50,000 inhabitants, and only another seven had more than 5,000 residents. Because many town parishes had landward rural areas beyond the burgh boundaries, Webster's town population statistics (Table 3) are probably an over-estimate.

Table 3 : *Urban populations c. 1755*

Town	Population (thousands)
Edinburgh	57.0
Glasgow	31.7
Aberdeen	15.6
Dundee	12.4
Inverness	9.7
Perth	9.0
Dunfermline	8.5
Paisley	6.8

In summary, Webster's estimate of population represented an annual average rate of net growth over the period from 1707 to 1755 of 0.5 per cent, and its geographical distribution and state of urbanisation reflected an expanding but traditional society.

Although the net growth of population between 1755 and 1801 was about 340,000, it seems likely, taking emigration into account, that the actual rate of population growth quickened significantly after 1780. However, despite surges and relapses in the rhythm of population growth, the average annual rate was remarkably steady over the century at about 0.6 per cent.

Census returns demonstrate that the most striking change in Scotland's population occurred in the seventy years after 1801 (see Appendix 1). By 1871 the total population was 3,360,018, an annual average net growth-rate of over 1.5 per cent and in total, more than doubling the 1,608,420 inhabitants recorded in 1801.

This dramatic increase in the population conceals the problem of deciding when Scotland escaped from its Malthusian chains, for the exact chronology of sustained population growth is difficult to determine. The most plausible impression is of slow growth until the American War of Independence, for the rapid increase of the early nineteenth century must have depended upon a decisive change in the generation before 1801. It follows that most of the net population gain of about 600,000 made in the eighteenth century must be explained in terms of the capabilities of an essentially rural society to achieve relatively slow growth. This was commonplace in agrarian Europe also; too commonly, Scotland's demographic experience in this period is related only to that of England and Wales.[6] On the other hand, a net population gain of one and three-quarter millions over the next seventy years was a victory gained by an industrial society over the problems of disease, famine and other human disasters which Malthus regarded as inexorable.[7] For that victory to be won, Gross National Product had to increase much more rapidly than the population. Structural changes in the economy, improvements in communications and transport, and particularly substantial increases in agricultural output had to be achieved.

More significant than a simple increase in population was the redistribution of Scotland's population in the two generations before 1801. Urban growth was apparent in most parts of Scotland. Every town of more than 4,000 inhabitants in 1755 showed some growth by 1801, with the solitary exception of Inverness. Glasgow and its environs in 1801 had 84,000 inhabitants, and Paisley's population increased from nearly 7,000 to over 31,000.[8] In consequence of structural changes in the economy, more Scots lived in towns than at the time of the Union, for this urban growth had proceeded at a faster rate than the growth of the population as a whole. The growing relative importance of the towns provides general evidence for two linked propositions. Since it is unlikely that natural increase could explain the increasing rate of urban growth, it follows that Scotland's population had become more mobile and that Scottish rural society was shedding labour. Indeed, there is a variety of circumstantial evidence reflecting short-wave migration to the towns as well as long-distance immigration by the Irish from the 1790s.[9]

Another feature of the mobility of labour was the development of new villages, planned and unplanned.[10] Some, like Tobermory, were consequences of increased investment in the fishing industry; most were products of agricultural improvement and/or industrial development. The textile villages of Renfrewshire, Lanarkshire and Angus, iron-working and mining communities like Muirkirk,[11] Glenbuck[12] and Wilsontown,[13] company villages such as New Lanark,[14] Deanston,[15] Catrine[16] and Stanley,[17] were progenitors of massive economic change. Significantly, these products of the late eighteenth century were overwhelmed in number by estate villages and planned communities where fishing or agriculture were meant to be combined with industry.[18] From Brora to Newcastleton, from Keith to Newton Stewart the countryside was dotted with new villages and small towns.

The relatively slight, but nonetheless important, net population gain of the eighteenth century was achieved by changes in the death-rate and/or the birth-rate for it is doubtful whether emigration or immigration had much effect on the total number of people. Mobility may have encouraged an increase in the birth-rate in some reception areas, since migrants may have married younger and started families earlier than in their place of origin, particularly since they commonly moved to high-wage areas.[19] Increasing urbanisation perhaps provided the socio-economic culture for earlier marriages, bigger families —and indeed, for more marriages. Yet death-rates in towns and among immigrants were likely to be higher than among those normally resident in the countryside. Local variations in birth, death and illegitimacy rates in a mobile society seem very likely.

Perhaps, changes in the sex composition of the population in the eighteenth century might be worth considering. It seems possible that the number of women of child-bearing age relative to the total population was increasing. By 1801 there were 1,176 females to every

1,000 males and this ratio increased by 1811 to 1,185 females for every 1,000 males.[20] If more women were surviving to the age of fertility, circumstances favoured an increase in population. Although we know that some areas had many more female inhabitants than males (Glasgow, for instance), it seems possible that generally the number of men in any generation who married was likely to increase in such an environment. Remarriage by widowers was more likely, as was a general trend to higher illegitimacy-rates and increased complaints about immorality. Imbalance in the sex composition of city populations continued to attract the attention of moralists well into the nineteenth century.[21] Continuous periods of prosperity in the eighteenth century might well have encouraged a higher proportion of the male population to marry young, and since men commonly marry younger women, greater marital fertility may have resulted. If families were started by parents at earlier ages than had previously been common, larger families could be expected, unless methods of family limitation were adopted.

Regionally, population growth might have particular causes that were not applicable everywhere. For example, illegitimacy-rates probably varied widely.[22] More important, productivity gains made in Highland agriculture and processing industries like distilling, fishing and kelping, the introduction and widespread application of the potato, the expansion of the pastoral economy (which had the important side-effect of increasing local milk supplies) made it possible for a larger population to be supported by the land. Subdivision of holdings without subsistence crises became more possible and made earlier peasant marriages likely. The evolution of a United Kingdom market for foodstuffs (especially for cattle and grains) was apparent to many contemporaries by the 1770s and the subject of comment by Adam Smith, and this must have operated to ease regional scarcities.[23] It is true that few peasants, because of lack of capital, could afford to carry excess food stocks, and there were certainly instances of widespread harvest failures producing some deaths by starvation in 1709, 1740, 1772, 1782–3, 1793 and 1800. Several periods, notably the 1790s saw sharp, short-term, upward movements in food prices. But there were no disasters on the late seventeenth century scale.[24]

Yet the Highland economy, with its dependence on cattle, fishing, illicit distilling, kelp, and ultimately oats, barley and potatoes, was exceedingly vulnerable to the prospect of mass starvation as the 'Great Destitution' of the 1840s was to show.[25] This weakness was masked by a variety of expedients for most of the eighteenth century, but the danger of over-population was occasionally exposed. From the evidence of the Duke of Argyll's estates, it is clear that, despite regular seasonal migration to the Lowlands and some emigration in bad years, the effect of agricultural improvement was to increase the population by twenty-five per cent between 1779 and 1792, a process which began well before 1779 and was to continue for half a century after 1792.[26]

The scale of such sub-regional increases can never be satisfactorily explained by a change in the birth-rate, and the linkages between vital statistics need to be explored more thoroughly. For in a pre-industrial, poverty-ridden society the greater the birth-rate, the greater the likelihood of widespread malnutrition and of infantile mortality. Webster's data of 1755 suggest that there was already a very high birth-rate, taking into account the age-structure which he advanced for the population, with 48,910 under the age of one.[27] A crude birth-rate of about thirty-nine per thousand in 1755 makes it difficult to believe that there was any great increase later. Nonetheless, it is true that employment opportunities in agriculture and industry for children certainly increased after 1760, and income additions by children to the family budget cannot be neglected as a factor favouring larger families.

A slight reduction in the infant death-rate, possibly coupled with earlier marriages, more children per marriage or shorter intervals between the birth of children, in periods of prosperity, might be sufficient explanation of why the population increased in the eighteenth century. These factors would tend to increase the rate of formation of new generations. Although infantile mortality, especially for males, was exceedingly high for all classes, there is evidence of some reduction after 1750. Trends in aristocratic families, according to modern research, exemplify this.[28] Similarly, data relating to government annuitants and life assurance suggest a fall in mortality from mid-century.[29] Whether the generality of Scotland's population was so affected cannot at present be firmly decided, but the results of current researches conducted by members of Edinburgh University are eagerly awaited.[30] If there was a slight decline in the death-rate, this might well help to explain the developing imbalance in the sex composition of the population, for even in modern under-developed societies female infants have a better survival-rate. The rôle of single medical advances in explaining a decline in the death-rate is in danger of being overestimated. Smallpox inoculation, used in Aberdeenshire first and then tried extensively in Dumfries-shire in 1733, was inclined to be very dangerous, until the Suttonian method was developed in 1765.[31] Jenner's much safer vaccination was very rapidly applied in Scotland with beneficial results but only after 1796.[32] It should also be remembered that there were many diseases fatal to children in the eighteenth century environment—typhus, measles, diphtheria, whooping cough—and in urban conditions, respiratory and enteric diseases were ubiquitous.[33] Thus, it is questionable whether a decline in the significance of one disease was sufficient to explain a decline in the death-rate. What seems very possible is that smallpox inoculation and the controversy surrounding it were signs of an improvement in the standard of general medical knowledge. The number of doctors seems to have increased faster than the rate of growth of the population, and there was an improvement in their training and education which made Scotland the subject of envy by observers from other countries. There was an increase in the number of hospitals and dispensaries; and the flow of medical treatises and popular medical works was substantial.[34] Obstetrics could be greatly influenced by simple environmental changes such as ensuring that the young were not born in close proximity to cattle dung.

In the late eighteenth century there were a number of scattered attempts to improve sanitation and water supply in places like Edinburgh, Glasgow, Dunfermline, Paisley and Perth, but the effect of these was insignificant, since it was not until the cholera outbreaks of 1831–3, 1848–9 and 1853–4 that the recognition of water-borne diseases produced ameliorative measures.[35] Yet these were pioneered by Scottish doctors. The developing insistence both in village and town that 'middens' or 'dunghills' should be removed for health reasons was an indication that the environmental causes of disease were being attacked. Improved village and town planning had little effect on the standard of housing of most people in the eighteenth century; overcrowding was common in town and country alike.[36]

A better and more variegated diet gradually became available to most of the people of Scotland in the eighteenth century. The potato, sown throughout the Lowlands by the 1770s and throughout the Highlands by the 1780s, was commonly an addition, and sometimes an alternative, to meal and kail; the failure of the oat crop was always a serious matter but it had ceased to mean absolute social disaster.[37] If the potato restricted mortality caused by dearth, its widespread availability—and that of fish and milk—may have been of substantial importance in explaining an improvement in general

Table 4 : The ten most populous counties 1871

County	Ranking 1755	Population 1801	Population 1871
Lanark	4	147,692	765,339
Midlothian	3	122,597	328,379
Aberdeen	2	121,065	244,603
Angus	6	99,053	237,567
Renfrew		78,501	216,947
Ayr	9	84,207	200,809
Fife	5	93,743	160,735
Perth	1	125,583	127,768
Stirling		50,825	98,218
Inverness	8	72,672	87,531

nutritional standards. The wealthier had increasing quantities of vegetables and fruit, meat, sugar and tea, made available to them from improved horticulture and the colonial trade, and their patterns of consumption were copied, as often and as far as income allowed, further down the social and economic scale.[38] If the countryside was healthier than the towns in the eighteenth century so that more children survived there, it was less capable than the urban centres of providing them with permanent employment as they grew to adulthood. Thus, although improved agriculture may have provided more employment in 1800 than earlier, the jobs were not always where the people were, nor were their numbers sufficient to match the increase in the population. In consequence, migration to the industrial districts proceeded as the countryside shed surplus labour.

After 1801 the course of population growth is much clearer. The population increased from 1,608,420 in 1801 to 2,091,521 in 1821, to

2,888,742 in 1851 and to 3,360,018 in 1871 (see Appendix I). By 1871 the distribution of population had markedly changed compared with 1801 or 1755, as can be seen from Table 4.

Lanarkshire had replaced Perthshire as the leading county and had more than twice the population of Midlothian, its nearest rival. The Highland counties had moved down the rankings and, in the case of Argyll and Ross and Cromarty, out of the first ten, their places being taken by Renfrewshire and Stirlingshire. In regional terms the contrasts were even more marked. Using the same geographical definitions given on p. 87, the redistribution of population was overwhelmingly in favour of the central belt at the expense of the northern and southern regions (see Table 5).

Table 5 : Percentage regional distribution of population 1755–1871

Year	Central belt	Northern region	Southern region
1755	37	51	11
1801	42.5	46	11.5
1871	61	31	8

This redistribution was essentially a consequence of the continuing structural changes in the Scottish economy, as agriculture lost its primacy as an employer of labour and as industrial concentration proceeded in the central belt. The west-central sub-division, including the counties of Dunbarton, Renfrew, Lanark and Ayr, increased its population from 331,000 in 1801 to 1,244,000 in 1871; the east-central division (Fife and Dundee, Clackmannan, Stirling and the three Lothians) from 352,000 to 803,000. Thus, even within the most rapidly advancing region, there was a marked shift in the proportions of total human resources from east to west.

The populations in the other regions continued to grow. That of the northern region increased from 741,000 in 1801 to 1,041,000 in 1871 and that of the southern from 185,000 to 272,000. Despite this growth, rural depopulation in these two regions, indicated by declining populations in some counties, became a significant problem. During this period there was a decreasing population in Argyll, Kinross and Perth from 1831, in Inverness from 1841, in Dumfries,

Kirkcudbright, Ross and Cromarty, Sutherland and Wigtown from 1851, and in Berwick, Caithness, Orkney, Roxburgh and Zetland from 1861.[39] 'Clearances' in the Highlands have received the romantic and tragic publicity, but many rural counties, especially in the south-west, were substantially affected.[40]

Urban growth was very apparent in 1871 (see Appendix 2). Those living in settlements of less than 2,000 inhabitants accounted for 1,141,386, while small towns (of 2,000 to 10,000 inhabitants) had a total population of 696,958; larger towns (10,000 to 25,000 inhabitants), 327,734 people, and the largest towns and cities (over 25,000 inhabitants), 1,193,940, i.e. over one-third of Scotland's population. Together, urban communities accounted for about two-thirds of Scotland's people in 1871. Glasgow, Dundee, Edinburgh and Aberdeen saw the most spectacular urban growth, but even in counties, such as Perthshire, where population had passed its peak, towns increased in size.[41]

The demographic experience of each of the large cities was different. Aberdeen increased its population by 1851 to 72,000 (from 27,000 in 1801) but remained a regional capital dependent on its own county. Fewer than 20,000 of its residents had been born outside the city or county, and of this number only 1,270 were Irish-born, slightly less than the English colony. By 1871 Aberdeen had a population of 88,000.[42] Dundee, on the other hand, with a population of nearly 79,000 in 1851, had about 15,000 Irish-born in the city, although two-thirds of the population was either born in Dundee itself or in the adjacent counties of Angus and Perth. In 1871 Dundee's population was 119,000.[43] Edinburgh and Leith had a combined population of 191,221 in 1851, over 106,000 of whom were native-born or from Midlothian. Fife, Lanark, Perth and East Lothian contributed over 5,000 migrants each, there were 12,514 Irish-born and 8,443 English. The population of Edinburgh and Leith had risen to 242,000 in 1871.[44] Glasgow's total population (excluding the independent burghs) in 1851 was 329,097 chiefly made up as follows: forty-four per cent or 145,022 born in the city; twenty per cent or 64,866 born in Lanark, Dunbarton, Stirling, Renfrew and Ayr; thirteen per cent or 42,928 born in Ireland; six per cent or 20,375 born in Argyll, Perth and Inverness. There were over 8,000 English-born in the city, but this was eclipsed by the number from Edinburgh and Midlothian. Independent burghs around the city accounted for another 18,000, and by 1871 Glasgow and its environs had a population of 568,000. Glasgow, relative to Scotland, was growing faster than London, relative to England, and in 1871 accounted for seventeen per cent of the total inhabitants.[45] This was the more remarkable because Scotland's population growth was less rapid than that south of the Border, for by 1871 Scotland's population was 14.8 per cent of that of England and Wales, as compared with 18.1 per cent in 1801. Although Edinburgh and Midlothian, together with the counties contiguous to Glasgow, were the main recipient areas for migrants in 1851, Glasgow gained a net inflow from all the other regions including Edinburgh and Midlothian. Also the 'industrial capital of Scotland' secured more people from other Scottish counties, except the Borders, than Edinburgh.[46]

Migration, immigration and emigration are constant themes in the social history of Scotland. There was a regular migration to London and commonly a return, as James Beattie's *London Diary* (1733) and Boswell's experiences with Dr Johnson indicate.[47] Soldiers, doctors, engineers and other professional men—examples like William Murdoch, James Watt, William Fairbairn, John Loudon McAdam, James Naismith and John Rennie—sought fame and fortune in England. Self-help, the code of Victorian Britain, was apotheosised by a Scot, Samuel Smiles who was born in Dunbar. Merchants on the grand scale, like James Shaw of Kilmarnock—and Lord Mayor of London—and his senior partner William Douglas, gravitated via Glasgow or Edinburgh to the commercial capital of the United Kingdom.[48] On a lesser plane, Scots retailers and pedlars could be found in most counties south of the Border. The traffic was not all one way, however. English and Welsh entrepreneurs, smelters and moulders for Carron ironworks, Lancashire spinners for Rothesay cotton mills, Irish bleachers and navvies, French weavers, Dutch sugar boilers, malleable ironworkers from Staffordshire and Wales, lead-miners from Weardale and Derbyshire—skilled men generally— made their way to Scotland before 1850. Yet in the period 1841–51 for instance, 50,000 Scots went to England as against 17,000 Englishmen who came to Scotland. In 1871 70,482 residents of Scotland (2.1 per cent of Scotland's population) were English- or Welsh-born.[49] Scots from Galloway commonly made their way to Liverpool and Lancashire; yet the experience of the Gladstones shows that other Scottish counties also had their representatives in the commercial life of the North-west.[50] London, naturally, continued to attract the greatest number of Scots because of the wide-ranging political, social and economic opportunities it offered: by 1871–81 19,000 Scots-born were resident in the capital (3.8 per cent of all immigrants).

Scottish ties with Europe were very strong, and Scots were to be found permanently settled in most countries in Northern and Western Europe. They formed a regular colony in Gothenburg and dominated the Swedish East India Company in the first half of the eighteenth century—and also the Russian navy.[51] James Keith (1696–1758) served as a mercenary in Spain and Russia and ended as Field-Marshal to Frederick II the Great of Prussia.[52]

Most emigrants went westward. The movement from the islands and western counties to Ulster was traditional. Yet more and more, Ulster became a staging post for America—and contemporaries recognised this: 'Scarce any of them [emigrants to Ulster] continue long there, but generally join the emigrants who annually go in great numbers from the North of Ireland to America.'[53]

Too commonly Scottish settlement in colonial America has been seen in terms of the failure of Jacobitism. Transportation of Jacobites possibly accounted for 1,000 settlers in America and the West Indies after the twin failures of 1715 and 1745.[54] More significant were the loyalist settlement of Highlanders in several of the colonies after the Seven Years War (1756–63) and the exodus of indentured servants both to America and the West Indies.[55]

The main periods for emigration in the eighteenth century were from 1763 to 1775, when, according to Knox, 20,000 left the Highlands for America, and from 1783 to 1803 when Canada was the main recipient.[56] Thomas Telford estimated that between 1801 and 1803 about 3,000 left the Highlands, mainly for Canada.[57] Earlier in the century there was some emigration from the Border counties and Galloway.[58] Generally, these Scotsmen, like the Highlanders, preferred to continue their existing way of life in another country rather than to change habitat and existence in their own.[59]

The movement abroad gradually built up a self-generated pressure, as those already settled wrote home or merchant factors from the tobacco colonies returned to Scotland. A glorious picture of a carefree existence with cheap land and plentiful crops was circulating widely in Scotland—what one called a 'Great Encouragement of Plowmen to go to America'.[60] One Highland clergyman believed that 'there is not a family, hardly an individual, who has not a father, brother, sister, cousin or kinsman in America with whom they keep up a regular correspondence'.[61] So close were the commercial contacts between North America and Scotland throughout our period that it was impossible to insulate wander-lusting Scots from the twin appeals of high wages and low land costs which contrasted in most Highland and Lowland experience with high rents and low wages, especially in the 1770s.[62]

Nor was emigration always disorganised. Commonly, the tacksmen led their subordinates from the Highlands, and would-be emigrants from other areas often formed emigration associations or land companies to plan settlement.[63] The efficiency of the arrangements for emigration was commonly regarded by affected landowners as criminal, since they feared a shortage of agricultural labour and high costs.[64] They welcomed the Passenger Vessels Act of June 1803 which laid down more stringent regulations to be observed in emigrant ships, thus increasing costs to the emigrants.[65] But Highlanders going to Canada, the main destination from 1783 to the late 1840s, evaded the effects of its terms by enlistment in the Canadian Fencibles and securing free passages for their families as a condition of service.[66]

Religious or political unorthodoxy was often a cause for movement. Episcopalian ministers tended to leave Perthshire, for instance, to serve Canadian congregations established by emigrants from the county.[67] On the other hand, presbyterian congregations in New York State kept in touch with Scotland in the eighteenth and early nineteenth centuries, mainly to raise money for church-building.[68] New Zealand saw the same phenomenon. Dunedin was founded in 1848 by the Revd Thomas Burns as a Free Church settlement.[69] Although aristocratic paternalism occasionally provided the spark, as for instance in the case of Lord Selkirk's Red River scheme,[70] it was the classlessness of the colonies and America (after 1850 the main reception area) which appealed to many radicals and Chartists:

> Uncursed with Tyrants, Kings and Lords
> And titled paupers proud and great
> Her nobles are her artisans
> The treasured jewels of the State.[71]

Handloom weavers and other workers from industrial areas formed the bulk of the male emigrants to the United States by the period 1846–54, according to recent research.[72] Although Australasia increased in significance as a reception area for Scottish emigrants in the 1850s and 1860s, the Clyde especially from 1864 to 1871 witnessed a substantial exodus and became the main embarkation point for Scots going to the United States.[73] Government and influential lay opinion by then favoured emigration as a solution to the problems of the Highlands—witness the foundation of the Highland Emigration Society in 1851—for the natural increase in the population, augmented by Irish immigration, more than compensated for any loss of population caused by the movement to North America and Australasia. It is notoriously difficult to assess the net migration loss before the 1860s, but in that decade it amounted to over 117,000.[74]

However, the influx of the Irish over a long period was even greater.[75] By 1841 126,000 residents in Scotland were Irish-born—about five per cent of the total population. This did not take into account those of the second and third generations who were of Irish parentage but Scots-born. The 1841 level was superseded in later decades, and by 1871 there were 207,770 Irish-born residents of Scotland, i.e. just over six per cent of the total population.[76]

The causes of the growth in Scotland's population in the period 1870–1 are no easier to determine than the factors behind the increase of the eighteenth century, for the compulsory registration of births, deaths and marriages did not begin until 1855. According to Stark, in the 1830s the annual average death-rate for 331 country parishes was 20.3 per 1,000 as against 26.68 per 1,000 for the fourteen main towns.[77] Between 1855 and 1871 there was no marked change in the national death-rate, usually fluctuating at between twenty and twenty-two per 1,000, but considering the increasing urbanisation of the population this was probably an improvement on the 1830s. The national birth-rate, at thirty-four or thirty-five per 1,000, was fairly steady from 1855 to 1871, little below the level of 1755.[78] How continuous or recent movements in the birth- and death-rates had been before 1855 is not known, but even allowing for cholera epidemics like those of 1831–3 which killed 10,000 people and of 1848–9 when about 8,000 people died, it is difficult to gainsay the judgment that the fall in death-rate probably explains Scotland's rapid rate of population growth from 1801 more satisfactorily than any other single factor.[79] Urbanisation almost certainly threatened any progress: the death-rate in Glasgow in 1837 was forty-one per 1,000 and 56.4 per 1,000 ten years later. Children remained the principal victims. Strang reported in 1858 that the death-rate for Glasgow infants (under five years of age) was 53.8 per 1,000. This, he described with biblical accuracy, as the 'Murder of the Innocents'.[80] At the same time, it must be stated that, as the example of cholera demonstrated, Scottish society was more and more capable of withstanding epidemics: in the 1866 visitation only 1,000 died out of a population of 3,000,000.[81]

By the mid-Victorian period abuses of the urban environment were recognised as dangerous to public health, but they were not tackled root and branch. Edinburgh's medical provision was very impressive; civic amenities like Glasgow's improved water supply, housing, and Improvement Trust began to blossom. However, their effect on death-rates in the 1860s and 1870s was slight, but without them, who knows—the death-rate might well have risen!

The relationship between the increase in population and economic growth is perhaps the most difficult problem in economic history.[82] Economic growth is always accompanied by an increase in the population, but not all population increases produce permanent economic growth—as Ireland and the Highlands demonstrated in the 1840s. We must accept that the second, very rapid phase of population growth after 1801 could have had little to do with the initiation of Scottish economic growth. The earlier phase of slower population increase before 1801 was, therefore, more critical. Gross National Product tended to grow as fast as, or faster than, population. Hence the Malthusian barriers were broken, for consumption per capita almost certainly increased.

But the population growth of the eighteenth century had to proceed in a most judicious manner to stimulate rapid economic growth. At too fast a rate, it would have put great pressure on capital and other factors of production. Too much of National Income would have been diverted to current consumption and not enough saved for future investment. For instance, if infantile mortality had been reduced at too fast a rate, there would have been too rapid an increase in the number of dependents, and current savings would have been bound to fall. Thus, capital formation would have been slowed, and structural changes in the economy prevented. Those sectors requiring most capital would have been severely affected, and in these we must include the capital goods industries.

However, agricultural output tended to grow faster than the rate of population increase at least until the 1750s for the Scots farmers clearly exported coastwise or by the drove roads increasing quantities of agricultural goods to England; and they still retained their traditional customers in Europe.[83] Domestic food prices remained remarkably steady, and in the period 1717 to 1750, allowing for upward movement of most wages, in real terms, actually fell.[84] Runrig agriculture and the pastoral economy were more capable of expanding output—without allowing domestic prices to go through the ceiling—than is generally supposed. Urbanisation was allowed to gather steam without provoking more than local or temporary food crises.

The movement of wages, because of regional variations, is difficult to disentangle, but by the 1790s regional differences, revealed by the ministers who prepared parish reports for the *Old Statistical Account*, were so marked that they could only have developed over a long period.[85] Those areas with the highest wage-rates in the 1790s were the most densely populated; rapid economic growth was occurring in them—and capital intensification. Relative to food prices and agricultural wages, therefore, the level of money wages in the urban areas and their surrounding regions was kept high. This encouraged labour mobility, migration and the development of regional markets for consumer goods. Even when food price rises became significant after 1750 (averaging about 2.5 per cent per year by 1790), their rate of increase did not always keep up with the rise in money wages in industrialising counties like Ayrshire.[86]

In such an environment the demand for consumer goods and food might be expected to rise, setting in train an upward trend in profits, capital investment and production. The growth of home demand and of inter-regional trade with other parts of Britain was the major cause of industrialisation. The expansion of foreign markets in the British Empire, especially in America and the West Indies, came as a bonus.

Entrepreneurship was stimulated by the growth of the market. Landowners and merchants strove to exploit regional scarcities and abundances. In the process, drastic changes in agriculture were undertaken, and improvements made in overhead capital—in transport facilities and the credit structure, for instance. More economic activity was generated as imperfections in markets were eased. Traditional methods of production were used as far as possible to meet demand, but as a national economy evolved, so revolutionary changes became inevitable. It is true that a growing population produced a larger labour force, but there is little evidence before 1815 of a permanent surplus of labour except in some Highland areas.[87] Enterprise ensured that an increasing labour force became better organised and better equipped to raise output. Increases in productivity were encouraged by piece-rate wage systems which became widespread.

The upward movement in rents and prices, apparent from the 1750s, might have been expected to eat into any advances in wages and thereby to affect demand adversely. Yet, as we know, the process of urbanisation and migration remained continuous. Differential growth possibilities were not obstructed by rigidities in the labour force. It is easy to point to the harshness of the Scots Poor Law and to suggest that the lack of social provision accelerated migration. But it is even more likely that urban and industrial wages acted as a magnet especially to those used to seasonal industrial employment. Yet a large domestic market for mass-produced consumer goods was essential to further economic growth, and this depended upon growing real incomes. Not all classes—and certainly not all the working classes—had to enjoy a higher standard of living continuously for the domestic market to expand. A redistribution of National Income favouring landowners, merchants and industrial workers most, in the period 1750–90, was all that was required. Investment was likely to increase most rapidly in an environment in which the rich and middling-rich anticipated greater returns. Yet they were also consumers and income-providers to others.

No doubt, life was hard and brutish for the vast majority of working people, but we must not assume that this made demand less than it had been before the Union or before 1750. There is much literary evidence to the contrary. The process of structural change in the Scottish market was clearly very complex. But as long as family incomes were above subsistence level (at which the effective demand for consumer goods would be nil), industrial growth and agricultural change would be encouraged. Adam Smith, a formidable contemporary observer, believed that real wages had increased generally up to the time that he wrote *The Wealth of Nations*.[88] But even if they were stagnant, it might be expected that family incomes would rise in consequence of the survival of more wage-earners.

Commercial interdependence was a consequence both of regional specialisation in production and increased migration after 1750. More people became dependent on intricate market relationships. In rural districts agricultural wages were increasingly paid in cash not kind, and this assisted the evolution of local markets. Alternative industrial opportunities forced up agricultural wages in some counties.[89] Differential urban wage-rates allowed consumers more choice in their expenditures, even if their real wages were no higher—and that is very doubtful—than those of nearby rural workers. Total and real purchasing power by 1790 must have increased for two reasons: there were many more consumers than in 1707; more of these consumers were living and working in areas where high wage-rates prevailed.

After 1795 the rate of inflation increased until 1813–15. But this did not affect all workers adversely. Urban workers lost most because of their dependence on the food market; agricultural workers were most protected because they were less exposed to rises in food prices. After the French wars ended in 1815, food prices tended to fall faster than money wages, and the real incomes of those in new industries who retained employment rose. But an abundance of labour, caused by population growth, immigration and migration, became most marked after 1815, too late to influence the initiation of industrialisation, but a decisively important factor in assisting the development of the transport system and the rise of the heavy industries which were labour-intensive. A saturated labour market might have delayed the application of labour-saving inventions—this again emphasises the significance of slow population growth in the eighteenth century —but a great increase in the number of consumers tended to offset falls in per capita purchasing power. Since profits were the main source of capital accumulation, an abundant supply of labour tended to accentuate the distribution of the National Income in favour of industrialists. By the 1830s the underlying profitability of the Scottish economy was apparent, and the widening of capital proceeded at an unprecedented level, with dramatic growth in the metallurgical and mining industries, followed in the 1840s by the great expansion of the transport system.

From the 1830s the upward trend in home demand was less significant, as an improved communications network allowed further penetration of British and foreign markets. But as urbanisation proceeded, so the opportunities for profitable investment increased.

Expansion at home, coupled with extensive sales in England and Ireland, was vital to improving export performance. If exports fell away, sufficient stocks could be taken up at home at least to meet fixed costs. The experience of the linen industry in the early eighteenth century makes the point. Between 1733 and 1743 when exports of linen were relatively slight, there was an increase in the production of linen priced at under 6d. per yard.[90] This part of output was taken up in the home market. As linen output expanded, the industry developed a wider market, but when foreign markets collapsed, in 1781 for instance, the amount of linen stamped for sale continued to rise.[91] In the 1830s the iron industry found a wider market in Britain which became the basis for an attack on foreign markets.[92] The rôle of the home market cannot, therefore, ever be regarded as secondary when explanations of Scotland's economic growth are sought.

Social capital was put under great pressure by the rapid increase in population. More of Scotland's National Income had to be spent on housing and public health. From a host of places there is evidence of increased social expenditures but usually at too slow a rate to satisfy demand. Thus, the health of towns and the lack of adequate social provisions remained to torment the late Victorian observers and modern spectators.[93] The age structure of the population changed as it increased. Productivity increases were likely when more of the labour force were healthy, young and adaptable,[94] but the moral and social life of towns and villages seems to have received more attention from Victorian statisticians—curious figures, e.g. one public house for every 255 Scots in 1861, bedevil deeper issues.[95] Considering the amount of child labour throughout our period it is clear that the working population was never overwhelmed by its dependents.[96]

Table 6 : Percentage of population
in different age-groups
1755–1871

Age-group (years)	1755	1871
0—14	30	36.7
15—64	60	58.1
Over 65	10	5.2

The population had to be not only geographically mobile but also prepared for occupational change. Employment patterns by 1871 reflect the change to an industrial society (Table 7).[97]

Table 7 : Percentage of population in different occupations 1871

Occupation	Percentage of occupied population 1871
Agriculture	17.3
Fishing	1.8
Mining	5.1
Building	6.3
Manufactures	34.7
Transport	4.9
'Dealing' (shops etc.)	7.1
Public and professional services	3.8
Domestic service	10.7

Occupational patterns varied between regions and cities. Edinburgh by 1831 had more middle-class occupations than Glasgow; there were more openings for professional people in the banks, courts and insurance firms. Its working classes in 1851 reveal a markedly craft bias—and there was a disproportionately large number of female domestic servants (16,601), 5,000 more than in Glasgow.[98] Middle-class occupations in the professions, commerce and public administration tended to increase in number after 1851, but Scotland had fewer people in this category and in skilled labouring groups relative to its population than England and Wales. This is why average income was less. Average estimated income per capita in 1867 was

£23.10s. per annum against £14 in Ireland, and £32 in England and Wales.[99]

Female employment varied little in its proportions to the total female population. About twenty-five per cent (nearly 450,000) of the female population were at work in the period 1851–71, little different from the pattern south of the Border. Domestic service was the most important occupation for women workers followed by the textile industries and agriculture.[100]

As Scotland's population had increased since 1707, so it had changed its occupational patterns. Urban growth raised problems of law and order and encouraged working-class cohesion and agitations. The rise of the Chartist press, equally with the development of 'respectable' daily papers (of which there were twenty-one by 1880), could not have occurred in a traditional agrarian society. These various manifestations of a more complex society were also indications of fundamental structural changes in the economy.

CHAPTER VIII

Agriculture and Economic Growth
1707–1871

THE significance of agriculture in the social and economic life of Scotland in the eighteenth century cannot be over estimated. In terms of employment, income and revenue, it was much the most important sector in the Scottish economy. Brigadier William Mackintosh (1662–1743) of Borlum, Inverness-shire, writing essays on agriculture during his term of imprisonment in Edinburgh Castle for his part in the Jacobite Risings of 1715 and 1719, expressed this in more figurative language. For him, agriculture was 'the main source from whence all the rivulets run and water the body, the main and first spring that must give motion and life to all the parts and branches of improving the nation'.[1] Yet to English eyes, Scottish rural society and its agricultural base appeared primitive—witness the opinions at different times of Daniel Defoe,[2] Thomas Pennant,[3] Samuel Johnson[4] and William Cobbett.[5] Of 19,000,000 acres only 5,000,000 were regarded as fit for cultivation; the rest were either irretrievable or beyond the technical competence of the period. Great stretches of the north and west were areas of natural poverty and likely to remain so. When John Naismith assessed the land of Lanarkshire in 1794, he concluded that fifty-five per cent of it was of minimal value for agricultural purposes.[6] Other examples might be added from parts of Ayrshire and the Border counties.

Nevertheless, if we consider only the cultivable area of 1707 and ignore later reclamation, land was the most abundant factor of production for there were five cultivable acres per inhabitant in 1707, over three in 1801 and nearly two in 1871. Landowners,

Whig or Tory, recognised that reform of the economic system depended upon improvement in the use of land and in the efficiency of agriculture. In general, they favoured change and efficiency and without their agreement, substantial economic growth would have been impossible in the eighteenth and early nineteenth centuries. For most wealthy people, investment in land represented the most secure and commonly the most profitable and prestigious form of investment. This is not to say that all the cultivable land was equally fertile or available in the land market. But it is certainly true that despite the hold over large estates exercised by aristocratic families, such as Argyll, Sutherland, Buccleuch and Breadalbane, there was an active land market for much of the period. Spectacular political failures like the 1715 and 1745 Risings and occasional sequestrations temporarily dislocated local aristocratic control over the market in land and encouraged speculation in leases; in the Lowlands, business failures by institutions like the Ayr Bank (Douglas, Heron and Co.) and A. G. Houston and Co., and by individual merchants, kept the land market very lively. Glasgow merchants, East India Company servants, West Indian nabobs, all acquired estates for a multitude of reasons; lawyers and bankers similarly penetrated landed society and made Scottish society remarkably fluid and mobile.[7] Population pressures in rural districts encouraged an upward movement in rents, as would-be tenants competed for leases. As industrialists acquired fortunes in the nineteenth century, they purchased land on a great scale—men like the Bairds of Gartsherrie, the Houldsworths of Coltness, the Monteiths of Carstairs, participated actively in the land market, usually for reasons of security, prestige and amenity.

An active land market encouraged economic change since new landowners were often less inhibited by any legal or financial restraint. Acts of the Scottish Parliament had made changes in tenure and business organisation very possible. A series of Acts of 1661,[8] 1669[9] and 1685[10] allowed enclosures to be made, and an Act of 1695[11] authorised sheriffs to divide land held conjointly. Another Act of 1695 gave power to the Court of Session to divide commons, except those belonging to the Crown or to royal burghs.[12] Thus, changes could be introduced into Scottish agriculture without the expense or delay of separate Parliamentary enclosure Bills so necessary in

England. Yet change very largely depended upon market considerations and long-term trends in prices.

Most farmers in the early eighteenth century regarded a surplus of agricultural products as an unusual blessing; they orientated production towards subsistence but not always with unerring success. Landlords, on the other hand, since they commonly received rents in kind, could be readily embarrassed by a surplus beyond normal food and seed stocks. In such circumstances farming methods were likely to remain primitive, even if sales were being made by the landlord in a wider market. Peasants generally lacked the capital to improve cultivation, lairds frequently the incentive.

Runrig (probably derived from 'roinn-ruith', Gaelic for parallel divisions) was the common method of landholding in 1707.[13] Tenants occupied a farm in strips of one-quarter to one-half of an acre. This variation in size depended upon the method of measurement, since a rig was intended to be about 240 paces long and 6 paces wide. The more tenants on the farm the more difficult it was to allot rigs, since they were reallocated sometimes annually but more usually every second or third year. Headrick's account of Arran (1807) gives a clear picture of the late survival of the system: 'The cultivated land is occupied in runrig, or in narrow strips called butts with intervals betwixt them, whose possessors are changed every second or third year.'[14] The rig of arable formed a ridge higher than the unploughed 'butt' or 'balk'. Thus, the field appeared as a collection of ploughed ridges—often serpentine in shape and varying in proportions—divided from each other by boundaries called butts or balks which might take up ten to twelve per cent of the total field area and be occupied by weeds and stones.

The farm was divided into two fields. The 'infield' or 'croftland' was the best land nearest the farmhouses and it was the most carefully cultivated area.[15] Usually, cultivation was carried out according to a primitive three-year rotation, with one-third of the infield occupied by barley or bere and the other two-thirds under oats every year. Numerous local variations in the infield rotation could be found. For instance, in the milder districts of Perthshire wheat was included, and in a number of counties, Fife for example, flax, peas and beans were added. The 'outfield', usually poorer land at greater distance from the farmhouses, was farmed by extensive methods, i.e. part was cropped year after year to exhaustion, usually with oats, and then allowed to lie fallow as cultivation shifted. Commonly the outfield was larger than the infield, but in rich soil conditions, such as prevailed in parts of Moray, Aberdeenshire and the Carse of Gowrie, it might be much smaller. Rainfall was often considerable—and unseasonable weather a normal hazard—and in such circumstances oats and barley or bere were the most reliable grain crops. Harvests ultimately depended upon the weather and were adversely affected in 1740, 1756, 1778, 1782–3, 1796 and 1800. Moor or waste land was common to all tenants and, apart from providing rough grazing, was often a source of fuel and sometimes thatch.[16]

The runrig system was intended to perpetuate a subsistence economy, and this made it widely applicable for communities like North Morar[17] on the one hand, where fishing augmented diets and incomes, and Melrose on the other, where small-scale wool-spinning and weaving added to agricultural surpluses. Weaknesses in the system were manifold. It provided little incentive to improvement of methods of cultivation, nor did it encourage efficiency. Disputes about the equity of the reallocation of rigs could not be avoided, and consequently continuous co-operation between tenants was unlikely. Visitors from south of the Border naturally compared runrig with the open-field system as practised in England and commented upon how primitive the former was. Nonetheless, the system of runrig would not have been so universal for so long had it not been most useful and flexible. Its backwardness should not blind us to its potentialities. Simple changes like adding more land to the outfield or planting turnips and potatoes could greatly affect productivity without changing methods or land tenure substantially. Nor should it be forgotten that runrig persisted in some areas well into the nineteenth century. For instance, in North Uist it prevailed until about 1814 and in other areas of the Highlands into the 1850s.[18]

'Improvement', which took many forms, increasingly placed traditional agricultural methods and tenure under strain. In some areas, enclosures were made for plantations of timber to replace natural endowments consumed over past centuries. Afforestation was a long-term investment, but returns could be very substantial. As demand for house and ship timber, pit-props and charcoal increased, substantial sums could be earned. In 1728 the York Buildings Company offered Sir James Grant £7,000 for 60,000 firs to be cut over fifteen years on Speyside, and English ironmasters offered landowners in Argyll and Galloway large sums for the chance to exploit their woods by coppicing.[19]

Pastoral farming was the most important stimulus to consolidation of landholdings, particularly just before, and in the fifty years after the Union. This was a consequence of better returns from cattle farming than from arable cultivation.[20] In Galloway the movement towards enclosure was so sustained in the 1720s that it provoked the 'Levellers' Rising';[21] in the Borders and West Highlands it was commonplace in the late 1730s and 1740s. Occasionally, as on the Argyll estates, economic motivation was augmented by political calculations, but in general pastoral 'improvement' depended upon the prices of cattle, horses, sheep, hides and wool.[22] So far, price data relating to these commodities are fragmentary, but some conclusions are possible. The 1730s was a period of depression whereas the earlier and later decades seem to have been relatively prosperous. The prices allowed by Archibald Campbell of Knockbuy (1693–1790) to his tenants for cattle in lieu of rent—and cattle were commonly used to pay rents—record a clear downward movement in the 1730s (Table 8).[23]

Table 8 : Prices allowed for cattle in lieu of rent 1729–49

Years	Average price per cow (£ Scots)
	£ s. d.
1729–31	15 17 0
1732–9	13 3 3
1740–9	17 19 0

Horse prices in Renfrewshire from the 1720s to 1740s and bounties paid by the Board of Trustees for flax cultivation confirm the general impression of the 1730s as a period of depression.[24]

At the time of the Union about 30,000 cattle per annum went to England, as war demand for fresh and salted beef for the army and navy was maintained. Lack of political stability and public order in the Highlands affected the profitability of this trade. However, as army control was reinforced after the 1715 and 1745 Risings, cattle thieving and 'protection rackets' were reduced. But as late as 1747 annual losses from theft of cattle were estimated at £37,000. Most contemporaries noted an increase in the volume of south-bound traffic in cattle, and some regarded this as the most important consequence of the Union. Scots cattle—or Irish, sent via Galloway —could be found fattening in Yorkshire and North-west England, in East Anglia and the Home Counties, ultimately destined for English urban markets.[25]

Over the period 1707–94 cattle prices rose fourfold, but most of the increase occurred after 1740. Upward price movements increased the pressure towards the consolidation of estates in pastoral districts and diverted marginal arable land to cattle production, particularly in upland areas. By the mid-eighteenth century possibly 80,000 cattle were going south from Scotland, and the trade in sheep, from the Borders especially, was running at about 150,000 per annum. By 1790 much of Galloway was devoted to fattening Irish cattle, and Port-patrick alone between 1786 and 1790 accounted for the import of over 55,000 head. About 1800 100,000 cattle, mostly originating north of the Forth-Clyde valley, went to England every year. The Hebrides sent 22,000 per annum to the mainland worth about £110,000, slightly more than the rentals of the islands.[26] The income effects of this trade for the Highlands and Islands were often considerable; high cattle prices, for instance, helped to finance emigration.[27]

The expansion of sheep farming in the Highlands in the century after 1750 completed the process of consolidation but, unlike the cattle trade, substantially reduced the demand for labour in counties such as Sutherland.[28] Apart from the slight growth in the Scots woollen industry by 1850, the main stimulus came from the expanding English woollen industry and also from a growing urban market for mutton. After 1818 Inverness became the most important market for wool-brokers who came from great distances, but by 1836 75,000 sheep were sold at Falkirk, previously the most important cattle market, and before mid-century sheep had displaced cattle as the most important commodity.[29] Taking pastoral farming statistics as a whole, the principal movements in the nineteenth century can be observed from the estimates in Table 9.[30]

Table 9 : Livestock numbers 1814–68

	1814	1856	1868
Horses	243,489	123,000	166,000
Cattle	1,047,142	967,000	1,051,000
Sheep	2,851,867	5,817,000	7,112,000
Pigs		127,000	140,000

Blackface and Cheviot sheep from the Southern Uplands were introduced into most Highland counties after 1760 and by 1800 had reached Caithness.[31] Sales of wool at Galashiels market multiplied nearly sevenfold between 1775 and 1800.[32] Yet the great increase in the sheep population occurred after 1815, as cattle prices declined and as wool and mutton became more attractive and profitable commodities. Highland counties exported sheep, fleeces—and people. Some sheep-walks were of very great extent: two in Inverness-shire and Argyll were over sixty square miles in area by 1815. In 1831 Sutherland exported annually 40,000 sheep and 180,000 fleeces, but many parts of the Highlands depended on meal imports and potatoes. Yet sheep and depopulation were twin possibilities if population growth in the Highlands was not to lead to mass starvation. Both landlord's and tenant farmer's incomes rose; the landlord's gain from changing to a sheep economy from cattle or mixed farming might be as great as 300 per cent.[33] It seems from the cattle figures that by 1814 the cattle economy had reached the summit of its expansion whereas the sheep economy had still much leeway to make up. The pity was that migration and emigration became inevitable social consequences of that expansion.

The decline in the number of horses from 1814 was occasioned by a number of circumstances. The long period of peace reduced demand for cavalry mounts and also for beasts of burden for the army. Scientific breeding of horses made for a reduction in total numbers as the quality and working efficiency of horses was improved. Canals, the application of steam-power to transport and the rapid development of the railways provided efficient competition for road transport which was heavily dependent on horses. The increase in the number of horses between 1856 and 1868 was partly caused by the expansion of arable agriculture and mining and partly by the demand for Scots-bred horses from England and overseas.

Yet mixed farming was most commonplace in Scotland throughout this period. This made Scottish agriculture far less susceptible than English to economic fluctuations within the British or international economy. But increasingly, Scottish arable agriculture, especially near towns or in counties with commercial or geographical connections with England, was influenced by market pressures and other influences from the south. In the Borders, for instance, there was early improvement of arable. Swinton of Swinton enclosed in the 1730s and then proceeded to drain and to marl his estate.[34] Dr Hutton of Sleighouses near Duns went to Norfolk and returned in 1754 with a Norfolk ploughman.[35] In the course of the following years he raised the capital value of his estate sevenfold. Dr John Rutherford who benefited most from the Melrose enclosure of 1742 began crop improvements such as sowing turnips by the drill in 1747.[36] John Smith, occupier of a farm upon the Cotswolds from 1744, wrote down his 'system of farm management'—a six-course rotation —and sent his notes for running a farm business efficiently to a Major Ogilvie at Montrose.[37] In the Lothians the landowners with large estates were commonly associated with improvement before 1707. From Edinburgh or London, seed merchants like Captain Arthur Clephane, David Dowie and William Miller found increasing numbers of customers for vegetable, flower and other seed as well as for plants and trees. But, in general, horticulture rather than agriculture benefited most from these services.[38]

However, in the late 1720s and early 1730s enclosed fields were becoming commonplace in the Lothians. The Earl of Haddington, having begun enclosures for timber c. 1707 and then planted trees as divisions between fields, introduced the English fallowing rotation at Tyninghame in 1725.[39] The Earl of Hopetoun, completing a gradual process of widening rigs at the expense of baulks, ended runrig on his West Lothian estates in the period 1754–6.[40] New crops like rye-grass and clover became a fundamental part of East Lothian rotations c. 1730, and the creation of temporary leys was common by 1750 in many Lowland counties. Potatoes and turnips became Lowland field crops in the late 1720s but only began to be widely exploited in the twenty years after 1740.[41]

In the Highlands, the idyllic life of Highlandmen basking in the occasional sunshine or more commonly consuming the pleasures created in the whisky house while the women did the hard agricultural work was not always far from reality. But the Commissioners for Forfeited Estates ineffectually encouraged the cause of improvement, as their abundant papers clearly indicate,[42] and in the south-west Highlands and in the Islands the tacksmen often undertook capitalist functions in the tenurial system known as 'steelbow' by which they provided a sub-tack, livestock, implements and seed and received the lion's share of the produce.[43] After 1770 energetic lairds like Archibald Campbell of Jura extended their economic power and influence, specialising in black cattle but also maximising their returns from arable farming.[44]

During the course of the eighteenth century many Highland landlords concentrated so effectively on cattle farming that they must be regarded as agricultural capitalists operating in a market economy. Retracing steps into the era of subsistence became less and less possible for the region as population increased, and several counties became importers of meal.[45] Mass starvation was avoided until the 1830s and 1840s because the potato became the linch-pin of Highland arable farming for the same land was used to support a growing population.[46] The consolidation of holdings pioneered by Argyll, who inherited a substantial debt and therefore had every incentive to improve his estates, became in the 1770s and 1780s part of the general movement of Highland and Lowland landlords to maximise their returns.[47] From Aberdeenshire by the mid-1790s general enclosure on the large estates was common, and Anderson, who prepared the *General View of Agriculture* of the county, commented in 1794:[48] 'Most of these gentlemen's farms are well inclosed, chiefly with stone fences, called here dykes, in a neat and substantial manner.' Between 1780 and 1800 the destruction of runrig for arable in many areas proceeded apace as grain prices moved sharply upwards. But small farms survived in many arable areas, simply because corn prices were so high that the relatively inefficient units of production were given a temporary feather bed. Potatoes were to be found as a prop to subsistence in Lowland counties in much the same fashion as they dominated small arable patches in the Highlands.

Reorganisation of landholding was commonly a piecemeal procedure as leases fell due for renewal; it is, therefore, difficult to track without a systematic examination of estate papers. 'Ornamental' enclosure for parks such as that at Inveraray played little part in the whole process; the enclosure of one estate commonly took several years.[49] Campbell of Knockbuy advocated enclosure in a letter to the Duke of Argyll in 1744, but Knockbuy and Minard were not completely enclosed until 1767 for he could only proceed as fast as his existing sub-tacks were terminated.[50] Arran similarly was enclosed over a period of years from 1766.[51]

Gradually the social and economic unit of the ferm toun was atomised and replaced by single farms or phased out of existence for sheep-walks as in Sutherland. In some parishes, as at Cranstoun, a whole village which in 1781 housed 200 people disappeared, to be replaced by the estate mansion and park.[52] In Lanarkshire, consolidation of holdings by the Dukes of Hamilton gave way to full-scale enclosure after 1766.[53]

From the evidence of estate plans the development of enclosure followed three phases:[54]

(i) 1720–60, a prelude of some enclosure by relatively few enlightened landowners who mainly enclosed for stock farming and plantations;

(ii) 1760–1800, the main movement towards enclosure with the peak of activity coinciding with the fifteen years after 1770;

(iii) 1800–20, when marginal land was enclosed on a large scale principally for sheep farming but also to gain from high grain prices.

From the 1750s the pattern for improvement and enclosure was set. Demand for food and raw materials was increasing, and prices were moving erratically upwards, sometimes with considerable urgency as in the early 1770s.[55] Grain exports were being replaced by slight imports, especially from the Baltic, although the coastal trade to England in agricultural commodities continued at a high level. The Corn Laws were suspended on an annual basis in the late 1760s and early 1770s before the liberal revision of 1773. Bad seasons hastened upward price movements and encouraged corn merchants to exploit regional opportunities for exceptional profit.[56] Government-inspired inflation in the 1790s particularly affected agricultural prices, especially from 1795.[57] Drastic changes in the organisation of production were stimulated by the very sharpness of some price increases. However, the very considerable price changes produced by the wars enabled small scale producers of grain and horses to survive against the general trend towards consolidation of farms and estates.

Economic explanations are no doubt fundamental, but it is also clear that agricultural improvement became a social fashion. The stream of advice on agricultural matters was constant; agricultural clubs and societies flourished; competitions and shows became regular features of county life. Most treatises were aimed at 'the gentleman farmer'—and Lord Kames entitled his major work exactly that! Improvement, like well-informed charity, had become socially prestigious.[58]

From the 1770s, detached observers like Adam Smith noted that enclosures carried higher rents than unenclosed land.[59] Another rough guide to the course of improvement is the activities of land surveyors, even allowing for their involvement in planning transport developments. The number of surveyors sharply increased from the 1740s when there were fifteen practising to nearly eighty in the 1770s. They varied from English incomers like Thomas Winter, brought from Norfolk in 1726 by Grant of Monymusk, to natives like Joseph Udney and James Richmond, who were nurserymen by training, to Charles Mercer, mathematics teacher in Dumfries, who made many plans for enclosures in the south-west in the period 1730–51.[60]

Just as it is mistaken to equate runrig with a total incapacity to expand output, so it would be wrong to assume that reorganisation of tenure inevitably led to outstanding and immediate gains. Andrew Wight's monumental *Present State of Husbandry in Scotland* (1778–84) in its four volumes documents both the persistence of antique methods of production and the survival of runrig in enclosed areas. The sharpest changes in methods of production clearly occurred in the last twenty years of the eighteenth century. The many volumes of the *Old Statistical Account* are an invaluable quarry of information about these changes.[61]

Despite 'Cocky' Cockburn's malicious and untrue comment that Robert Forsyth, an Edinburgh advocate, wrote his *Beauties of Scotland* 'sitting by his fireside, as the usual extent of his peregrina-

tions was from his rooms to the Court', this five-volume tour of
Scotland (1805) provides valuable testimony about agricultural
practices. He commented on the earliest of enclosures around
Edinburgh, some of which preceded 1707, and expounded on how
the city market for food acted as a stimulus to improvement in
neighbouring counties.[62] Efficiency, he tended to equate with size,
and his admiration of large farms was generally uncritical.[63] He
commented favourably on the great farms of Berwickshire, for
instance, where changes in scale were produced by landowners
anticipating better rentals from enclosed land. The extensive use of
lime impressed him and also the importation of horses from
Lanarkshire—£8,000 was spent annually on this trade in horses.[64]
The links between the improvement of grass and the introduction of
the turnip to stock farming he demonstrated by reference to
Roxburghshire where winter feed had to be provided for 260,000
sheep. Most of this county was unenclosed in 1805, but farms had
been consolidated.[65]

Ayrshire, by contrast, suffered from lack of capital, and its
agriculture, according to Forsyth, was relatively backward when
compared with the eastern counties. Dairy farming was prosperous
and organised reasonably well, but most arable farms were small and
inefficient. Improvers brought in experts from the Lothians, and
demand from the Glasgow market acted in favour of better methods.
John Smith of Swinridge Muir near Beith turned peaty land into
model farming country by extensive liming.[66]

In Lanarkshire he noted the widespread cultivation of potatoes
and turnips, the latter used for winter feed for cattle and sheep.
There was considerable experimentation with rotations, alternating
barley, grasses, turnips, potatoes and oats. Wheat was sown on lower
ground, where the climate was less severe than in upland areas of the
county, and also pease and beans. In Clydesdale the orchards and
dairies were numerous, and their production was clearly affected by
Glasgow's demand for fresh milk, fruit and vegetables. Liming was
commonplace, and limekilns were numerous in the Closeburn and
Lesmahagow district.[67]

Dunbarton in 1805 was a county still dominated by small farms
of thirty acres or less where agriculture was linked to part-time
industrial employment such as handloom weaving and cloth finishing.

The general standard of agriculture was poor. Potatoes and oats were the most common crops, and a fair amount of flax was grown, probably for domestic use. Some attempt had been made to cultivate vegetable dyestuffs, woad and madder, but with little permanent success. Black cattle were very numerous but from the late 1740s were being replaced by sheep in upland districts and also in adjoining Argyll. By 1805 there were 26,000 sheep in Dunbartonshire but about one-third of the county was still unenclosed, although there had been rapid changes since 1760.[68]

Stirlingshire had much bigger farms than Dunbartonshire, arable farms of up to 100 acres being common while some stock farms had up to 1,000 acres. This county had pioneered potatoes as a field crop; they were first planted in 1728 by Thomas Prentice (1706–92), a labourer at Kilsyth, as a result of which he accumulated £200. Glasgow's demand for potatoes encouraged more substantial farmers to try them. About two-thirds of this county was enclosed by 1805.[69]

Table 10 : Arable crop acreages in Fife
1800

Crop	Acres (thousands)
Oats,	30
Barley,	20
Wheat,	10
Beans and pease,	7
Potatoes,	6
Turnips,	5
Flax	1.5

West Lothian was owned by thirty or forty landowners, and large farms were the rule. Commonly, leys were created and leased to graziers who supplied meat, hides and dairy products to the Edinburgh market. But there was much mixed farming and about one-sixth of the county remained to be enclosed.[70] The best county as an example of mixed farming was Fife, and in 1800, varieties in crops were usual; 230,000 acres were under arable crops and pasture (Table 10).[71]

Forsyth explained the predominance of oats:

> Oats are more generally adapted to the soil and climate; oatmeal still continues to be the principal article of food among the lower classes of the people; and the consumption by horses has been on the increase for some years past.

Black Fife cattle were well-known in the London market, commanding high prices at Smithfield; dairying was also widespread, especially in association with breweries and distilleries in the county, for draff was excellent fodder. Despite the variations within the agriculture of Fife, relatively little of its land was enclosed—about one-third in all. Even where farms were enclosed, it was common to find field cultivation dominated by runrig.[72]

Further north there was also great variety in agriculture and tenure. In Caithness thirty-five landlords owned the county, but the number of small tenant-farmers was considerable. Rents previously paid in kind had been replaced by money payments. As the county of Sir John Sinclair (1754–1835), the founder of the Board of Agriculture and the indefatigible editor of the *Old Statistical Account*, Caithness had been the scene of considerable improvement, and much marginal land was being brought into cultivation, no doubt inspired by wartime price rises. Pastoral farming for sheep was, by 1805, beginning to displace black cattle.[73]

Orkney had its own special emphasis on pastoral farming: about 24,000 acres of the 84,000 cultivable were arable and the rest devoted to livestock. But little improvement in livestock breeds had occurred. Yet these islands developed a surplus of agricultural commodities—even while persisting with runrig—which had doubled in value between 1770 and 1790.[74] Further north, the Shetlanders mixed farming with fishing, but the latter was the dominant activity. Bere and horses were prime products but sheep, becoming the most important element in stock farming, provided the basis for the local hosiery industry.[75]

Agricultural improvement led to greater output but also greater employment. Although there were clearly productivity gains from better organisation, there was little sign of any decline in the numbers employed on the land before 1815. Essentially, agriculture remained labour-intensive in most areas. Technical improvements were slow to be applied. The chain plough, developed in 1767 by James Small (*c.* 1740–93), a Berwickshire ploughwright, was long in use before it finally replaced the old Scots plough,[76] and the harrow, described as 'more fit to raise laughter than soil', saw little technical change save the increasing use of iron parts.[77] The principal change was the increasing use of wind-, water- and horse-power in such tasks as threshing and milling. James Meikle, inspired by Dutch experience, produced the winnowing machine *c.* 1710, but its use was confined to a small area of the Lothians until after 1740. His son, Andrew, *c.* 1775, produced a threshing machine which was widely pirated on both sides of the Border. For a cost varying from £40 to £70 (compared with a windmill's cost of £200 to £300 and a watermill's cost of about £100) it reduced threshing costs by thirty to forty per cent averaging sixty-three bolls of grain in ten hours and saving more grain from the chaff than was possible with the hand flail.[78] Other improvements included the flax scutching mill, also introduced from Holland in 1729, and the gradual replacement of the sickle by the scythe.[79]

The more scientific use of the land by many in the period to 1815 did not inevitably lead to the best practices being used everywhere. Nor did it follow that principles of veterinary science were universal if a few were breeding cattle, sheep and horses in a scientific fashion.[80] The full implications of capitalist agriculture were slowly realised; there is no bigger misnomer than to describe improvement as a revolution confined to the period before 1815.[81]

Certainly, prices and rents started to move downwards before the end of the war with France, and under these deflationary pressures improvement took on new forms. Because Scottish agriculture was so varied, it is difficult to generalise about experience after 1815. Wheat prices were most adversely affected, and farmers tended to respond to this by leaving wheat out of their rotations. Oats and barley were both more reliable crops and less affected by the fall in cereal prices. In most arable areas, they replaced wheat, but marginal land tended to revert to leys or pasture.[82]

Estimates of cereal crop acreages are given in Table 11.[83] The arable acreage devoted to cereals markedly fell, but this trend was less apparent in the period after 1850. The wheat acreages fluctuated inversely with the barley acreages, while oats maintained a

Table 11 : Cereal crop acreages (millions) 1814–68

Crop	1814	1856	1868
Oats	1.25	0.919	1.011
Barley	0.28	0.18	0.219
Wheat	0.14	0.263	0.125
Total	1.67	1.413	1.386

reasonably constant position. Flax ceased to be a significant crop as the nineteenth century proceeded, but turnips and potatoes became more important.

Farmers everywhere were increasingly intent on cutting their labour costs. With the application of power to threshing exceedingly commonplace by 1830 in all districts, the activity of threshing by the flail, the mainstay of agricultural labourers' winter incomes, was displaced. Much social dislocation resulted, and rural poverty was ubiquitous and stark, especially in the period from 1815 to 1832, and again from 1837 to 1846. Reform of the Poor Law became a pressing social and political question.[84]

In many areas tenants found it difficult to meet the terms of their leases which had commonly been negotiated during the wartime inflation. Rack-renting was a well established phenomenon, especially in the Highlands, as witness the plaintive query of 1773: 'What greater sign of hating their fellow creatures can there be than men [landlords] grinding their very faces?'[85] Enlightened landlords stimulated improvement by carefully calculating rent remissions; in many districts, after 1815, rents in kind once more became common.

But the astringency of the new farming economics was most marked in the Highlands, where Lowland tenants and other incomers set the tone. Patrick Sellar (1780–1851), an Elgin capitalist-farmer, assaulted the existing traditions of Sutherland and in the process achieved remarkable opprobrium. He concentrated on the economics of sheep farming on the Sutherland estates to such a degree that extensive depopulation became inevitable. Through his career in Sutherland, he made a great sum of money from which he spent almost £30,000 on an Argyll estate in the 1840s.[86]

The fall in wool and mutton prices from 1818 down to 1824

was not so devastating as the collapse, especially in the North-west, of cattle prices. By the 1830s sheep numbers in Scotland began to increase substantially (3.4 million by 1841), following the pattern already established in the 1780s. After the period of the 'clearances', Sutherland, for instance, was noted as a county with high quality farming practices. Rack-renting had been generally exposed by the 1830s as a short-sighted policy, and factors in counties such as Caithness were pursuing leasing and rent remission policies designed to avoid tenant indebtedness.[87]

A slight decline in cattle numbers until the 1850s was accompanied by considerable improvements associated with scientific breeding. Breed societies were formed and herd books compiled. Highland cattle farms especially in Aberdeenshire were very impressive to visiting stock-breeders, both on account of size and because of breeding experiments.[88] Fattening cattle on home pasture became much easier for two main reasons. First, fodder crops—oats and roots and cattle cake—increased in supply, and secondly, easier access to markets was provided by steamships and by railways. Thus, carcasses or live beasts could be sent long distances to market without any appreciable weight-loss.[89] The Aberdeen Angus, a breed developed by men like William McCombie (1805–80), a drover in early life, developed a wide market in England as well as in Edinburgh and Glasgow. However, until 1870, the short-horn produced most of Scotland's beef, and the stimulus of Lancashire's market inspired the farmers of Ayrshire and Galloway to send Ayrshires and short-horns to Liverpool via regular steam packet services.[90]

The North probably gained more than the West from improved communications, since it had previously been furthest from urban markets. Beef prices in the twenty years after 1850 were generally rising—by as much as sixty-six per cent according to season in the period 1850 to 1864—and cattle numbers increased substantially. By 1870 many farmers were finding it more profitable to fatten cattle and sheep than to grow cereals. Dairying also gained substantially from transport improvements which allowed quick, safe traffic in perishable foods. South-west Scotland increasingly specialised in dairying, but sheep farming in upland areas still remained most profitable.[91]

Most areas in the period 1815 to 1870 found mixed farming most reliable in changing profit circumstances. In the Lothians, many farms provided models of ideal land utilisation even to the English, and by 1840 returns of the order of twenty per cent on capital per annum could be achieved in normal times. Tenant-farmers in these counties, like George Hope of Fentonbarns, became the cynosure of all would-be farming experts. But these men had learned the error of specialising in cereals.[92]

Improvements such as liming, long-established, and draining—the latter aided by better tile production—became even more common from the 1820s.[93] Under-drainage, popularised by James Smith of Deanston (1789–1850) in the 1830s and 1840s, significantly raised yields on wetter lands,[94] and Peel's Public Money Drainage Act (1846) made loans available to farmers for this purpose. These funds were extensively used by Scottish landowners.[95] The wider use of better implements also made productivity gains possible. But agriculture remained labour-intensive, primarily because labour was cheap. For instance, despite experimentation with mechanised reaping, particularly by James Smith (1815) and Patrick Bell (1828), the main change in harvesting before 1850 was from sickle to scythe.[96] In the 1850s American ploughs and reapers became relatively commonplace, and increased mechanisation, particularly by using the reaper, cut labour costs significantly, especially for expensive scythesmen. Farmers found it easier to get the harvest in, as grains and hay could be cut so much more quickly. Demand for casual labour was cut, but increased numbers of horses were needed.[97] In turn, oat prices were affected; as they moved upwards in the 1850s and 1860s, there was increasing encouragement to reclaim land both for cereals and pasture. The increased use of artificial fertilisers, notably bone-meal, guano and, from the late 1860s, cheap sulphate of ammonia (a by-product of the native shale-oil industry), was marked by the foundation of the Agricultural Chemistry Association of Scotland in 1842.[98] The increasing use of steam-power for threshing and ploughing after 1850 aided productivity and reclamation.

Enclosure was finally completed in several counties in the 1850s and 1860s, and the concentration of property ownership proceeded. This was aided by the upward movement of rents and land prices in most counties after 1830; the amount of capital required to begin farming steadily increased.[99] Despite the tendency towards larger farming units, in many counties the small farm of less than one hundred acres remained typical. In 1851 there were 44,469 farms in this category as opposed to the 360 of 1,000 acres or more.[100] Industrialisation in some counties had the effect of allowing small farms to survive as suppliers of produce or of outwork; in others, crofting with fishing assumed considerable social significance. By 1874 the concentration of property ownership had proceeded further, and cries of 'land monopolists' by extreme Liberals were being raised against the relatively few proprietors, variously estimated at between 1,700 and 8,000 individuals, who owned the land of Scotland.[101] But in 1875 there were 80,796 farms, of which 56,311 had less than fifty acres, and only 817 exceeded 500 acres.[102] By that date landed incomes rarely depended on rents alone. Mineral-mining, quarrying, railway building and urban growth provided royalties, way-leaves, compensation and other capital windfalls.[103]

The contributions of agriculture to Scottish economic development during the period 1707–1871 were numerous. English observers could be scathing about unimproved and improved Scottish agriculture; John Marshall, the Leeds flax-spinner, for instance observed in his diary in 1800 about the farmers at work between Elvanfoot and Lanark:

> They were getting in their corn, which they said was a remarkably good crop, but it was very short & thin. One acre near Selby would yield more than six of it. They were cutting some of it very green. They do not expect to reap on the average more than 2 crops in 3. I suppose the state of cultivation here is much the same as in Russia. They scratch up a bit of ground on the common & sow corn or flax without any sort of fence to preserve it from the cattle, & when that is exhausted they leave it & choose a bit somewhere else.[104]

For someone used to the fertility of the Vale of York, such reactions were perfectly reasonable, but Scottish agriculture had made notable strides by 1800, and linkages with other sectors of the economy were numerous. As the nineteenth century proceeded, agriculture became less significant in the general process of economic growth, but a wide-ranging industrial diversification would not have been initially possible without substantially growing and increasingly efficient primary production.

Inevitably, agriculture had to act as the most important domestic prop to the balance of payments, since the industrial sector immediately after the Union was too small to serve any such function. A favourable balance of payments was essential to the process of industrialisation, particularly in a country with an intricate and extended credit structure formed and conditioned by an inadequate supply of specie. A balance of payments crisis naturally led to bullion exports, financial collapse, higher interest rates and depression; these were inimical to the development of a market economy and to industrialisation. Bullion imports produced by a favourable balance of payments, on the contrary, improved the cash basis of the credit structure and enabled banks to lower interest rates. Under such circumstances expansion was very likely to occur. To achieve a favourable balance of payments, it was necessary for Scottish agriculture to increase its productivity—thereby releasing labour to industries with export potential—and to raise the volume and value of its contribution to trade with England and other countries.

The treaty of Union greatly aided trade in agricultural commodities with England, particularly during periods of peak production in Scotland. Had the Scots had to face hostile Corn Laws and embargoes on the cattle trade, agricultural improvement and industrialisation would have been retarded twins. Instead, considerable consignments of grain, cattle and other agricultural produce flowed to England, and in addition, the corn bounty (extended to Scotland in 1709) stimulated exports, particularly during the period before 1760 (Table 12).[105]

No doubt, this performance was aided by good harvests, stable domestic prices—and the weather. When imports of oats became more common, especially from the 1770s, increasing domestic prices stimulated agricultural improvement, but credit crises also intervened. These would have been more disastrous, had not the economy already achieved a considerable degree of diversification.

Grain imports should, of course, be balanced against the increasing trade with England in cattle, wool, potatoes and processed (i.e. value-added) agricultural goods. Raw spirit exports to England (Table 13) dramatically increased after 1780, for instance, despite government ambivalence about the use of barley for distilling.[106]

Table 12 : Exports of grain from
Scotland 1707–52

Years	Annual average (bolls)
1707–12	55,900
1713–17	95,300
1718–22	115,000
1723–7	59,200
1728–32	40,300
1733–7	71,200
1738–42	53,900
1743–7	79,500
1748–52	98,000

Malt for English breweries also left Scottish ports in greater quantities as did beer. Thus, the value and volume of trade in agricultural goods continued to provide substantial aid to the balance of payments throughout a period of developing industrialisation.

An increased output from agriculture stimulated domestic trade and entrepreneurship by easing the evolution of a national market for food and by encouraging greater regional specialisation in agricultural and industrial production. Landowners and merchants were activated alike by the anticipation of greater profits from inter-regional trade. Farmers commonly became processors, and processors occasionally became farmers; landowners frequently owned cornmills and leased them to millers. John Lawson, junior, of Oldmills, Elgin, was both miller and farmer, his property being insured in 1795 for £1,100. This included, apart from the farm and mill, a distillery and associated buildings.[107] Patrick McAlister of Ballochmill, Dunbartonshire, owned farm property and three mills in 1797; one for corn, a second for flax and madder and a third for logwood.[108] Robert Davidson of Findhorn was farmer, miller and merchant, apparently trading extensively in grain.[109] From Perth, Stirling, Edinburgh and Leith, and Glasgow similar examples of corn merchants with farms and processing plant could be drawn.

Table 13:
Spirits exported
to England
1780–1820

Year	Gallons
1780	34,067
1786	881,969
1787	32,267
1812	1,294,211
1818	1,637,724
1820	1,341,978

The linen and paper industries, brewing, distilling and tanning were commonly associated with landowners, farming families and groups. Charles and Robert Kerr, paper-makers of Edinburgh, for instance, owned a paper-mill and farm at Ayton, Berwickshire, in 1793;[110] William Davidson of Kirkton of Largo, Fife, was both a farmer and flax-dresser;[111] William Welsh, farmer of Inverness, owned and worked a tannery;[112] Thomas Rannie of Cullen, Banff, described himself as a manufacturer—he insured a heckling house, weaving shop and lint mill—but he also owned a farm.[113] Closest personal connections between farming and industrial entrepreneurship existed in brewing and distilling. Robert Bowman and Company of Stonefield, near Paisley, were farmers, maltsters and brewers, for instance.[114] The Glendronach Distillery Company of Aberdeenshire had six partners in 1833, all farmers.[115] The most perfect cycle of economic operations, from farm to distillery and back to farm, was provided by the Steins, the greatest of the Lowland distiller-capitalists. The Steins in 1797 owned over 1,500 Scotch acres at Kilbagie; 200 acres were sown with wheat and barley, and they also fattened 700 oxen and 2,000 to 3,000 pigs.[116] Their own grain they malted for the distillery; the draff from the stills was used to feed the livestock; the dung from the byres went back to the land. Most brewers and distillers kept cattle and pigs, and the draff was particularly valuable as animal feeding stuff during the colder months when other fodder tended to be both scarce and expensive.

Raw materials were provided for a number of industries from agriculture. Flax cultivation, although never sufficient, also aided the balance of payments. A rough indication of its expansion in the eighteenth century can be gathered from the bounty figures. The highest sum paid in the first decade of this subsidy was £412 10s. in 1733–4;[117] by 1774 expenditure on this bounty was £2,583.[118] Madder and woad were cultivated in several counties and used as dyestuffs by the textile industries before the development of synthetic dyes (c. 1800). Sour milk was widely used as a bleaching agent before the technique of applying dilute sulphuric acid was perfected (c. 1750). The introduction of sheep-farming to new farming districts expanded the supply of wool to native and English woollen industry alike, and as the nineteenth century proceeded, quality as well as quantity improved. From afforested areas charcoal was conveyed to a range of industries, and timber came for the mines and the building industry. Hides went to the tanners and then to saddlers and boot- and shoe-makers; animal fats were used in soap and candle manu- facture; bone went to the glue-makers and from the 1840s to the fertiliser producers; horn was an essential material to the cutlers. Because transport was heavily dependent on draught animals for much of the period, animal fodder was its essential raw material. Straw was used as a filler for cheap mattresses and as a packing material for glass, pottery, wines and spirits. Naturally, grains and hides were the most significant and universal raw materials for a range of processing industries, commonly located in rural burghs as well as concentrating in the larger ports and cities.

One significant indication of the development of agricultural processing, because of its association with brewing and distilling, was the quantity of malt charged for duty. In 1809–10, 784,527 bushels (2.87 per cent of British output) was produced in Scotland; by 1840 malt production had increased 550 per cent to 4,309,656 bushels (10.77 per cent of British output). The intermediate phases can be traced from Table 14.[119]

The extent of direct involvement by landowners in mining and manufacturing varied according to personality, industry and time. Before 1780 Scottish landowners in a number of areas were vitally involved in improving the linen and woollen industries.[120] The

Table 14: Quantities of malt (imperial bushels) charged for duty 1810–40

Year	Scotland	United Kingdom	Scotland's share % of UK total
1810	784,527	27,359,120	2.87
1815	1,319,472	30,693,801	4.30
1820	1,400,309	27,874,327	5.02
1825	2,784,477	32,950,757	8.45
1830	3,944,406	28,844,909	13.67
1835	4,437,220	40,662,023	10.91
1840	4,309,656	40,000,018	10.77

promotors of the British Linen Company (1746) were primarily aristocrats; gentlemen and nobles who planned villages like Inveraray usually included a cornmill, a brewery and a variety of facilities for textile industrialists in their design. Merchant-landowners after 1780 like the McDowalls of Castle Semple, the Caldwells of Lochwinnoch and the Houstons of Johnstone financed cotton mills. James Kerr of Flemington described himself in 1801 as 'cotton spinner and farmer';[121] Sir John Stirling of Glorat in the 1790s financed cotton spinning at Kirkintilloch.[122] The sources of capital for the cotton industry become difficult to disentangle, since men like Archibald Campbell of Jura lent money to David Dale and later to Robert Owen on a personal basis.[123]

Mineral-mining, essential to a variety of commercial and industrial development, expanded greatly after 1760, mainly at the behest of landowners and merchant-landowners. The Dukes of Hamilton, Sutherland, Buccleuch and Portland, the Earls of Dundonald, Eglinton, Leven, Wemyss and Rothes provided the vanguard for an army of lesser gentlemen and merchants, coal-masters all, such as the Clerks of Penicuik, the Halketts of Pitfirrane, the Cunninghams of Saltcoats and the Dunlops of Garnkirk.[124] Lead-mining was largely financed by landowners, notably by the Hopes at Wanlockhead, by Buccleuch at Leadhills and in Galloway by Admiral Sir Keith Stewart of Glasserton and his brother, the Earl of Galloway.[125] Leases for ironstone-mining were inevitably controlled by landowners, and the growth of the iron industry after 1759 would not have been possible without the connivance of landowners.

Transport improvement concerned landowners for a number of reasons. Statute labour for road maintenance was organised by the Justices, and the majority of Scottish turnpikes before 1800 were adaptations implemented by county administrations which were, of course, controlled by the landowners. The gradual commutation of statute labour for money payments, common by 1780, occurred because landowners found the old parochial system unsuitable for their needs. Better roads, they recognised, widened the market for agricultural goods but increased the competition for local industries, craftsmen and producers. Highland roads were partly financed by landowners, even when their purposes were commonly military. Canal development was often promoted by landowners and so was port improvement.

Early railways often evolved as an ancillary to coal-mining, salt-boiling and lime-burning; in consequence, they were both promoted and financed by landowners.[126] The Erskines of Mar, Sir John Hope of Pinkie, the Earls of Eglinton and Elgin, the Duke of Portland were all pioneers of wagonways in the eighteenth and early nineteenth centuries.[127] Later, landowners often dominated railway promotion committees and aided the passage of railway Acts through Parliament. Sometimes the early history of a company was dictated by its land-owning adherents, as, for instance, J. J. Hope-Johnstone of Annandale controlled the destinies of the Caledonian Railway before 1850. Scottish landowners were expected to become significant railway investors: the Glasgow, Paisley, Kilmarnock and Ayr Railway Company set aside a thousand shares for local landowners, and the Caledonian had one-fifth of its initial Scottish subscribers from the landed class, representing over one-third of the capital promised from Scotland.[128] In total, landowners' investments in Scottish railways before 1860 were secondary to those of merchants—but important nonetheless.[129]

Scottish landowners also helped to form the banking system and the credit structure. The old chartered banks began their existence— the Bank of Scotland in 1695, the Royal Bank in 1727 and the British Linen Company in 1746—when agriculture was the most important sector of the economy, and the nobility were the most numerous and influential group on their directorates. Involvement in the affairs of the provincial banks were also common. John Coutts and Company evolved from a firm of grain merchants; the Maxwells of Pollok and the Mures of Caldwell were associated with the Glasgow Thistle Bank (1761); Hunters and Company of Ayr (1773) included several lairds as partners, notably Colonel William Hunter of Broomhill. In the North-east Aberdeen's banks included several of the county's leading families as shareholders. Among the failures, Douglas, Heron and Company or the Ayr Bank (established 1769) became notorious as an example of over-speculation undertaken by the landed interest.[130] Tenant farmers in East Lothian were the main support of the ill-fated East Lothian Bank (1810).[131] Commonly, branch banking by these provincial banks grew from the needs of an agrarian society and, in particular, from the demands of the cattle trade and of merchants trading in agricultural commodities. The flow of capital from agriculture into trade and industry in the eighteenth century is currently impossible to chart, for more research needs to be undertaken. The process was often personal, as landowners and farmers supported ventures by relatives or friends, but it was also institutional, as banks channelled trading capital to industry via the discounting of bills of exchange. Significantly, the humble savings bank movement began at Ruthwell in a rural area.[132] However, the use of Edinburgh-based lawyers as factors by the nobility, and the development there of insurance and assurance companies also aided the evolution of a national capital market. For the long-term development of the Scottish economy such a refined credit structure was very necessary.

Just as all landowners did not favour industrial development of their estates—the Duke of Buccleuch, for instance, held up the rise of the woollen industry at Hawick—so the costs of agricultural improvement may have diverted capital from time to time away from investment in trade and industry. This counter-attraction was less important as the nineteenth century proceeded, for industrialisation itself created surplus pools of capital. However, it is significant that the costs of the long wars in the seventy years before 1815 were largely met from land taxes and indirect taxation and not directly from commercial and industrial profits. A generally prosperous agriculture made such a fiscal policy possible and thus, indirectly, aided the rise of commerce and industry.

The income effects of agricultural progress also require more investigation. Low farm prices before 1750 may have encouraged the spread of manufacturing and the growth of local markets in rural districts, as communities attempted to supplement incomes by seasonal weaving or bleaching work. Such price levels raised the real incomes of consumers and released a greater margin of income for spending on industrial goods such as clothing. Processing industries like brewing and distilling were also encouraged. The migration of labour from the countryside was likely to be stimulated, and as population increased in relatively high money-wage areas so demand for industrial goods was likely to rise. As money wages tended to become more significant than wages in kind, so the structure of the market changed in favour of economic development. Any temporary falls in per capita purchasing power through wage reductions or food price increases were likely to be offset by increases in the population, which would aid the growth of aggregate demand. In wartime, demand for labour tended to rise, and opportunities for employment in the services tended to keep up wage levels. Without an increasingly efficient agriculture, the cost of living would have risen much higher after 1750 than, in fact, happened. This would certainly have restricted the growth of demand. Hamilton's examination of wages in the eighteenth century suggests that wages were rising more rapidly in Scotland than in England, and the perennial complaints in the *Old Statistical Account* suggest that ministers were of the opinion that most workers and all members of 'superior classes' were subject to increasing temptations from the market-place.[133]

One contribution of agriculture to economic growth has been mentioned *en passant*. Agricultural labour was commonly used for non-agricultural purposes, in particular in the textile industries and their finishing trades. Also the development of the transport system depended upon navvies, many of whom were recruited locally. It was not until the era of railways that imported labour became a substantial component in the building trades. The skilled labour of land surveyors, millwrights, masons, joiners and clockmakers, so necessary for the early stages of industrialisation was primarily recruited to serve the needs of a growingly affluent rural society. Improved agriculture required more skills and commonly more labour and not less. Rural society with its clear divisions of laird, tenant-farmer and landless labourer possessed also a variety of inter-mediate grades, some of whom deserve greater research. The ploughman, for instance, was an 'aristocrat' of farm labour until 1815, with his own status in society and commonly his own club or Friendly Society. In contrast, the seasonal labour of the farms was often undertaken by unskilled men with little status and fewer prospects. Social change emanated from agricultural improvement in much the same way as the size of industry and commerce produced new or more numerous occupational groups.[134]

Despite the vast economic changes which occurred in the period from 1707 to 1871, landowners remained dominant in Scottish society. In material terms, landed wealth was still growing sub-stantially as this period closed: income from lands under Schedule A of the income tax rose forty-one per cent between 1851–2 and 1878–9.[135] Landowners were reinforced from the commercial and industrial sectors and not displaced by the 'capitalist' revolution. They dominated local administration, controlling church patronage, poor relief and education; they remained the principal employers of labour in most counties; they gave active support to all sorts of agencies of economic progress provided these did not jeopardise their social position. Where their support for the forces of economic change was generally passive, this was commonly critical, since they often controlled the land, the minerals, the food supply and the people.

CHAPTER IX

Commerce and Credit
1707–1871

IN A private enterprise situation, economic growth depends upon
the expansion of effective demand. A trend of increasing exports was
one important feature of the Scottish economy during industrialisation but more significant was the development of the United
Kingdom market for Scottish goods. David Macpherson, for
instance, thought in 1805 that there was good evidence for believing
'the people of Great Britain being the best customers to the
manufacturers and traders of Great Britain'.[1] The rate of growth of
this wider domestic market was aided by the Treaty of Union and
by the gradual increase in protectionism in the eighteenth century.
Increasing customs duties protected the British market from foreign
competition—French linens, for instance, by 1779 faced a duty of
sixty-two per cent; after 1717, in contrast, there were no export
duties on Scots linen, and commonly subsidies.[2] Foreign trade was
much more volatile in its behaviour than the rate of domestic consumption; indeed, the underlying stability and buoyancy of the domestic market were the subjects of many eighteenth century statements,
often accompanied with unflattering puritanical comments about the
spread of decadent and luxurious tastes among the middle and
artisan classes.

INTERNAL TRADE

The growth of internal trade, considering the marked poverty of
Scotland before the Union, was one of the main features of economic

136

change in the eighteenth century. Population was an obvious source of increased demand in Scotland particularly as the community became more mobile and urbanised in areas where wages, on average, were higher than in rural districts. The very transfer to monetary incomes from payment in kind—despite the long survival of the latter practice—was likely to raise demand. A more vexed question is whether income per family or per capita increased. For every occupational group this seems most unlikely, if only because structural changes in the economy were likely to make some skills redundant. In addition, as a market economy evolved, the effects of downswings in the trade cycle—and in foreign trade—would be more widely felt. For these reasons the rate of growth in domestic purchasing power could not be consistent. Yet there is much evidence to suggest that the expansion of middle- and upper-class demand was less affected by these economic circumstances than might be supposed and that new jobs were generally being created faster than declining crafts decayed. It is important not to regard the victims of mechanisation, such as the cotton handloom weavers after 1815, as in some way representative workers in the new industrial economy. By 1870 the course of living standards for most workers was clearly upwards, and the material condition of urban and rural workers was incomparably better than at the time of the Union.[3]

One restraint on the growth of demand was the cost of transport, but the drive to improvement, manifest in better roads and in canal and railway promotion, united congeries of local economies and reduced prices for many staple articles without cutting profits.

As traditional methods of production were replaced, the substitution of cheaper industrially-produced consumer goods, such as Paisley silk gauzes, tended to widen demand where price elasticity had some significance.[4] Social and religious attitudes against consumption, commonly expressed by the relatively affluent, weakened. The Calvinist ethic which emphasised work rather than leisure ensured that Scots consumed gains from extra productivity, not in the form of more holidays and less labour, but in greater quantities of food, drink, goods and services. In its report on the state of the linen manufacture for 1740, the Board of Trustees commented that 'a Taste for wearing of Thread Stockings did now begin to prevail in the Country'.[5] Earlier, in 1738, the Board had noted that the gentry, had abandoned 'Linen brought from Holland for Shirting' in favour of Scots fine cloth.[6]

Most obvious were the symptoms of middle-class well-being from c. 1750:

> a new stile [sic] was introduced in building, in living, in dress, and in furniture; the conveniences, the elegances of life began to be studied, wheel carriages were set up; public places of entertainment were frequented; an assembly room and a play-house were built by subscription.[7]

John Gibson's comments (1777) about Glasgow could have been equalled by the experience of Aberdeen, Dundee and Perth and more than matched by that of Edinburgh, described in 1805 by Robert Forsyth as 'the principal seat of luxury and ostentation'.[8] As an academic, legal, administrative and recreational centre, the capital demonstrated most aspects of upper-class consumption, but the extent and scale of its markets indicate its wider economic significance to the region that they served.[9]

Fairs and markets rather than shops were the main institutions of internal trade at the beginning of this period, but in his analysis of the *Old Statistical Account* published in 1825 Sir John Sinclair commented: 'The inland trade is principally carried on by shop-keepers, who buy and sell foreign, colonial and domestic commodities'.[10] They provided employment for a host of carriers and shippers; they urged the necessity of transport improvement. It was not that fairs and markets disappeared overnight: in general, farm labour was hired, and country commodities and livestock were extensively sold at these gatherings. In the 1830s a place like Newton Stewart still had four fairs during the year, a general market every Friday, a horse fair three times a year and a cattle market once a month.[11] In the nineteenth century, urban markets were greatly extended, and this often meant the provision of purpose-built accommodation, notably in Edinburgh and Glasgow.[12] However, the great increase in the number and variety of shops in the towns was most marked from c. 1750 and by the 1820s was a feature of rural society also, as a glance at *Pigot's Directory* for 1825 indicates.

The organisation of internal trade was varied for most of this period. Trading from dwelling houses or outbuildings was common.

Tradesmen and craftsmen like weavers, tailors, milliners, shoe-makers, smiths and wrights together with grocers and innkeepers often combined their living and trading premises.[13] There was also some conversion: 'The house of the late President Dundas [in Edinburgh] who died in December 1787 is now possessed by an ironmonger, as his dwelling house and wareroom', reported the local minister.[14] 'Scotch' pedlars were found far afield, so much so that the expression in many English areas came to mean any travelling salesman of whatever nationality. Some made their fortunes and settled as linen drapers in England, like James McGuffog, Robert Owen's first master at Stamford.[15] Hawking was commonplace in urban districts, simply because retailing services were often slow to penetrate working-class areas. A sign of the widening market—and of the extent of literacy—was the great increase in the number of hawkers who sold books. 'A new trade since 1796', book hawking had 414 licensed operators by 1820.[16]

The most numerous group of retailers were concerned with selling food, drink and clothing, but many shopkeepers were general dealers. The development of specialist shops in the towns and cities was generally a product of the late eighteenth century. The first shoe shop in Glasgow was opened as a speculation in 1749, and the first haberdashery c. 1750 while jewellers and silversmiths started retail shops in the city in the 1750s.[17] After the American War specialist shops became very common. South Bridge, Edinburgh, built from 1785, was soon crowded with shops; Cockburn described it as 'taken possession of by haberdashers', but it also housed Blackwood, the publisher, and Thin, the bookseller.[18] The development of such central shopping areas in the cities and towns was a feature of speculative building operations in the fifty years after 1820.

Some retailers were also manufacturers and occasionally, even exporters. The Glasgow firm of John Buchanan and Company (fl. 1790) had two hat shops, with a stock of hats made in London, Sheffield and Manchester. Operating with a capital of about £2,000, this firm also employed their own hat-makers and had two apprentice salesmen. John Buchanan had as his partner, John Paterson of Castlehill, a merchant-landowner. Apart from selling retail, Buchanan was a wholesaler with a clientele of retailers scattered throughout

Scotland, and among his other customers was a Scots merchant in Virginia.[19]

Capital requirements for retailing were often relatively modest. The shop could be rented; fittings were often rudimentary and cheap; stock could be obtained on credit. Sometimes the shop was merely a side-line managed by the wife while the husband operated a wholesale business.[20] Because entry to retailing was relatively simple —stallholding at markets and fairs interspersed with periods of itinerant peddling could provide both initial capital and experience— the real problem was often to stay in business. Mortality among such businesses was generally high. The progress of John Connell of Melville Street, Portobello, may help to illustrate this process. Having the right connections, Connell began in 1817 as the junior partner in the firm of Patison and Connell, 28 Princes Street, Edinburgh, dealing in general grocery—cheese, bacon, ham—but this firm failed in the general depression of 1819. Within a month Connell found a position as manager of a shop belonging to John Jamieson and Company, also of Princes Street. He saved and eventually obtained a discharge from bankruptcy in 1825. Almost immediately he set up on his own in another shop, obtaining the necessary credit by using his Portobello house as security. In 1830 he was pressed to repay this loan and could not do so. Then followed his second sequestration. With the help of friends he bought his shop and stock from his creditors and restarted. In 1833 he retired from this business and began wholesaling in Glasgow; by 1834 he was bankrupt for the third time.[21]

Some indication of the economic standing of shopkeepers and wholesalers can be obtained from the insurance policies taken out in the 1790s with the Sun Fire Insurance Company. Outside Glasgow 119 shopkeepers took policies for an aggregate value of £61,798, averaging £519 6s.; ninety-four Glasgow shopkeepers' policies averaged £890 6s. [aggregate £83,685]. Many owned property beyond shops and stock. As one might expect, the more substantial wholesalers insured assets on a greater scale. For Scotland outside Glasgow 104 wholesalers took policies for £182,455, an average of £1,754 8s., while nineteen Glasgow wholesalers averaged £1,518 8s. [aggregate £28,849].[22] Most of Glasgow's wholesale trade in the 1790s, it should be remembered, was conducted by general merchants who also had import-export businesses. By the 1850s retail and wholesale distribution had become both more specialised and more complex. Some indication of this is given in Appendix III.[23]

As noted already, the wholesalers had ties with coastal and foreign trade and often sold retail as well as supplying retailers. Although specialisation was increasingly the fashion, general wholesaling remained relatively common throughout this period, primarily because it reduced the risks of failure and enhanced the opportunities for profit. The size and social structure of the population—and its purchasing power—of towns and cities made specialisation much less risky as time passed. Glasgow importers sold a number of commodities wholesale. For instance, William Coats, according to *Jones's Directory* (1789), was a general merchant, a wholesale hardware merchant and a wholesale linen merchant.[24] Thomas Baird, Glasgow merchant and broker (*fl.* 1815) dealt in sugar, coffee, rum, gin, spices such as ginger, logwood, yarn and wines.[25]

Sometimes a sound base in retailing became the spring-board to a career in wholesaling. Andrew Melrose (1789/90–1855) began his business career as an apprentice to Robert Sheppard, tea and spirit dealer of South Bridge Street, Edinburgh. Sheppard had four shops, two in Edinburgh, one in Leith and one in Aberdeen. His apprentices, as well as Melrose, made fortunes and occasionally reputations for themselves—James Richardson as a sugar dealer, William Law as a coffee merchant and John Christie as a wholesaler of butter and groceries. The tea trade, which became Melrose's speciality, was dominated by the East India Company until the 1830s; in 1834 the first shipment of China tea reached Greenock direct from Canton. Melrose operated shops in Edinburgh and was supplied with groceries from a wide area of Scotland and England; in turn, he supplied retailers throughout Scotland and northern England, using circulars and newspaper advertising as methods of recruiting his customers.[26]

Some producers were also wholesalers and increasingly exporters. This was particularly true of industrial firms in sectors such as iron, textiles, coal, glass and distilling, but it applied equally to firms as diverse as tobacconists and ships chandlers. For instance, John Laing of Port Glasgow (*fl.* 1801), sea-biscuit bakers, also sold bread and confectionery retail and wholesale.[27]

The range of capital size and the opportunities for upward mobility among wholesalers were considerable. But some were doomed to fail, either because of their own shortcomings as businessmen or, more often, on account of the economic environment. Such a case was the firm of Hugh Walker and Company of Paisley (*fl.* 1817). Hugh Walker began in business at Whitsuntide in 1815 as a merchant and shopkeeper, dealing wholesale and retail in a range of textiles supplied from places as far afield as London, Kidderminster, Leeds and Huddersfield. His capital was only £460. Of this, £200 was lent to him by his father and the remaining £260 by his brother, James, a farmer. Further trading capital was made available by an uncle, also a farmer, who provided between £200 and £300. Under-capitalisation was the prime cause of failure, two years later.[28] The incapacity to find cash when credit was difficult to obtain was a very common reason for business failures, even when the long-term trend favoured the expansion of business operations. For instance, when the boom of 1825 collapsed, John Craig, a silk warehouseman of South Bridge Street, Edinburgh, failed, primarily because his stock fell in value and he could not collect the debts owing to him. His stock, valued cheaply at £1,128 2s. 10d., included supplies from London, Coventry, Manchester and Halifax.[29] Specialisation often began in consequence of a shortage of capital, but as urban middle-class markets became more substantial, it became more viable. From 1828 John Robertson of Argyle Street, Glasgow, for instance, ran a successful warehouse specialising in cutlery.[30]

The opportunities for wholesalers and retailers constantly widened from the 1830s. The growth of industry and the development of foreign trade encouraged expansion of the distributive trades. Urban growth and railway development altered the structure of the market and increased the profit potential available to middlemen. Improved commercial intelligence enabled regular patterns of business to become discernible. Multiple-branch firms increased in number, and 'higgling' [haggling] over prices gradually ceased to be a feature of retail trade. The benefits of regional specialisation in production—and the great trade between England and Scotland—were appreciated by merchant groups in many Scottish towns.

New advice was offered to retailers by the 1850s:

Save discounts in buying goods.
Give short credits to your customers.
Run no risks.
Sell at small prices.
Turn over large amounts yearly.

Thus, Peter Scott, clothier and shirt merchant of South Bridge, Edinburgh, advertised his services in *The North British Advertiser* on 10 May 1856. Most towns had specialised shops and wholesalers in variety by that date.

The working classes, led by skilled artisans, had also entered retail trade, adopting some of Scott's precepts. The co-operative society, a mixture of social idealism and economic practicality, was a reaction against the employers' truck shops, adulterated food, bad weights and the concept of 'capitalist profit'. Although beginning early in Scotland with the Fenwick Weavers Society (1769), the great period for retail society formation was the 1850s and 1860s. The Scottish Co-operative Wholesale Society, formed in 1868, had, by 1872–3, 107 member societies and over 100 others making purchases. Sales reached £262,434; share capital was only £7,883; net profit was £5,434.[31]

Yet the truck shop survived and, despite government legislation, remained 'big business' in mining and iron-working areas. Commonly, truck shops existed in industries notorious for 'long pays' (sometimes at six-monthly intervals), and extensive credit given by employers soon brought back wages paid and restricted the mobility of labour. For instance, the Coltness Iron Company in 1869–70 advanced £47,797 2s. 10d. to its workmen via its truck shops, and any bad debts were recovered from wages.[32]

Bad debts were common in most types of business. In Edinburgh the Scottish Trade Protection Society was formed in the 1850s with Charles Cowan M.P. as its president. Its members—bankers, merchants and traders—were offered a number of services, but foremost were protection of members from fraud, the testing of credit-worthiness and the collection of overdue accounts.[33]

By 1870, in retail and wholesale trade, there had been an astonishing change in scale, business methods and organisation. The ground had been prepared for what has been usually described as a 'retailing revolution'.[34]

COASTAL AND FOREIGN TRADE

An outstanding feature of the Scottish economy after 1760 was the growth of the shipping industry, a reflection of the significance of coastal and foreign trade. By 1860 the number of Scottish ships had increased from 999 to 3,486, and capacity from 53,913 tons to 523,771 tons. After 1840 steam vessels played an increasing part in commercial operations. By 1867 there were 138 steamers of under fifty tons and 363 of over fifty tons—steam tonnage accounted for about a fifth of total shipping capacity of 820,657 tons.[35]

There were always more ships engaged in the coastal trade than in foreign ventures, but the larger the vessel the more likely that it was purpose-built for overseas trade. In 1771, for instance, 604 ships (total tonnage: 48,844) were engaged in foreign trade and 677 (tonnage: 28,623) in the coastal trade. The turn-round of shipping in Scottish ports is perhaps more instructive than other quantities. Vessels cleared in Scottish ports in 1771 represented a total tonnage of 777,105, of which 548,984 tons was accounted for by coastal, and 228,121 tons by foreign trade.[36]

Until the coming of the railways coastal shipping had no real rivals for transporting goods between Scottish and English ports, although the cattle trade—according to Adam Smith, the prime beneficiary of the Treaty of Union and certainly Scotland's great money-spinner before 1815—was a prominent exception to the general rule that land carriage was inordinately expensive. The ties between Scottish and English ports were long-standing, and the sea-borne flow of goods between the two countries was clearly an important component in the aggregate of Scottish trade. Until the history of individual ports has been written, the exact quantities of commodities moved coastwise cannot be accurately assessed.

However, there are a number of indicators. Even before the Union, linen cloth and yarn were important in the trade with England, and as the eighteenth century proceeded, their significance grew.[37] One-third of the total value of Scotland's trade with England in 1700 was represented by cloth and yarn.[38] The Board of Trustees commented regularly that the coastal trade in yarn, particularly to Lancashire and via the Trent to Nottingham, was so substantial as to raise the internal price level, adversely affecting the manufacture of coarse linen. In 1736 their report noted:[39]

> there was a considerable decrease on the coarse [manufacture], which was attributed to the great quantity of yarn exported to Manchester and other parts of the North of England, By which means the price of yarn was so advanced that many of our poor weavers had not stocks for purchasing a sufficient quantity for keeping their looms going.

A rise of twenty per cent in yarn prices in 1738 was attributed to English demand for Scottish yarns.[40] About the same time London merchants were warning their agents in Holland that Scottish fine linens were becoming competitive in quality and price.[41] An estimate in 1765 placed the value of linen sent to London annually at £300,000, and the yarn trade in 1766 was estimated by Lord Kames at £100,000.[42] Variation in textile production was also represented in the coastal trade—Paisley silk gauzes to London from 1759 and an extensive trade in stockings and sailcloth from the North-east for most of the century.[43]

Agricultural goods and processed commodities, such as malt, raw grain spirit, beer and whisky, butter and cheese, passed freely among the Scottish ports and between them and England—from Galloway to Lancashire and London, and from the Lothians, Fife, Angus and Perthshire to many east-coast ports to the north and south.[44] From the forests of Abernethy and Rothiemurchus timber was floated down the Spey to the sea and thence to Edinburgh, the naval dockyards on the Thames, and Hull. From Hull came entrepreneurs who established their shipbuilding yard at Kingston-upon-Spey.[45]

The colonial trade in tobacco, sugar and, ultimately, cotton acted as a stimulus to the coastal trade. During the early post-Union years, for instance, three-quarters of the tobacco imported into Scotland was sent coastwise to England, principally to Bristol and London.[46] Recent research reveals that in 1775 tobacco, linen goods, cloth and yarn from the ports of Bo'ness and Leith featured significantly in the trade of Hull together with smaller shipments of coal, metal goods, sulphuric acid and books.[47] The opening of the Forth and Clyde canal further aided the trade in colonial produce along the east coast via Grangemouth.[48]

Industrialisation had the side-effect of diversifying and stimulating the coastal trade. Progressive Scottish firms, like William Stirling and Company (calico printers), Carron Company and the Dumbarton Glassworks, opened warehouses in important English markets— London, Hull and Liverpool.[49] The scale of coal movements greatly changed, and in 1846 the port of Irvine, for instance, sent 177,635 tons coastwise.[50] Pig-iron, sent southwards in penny numbers in the early eighteenth century, became after 1830 a prominent commodity in the coastal trade; usually, about one-third of total output went to England, mostly from the Clyde.[51] The tradition of Scottish textiles seeking an English market was continued and extended by cotton, tweeds and jute.[52]

From the south came luxuries and capital goods—fine woollen cloth, hats, Manchester cottons and yarns, silks, specialist metal goods like Sheffield cutlery and Birmingham ware, machinery and rails. From James Watt's Soho works came steam engines to Leadhills and Wanlockhead, to cotton mills at Glasgow, Paisley and Johnstone and to mines in the Lothians; they were carried by canal and river to the sea, and their coastal journey then began.[53] However, no matter how sophisticated the products of the south, the trade was almost always in Scotland's favour; the significance of this surplus was that it offset debits with other countries.[54]

Scotland's foreign trade was protected after the Union by the Navigation Acts, but as we have seen, Scottish merchants had developed an illegal trade with English colonies in America and the West Indies before 1707.[55] Thus, the Union's immediate commercial advantages were likely to be minimised. However, there was a spectacular increase in the tobacco trade up to 1775. Despite the existence of smuggling, for which there is a miscellany of evidence, the official (and, therefore, low) figures, beginning in 1755, indicate by 1775 a rise in tobacco imports of the order of 300 per cent.[56]

This trade concentrated on the Clyde ports immediately after the Union and was essentially controlled by Glasgow merchant partnerships. By 1769 they were importing as much tobacco as London and the outports combined; in 1772 tobacco (at official valuation)

Table 15 : Tobacco imports and
re-exports 1755–75

Year	Imports (lb.)	Re-exports (lb.)
1755	15,200,698	10,477,024
1760	32,182,508	24,771,724
1765	33,159,815	28,642,935
1770	38,708,809	39,490,824
1775	45,863,154	30,228,949

accounted for eighty per cent of all Scottish imports from North America.[57] Such commercial success can only be explained in terms of the economic advantages available to Glasgow merchants.[58] Clyde-based ships had the quickest passage to Virginia and Maryland, and the route round the north of Ireland was safer in times of war. By means of joint-stock partnerships and banks, Glasgow men were able to draw far and wide on the capital and credit of Scotland. Goods in demand in the plantations—cloth, guns, tools, leather goods, dried fish—were in ready supply in the West of Scotland, even if, from time to time, merchant investment was necessary to increase the scale of their production. Operating costs, notably cheaper labour and ships and better outgoing cargoes, favoured the Scots. So did superior commercial organisation in the colonies where the store system prepared the way for the arrival of ships, as salaried employees—occasionally junior partners—of the partnerships bought cargoes of tobacco from the planters. Thus, Clyde ships achieved a quick turn-round; two voyages in the year instead of the more normal one greatly reduced costs. Meanwhile, Whitehaven concentrated more on trade with Ireland, and Bristol and Liverpool specialised in other commodities.

As Glasgow's tobacco trade grew, its commercial élite became a tighter group, interlinked by blood, marriage and common economic interests. Partnerships were often interlocking; kindred companies pursued mutually agreed trading policies and reinforced one another with credit. Common action of this sort was likely to reduce costs and risks, to increase profits and to make entry to the trade more difficult. Thus, when the American War of Independence broke out, there were few failures, and the larger merchant groups of

Glasgow, with stocks of tobacco in hand, made substantial short-term gains because of the interruption in supplies. That some losses were made by tobacco importers—and especially by those firms who owned plantations in America—seems irrefutable; that they were catastrophic for the merchant community is nonsense.[59]

For the Glasgow tobacco merchants were also general exporters, able by a combination of mercantile expertise and the skilful rearrangement of partnership agreements to offset the effects of the conflict and to exploit the opportunities presented by other areas, notably the West Indies.[60] Those possessing liquid capital could invest it in land or grow fat on their returns from government stock, for during the war interest-rates rose substantially.[61] They did not require to move their capital into the cotton industry—there is little or no evidence that they did so—and although there is a common view that the American War was a watershed for mercantile capital investment in industry, this is certainly fallacious.[62] Indeed, the intervention of the government in the capital market by profusely issuing loan stock at attractive discounts may have halted the switch of mercantile profits into industry, just as increases in taxation might be expected to have depressed home demand.[63]

The tobacco trade, because it was the basis of extensive re-exports, had few direct income effects on the economy. There was some processing of snuff and tobacco, but Holland and France were the principal customers for raw tobacco which formed the bulk of Scotland's exports before the American War. The Dutch also purchased quantities of knitted stockings and from the 1750s vitriol (sulphuric acid) mainly used in linen bleaching. France and southern Europe, in addition to tobacco, bought barrels of herrings, this export being supported by bounties. As Scotland's trade with the West Indies developed, so the re-export of sugar, rum, and cotton became more important.[64]

Thus, re-exporting dominated the pattern of Scottish trade before the American War: in 1771 seventy-six per cent of the value of exports went to Europe, and eighty-seven per cent of this represented re-exports. The main overseas markets for Scotland's industrial products during this period were the American colonies, and the expansion of American purchasing power had substantial indirect effects on the pace of industrial development in Scotland. This phase of overseas trade also conditioned the quality of Scotland's overhead capital—river improvement, port development, warehouse building, marine insurance and credit institutions.

The collapse of the tobacco trade had significant effects on trade. Even when the American trade was resumed, it was never so important to the Scottish economy again. Europe, particularly Germany and Russia, shared with the West Indies in a general boom in Scottish trade after 1783. Exports to Europe increased in quantity and value, but were also markedly different. Linen, cotton yarn and goods, coal, vitriol and fish replaced tobacco; sugar re-exports increased in significance. Imports from Europe also diversified: flax, hemp, tallow, timber, tar and bar-iron were basic commodities of increasing importance in the Baltic trade and to them was added a range of wines and agricultural goods from southern Europe intended for the tables of the wealthy. To the West Indies, linen and cotton cloth, dried fish, a range of plantation equipment, leather goods, guns and gunpowder went in exchange for sugar, cotton and rum.[65]

After 1800 Scotland's trade was increasingly divergent—Asia, South America and Australasia became important markets and suppliers of raw materials. The expansion of the American cotton production was accompanied by a rapidly developing trade in raw cotton to the Clyde, and Scots firms established agencies in the southern states, particularly in New Orleans. After 1840, however, Liverpool gradually dominated this trade. The expansion of Dundee's jute industry in the 1840s aided the growth of the existing trade with India and Ceylon; equally, the Borders woollen industry was fed with rising imports from Australasia. Textiles, pig-iron, metal goods and machinery, chemicals and coal formed the bulk of Scottish exports by 1870: Scotland was firmly drawn into the world economy.[66]

Although official statistics are defective—and, in any case, do not take into account goods sent coastwise to England and then exported —the change in the scale of foreign trade can be readily appreciated from Appendix IV which shows the average trend in the official values of imports and exports from 1755 to 1850. Whereas in the five-year period 1755–9 imports averaged £566,145 and exports £750,053, by 1845–9 the figures were respectively £7,899,017 and

£13,634,687. Such an expansion, which outpaced the rate of growth in the population, suggests that Scotland became more dependent on foreign trade as a consequence of industrialisation. Relatively low costs of industrial production kept foreign demand for manufactures buoyant, and the growing textile sector, in particular, depended upon the sustained inflow of cheap raw materials.

Directly, the effects of increasing foreign trade were most marked on shipping services which expanded considerably. In turn, shipbuilding was stimulated. Glasgow, in consequence, became the headquarters for shipping lines, and the Clyde the most important river for shipbuilding. Indirect effects included further harbour and river improvement, and extensive building in the seaports of Aberdeen, Leith, Dundee and Greenock as well as in Glasgow. The physical expansion of dock areas and commercial sections of these towns and cities increased the demand for building, dock and clerical labour. The social structure of these seaports mirrored their economic roles.

BANKING AND CREDIT

Most observers were struck by the poverty of the economy in the late seventeenth and early eighteenth centuries. Badly damaged by the failure of the Darien scheme, the credit structure was primitive and in disarray; the deficiency of the money supply was widely recognised as an obstacle to commerce; the coinage was in poor physical condition; a drain of bullion to London was an ever-present threat for the balance of payments was unsteady.[67] The capital market was likely, therefore, to be grossly imperfect—credit was given to personal friends and acquaintances, and because confidence easily faltered, there was no sustained possibility of tapping the savings of the community and changing them into investment funds.

In the general euphoria surrounding the Darien scheme the Bank of Scotland was founded by Act of the Scottish Parliament in 1695, principally to serve the borrowing interests of the state. This venture, the first of the chartered banks, was promoted by London Scots. It had the twin privileges of limited liability and a legal monopoly of formalised banking for twenty-one years. Its nominal capital was

£100,000 to be subscribed by not less than sixty and not more than 1,200 shareholders.[68]

Similarly privileged was the Royal Bank of Scotland chartered in 1727. This evolved from the Equivalent Company (founded in 1724 to guard the interests of the debenture holders of the Equivalent Debt), and its nominal capital was calculated at over £110,000 with powers to raise another £40,000 if required.[69] Thus, the monopoly of the 'Auld Bank' was broken, after it had itself repulsed the overtures of the Equivalent Company for an amalgamation.

Both these banks had significant numbers of London share-holders,[70] but relations between them were initially bad. The Bank of Scotland, with a paid-up capital of over £10,000 in 1720, was not able to cope with the financial pressures engendered by increasing economic activity, but it was jealous of its own position, its directors protesting against the Royal Bank's receiving a charter. Each bank practised the tactic of collecting large numbers of the other's notes and then, in an attempt to close down or to embarrass its rival, presenting them for payment in coin. This behaviour was an indication that banking was still in its infancy and bankers were still learning the basic principles of sound finance. For each bank was testing the liquidity of the other: it did not matter that sound assets existed capable of more than matching liabilities; it was necessary that these could be quickly mobilised to beat off any dangerous runs on cash reserves. On 27 March 1728 the 'Auld Bank', although soundly financed, had to suspend payments in consequence of the Royal Bank's pressure over the previous three months.[71] The Royal Bank, on the day of the temporary closure, held £9,374 of the Bank of Scotland's notes, while the 'Auld Bank', after the persistent run, had only a cash reserve of £585 4s. 9d.[72]

The Bank of Scotland re-opened on 27 June 1728, having made a call of £10,000 on its shareholders, realised some of its previously illiquid assets and published its balance sheet to raise confidence in its notes. In addition it offered a five per cent bonus to those who took its notes. Thus, the 'Auld Bank' learned the liquidity lesson the hard way. One reason for the relatively high liquidity ratio of bank assets later in the century—reserves were commonly held in cash, or government or Bank of England stock—was the bankers' memory of this experience.

The Royal Bank also learned the significance to general confidence of a run on one bank. After forcing the crisis, its directors accepted its rival's notes, knowing that its assets were sound. Both banks had realised the importance of co-existence.

The third chartered bank, the British Linen Company (1746), began, also with London support, granting and discounting bills of exchange generated by the linen industry's requirements. Gradually, it made advances to landowners and businessmen outside the industry and after 1763 it concentrated on banking.[73]

For generations before the chartered banks were established, various banking functions had been undertaken by merchants, partnerships and joint-stock companies, as part of wider economic interests. Notable in Edinburgh were the lawyers and goldsmiths. To these were added the grain dealers, maltmen, brewers, distillers, wholesalers and retailers. In Glasgow, merchants dealt in bills of exchange and received deposits upon which they allowed interest. Merchant partnerships, involved in tobacco importing, shipowning and marine insurance, had a natural requirement for loan capital which they could invest in their own activities at a greater profit. Co-partnerships concerned in sugar refining, tanning, shoe-making, and soap manufacture also accepted deposits.[74] In other cities and burghs, merchant partnerships existed performing the same functions and from these groups evolved the private banks and later the insurance companies.

Because some of these groups were engaged in highly speculative operations, notably the corn dealers and distillers, failures were very possible. Corn importers moved to banking because they were often concerned in the negotiation of international bills of exchange. This was the origin of the Edinburgh firm of John Coutts and Company, later Forbes, Hunter and Company, and this banking house carried on corn-dealing until 1761, when Sir William Forbes, then senior partner stopped the practice.[75] A less happy example—because the firm did not survive—was Adam and Thomas Fairholme which failed in 1764.[76] The cloth trade threw up a number of bankers and banking firms in Edinburgh: Mansfield, Hunter and Company began as a draper's business, as did William Cumming and Sons.[77]

Because of the inadequacies of the services provided by the Edinburgh banks, provincial banking firms developed. They usually faced competition from branches of the chartered banks but some-times they began with the short-sighted support of the Bank of Scotland or the Royal Bank who regarded them as substitutes for branches. Provincial banks reflect the pace of urban economic development and also the increasing specialisation and formalisation of the money market and within merchanting. The merchant partners of these banks often retained other economic interests—commonly in trade and occasionally in manufacturing.

The first provincial note-issuing bank was opened in Aberdeen in 1749 by Livingston, Mowat, Bremner and Dingwall with a modest capital of £600. This venture was short-lived; the Bank of Scotland and the Royal Bank eventually bought up its notes and presented them for payment in sufficient quantities in 1753 that voluntary liquidation inevitably followed.[78]

In Glasgow, banking was greatly influenced by merchants involved in foreign (especially the tobacco) trade. The Ship Bank, founded in 1750 and aided by the Bank of Scotland, consisted entirely of foreign traders, mostly tobacco lords, who hoped to mobilise the savings of the region in their efforts to extend an obviously lucrative activity. Cochrane, Murdoch and Company, the Glasgow Arms Bank, also founded in 1750, but with the help of the Royal Bank, was composed of merchants involved in foreign trade.[79] The six partners of the Thistle Bank (1761) had among their number four tobacco importers —James Ritchie, John Glassford, John McCall and John Campbell.[80]

The provision of credits—to the Ship Bank by the 'Auld Bank' and to the Arms Bank by the Royal Bank—was the honeymoon before the quarrel. The two chartered banks were intent on policing the credit structure and they decided in 1751–2 to adopt common cause against the Glasgow banks which they regarded as infringing their monopoly. In March 1752 they agreed to cultivate 'a Mutual friendship and harmony' and began by establishing a clearing house for their own notes.[81] Having forced the Aberdeen bank to succumb to their pressure, the two chartered banks withdrew their credits from the Glasgow banks and attempted to stop the Edinburgh private banks from acting as their agents. However, the Glasgow banks had greater resources than the Aberdeen bank and successfully resisted all attempts to close them.[82]

Despite their failure against the Glasgow banks, the chartered banks did set the limit of banking practice. Over the tripartite system of provincial banks, private banks and their own branches, the Bank of Scotland and the Royal Bank exerted considerable power. By developing branches they pre-empted control over great areas of the country and were able to mop up rural and urban savings. In the process it was made difficult for other joint-stock banks to extend their operations.[83] Provincial banks were likely to be limited in numbers, and the geographical availability of credit would be uneven.

The chartered banks also developed the acceptable practices or assimilated them from other sources. Most banks of any longevity followed their practice of investing their reserves in easily realisable government and Bank of England stock. It was the Royal Bank that developed in 1728 the cash credit, a device which became a fundamental part of Scottish banking.[84] Cash credits were really overdraft facilities: credit was allowed to an agreed amount but without a fixed repayment date; interest was calculated daily on the actual sum borrowed. This credit was only given after a careful scrutiny of the recipient's ability to repay, and, in addition to his own signature, those of two sureties were also required. The credit rating of these could be checked, and usually the possession of urban property or rural rent-rolls provided the best guarantee that cash credits would be granted. By 1800 all banks operated them.[85]

From the evidence of trusteeship operations, bankruptcy proceedings and, most conclusively, the registers of deeds, it is clear that long-term loans before 1820 were most commonly provided through the medium of bonds rather than by cash credits from banks. Used extensively in agriculture and trade at first, the bond was an important agency in the creation of regional, and then national capital markets, for after 1780 it was increasingly part of industrial financing. A legally enforceable deed, the bond was often heritable, i.e. secured by specified property of the borrower; this gave the creditor preferential status in the event of bankruptcy. Sometimes, the bond merely stipulated that the maximum legal interest of five per cent should be paid in accordance with the provisions of the usury laws, but often when interest rates were moving upwards, these were evaded by the insertion of a penalty clause allowing for the payment of a fixed sum at a stated date if the bond was not redeemed then— and both partners in the transaction were aware at the outset that the due date for repayment would not be met. Thus, the market price for capital might be higher than the legal maximum bank rate.

In the early eighteenth century private banks did more discounting of bills of exchange than the chartered banks, but gradually the extension of branch banking led to an increase in discounting, particularly at the Glasgow branch of the Royal Bank, where David Dale, cashier from 1783, had a unique ability to check the credit ratings of his customers. Discounting bills of exchange was the most important banking service as far as businessmen were concerned. In a sense, this developing practice was also a credit operation, since the businessman would have found it inconvenient to await the due term for every bill of exchange he received.

The great expansion of private banking was inevitably accompanied by financial crises. However, there were relatively few failures among Scottish banks—a notable example was the Ayr Bank in 1772[86]—and where banks ceased operating, they commonly paid off their liabilities. The tendency to issue notes for very small sums which turned into a mania in 1763 was restrained in consequence of the Act of 1765 which prohibited the issue of notes of a lower denomination than £1.[87]

By 1800 all the banks together had sixty-four branches; eighteen banks issued notes—three in Edinburgh, two in Glasgow, Aberdeen, Dundee, Stirling and Paisley, and one in Perth, Greenock, Falkirk, Ayr and Leith; there were eleven private banks providing discount and deposit facilities but not issuing notes.[88] Despite these facilities Scotland lacked adequate credit in deep recessions. As Gilbert Innes of Stow, a director of the Royal Bank, indicated to the Committee on the State of Commercial Credit (1793) long-dated bills of exchange were anathema to bankers when times were bad, and William McDowall M.P. gave instances of Glasgow, Paisley and Greenock banks refusing to discount any bills.[89]

The capital sizes of banks tended to increase substantially after 1780. About 1810 the average capital of Scottish joint-stock banks was £50,000 compared with Pressnell's estimate of £10,000 for English country banks. The chartered banks, in particular, were mammoth creations—the Bank of Scotland and the Royal Bank having about £1.5 million each, and the newly chartered Commercial Bank aiming for £3 million.[90]

Although there were fresh spurts of bank formation notably between 1800 and 1810, in 1825 and again in the 1830s, the general trend was towards consolidation. There could be set-backs, particularly to provincial note-issuing banks, as the crisis of 1812 makes clear. On 5 January 1811 there were twenty-six country banks with 1,068 partners licensed to issue notes; two years later there were nineteen such banks with 920 partners.[91] The number of banks of issue settled at about thirty between 1815 and 1840, and fell rapidly after Peel's Act of 1845 (which extended the principles of the Bank Charter Act of 1844 to Scotland).[92] By 1864 there were thirteen banks with 594 branches.[93] The trend was clearly to bigger banks with more branches: in 1865 there were only twelve banks but the number of branches had risen to 682.[94] Even the ill-fated Western Bank which failed in 1857 had over a hundred branches by that date.

Amalgamations were commonplace after 1830. The Union Bank of Scotland perhaps demonstrates this best. By 1843, the date of its formation, it consisted of eight other banks, most of which had joined the Glasgow Union Bank (established in 1830).[95] Other banks followed this example, particularly in the 1860s.[96] As assets and aggregate profits of banking increased, so the cry of monopoly was raised. *The Railway News and Joint Stock Journal,* January 1870, reported on the Scots banks in caustic terms. The eleven companies had nominal capitals aggregating £9 million, deposits were £63.5 million, and profits £1.141 million. Comfortable profits were the product of monopolistic practices, the leader-writer proclaimed, and Peel's 'highly obnoxious' Act had produced several perils. No new Scottish bank had been formed since 1845 except by amalgamation; the authorised circulation of £3,087,000 was too small for the good of the economy. The writer ended:

> Toleration for a gold currency is extending to Scotland, but it is the fact that the people there do not like gold. Nineteen persons out of twenty, strange as the statement may appear to our English readers, would infinitely prefer the most worn and well-thumbed note of local banks to the newest sovereign from the Mint....

But the 1845 Act had merely attempted to put into law the 'sound' principles of banking which Edinburgh bankers had enunciated and practised from the time of the battle between the 'Auld Bank' and the Royal Bank in 1728. Nonetheless, the willingness of the Scots to accept notes rather than coin had ensured that before 1845 money supply could be more elastic than the gold supply.

Savings banks rapidly became popular. After the Revd Dr Henry Duncan had pioneered the idea at Ruthwell (Dumfries-shire) in 1810, one was opened in Edinburgh in 1813, and by 1839 they were widespread, as Table 16 indicates.

Table 16 : Distribution, depositors and deposits of savings banks 1839

County	Savings banks	Depositors	Deposits (£)
Aberdeen	4	845	8,776
Banff	2	194	194
Edinburgh	1	13,501	149,751
Elgin	2	1,068	13,247
Fife	3	1,727	21,648
Forfar	1	2,233	20,973
Kincardine	1	677	10,774
Lanark	2	9,492	114,740
Perth	1	1,839	15,163
Renfrew	1	2,054	20,752
Roxburgh	1	517	13,061
Selkirk	1	176	1,682
Totals	20	34,323	393,460

Source: *BPP* (1841), XXIV, Accounts and Papers, 11

As might be expected, about eighty per cent of depositors had savings of less than £20 (Table 17), but it is certain that the self-help concept, popularised by Samuel Smiles of Dunbar, had a sound Scottish base. The experience of the Glasgow Savings Bank (founded in 1836) was fairly typical; the two main groups of depositors were domestic servants and skilled artisans.[97]

Unlike the English trustee savings banks, the Scottish banks were not protected by law until 1835, and their investment policies tended to favour opening accounts with the local joint-stock banks at first, since five per cent was the normal interest allowed on these. From the 1820s when bank interest rates began to fall, they began to invest in government stock and in municipal loans. In 1846 total

Table 17 : Denomination of savings and average deposits
1839

Denomination	No. of depositors	Average deposit (£)
Less than £20	27,312	5
£20–49	5,820	29
£50–99	1,073	65
£100–49	111	116
£150–99	7	157
Over £200	None	

deposits amounted to £1.384 million, an average of over £15 per depositor.[98] The general progress of savings banks in the period 1845–70 is indicated in Table 18.

Table 18 : Capital of Scottish savings
banks 1845–70

Year	Capital (£)
1845	1,278,929
1850	1,325,063
1855	2,033,925
1860	2,414,073
1865	2,859,277
1870	3,828,294

Source: Annual Abstract of Statistics

There was some slight involvement of artisans in building societies from the late eighteenth century, but far more significant were the friendly societies. Between 1793 and 1824, in the county of Aberdeen alone, the Justices approved the rules of 200. When the Highland Society was seeking information about them in 1820, seventy-nine provided data.[99] Weavers' friendly societies were very common in the burghs of eighteenth century Scotland, but ceased to be accurately designated, as the occupational group became more depressed after 1810. The temperance movement brought with it special friendly societies, several of English origin, notably the Rechabites.[100] Substantial savings by artisans were also made in the form of co-operative society share accounts, especially in the 1850s and 1860s.

Insurance premiums paid to fire and life insurance companies were another source of community savings. The Friendly Insurance Company, possibly the first in Scotland, was established in 1720, and fire insurance companies based in England did considerable business in Scotland, notably the Sun and Phoenix companies. The earliest Scottish life assurance company was the Scottish Widows fund, founded in 1815 and by 1870 the largest mutual office in Great Britain with a realised capital of £4.67 million. A proprietary office, the Edinburgh Life, was founded in 1823 with a nominal capital of £500,000, but only £15 was paid up on the £100 shares. In the same year the North British Insurance Company, founded as a fire office in 1809, extended its activities into life assurance. The Standard Assurance Company evolved similarly in 1825 from the Insurance Company of Scotland which had been established in 1821. Altogether, thirteen companies for life assurance developed in Scotland between 1815 and 1838, and by the 1850s assurance policies totalled about £33 million. By the 1870s there were sixteen Scottish insurance companies—and there had been amalgamations from the 1840s—many based in Edinburgh, controlling over twenty-five per cent of British insurance funds and about thirty per cent of the policies. In general, these followed earlier bank practice—investing in government stock and annuities for selected lives, and using Bank of England stock to keep funds relatively liquid. By the 1840s substantial loans were being made to landowners for drainage schemes and in the 1850s personal loans secured on land and rent rolls. Many companies also took up railway debentures and made loans against their own policies; this latter practice allowed small businesses to accumulate loan capital.[101]

Commerce, banking and the credit structure had become more complex and sophisticated by 1870. Relations between the Bank of England and the Scottish banks had grown as the eighteenth century proceeded, and correspondence with London agents, several of Scottish descent, was normal. Spare funds were increasingly channelled to London from Scotland in the nineteenth century and reclaimed via the Bank of England's Newcastle branch when needed.[102] Walter Bagehot, after describing how English country banks kept their reserves in London, goes on to assert that 'The habit of Scotch and Irish bankers is much the same. All their spare money is in London'.[103]

In the 1860s the Scottish banks began a policy of opening branches in the capital, and most of them by 1883 possessed both a London office and an independent note-issue, the latter privilege having been surrendered by English banks in the metropolis to the Bank of England.[104] Linked to the London money market as well as to economic activities in Scotland, the credit structure had become equipped to sponsor massive foreign investment after 1870, although earlier experiments with this aspect of the international economy had not always ended happily.

CHAPTER X

The Rise of Industry
1707–1871

DURING the eighteenth century several regions in Britain demonstrated social and economic trends which may be broadly associated with the rise of industry: the accumulation of capital in the form of industrial buildings and equipment, the concentration of labour and the growth of towns, and the exploitation of natural resources to produce greater quantities of industrial goods. Many explanations of this complex process have been forthcoming, usually framed in an English context, particularly as theories of economic growth have developed an international importance in recent years.[1]

In his pioneering study, *The Industrial Revolution in Scotland* (1932) Professor Henry Hamilton devised a two-phase theory:[2]

> There were two stages in the Industrial Revolution in Scotland
> —the first from about 1780 to 1830, when the cotton industry
> sprang up rapidly to the position of Scotland's premier industry,
> and the second commencing in the 'thirties and extending to
> about 1880, when the metal industries gained very quickly on
> the textiles and soon surpassed them.

However, his later book, *An Economic History of Scotland in the Eighteenth Century* (1963) concentrated more on the general growth of the economy rather than on sectoral advance.[3]

These two approaches to the problem of industrialisation mirror a wider debate. Was industrialisation the consequence of growth in a leading sector or did it consist of broader aggregate development upon which very rapid growth in one industry or a group of industries was superimposed? If there was a leading sector, would it not be reasonable to give pride of place to agriculture because of its contribution to national income and on account of its complex relationship with economic growth?[4]

Recently, scholars, notably Professors Campbell[5] and Smout,[6] have emphasised the many strands in the tale of economic development and the gradual nature of change. This has raised problems of chronology and, in particular, the question as to when it is reasonable to describe Scotland as an industrial nation. Hamilton felt confident about the decade of the 1780s because of the rise of the cotton industry; others express doubts as to whether self-sustained industrial development predates the 1830s, the beginning of Hamilton's second stage. In terms of national income, it seems likely that agriculture was not displaced as the major contributor before the 1820s, but this demarcation requires much greater examination than is possible here. Sufficient to say that the onset of industrialisation was a slow, evolutionary process with many antecedents which preclude single-cause explanations or emphasis on one sector!

The ingredients of the growth process are less controversial than the exact recipe. Scotland had abundant natural endowments but these were slow to be exploited. As John Chamberlayne indicated in his *Magnae Britanniae Notitia* (1710), 'Scotland is said to be richer underground than above'. All the minerals necessary for economic development—coal, limestone and ironstone—were available in substantial quantities but they were at first indifferently exploited since the cost of transport limited the size of the market. The coal industry, for instance, saw little change in the period before 1760; most units of production were either near the sea or relatively close to Edinburgh and Glasgow. The leading coal-masters were usually associated with salt-works or limekilns.[7] Demand was relatively stable, and this was reflected in pit-head prices.[8] A combination of agricultural, industrial and urban development after 1760 gradually increased the level of demand—the growth of the glass industry, the expansion of lime production and of the chemical industry, the founding of coke-based iron production are merely examples of this process. In consequence, the coal industry increased its output as prices rose, so that by 1800 probably two million tons were produced, compared with about half a million in 1707.[9] The range of customers for coal continued to increase after 1800, and the upward movement of coal prices was steep from 1790 until 1809–10.[10] Demand from domestic and industrial consumers was also augmented by the needs of the coastal and export trades. When the first official statistics were published for 1854, there were 368 collieries employing 32,971 miners and producing seven and a half million tons of coal.[11]

Perhaps, the case of the coal industry illustrates the broad spectrum of mutually reinforcing changes which was characteristic of industrialisation. Population growth, agricultural improvement, and general industrial development within the economy created supply pressures for the coal industry. In turn, its changes in technology, scale and organisation made demands upon the economy at large and stimulated further social and economic changes, notably the creation of a free labour force and of better methods of transport.

Assessment of the role of capital in industrialisation is fraught with problems, but it would be unwise to assume that a rapid acceleration in capital accumulation in the eighteenth century was primarily responsible for structural changes in the economy. Although it may appear reasonable to point to gains made in colonial trade or in agriculture and to suggest that these were ploughed substantially into industry, thus provoking rapid increases in output, it is by no means self-evident, from the experience of present-day developing economies, that capital investment must inevitably produce rapid economic change. It would be equally valid to argue that increased capital formation comes from industrialisation rather than precedes it. In other words, the rate of economic growth in eighteenth century Scotland may have determined the rate of capital accumulation rather than the converse.

Exact measurement of the sources of capital is impossible, and it is doubtful whether we shall ever know what the totality of the Industrial Revolution cost. There is little doubt that capital gains made in agriculture aided the development of mining, transport, building, banking and other ventures.[12] Foreign traders contributed significantly to the development of industry, but there was no special magic about the years of the American War of Independence and no dramatic transfer of funds from the tobacco trade to industry. Indeed, it seems most likely that the major contributions of foreign traders were made before 1770 and that in the shadow of the understandable exaggeration of the amount of capital required, smaller capital flows than those that went into their trade, government stocks, houses and land or banks have been underestimated for their qualitative significance.

Some of this investment was clearly complementary to existing trading interests. The Oswalds of Glasgow, wine importers, West India merchants and also tobacco importers, invested during the 1740s in the Glasgow bottleworks.[13] Sugar importers were naturally found as partners in sugar houses;[14] grain dealers and importers, such as the Falls of Dunbar, were also owners of malt barns.[15] The rope-work and sailcloth factory at Greenock was owned in 1748 by a partnership headed by Robert Donald, George Bogle and Andrew Buchanan, three Glasgow foreign merchants, and insured for £4,400.[16] The need for plantation tools and equipment, particularly saddlery, edge tools and nails, encouraged foreign traders to spread their industrial investment into tanneries, slitmills and forges. Fourteen of the sixteen shares in the Dalnotter Iron Company, established in 1769, were owned by tobacco merchants, including Robert Dunmore and the great William Cunninghame of Lainshaw;[17] the Smithfield Company, founded c. 1732 according to Gibson, was owned by tobacco importers and West India merchants.[18]

Demand for luxury goods at home and abroad may have stimulated foreign traders to diversify into the production of consumer goods. What is most likely, however, is that firms requiring abnormally large quantities of capital by the standards of the generation of businesses between 1740 and 1770 sought wealthy partners, and these were most commonly found among the foreign traders. Andrew Aiton (d. 1772), tobacco importer in 1743, was a partner in the Haarlem Linen and Dye Manufactories (founded in 1732) and in the Broomley Printfield Company.[19] Walter Brock, also a tobacco importer, was associated with the Glasgow tartan manufactory in the period 1740–6, and tartans were in considerable demand in America.[20] The Glasgow Inkle Factory Company, established in December 1741 to produce tape and small textile goods in Montrose Street, acquired its capital from foreign traders.[21]

The Scots governor of Virginia, Robert Dinwiddie, was a partner along with his brother, Lawrence and three other merchants in the Glasgow Delft factory (founded in 1748) which they insured in 1752 for £1,500.[22]

Some names were associated with a number of ventures. Lawrence Dinwiddie (1696–1764) was also a partner in the rope-work at Port Glasgow and the 'Old Tannery' in Glasgow.[23] Archibald Ingram (c. 1699–1770) was involved with John Glassford in most of the larger industrial concerns in Glasgow, including the Pollokshaws Printing Company, the first textile printers in Scotland, and the Inkle Factory.[24] John Glassford (d. 1784), his brother-in-law, the greatest of the tobacco merchants, invested also in Prestonpans Vitriol works, the Glasgow Cudbear works, the Anderston Brewery and the Banton ironstone mines near Falkirk, significantly all ventures requiring substantial capital.[25]

Glassford's wide-ranging investments indicate significant characteristics of the association of foreign traders with the larger firms before the American War. These merchants were essentially prestigious rentiers able to secure access to credit for their partners by their reputations; they did not involve themselves often with direct control or management. Yet their association with such businesses might be long-lasting. Industrial ventures, smaller in scale, of which there were great numbers by 1776, rarely had such direct relationships with foreign traders for their capital requirements for buildings and equipment were often modest, and trading capital could be obtained by a variety of other expedients. However, it should be noted that they derived indirect benefits from the expansion of foreign trade—cash credits from banks (with which foreign traders were linked), discounting facilities and raising loans on bonds were financial facilities gradually extended to industrialists; in the case of textile manufacturers, raw materials were often supplied by importers on credit.

After 1770 capital from foreign trade remained a significant source of funds for industrial investment. Recent research into Glasgow's colonial merchant community, between 1770 and 1815 for instance, revealed that about half—at least seventy-seven merchants—had interests in industrial co-partneries.[26] Sugar-refining capacity was extended considerably, for example, and there was a substantial investment in coal-mining, often a consequence of estate purchase and/or other industrial interests. For investment in coal-mining encouraged integration into coal-using ventures: the Dumbarton Glass Works Company began *c.* 1776 as a speculation by James Dunlop (1741–1816), probably the greatest coal-master among the colonial merchants. Dunlop was involved in many other industrial ventures for which he often raised funds on heritable bonds, and when his industrial and financial empire collapsed in 1793, he was replaced in the Dumbarton co-partnery by Alexander Houston of Clerkington, another foreign merchant-landowner.[27] The Muirkirk Iron Company in its early years was controlled by a majority of foreign traders, who, as already indicated, had a special interest in malleable iron-works and wanted a regular supply of bar-iron.[28] Wilsontown, the first coke-based iron-works in Lanarkshire, was founded with money made in foreign trade.[29] Boot and shoe production in Glasgow was still dominated in the 1780s and 1790s by merchants with extensive interests in overseas trade.[30]

The idea that the sector concerned with foreign trade could remain an enclave within an industrialising economy perhaps received greater credence among historians because of the tendency to concentrate on the period of the American War.[31] Certainly, it is a mistaken view of Scottish economic development. The well-known association of mercantile profits with investment in land had implications for estate exploitation—coal-mining, lime production, quarrying, the development of water-power sites for a host of agricultural-processing ventures—and for the rural diffusion of erstwhile urban industrial techniques. The putting-out or 'domestic' system of production was greatly extended, the more the barriers between merchanting and landowning decreased in social and economic significance. Equally, the trend to concentration of production, particularly of fine textiles, preceded extensive mechanisation and the pace-setters were often partners of firms engaged in foreign trade. James McDowall (d. 1808), a partner in the great West Indian firm of Alexander Houston and Company, was involved in a number of industrial ventures including the handloom weaving factory of John Renfrew in Anderston, which was established in 1789.[32] The Bell's Wynd area of Glasgow was associated before the American War with fine linen weaving and afterwards with the manufacture of muslins.[33] In many of these ventures, foreign traders, putting out merchants, and those engaged in the finishing trade such as bleaching and dyeing were often associated.

This association was also common in the early cotton-spinning factories, but as general merchanting was faced with competition from industrial firms exporting directly, the importance of having experience and capital derived from specialist foreign trade decreased. Robin Carrick, the Glasgow banker with many industrial interests, also invested in the West Indian and American trade and was a founding partner in Rothesay Cotton-spinning Company (1779).[34] When this firm was sold in 1785, its purchasers included Greenock merchants engaged in the West Indian trade.[35] David Dale was associated with a number of partners who had made money in foreign trade. With Claud Alexander of Ballochmyle, he founded Catrine mills (Ayrshire); with William Douglas he became involved in cotton-spinning at Newton Stewart (Kirkcudbright); at Spinning-dale (Sutherland) he had a variety of partners, mostly Glasgow foreign traders.[36] Robert Dunmore, tobacco merchant and West Indian trader, in association with the Buchanan brothers (like Dale yarn dealers) invested money in cotton mills at Balfron in 1790 on his Stirlingshire estate of Ballindalloch where he was also a partner in the Endrick printfield. With James Dunlop in 1788 he was also involved in the Duntocher Cotton Wool Company (Dunbarton-shire).[37] In Renfrewshire William McDowall (d. 1810) like his brother a partner in Alexander Houston and Company invested £20,000 in cotton mills, his share in the co-partnery of Houston, Burns and Company (1788).[38] Profits earned by one generation in the colonial trade were invested by the next in cotton mills. This was the experience of the Culcreuch Cotton Company (Stirlingshire) in which Peter Spiers and James Murdoch, both sons of colonial merchants, allied themselves with domestic system merchants in 1792.[39]

In the 1790s the great cotton empire of James Finlay and Company, begun as a putting-out linen business, was developed by Kirkman Finlay, industrialist and later foreign trader and banker, using money provided by West India merchants.[40] Robert Owen's partners between 1810 and 1814 were also principally concerned with the West Indies trade.[41] One of them, Alexander Campbell of Hallyards, provided the £42,000 for Robert Humphrey and Company, the largest cotton mill in Glasgow by 1817.[42] George Yuille who was a partner in the London firm of Leitch and Company importing tobacco and cotton from the United States was also the owner of the Duke Street cotton mill in Glasgow, valued in 1819 at £8,432 4s. 10d.[43] Despite the growing determination of industrial producers to handle their own exporting business, thereby maximising profits, there was, as these few instances indicate, a continuity of investment in industry by foreign traders which persevered into the nineteenth century.

This new age in which the industrial firms were also exporting through their own agencies is perhaps best exemplified by the case of Sharp and Mackenzie. They were shipowners (trading in American cotton, flour and rice, and West Indian cotton and hardwoods) by 1799 with stores in Nassau, Charleston and New York; in addition, they were putting out yarn to weavers in Scotland and exporting the textiles produced. John Mackenzie, one of the partners, owned the cotton mill, houses and land at Cromwellpark in Perthshire, which was valued at £4,000 and let to Wright, Mellis and Company, but his principal asset was the estate of Garnkirk valued at £47,000.[44] The relative capital sizes of these two assets perhaps mirror a possible source of confusion. Because it has been assumed that the new textiles firms required larger amounts of capital than was in fact the case, there has been recently a natural reluctance to attach much significance to investments in industry made by foreign traders.

However, since the West Indies was the principal source of cotton before 1800, nothing was more natural than that those importing cotton should invest in its processing just as they had continued to exercise a direct interest in sugar-refining. Two further examples must suffice. The Linwood Cotton Company near Paisley had among its partners James and Alexander Oswald, and Reynolds, Monteith and Company of Bridge of Weir, the Dennistouns—both these families were engaged in the West Indian trade.[45] Their investments in cotton did not mean that they were leaving foreign trade, merely that they were establishing complementary interests to it, a continuous process as we have already seen.

What was particularly new after 1770 was the increasing profitability of textile production which allowed growth through re-investment of profits and through the transfer of capital within the industrial sector. Most obvious in this latter respect was the continuity between fine linen production in the West of Scotland and the growth of the cotton industry. The most normal recruits to factory production of yarn and cloth came via the 'domestic system'.[46] Beginning as weaver's apprentices often, as David Dale did, these embryonic entrepreneurs proceeded from journeymen to master-weaver and then either into the network of weaver's agents or directly into putting out work to spinners and then to weavers. Concentration of labour often followed in the loom shop or linen factory as a preliminary to full-blown factory production with the new English textile inventions. Productivity gains were made, even without the more elaborate capital equipment, because stricter supervision and control of labour was possible than the putting-out system allowed, and often better stock controls reduced waste of expensive raw materials or incidence of embezzlement of fine yarns or cloth. Common features of this preliminary phase were the creation of purpose-built accommodation and the integration of both spinning and weaving in the same factory. Even then, most of these 'manufactories' employed relatively few people compared with the labour forces partially controlled by some domestic system merchants who were also often importing fine yarns by the 1780s.

Putting-out had great flexibility: merchants did not require to have much fixed capital beyond their warehouse and its equipment; this was because their workers provided spinning wheels and looms in their own homes or workshops. Trading capital for wages (usually paid according to a list of piece-rates), raw materials and stocks were their principal needs. Their business problems, in times of depression, were relatively small, provided they had liquid assets, since they could sit tight in their counting houses and pass on the effects of bad trade to their workers by lowering piece-rates or by refusing to contract for more work. Because of the steady expansion of the labour force, consequent upon rural population growth and gains in agricultural productivity, putting-out continued to spread to fresh areas until the 1830s, in the case of cotton, and even later, in the linen, hosiery and woollen trades.

Pressures to change to factory production were many but depended principally upon the expansion of demand. Spinners and weavers in boom circumstances tried to raise piece-rates and found that competition between would-be employers gave them a powerful bargaining position. Attempts to increase production were necessary for the merchant if he wished to avail himself of market opportunities but unnecessary to outworkers on better piece-rates for they earned more from the same output. Employing additional workers presented problems and extra costs, since they would probably be not so efficient as the existing labour force—otherwise, why were they not fully employed already? Experienced and skilled labour was often well organised in weavers' societies and, consequently, better equipped to raise wages. Thus, the classic features of rising marginal costs tended to occur in booms.[47]

As we have already noted, other circumstances sometimes favoured concentration of production. Examples could be found from earlier times, such as the relatively unsuccessful woollen manufactory at Newmills, East Lothian, founded in 1681 with a nominal capital of £5,000.[48] Information about less grandiose ventures from a range of textile industries is available from fire insurance policies. James Cockburn, an Edinburgh hosier, insured his assets for £300 in November 1739. His dwelling-house, part stone, part timber and slated, was assessed at £50, and his household goods at £10. In the first storey he had a shop (£20) from which he sold his stock of worsted thread and cotton stockings (£50); the garrets were insured for £30 and in them were stocking frames, probably a dozen, valued at £120, together with a throwing mill and other utensils, assessed at £10.[49] The practice of combining manufacturing, living and selling premises in one building was very common until 1800.[50]

Pollok and Keir of Paisley took two policies in March 1745, one for 'their tenements called Old Factory, stone and slated' and the other for an extension to it. The old factory valued at £200 contained looms and utensils insured for £120, with webs in the looms (i.e. materials in the process of manufacture) assessed at £180. Linen yarn and cloth 'in the Wareroom of the said House' apparently represented the greatest value—£500. The stone and slated house adjoining the old factory was valued at £50, looms and utensils at £50 and webs in the looms at £100.[51]

Five Kilmarnock merchants, William Gilchrist, Alexander

Cunyngham, William Bankhead, James Wilson and Robert Boyd, insured their factory, looms, cloth and yarn for £1,000 in 1747, a large thatched storehouse nearby for £200 and the stock of wool and woollens in this for a further £200.[52] In Montrose, the same year, Robert Ouchterlony and Company insured their 'Sail Duck Manufactory' for £1,000.[53]

Thomas Bell and James Murray, linen manufacturers in Leith, rented premises belonging to a merchant, William Mitchell. In 1748 linen cloth, webs and yarn in this factory were insured for £750, dressed lint for £20, and utensils for £130. They also hired warehouse space from Joan and Jannet Halliday in which they stored flax valued at £350 and had it prepared for spinning with utensils assessed at £50. In two weaving shops adjoining this warehouse they had handlooms and webs assessed at £100 and £200 respectively.[54] In 1754 Thomas Lindsay of Kirkwall, Orkney, insured flax, linen, wool and woollen cloth in a house 'usually known as the Bishop's Palace' for £700 and more raw materials and cloth together with his household possessions in another house for a further £300.[55] Another fifteen textile manufactories were insured with the London-based Sun Fire Insurance Company during the 1750s.[56] Thus, it is clearly mistaken to associate factory production with the development of the cotton-spinning industry after 1779.

Concentration of production was also apparent in the metal trades. Imported Swedish and Russian bar-iron was turned into a range of products under factory-type conditions. In addition to the slitmills and forges owned by the Smithfield (1732) and Dalnotter (1769) companies, there were a number of other similar ventures. The Smith and Wright Work Company of Leith established a slitmill at Cramond in 1752 which was sold in 1759 for £1,010 to Dr John Roebuck of the recently founded Carron Company.[57] Cramond's output included iron hoops, which sold in 1769 at £22 per ton, handle-iron for fitting to cast-iron pots and pans made at Carron and the principal product, nail rods, which were put out to cottage-workers who produced many varieties of nails.[58] In Calton, Glasgow nail-makers using traditional equipment were concentrated in a nail-making factory (1764) which was partly financed by John Anderson, a tobacco importer.[59] Glasgow ironmongers financed a partnership in 1766 and established a file-making factory at Strathbungo. Metal-ware factories existed also at Aberdour, Inverkeithing, Kilsyth and Rutherglen.[60]

Some businesses were naturally more capital-intensive than others. Bleachfields, distilleries, breweries, glass-works, blast furnaces, soap-works and paper-mills, for instance, had by 1770 attracted substantial investment, although the norm for the particular industry might still be relatively small. In consequence, it would be reasonable to conclude that industrialisation represented a joint victory for a multiplicity of unsung small firms and a minority of larger better-known enterprises. This conclusion is reinforced by evidence from fire insurance policies in the decade 1790–1800. Admittedly, there is some risk of undervaluation of assets, but even allowing generously for this, it seems reasonable to assume that the quantity of capital invested was less significant in producing increases in output than might be supposed. A sample of 1,286 firms, which excluded those taking insurance policies for assets of less than £200, insured buildings and other fixed capital, stock, household goods and sometimes unassociated property for £4,076,594 in these years, an average of £3,170 per firm. A more detailed selection, differentiating between Scotland and the city of Glasgow in some cases, is given in Table 19.

These data, admittedly fragmentary, confirm many established notions that with few exceptions the business class in Glasgow was operating with larger capital than other businessmen. The exceptions may require more explanation than is currently possible. Edinburgh's printers dominated that industry and the sample. The building industry of Glasgow may have provided more openings for small-scale operations than the country at large, but this industry was notoriously dominated by small businesses until well into the nineteenth century. The control of Glasgow's merchant class over its regional textile industries was only possible because of its accumulation of capital. This is decidedly verified by the evidence of this sample.

A similar examination of the cotton-spinning industry c. 1795 demonstrates that firms in this sector, for which we have information, could be readily matched from other sectors of the economy. The problem of undervaluation may, however, be more serious for assessing cotton firms than for the generality of businesses.[61]

Table 19 : Insurance valuations for Scottish businesses 1790–1800

Category of business	Location	No. in sample	Total insurance (£)	Average (£)
Distillers	Scotland	70	517,100	7,387
Millers	Scotland	63	86,726	1,377
Foreign traders	Scotland	57	218,295	3,829
Foreign traders	Glasgow	7	79,100	11,300
Domestic system merchants	Scotland	51	94,800	1,859
	Glasgow	11	136,600	12,418
Weaving partnerships	Scotland	6	5,200	867
	Glasgow	49	85,592	1,747
Family weavers	Scotland	15	7,050	470
	Glasgow	86	1,572,766	18,288
Chemical manufacturers	Scotland	55	88,500	1,609
	Glasgow	9	13,800	1,533
Woollen manufacturers	Scotland	30	58,199	1,940
Rope-makers	Scotland	7	14,050	2,007
Wrights and builders	Scotland	16	13,450	841
	Glasgow	31	21,658	699
Shipbuilders	Scotland	9	16,550	1,839
Paper-makers	Scotland	18	54,200	3,011
Printers	Scotland	8	32,700	4,088
	Glasgow	3	3,050	1,017
Tanners	Scotland	18	31,500	1,750
Cabinet-makers	Scotland	10	34,250	3,425

Source: Sun Fire Insurance Company Policy Registers 1790–1800

Twenty-five small firms insured assets totalling £26,400, and the remaining thirty-eight accounted for £302,530. The average insurance valuation for this sector was £5,220 i.e. about sixty per cent greater than the average for the larger sample of other Scottish businesses between 1790 and 1800. However, this average is markedly less than for Glasgow weaving family firms, for the city's domestic system merchants and for distillers. Taken against the valuation of assets of the untypically large 'manufactories' of the period 1740–60, however there is a marked difference in the scale of the 1790s, although one must bear in mind the possible effects of changes in the value of money.

Table 20 : Sizes of cotton-spinning firms
according to insurance valua-
tions c. 1795

Insurance valuation	Number of firms
Up to £1,000	17
£1,001 to £2,000	8
£3,000	4
£4,000	6
£5,000	5
£6,000	4
£7,000	4
£8,000	5
£9,000	4
£10,000	4
Over £24,000	2

Technical innovations and attempts at better organisation found many supporters in Scotland varying from 'improvers', who visualised planned villages with a balance between agriculture and industry, to merchants and manufacturers who applied better methods to production. Coal was increasingly used in metallurgy in place of charcoal; better and more extensive use was made of water-power, wind-power and horse-power; agricultural changes and the development of factory production raised productivity and hastened the division of labour. Technical and organisational changes began to occur on a broad front from the 1780s, but the prehistory of this process was much more piecemeal.

New methods were imported from abroad and often skilled workers. The first lint mill for breaking and scutching flax was constructed in 1729 by James Spaulding, after a fact-finding tour in Holland; by 1770 there were 253 in existence, mainly concentrated in the belt of counties between Ayrshire and Perthshire.[62] Linen bleaching was subject to many improvements ranging from the use of sulphuric acid from the 1750s—again based on Dutch practice— to the introduction of the Irish rubbing board which was rapidly modified by Scots millwrights and produced in such quantities that the new, better Scots model was reintroduced to Ireland.[63] Holland was also the source from which better looms and weavers were introduced in 1733 by the Board of Trustees; the thread twisting mill (1722), the inkle loom for tape manufacture (1732) and the Dutch press for folding cloth (1730) similarly indicate the significance of Dutch technology for the Scots textile industries.[64] French Huguenot paper-makers had been encouraged to come to Scotland before the Union, but the Board of Trustees made a singularly systematic attempt to improve fine weaving by introducing a small colony of ten cambric weavers with their families to Edinburgh in 1729.[65]

As in the case of agricultural improvement, England was also a main, if occasionally indirect, source of new processes, machinery and skills. Newcastle and Whitehaven were the founts from which the best mining methods flowed into Scotland, and a few Newcomen engines were in operation by 1770 draining deep mines in Clackmannanshire, the Lothians and Ayrshire.[66] The blast furnace and the coke process of smelting were both introduced from England in the course of the eighteenth century, the former from the Furness district and the latter from the Midlands.[67] Lee's stocking frame only penetrated slowly; it was in Edinburgh *c.* 1740 and Nottingham men introduced it to Glasgow *c.* 1750. However, it was not in use in the Borders before the early 1770s.[68] This was the fitful prelude to the widespread adoption of English textile technology in the period after 1778. The chemical industry also made significant gains from England. Sulphuric acid manufacture was pioneered in 1749 at Prestonpans by Dr John Roebuck (1718–94) and Samuel Garbett (1717–1805) after an initial venture in Birmingham.[69] Production of copperas, essential for the development of dyeing, was introduced to Hurlet by a Liverpool firm in 1753.[70] The coal-fired reverberatory furnace, an essential part of glass, pottery, chemical and brewing technology—but with several other applications—was gradually introduced into relevant Scottish industries after 1750.[71] Early transport improvements were often guided by English practice, itself a reflection of the best international standards. Wagonways began their career in Scotland with the York Buildings Company's scheme to connect the collieries at Tranent with the harbour at Cockenzie in 1722 and there is some evidence to suggest that Tynesiders, familiar with horse wagonways as part of colliery complexes introduced them to Scotland.[72] The desire for river improvements, such as those on the

Clyde from the 1750s, at first brought English engineers northwards
—to Glasgow came John Smeaton in 1755 and John Golborne of
Chester in 1768.[73] Smeaton was also associated in 1763–4 with an
influential survey of a route for the Forth and Clyde canal.[74]

Technical skill and innovations were readily assimilated into the
Scottish environment, and it is in explaining the readiness of society
to welcome change that most uncertainty prevails.[75] Certainly, it is
never sufficient to explain rapid economic growth in terms of
inventions being readily available. True, they alter the quality of
fixed capital and make increases in the scale of output possible.
The application of inventions in many different parts of the economy
in the late eighteenth century represented the recognition by
businessmen that new forms of production were preferable to the
old. This willingness to discard the economic continuity of past
production may be partly explained in economic terms: inventions
saved capital, labour or raw material—or all three. But without a
versatile labour force prepared to accept them and to obey more
stringent forms of labour discipline, the economic wisdom of
applying inventions would have been doubtful. Skills had to be
learned quickly, and in turn this depended upon the general
educational level of society. It is customary still to refer to the
inexorable deterministic logic of the spate of inventions, and to
explain them as products of economic necessity. How meaningful
this really is must be questioned, for why was there such a time-lag
between Darby's coke process and the foundation of Carron or
Edmund Cartwright's invention of the power loom and its application in Scotland—as merely two instances—if economic pressures
really called inventions into being?

To demonstrate that necessity as the mother of invention relied
upon scientific curiosity and application, which in turn might depend
on the characters and family training of individuals, is simply to
state a truism about societies prepared to absorb and apply novelties.
Social structure and cultural patterns can inhibit change; in British
society they did not: 'The prevailing talent of the English and Scotch
people is to apply new ideas to use, and to bring such applications
to perfection...'.[76] Just as the Scottish Enlightenment when vulgar-
ised made its way into the market-place in the form of the
idolatrous worship of the invisible hand of market forces, so the

emphasis of the powerful social classes on science and 'mechanism', on spinning schools and other practical forms of education was likely to manifest itself in wide-ranging intellectual curiosity and better workmanship. The quality of the work of Scots masons and craftsmen is never doubted when country houses, churches and grandfather clocks are discussed; to imagine that factory buildings, water-wheel and lade construction and machine-making were the products of practical but relatively unintelligent men is to divorce two sectors of human activity for which often the same people were responsible. It is no accident that insurance assessors described the new cotton machinery in their policies as 'clockmakers work'.

As an examination of the statistics in Appendix V will clarify, output per capita rose substantially for those industries for which we have good information. But this process was not uniform. It was first apparent in the linen and paper industries particularly from the 1750s, in the production of spirits from the 1820s (although here the Act of 1823, by conceding more liberal regulations and lower duties may have made evasion less worthwhile), in pig-iron output from the 1830s, in railway building and house construction from the 1850s. Coal production, as we have seen, rose less dramatically than pig-iron output because Neilson's hot-blast process produced very significant savings in its use, but even here the annual average increase in output was about seven per cent between 1800 and 1854.

For the cotton industry we have no good output statistics. However, there are many indications of a substantial increase in production: cotton imports, for instance rose from a mere 137,160 lb. on the eve of the American War to 1,757,504 lb. in 1790; by 1812 11,114,640 lb. were imported and about forty million lb. by 1840.[77] In addition, English textile technology, notably Arkwright's water-frame, Hargreaves' jenny and Crompton's mule, were adopted in rapidly increasing numbers of factories in the 1780s and 1790s. The power loom was the subject of much experimentation in Scotland after its invention by Cartwright in 1785 but there is little indication that it was applied on any scale before 1810.[78] Significantly, the linen industry continued to expand its production at an annual average rate of about six per cent between 1790 and 1822, even though the growth of the cotton industry was largely at the expense of fine linen production in the West.

A number of circumstances made the increased productivity of the economy possible. Improved technology was available, but although some industries were more aided by it than others, the general story was still of hard physical effort. Gradual changes in the structure of the economy allowed the transfer of labour from less to more productive sectors. Most notable in this regard, of course was the progress of agricultural improvement. Productivity gains were made through the increasing application of factory organisation which allowed the specialisation of labour, the control of production by management, and the transport of materials and goods to be better co-ordinated. Regional specialisation and the localisation of industry encouraged the improvement of distribution and marketing, the evolution of a disciplined labour force and the emergence of specialist credit facilities. Productive employment was made available for a higher proportion of the working population: many more opportunities were open, for instance, to female and child labour. Underemployed labour resources, notably in Ireland and the Highlands were very important to the development of industries such as cotton, sugar-refining, chemicals, construction, mining and metals.

Self-sustained growth required not only the mobility of labour and the diffusion of technical progress but also a relatively elastic supply of capital and business enterprise. Underpinning these were growing markets which made expansion in output seem a desirable preliminary to increased volumes of profit. If economic change was accompanied by gains, it was also the occasion for losses, and the accounting exercise, balancing, for instance, rises in output and living standards against the exploitation of child labour or the dangers implicit in urban living, is exceedingly difficult. Three groups of industries, because of their extensive linkages with other sectors of the economy, perhaps mirror this dilemma best—textiles, metals and transport.

LINEN

Textiles were headed by linen in 1707, an industry which by 1780 had reached a high level of technical organisation. More than any other industry, linen demonstrates that the domestic system was not static but capable both of achieving substantial increases in output and of stimulating piecemeal technical changes.[79] Its products were of bewildering variety, varying from cheap cloth for slaves to more expensive imitations of East India wares designed to appeal to the fashion-conscious. Despite continental competition, which was gradually hampered by government mercantilist policies that squeezed imports, markets for linen cloth within the British Empire were widening. In 1760 total consumption in Great Britain and the colonies was estimated at eighty million yards. Of this the Irish produced over twelve million yards, the Scots slightly less, the English nearly twenty-six millions, and imports, principally from Holland, France and Germany, accounted for about thirty million yards.[80] In addition, the lace and hosiery industries of the Midland counties, notably Nottingham and Leicester, developed close connections with yarn-producing areas in Scotland.

Influential groups favoured the expansion of the linen industry, although there were those like David Loch who in the 1770s advocated more support for the woollen industry. Landowners stimulated the spread of industry, partly because seasonal demands for agricultural labour could thereby be more readily met without raising local wage levels and partly because rent-rolls were likely to rise. Together with the Convention of Royal Burghs, the Society of Improvers in the Knowledge of Agriculture (founded 1723) pressed for the government to encourage industry, and the outcome was the establishment of the Board of Trustees for Manufactures in 1727 with an annual income of £6,000, of which £2,650 was allocated for the improvement of the linen industry.[81] The Board tried to improve the manufacture of linen by introducing foreign workers and techniques, by paying premiums and prizes for mechanical and chemical improvements and by subsidising flax-growing and the establishment of bleachfields. Much emphasis was placed on quality control, and fifty stampmasters were appointed to ensure that linen sold met specified standards.[82] These men produced the figures which appear in Appendix V, but it should be noted that much linen was also made for local consumption and not for sale. Thus, we lack true figures for output.

Members of the Board, notably Lord Milton, also took an interest in marketing and from this developed the British Linen Company which was originally intended to provide short-term finance to merchant-manufacturers by paying for linen as it was delivered.[83] Since we still lack a definitive assessment of the rôle of the Board of Trustees, it is difficult to judge their performance, although there can be no doubt that they symbolised a patriotic concern for economic development.

Parliamentary regard for the linen industry was at first ambivalent. The home market for linens was so extensive that bounty and tariff policy, for instance, was difficult to formulate. Was it reasonable to encourage exports by bounties when home demand was so certain? Should home products be free from foreign competition, when there was some doubt about their ability to satisfy demand? Would it not merely encourage smuggling? These questions were gradually answered in the 1740s and 1750s by positive protection for the fine linen trade which was most under foreign pressure and by bounties on all cloth exports.[84] In these two decades, linen output probably increased at an average annual rate of ten per cent.

Much imitation of fine continental and East India cloths was a feature of this period. Dairsie (Fife) became known as Osnaburgh as a flattering but utilitarian tribute to the quality of German linens; the Board of Trustees, not to be outdone, decided to rename Osnaburgs Edinburgs and cambrics Carolines.[85] The geographical range of putting-out operations by merchants widened, and an intricate network of middlemen and yarn dealers spread from the burghs and seaports through growing hinterlands.[86] The Commissioners established to administer the estates forfeited after the Jacobite risings in 1715 and 1745 aided the spread of the domestic system into the Highlands, but again it is difficult, in the present state of knowledge, to test the efficacy of their policies.[87]

After 1748—and an Act prohibiting the import of French lawns and cambrics—there is evidence that home demand principally for handkerchiefs and shirts was a major stimulus to an expansion of output. This encouraged an existing trend to regional specialisation within the industry, for the West of Scotland and Edinburgh concentrated increasingly on the fine end of the trade, leaving Angus and Fife as the principal counties for the production of coarse linens. The east-coast counties had the advantage of being best served by the Baltic trade from which seventy-five per cent of the flax came by 1770; in reverse, the western counties around Glasgow concentrated on fine mixed fabrics (with linen warp and cotton weft) which had a higher value-to-volume ratio and could, therefore, withstand inland transport costs.

In the period from 1763 to the outbreak of the American War, the linen industry appeared to be approaching a plateau in output. One problem was rising flax prices, a second was a tendency for marginal labour costs to increase, and a third was provoked by the reluctance of the American colonists to buy British goods in general. Added to these difficulties was the squeeze on domestic purchasing power occasioned by poor harvests and high food prices.

The coarse linen trade probably felt these difficulties most, judging by the evidence of destitution in eastern manufacturing districts reported to the Commons committee appointed to enquire into the depressed state of the linen trade.[88] Attempts were made at integration such as that of Sandeman of Luncarty who dominated a business empire stretching north from Perth into the Highlands, putting out yarn and taking in cloth for finishing.[89] There were also early efforts to concentrate production in manufactories, but the main incentives to do this occurred most forcibly in the fine manufacturing districts of the West. There embezzlement of raw materials and finished goods, because of their relative value, was a significant factor favouring concentration. In the urban centres of Paisley and Glasgow the road to the factory had already been well trod, and labour in rural areas had frequently reached a fairly high price, even though it did not display the militancy of the Paisley weavers who combined in 1773 to resist reductions in piece-rates offered by merchants and prevented work from being taken out of the burgh.[90] Glasgow merchant-manufacturers were subjected to a similar demonstration in 1787 when webs were cut from looms and masters attacked.[91] It seems possible, therefore, that attempts to concentrate and to control linen production would have increased, even if cotton-spinning had not developed.

The factory system did not pass the linen industry by. In 1787 John Kendrew, an optician, and Thomas Porthouse, a clockmaker, both of Darlington, patented a machine for spinning flax and licensed Scottish manufacturers to use their invention.[92] They were rewarded by a concerted but unsuccessful attempt on the part of Fife and

Angus manufacturers to break their patent.[93] At Brigton (Angus) William Douglas, using capital from Dundee interests, in 1787 converted a cornmill and secured a licence from Kendrew and Porthouse at a cost of about £1,000 and began yarn-spinning. In 1789 James Ivory, a mathematics teacher at Dundee Academy, became managing partner, and a new mill was built. This company was under-capitalised and became bankrupt in the depression of 1802–3; Douglas paid its debts and bought the mills but in 1808 was still apparently seeking capital and offering shares at £800 each.[94] Sim and Thom in 1787 began the factory spinning of linen thread at Inverbervie (Kincardineshire).[95] These firms represented the beginning of mechanical production of linen. Cornmills were converted, and new buildings erected in many parts of eastern Scotland from Aberdeen to Dunbar, often at first at inland sites to exploit water-power but gradually after the application of steam-power tending to concentrate on coastal towns.[96]

Flax-spinning machinery remained primitive, however. Because flax contains a gum, its fibres tend to stick together. Hand spinners moistened the flax as they worked or simply separated the glued fibres, but machines tended to block or to break fibres. This problem was not solved until James Kay of Pennybridge, Lancashire, invented wet-spinning in 1825.[97] However, after 1783 demand for coarse linens, notably for sailcloth, tentings and horse blankets during the French wars, continued to increase, except for the period between 1803–7 when flax supplies and prices were badly affected by the mercantilist policies of the Russian government and interruptions to the Baltic trade consequent on war.

Ineffectual experiments with power looms at first using water-power, notably by Alexander Robb, a schoolmaster at Tongland (Kirkcudbright), were numerous, and in 1810 coarse cloth for government contracts was being made by steam-driven power looms at Brechin by Wilson and Company.[98] Nontheless, handlooms dominated linen weaving, especially before the 1820s, and it was over fifty years after Cartwright's invention of the power loom that it was used on any scale in Dundee, the city that dominated both the linen and jute industries.[99] Where fine linen remained an important manufacture, as, for instance, at Dunfermline, where the production of table linen was a speciality, the power loom took even longer to prevail, and handloom weaving survived well into the 1860s.[100]

There are several indications of the industry's expansion after 1820. Flax and hemp imports (discounting negligible quantities of dressed flax and hemp) were running at about 300,000 cwt. in the years just before 1820; by 1840 Dundee imported about 500,000 cwt. Jute introduced to the city in the late 1830s became an important addition to the industry in the 1840s and 1850s; by 1863 total imports of flax, hemp and jute were running at about 1,500,000 cwt. of which jute accounted for just less than two-thirds.[101] The Crimean War and the American Civil War brought massive booms and profits to the industry and much speculative activity.[102]

The introduction of jute was partly conditioned by costs and partly by technical considerations. Flax was a better raw material producing a product with a higher selling price, but it could often be both expensive and poor. Mechanical improvements designed to cope with poor flax made the introduction of jute, a lower quality but much cheaper material, relatively easy.[103]

As Dundee grew in significance, other towns declined as linen producers. Before 1800 only five mills had been built in the burgh; by 1851 there were forty, mostly erected since 1820, and in 1864 there were sixty-one.[104] The total number of flax-spinning mills in 1836 was 170 with 13,409 employees, concentrated in Angus where there were eighty-two and in Fife which had forty-seven. By 1870 the industry had seventy-six spinning mills, eighty-eight weaving factories and twenty-four integrated complexes combining spinning and weaving, a total of 191 flax factories. Additionally, there were forty-eight integrated jute factories, of which twenty-six were in Angus. In linen three counties, Angus (eighty-three factories), Fife (sixty-six) and Perth (twenty-one) predominated. The labour force in linen numbered 49,917 and that in jute 14,911. The average unit in flax-spinning in 1836 employed seventy-nine workers; by 1871 the average linen factory employed 261 people—and jute factories 312 each.[105] Several firms were of considerable size by 1871; Baxters of Dundee, for instance, employed one-tenth of all those working in jute flax and linen.[106]

COTTON

Just as the linen industry encountered rising flax prices, the costs of raw cotton began to fall. This trend was most marked in the early years of the American War of Independence when the first water-powered spinning factories were planned. By November 1778 cotton, which had sold at 1s. 6d. per lb. two years before, was available at 1s. 3d., and during this period had, from time to time, been 'perfectly unsaleable'.[107] World production of cotton, especially in the West Indies, was increasing faster than demand. The transition from linen to cotton in the 1780s, therefore, made good economic sense in terms of changes in raw material prices, but the process would have met more difficulty had not Scotland already accumulated resources of capital, entrepreneurship, technical skill and labour. In England there was available a new technology, based upon the inventions of Kay, Hargreaves, Arkwright and Crompton, and this was readily assimilated.

A legacy of other facilities was bequeathed to the cotton industry in the West by its predecessor: the commercial network of the domestic system controlled by Glasgow's merchants, the more important of whom had also been yarn importers (commonly called 'English' merchants), able, because of their experience, to assess markets for warps and wefts; the bleachfields and dyeworks; the credit facilities. Contacts between Glasgow and Manchester and the English Midlands, the main locations of the new industry, were longstanding consequences of the linen trade.

Trade to the West Indies, financed and controlled, as we have seen, by the great Glasgow firms, made possible the extensive importation of the basic raw material. With the introduction of long-staple sea-island cotton to the American mainland and the expansion of production of short-staple cotton inland, the cost of raw materials continued to fall, despite temporary interruptions to this trend. Eli Whitney's invention of the cotton gin (1793) accelerated this development for, even if operated by hand, it enabled one man to clean as much cotton as ten had done before. American planters commonly applied horse-power to Whitney's gin and this allowed one man to do the work of fifty. Raw material supplies, therefore, were assured.

Yet the growth of the cotton industry did place pressures on Scotland's resources. Water-power sites in the burghs, generally controlled by the millers and tanners already, were often inadequate for cotton-spinning. Hargreaves' jenny was a hand machine, of course, and small 'jenny houses' were erected in Glasgow and Paisley, but, in general, the big Arkwright-type mills were built in the countryside, where often inadequate rivers could produce good falls of water through efficient lade construction. Commonly, existing mill-steads were converted to cotton-spinning, as, for example, at Woodside in Glasgow. Water-rights, therefore, were often the source of initial problems, and many were the local disputes about them. However, the retention of hand machinery was common even in the largest cotton firms until the 1830s for it was often difficult to maintain adequate power, especially in the summer when rivers were low or in severe winters when lades froze.

Recruiting skilled labour to supervise mill building, lade construction and machine-making was often difficult and best achieved by regular contract. When Arkwright came north in 1783, ostensibly to use Scotland as a razor to the throat of Lancashire, he introduced his own millwright, Lowe of Nottingham, to Dale and Alexander, and they contracted for him to build the first four water-wheels at their Catrine mills.[108] From Arkwright's Cromford mills came not only the basic design for mills like Catrine and New Lanark but also the technical skills and plans for machinery which were essential to the new cotton partnerships of Scotland. Peter Brotherston of Penicuik mill, who claimed to have invented a new twist mill in 1780, had, in fact, modified an Arkwright water-frame; it seems, however, that he had special mechanical abilities for after he went to Paisley in January 1779 to inspect machinery 'from Indostan', the Board of Trustees paid him five guineas for his expenses.[109] James Kenyon, a Sheffield merchant and mechanic, came to Scotland to evade Arkwright's patent for he established the mills at Rothesay in 1779 to use the water-frame.[110] Robert Burns (d. 1809) introduced Arkwright's invention into Renfrewshire c. 1783 and was involved in at least two partnerships to which he contributed no capital but considerable technical skill.[111]

Technical men with experience of English mill practice often became managers of these early mills. Apart from Brotherston,

Kenyon and Burns, at least ten other individuals between 1779 and 1795 were associated either directly or indirectly with English mill practice. Perhaps the greatest of them was Archibald Buchanan, formerly an apprentice at Cromford and the technical brains behind the success of James Finlay and Company. In turn, he trained others, notably his talented nephew, James Smith of Deanston.[112]

Recruiting, training and retaining ordinary labour for rural mills were more difficult problems than might be supposed. Entrepreneurs turned to pauper apprentices or to Highland and Irish labour; Lowland Scots were normally reluctant to enter mills, nor did they favour putting their children into them if other more respectable employment could be found. Thus, a number of millowners built apprentice houses and provided tied houses or 'barracks'. Gradually, factory villages developed their own social hierarchies with spinning-masters in better housing than spinners; the factory-master became also the laird. Truckshops were a common feature of these villages, as were schools. Yet, despite elaborate social provision, labour turnover often reached staggering proportions. At Newton Stewart mill, in the full year September 1800 to August 1801, forty-eight per cent of the workers completed the year, nearly thirty-five per cent began the year but did not end it, and a further ten per cent neither began the year nor finished it.[113]

Because investment was unplanned, it tended to occur in waves, which were halted by crises of confidence during which credit was difficult to obtain. The industry was, at first, widely dispersed, as Table 21 indicates.

Paisley and Renfrewshire were clearly more important than Glasgow and Lanarkshire during this water-power phase of the industry's development. Because cotton spinning was highly profitable and intensely speculative, capital requirements, as we have seen, were slight in the early years and sometimes most unlikely sites were selected. At Spinningdale (Sutherland) a spinning mill was built in the period 1792–4 with the idea of offsetting its disadvantages by training local weavers to produce calicoes, shawl cloths and shirtings from the yarn at well below Glasgow prices.[114]

Gradually, as steam-power began to dominate the industry's technology, the industry concentrated on Glasgow, and outlying areas were steadily squeezed of their competitive strength or resorted

Table 21 : Distribution of cotton firms c. 1795

Place	No. of firms	Insurance valuation or, where known, capital (£)	Average (£)
Aberdeenshire	2	15,600	7,800
Ayrshire	2	15,600	7,800
Bute	1	25,000	25,000
Fife	5	28,180	5,636
East Lothian	1	8,400	8,400
Midlothian	2	10,300	5,150
West Lothian	1	400	400
Galloway counties	5	20,750	4,150
Glasgow	11	35,500	3,227
Rest of Lanarkshire	6	30,850	5,140
Perthshire	3	26,200	8,730
Stirlingshire	2	14,300	7,150
Paisley	11	44,300	4,027
Rest of Renfrewshire	12	53,550	4,462
Sutherland	1	2,300	2,300

to the production of other textiles. Galloway felt the pinch in the late 1830s and Aberdeen a decade later.[115] Fife's factories reverted to linen more quickly, and most of Perthshire's mills followed suit.[116]

However, the industry grew in terms of capital and labour employed. Against the nineteen mills of 1787, there were ninety-one in 1795, 120 in 1812 and 192 in 1839. Glasgow, at the latter date, had ninety-eight mills within the city and its environs. The application of the power loom slowly increased after 1815, and many firms by the 1830s included spinning and weaving mills. Probably, the industry, including spinning, hand and powerloom weaving, and finishing, represented a capital investment of about £4½ million by 1840.[117] Ten years later the number of mills had fallen to 168, but the tendencies to concentration, integration and to bigger units were even more marked.[118] Clearly, capital requirements had greatly risen since the early days of the industry.

The labour force also expanded. By 1861 41,237 people were employed in cotton factories; 27,065 of these were working in Lanarkshire.[119] Increasing employment in factories only partly compensated for a decline in opportunities for handloom weavers, since women took the factory jobs, displacing men who had either worked in their own homes, or more commonly, as time passed, in loom shops. Total employment in the industry gradually fell after 1861, but 34,873 people, mainly women, were still working in 1890.[120]

The reasons for the industry's relative decline were varied. Too much has been made of the long-term effects of the American Civil War (1861–5). The 'cotton famine' greatly disturbed production in the war years, of course, but there were fresh surges of investment in the 1870s and 1880s.[121] Although spinning began to contract before 1861, power loom capacity reached its highest point in 1868, after the war was over.

Entrepreneurs probably encountered greater problems in raising credit from the 1830s, as developments in other sectors of the economy increased the competition for capital. This business problem was certainly accentuated by the difficulties which some banks, notably the Western Bank of Glasgow, encountered as a consequence of association with textile firms.[122] Compared with the United States or even Lancashire, there was a substantial lag in the application of the latest machinery. Short-term, this seemed to make good economic sense because the emphasis on fancy weaving reduced pressures to mechanise further as did the employment of women which reduced labour costs.[123] But as profits fell, it became less possible to finance re-equipment from reserves or to raise capital outside, even if businessmen tardily recognised the need for technical changes.

International competition became more intense. As early as the 1830s Scottish firms complained of American competition in Central and Latin America and also in the Far East.[124] Gradually, European, Indian and Japanese production increased, as the second half of the century proceeded, and these economies were closing to Scots producers.[125] In the markets of underdeveloped countries, competition became even more keen.

Within Britain, of the cotton regions, Lancashire adjusted best to changing world circumstances. Liverpool had become the undisputed cotton port of the 1850s, and cotton-broking in Glasgow became a less significant activity. This may have increased the Scottish industry's costs and contributed to its falling profitability. Equal in importance was the fact that Lancashire possessed a much more efficient cotton machine-tool industry than Scotland.[126]

However, the Scottish cotton industry nurtured its own problems. Specialisation on fancy cloths made firms vulnerable to changes in fashion—as Paisley shawl-makers found to their cost—and to contractions in world trade.[127] Businessmen were generally slow to combine and, with the notable of exception of J. and P. Coats, the Paisley thread firm, rarely reached the eminence of dominating markets and of determining trade policy.[128] A highly competitive industrial structure did not aid the rationalisation of the industry, nor did the inadequacies of the unprotected home market where purchasing power was too low to encourage cotton firms to integrate forward into the clothing industry. Thus, after 1890 employment in the cotton industry fell rapidly and the classic success story of the Industrial Revolution concluded in failure.

IRON

Metal working, especially with Baltic bar-iron, had a long history, but, as indicated in Chapter IV, the production of pig-iron did not take permanent root in Scotland until the eighteenth century. Despite the development of coke-smelting by Abraham Darby I c. 1709, this new process was only slowly adopted, and English entrepreneurs came to the Highlands attracted by abundant and cheap charcoal.[129] Furnaces were erected at Invergarry (1727), Bonawe (1753) and Furnace (1755) by partnerships from Furness and district, and at Glenkinglass (1727) and Abernethy (1728) by the York Buildings Company.[130] Apparently, coke-smelting remained generally uncompetitive with charcoal-smelting until the 1750s, and this impression is reinforced by the cost evidence from these charcoal furnaces.[131] Costs of imported high-quality English ore were offset by cheap charcoal, but the Scottish demand for pig-iron was inadequate and therefore, these firms—apart from Bonawe and Furnace—operated only for short periods, and, because they were principally concerned with supplying the English market, were dogged with high transport charges.[132] Imported bar-iron for use in the forge continued to be a substantial component in foreign trade and thus the iron industry contributed little to the economy in the period before coke-smelting became competitive.

As British pig-iron prices rose sharply in the 1750s, output increased—but so did charcoal costs. Ironmasters, therefore, began to transfer to the coke-smelting process.[133] In Scotland, this process of applying the techniques pioneered at Coalbrookdale was marked by the foundation of Carron Company in 1759 by Samuel Garbett, John Roebuck and William Cadell of Cockenzie.[134] However, charcoal pig-iron was still used in the forge and even at Carron for some years after 1759.[135] Despite changes in ownership and difficulties over finance and technical processes, Carron Company became an outstandingly successful firm, specialising in fine cast-iron work, stoves and grates, and in particular supplying cannon, the famous 'Carronades', and shot, far and wide.[136] Nail iron was also supplied to nailers working in their own homes from the rolling and slitting mills at Cramond; apart from cast-iron, this was probably the most significant product supplied to the Scottish market, for much of Carron's output was sold externally.[137]

From 1779 to 1801 the progress of Scotland's iron industry was dramatic. Nine iron-works were founded during that period of rapid industrialisation—Wilsontown (1779), Clyde (1786), Omoa (1787), Calder (1800), and Shotts (1801) in Lanarkshire; Muirkirk (1787) and Glenbuck (1795) in Ayrshire; Devon (1792) in Clackmannanshire; and Balgonie or Markinch (1801) in Fife. In contrast to Carron, these later partnerships began with little capital and relied almost exclusively on reploughing profits. Capital flowed from a range of sources, and several partners were connected with more than one iron-works. Because of their wide business interests, partners tended to judge their investment not only in terms of the profits they anticipated from iron sales but also according to the relative profitability of the other businesses with which they were associated. This may have restricted investment when other sectors were markedly more profitable.[138]

Iron firms were usually founded at the peaks of trade cycles when demand for capital goods was buoyant, but because furnaces normally took two years to build, booms had often given way to depressions before their completion. Thus, high hopes commonly ended in disappointment, recriminations among the partners and failure.

There is a natural tendency to assume that the influence of war was bound to be beneficial to the development of firms. Significantly, Carron was founded in the Seven Years War, Wilsontown during the American War of Independence and four of the other firms noted above in the French wars (1793–1815). Certainly the demand for armaments stimulated the iron industry, but only the largest firms such as Carron received substantial war orders. The smaller firms were often in difficulties as soon as war demand declined or trade became less buoyant.

Peacetime demand was probably more influential if less standardised. In general, the industry was heavily dependent on external sales, and several companies, notably Carron, Glenbuck and Balgonie, were founded with the aid of English capital, entrepreneurship, specialised equipment or skilled labour, principally to supply growing English demand. Although Wales, of all the iron-producing regions, had the lowest costs of production, particularly for bar-iron, before 1830, Scotland had the advantage over the English regions in terms of fixed costs—land, mineral royalties, raw materials and unskilled labour—and mineral endowments. Trade with Ireland, the West Indies and the United States was an additional stimulus, but as distinct from the coastal trade, overseas ventures were often adversely affected by war or diplomacy. Most iron firms encountered trading difficulties, for instance, when President Jefferson enforced an embargo against British trade after 1808, the very period when Napoleon's continental system was beginning to bite into Britain's European markets.

The Scottish market for iron goods was growing as a consequence of agricultural improvement, industrialisation and urbanisation. However, the metal manufacturing industry was dominated by small, non-specialist firms with skilled labour forces and high costs. Demand at home was, therefore, held back by this industrial structure. Since many iron firms were resource-orientated, their inland location involved high transport costs and reduced their competitiveness in distant markets.

Another major obstacle to expansion was lack of trading capital. Initial under-capitalisation made most firms over-dependent on external finance, and unless profits were more than adequate, reserves were difficult to acquire. Banks did provide long-term credit to both Carron and Wilsontown, and iron merchants, acting as agents, tended to issue bills of exchange after delivery of iron but in advance of sales. Nonetheless, many firms failed before 1830 because they lacked capital at critical moments.

As will be gathered from Table 22 there was stagnation in capacity until the mid-1820s.

Table 22 :   *The Scottish iron industry : output and capacity 1780–1840*

Year	Total furnaces	In blast	Out of blast	Output	Capacity
1780	4	4	0	4,000	4,000
1788	8	8	0	7,000	8,000
1796	21	17	4	16,086	20,000
1805		18			
1806	29	20	9	23,240	32,000
1812	29	14	15	15,000	32,000
1813	29	10	19	11,000	32,000
1820				20,000	
1823	28	22	6	24,500	
1825				29,000	
1828	25	18	7	36,500	45,000
1830	27	24	3	40,000	48,000
1835	29				
1836	34	34	0	110,000	
1838	56				
1839	61			195,000	
1840	70			241,000	

Despite this, there was some technical progress and also improvements in business organisation. The application of Watt's double-blast engine, improvements in coking techniques, the introduction of Cort's puddling process for bar-iron production and increasing furnace efficiency were symptoms of this development. In 1801 David Mushet discovered blackband ironstone, but it was only used at first with other ironstones; after 1825 the Monkland Company used it successfully on its own.

Traditional explanations of the great expansion of the industry after 1830 emphasise the significance not only of the discovery of blackband ironstone but also the importance of J. B. Neilson's invention of the hot-blast process (1828). Generally, the argument runs that only high transport costs before 1830 protected the high-costing Scottish industry from extinction by other producers in Britain.[139] Certainly, data available about furnace production costs in the 1820s prove that Wales was the lowest costing region in Britain, but high transport costs protected all the English regions as well as Scotland from Welsh competition.[140] In terms of English production, Scotland was highly competitive, but its fuel costs were higher. The major saving made possible by the hot-blast process was in fuel costs, and thus Scotland's iron industry gained most from the new process.[141]

Investment only proceeded, however, because of an expansion in external sales. Scots pig-iron was in great demand from England and abroad, as markets for railway metal and engineering products increased. Development of the engineering trades in Scotland further stimulated production, but sales depended most heavily on foreign and coastal trade. In 1846, for instance, 119,000 tons were shipped abroad (twenty-one per cent of production), and 257,000 tons (forty-six per cent of production) went coastwise to England.[142] The commercial organisation of the iron trade greatly improved, as the Glasgow commodity market became more specialised and sophisticated.

Entrepreneurs such as the Bairds of Gartsherrie and Wilson of Dundyvan took great risks and made considerable profits.[143] They were enabled to expand their plants unchecked and to increase their output because the credit structure was less necessary but more open to them as the profitability of pig-iron production became more obvious to the commercial community. Cheap Irish and Highland labour kept down labour costs to add to capital and raw material savings. Thus, output and number of furnaces greatly increased, as Table 23 indicates.

From five per cent of British production the Scottish iron industry increased its share to twenty-five per cent by the mid-1840s and remained roughly in that position for the next two decades.[144] There were changes in the location of the industry, however. Lanarkshire had seen the greatest expansion before 1845, but Ayrshire from the late 1830s was increasingly affected by industrial development, as its mineral endowments unfolded.[145] By 1869 the Bairds, employers of 9,000, made twenty-five per cent of total Scottish output at their

Table 23 : Furnaces and output 1840–70

Year	Furnaces	In blast	Production (tons)
1840	70		241,000
1843	98	56	280,000
1844			412,000
1845	109	94	475,000
1850	143	105	630,000
1855	157	122	820,000
1860	171	133	1,000,000
1865	165	136	1,164,000
1870	156	123	1,206,000

twenty-six Ayrshire and sixteen Lanarkshire furnaces, and reputedly, earned £750,000 a year.[146]

Relatively little output was made into malleable iron in Scotland in the 1830s and 1840s, although Scots iron was mixed with other varieties for this purpose in England and Wales. Some of the earliest malleable iron firms were abysmal failures, bordering on fraudulent promotions, and apart from Wilson of Dundyvan and Dixon of Govan few established iron-masters concerned themselves with this branch.[147] Demand for railway metal was often supplied from England or Wales, but gradually the needs of the shipbuilding and engineering industries were met by Scots firms. In 1869 there were forty-four rolling mills and 338 puddling furnaces in Scotland, producing nearly 144,000 tons of malleable iron.[148] Considering total iron output, however, this progress was relatively insignificant. Dependence on external sales of pig-iron discouraged iron-masters from diversifying production, even if they had the inclination. Yet they were really equipping Scotland's future competitors and increasing the vulnerability of her economy.

The social costs of this expansion were great. Amenity was often disregarded in the pursuit of profit. For Bremner in 1869, Coatbridge had to be seen at night in all its spectacular glory; but he did not live there! Even he noted:

> Dense clouds of smoke roll over it incessantly, and impart to all the buildings a peculiarly dingy aspect. A coat of black dust

overlies everything, and in a few hours the visitor finds his complexion considerably deteriorated by the flakes of soot which fill the air and settle on his face.[149]

Overcrowding, inadequate sanitation and poor health were the lot of many. Paternalism was the keynote of many settlements associated with the iron and associated extractive industries—tied housing, company stores and occasionally, as at Gartsherrie, company churches!

RAILWAYS

Of all innovations in transport, railways had the most significant effects on the economy and society. Their prehistory began with wagonways built usually to allow the profitable exploitation of coal, but because of their limitations, canals, such as the Monkland, which had been devised for the same purpose, were more important before 1825.[150]

However, the potential of railways and locomotives was being recognised more and more, partly because of the success of ventures such as the Kilmarnock–Troon line, financed by the Duke of Portland and opened on 6 July 1812.[151] Charles Maclaren, editor of *The Scotsman*, propounded the view in December 1824 for anyone to read that the railway was 'destined perhaps to work a greater change in the state of civil society than even the grand discovery of navigation'.[152] Much the same sentiments were being expressed elsewhere in Scotland by knowledgeable people. Yet the early local ventures, notably the Monkland and Kirkintilloch Railway (Act obtained in 1824) and the Garnkirk and Glasgow (1826) were still promoted with the intention of exploiting mineral deposits.[153]

Substantial investment in railways in several parts of Scotland—in the Monklands, around Dundee, Arbroath, Glasgow and Edinburgh —was the prelude to the promotion of trunk lines in the late 1830s and early 1840s, but as Table 24 indicates, the major period of development came in the thirty years after 1840.[154] The granting of Acts to the Glasgow, Paisley, Kilmarnock and Ayr Railway (1837), Glasgow, Paisley and Greenock (1837) and Edinburgh and Glasgow (1838) was followed by the promotion of east- and west-coast routes to England.[155] Yet the depression of the early 1840s damped down these ambitious schemes, although by June 1843 railway revenue was £284,672 for the previous year, more than half of which came from passengers.[156] The shortage of capital appeared to be crucial. In a changing economic climate within the next three years capital raised by railway companies had more than doubled, and a railway mania spread to Scotland, with newspapers proudly announcing new railway promotions at regular intervals. By December 1845 plans for 115 new railway lines were deposited with the Board of Trade.[157]

Table 24: *Capital raised by Scottish railway companies 1825–70*

Year	Share capital (thousands)	Loan capital (thousands)	Total
1825	32		32
1826	45	5	50
1827	71	15	86
1828	93	22	115
1829	117	29	146
1830	151	53	204
1840	1,960	722	2,682
1844	3,839	1,457	5,296
1845	5,807	1,538	7,345
1846	9,831	1,623	11,454
1847	14,276	3,116	17,392
1850	20,351	6,277	26,628
1855	23,367	9,073	32,441
1860	28,505	9,772	38,277
1865	38,570	11,636	50,206
1870	45,628	16,874	62,502

Source: G. R. Hawke and M. C. Reed, 'Railway Capital in the United Kingdom in the Nineteenth Century', *EcHR, XXII* (*1969*), *270–1*

Despite the financial crisis following this mania, capital formation was only temporarily halted. A period of recrimination directed against Boards of Directors about financial mismanagement, commonly accompanied by shareholders' committees of investigation into the affairs of companies, gave way to slower rates of investment in the 1850s.[158] However, capital formation more than doubled again in the 1860s.

During the mania of 1845–6 seventy-three Acts relating to railways in Scotland emerged from the plethora of plans.[159] The Caledonian, the North British, and the Great North of Scotland were products of this frenetic investment activity.[160] In the 1850s the Glasgow and South-Western and the Highland Railway were founded from amalgamations while the North British and Caledonian gradually extended their control by absorbing other companies or leasing their lines.[161] By the mid-1860s this process of horizontal integration was far advanced: of forty-eight railway companies in 1866, all but three were either leased or owned by the five companies mentioned above.[162]

The great investment in railways, apparent from Table 24, conveys a false impression about the difficulty of raising capital in Scotland. The stock exchanges of Glasgow and Edinburgh were but infant institutions, unable to cope with the necessary flow of funds; banks, reluctant to invest in railway shares before the mid-1850s, provided short-term loans, as did a few insurance companies. More significant railway investors were the newly created exchange companies, but these commonly ended a brief existence in ruin.[163] Most shareholders were not institutions but private individuals, and much of the share capital came from England, particularly from London and Lancashire. Merchants were much the largest occupational group among shareholders followed at some distance by landowners. Among Scots investors, Glasgow merchants were clearly preponderant. Industrialists were relatively insignificant, principally because they were disposed to replough their profits into their firms rather than into transport. Merchants had more to gain through improvements in distribution; landowners anticipated increased land values and better markets for agricultural and other commodities, particularly for coal.

On the relative rôles of London and Lancashire as investing regions, controversy still prevails over certainty. After examining subscription contracts, in the absence of share registers, Dr Vamplew concluded that, for Scottish railways as a whole, Lancashire was more important during the mania.[164] Experience certainly varied, and his conclusions have been questioned.[165] In the initial financing of the Caledonian and the North British, Scotland's two largest railways, London seems to have been more important than Lancashire.[166] Clearly, more research is necessary before firm conclusions will be possible.

About the effects of the railways on the economy and society more certainty apparently prevails. Alternative forms of transport still survived: railways were not cheapest under all circumstances, and sometimes they generated more business for canals and roads rather than less. Steamers in 1837 conveyed 692,000 passengers along the Clyde, and the advent of the Glasgow, Paisley and Greenock Railway was heralded by intense competition.[167] Generally, steamboat companies refused to concede their passenger traffic to railways until they were bought out. However, passengers could travel more quickly by rail, and over longer routes the railways had a clear advantage, but not necessarily in terms of price.[168]

Perishable goods attained wider markets as a consequence of the speed of railways, and savings on stocks could be made by wholesalers and retailers, arising from quicker deliveries. Railways tended to be more convenient for carters than canals, since loading and unloading freight was a relatively simple operation. Turnpike companies were, however, affected adversely, and most railways in direct competition with them had to pay compensation, because the anticipated losses in road revenues did, in practice, materialise.[169] Yet where roads complemented rail services and acted as short distance feeders to them, both forms of transport tended to gain. Generally, long distance carriers tended to decline, but suburban cartage services benefited.

Evidence about canals is difficult to interpret. The Forth and Clyde canal remained profitable, despite extensive competition from the Edinburgh and Glasgow Railway, and one can only assume that the coming of railways tended to increase efficiency in canal management. Indeed, when the Caledonian Railway bought this canal (1867), it was still profitable. The Monkland canal, also a profitable mineral carrier, continued to make money up to 1867 when it too was purchased by the Caledonian.[170]

Coastal shipping was the most serious competitor facing railway companies. Cattle and meat, it is true, increasingly went from Aberdeen to London by rail, and no doubt, trade in such perishables as fish gained much from the new form of transport. However, for bulky non-perishables—and for passengers unworried by sea-sickness or by time—the coaster provided a reliable and cheaper service until the 1890s.[171]

Nonetheless, the railway's impact on inland trade far outweighed its competitive disadvantages elsewhere. The woollen trade of the Borders, for instance, greatly gained as its geographical isolation was broken and its transport costs fell.[172] Equally, the coal trade and the urban gas industry enjoyed reduced costs and better supplies. Price differentials between town and country for bulky low-value-to-volume commodities did not entirely disappear but they were much reduced.

That the railways stimulated the development of the coal, iron and steel engineering industries is certain, but it is easy to exaggerate the demands made on these industries. Although railways were significant, but not the only, carriers of coal, as indicated above, they were less important as consumers of fuel, probably accounting for less than three per cent of production in 1854. Since coal was used in the manufacture of articles needed by the railways, total railway demand, direct and indirect, probably ran at only ten per cent of coal production in the 1850s and 1860s. It is equally important to bear in mind that much of the rolling stock supplied to railway companies in their early days came from England, and that English private builders of locomotives remained very significant suppliers until the 1860s. However, the railway companies built most of their own rolling stock as the century proceeded. Therefore, relatively few firms emerged as locomotive builders and remained in the business —Hawthorn of Leith, Neilson of Glasgow and, from 1861, Dübs of Glasgow. Significantly, these firms were increasingly concerned with exporting. Machine tool production before 1870 was little affected by railway demand; shipbuilding was a more formative influence. Rail-making was dominated by the Welsh, who supplied Scottish railways extensively, but they often mixed Scots-made pig-iron with their own native brands, and, therefore, it is difficult to estimate with any degree of accuracy the demand generated by Scottish railways for pig-iron. Possibly, ten to fifteen per cent of production in the 1850s and 1860s may be near the mark.[173]

On investment and employment, their forms and quantities, railways had a significant general influence. Alternative methods of financing to partnerships, the traditional methods previously used in industry, gave way to limited liability very gradually, but this process was sure if only steady. The capital market became, in consequence, better organised and slowly more perfect. As total purchasing power tended to increase as a general result of railway development, so investment was indirectly stimulated.

Effects on the labour market were wide-ranging also. Labour tended to become more mobile and in greater demand as a consequence of railway development. New employment opportunities were created in abundance; these were of particular significance as far as the level of rural wages was concerned; temporarily, this rose. Unskilled labour was in great demand during phases of construction, and the navvy became a familiar, if occasionally fearsome, sight in the countryside. Migrant labour, especially Irish immigrants, prepared to endure considerable privation for high wages, was attracted by the apparent bonanza, but local communities were faced with temporary problems of assimilation which they did not solve.[174] Once railways became operational, new occupations such as driver, fireman, signalman, level-crossing keeper and porter took their places in a diversifying structure of employment.

The influence of railways on the economy merely confirms the opinion, earlier stated, that industrialisation was a broadly based phenomenon, an aggregate development rather than a sectoral advance. Into the story could have been woven increases in the production of a great range of other products—chemicals, oil, gas, tar, woollens, ships, metal manufactures, leather, glass, rubber, floor-cloth, bricks, pots, tiles, granite, slates, houses, beer, whisky, sugar, bread, confectionery, preserves, and newspapers, to mention but a few! The rise of industry, as earlier chapters have attempted to demonstrate, had many complex interrelationships; its triumph in the economy was accompanied by vast changes in social and economic organisation, occupational structure and output.

CHAPTER XI

Scotland in the International Economy
1870–1939

INDUSTRIALISATION became an international phenomenon during the course of the nineteenth century, but the full effects of this were not felt in Scotland until after 1870. The transcontinental railroads of the United States and Canada and the abundance of resources in all the continents provided opportunities for Scottish settlers, investors, merchants and industrialists. Thus, part of the story of Scotland in this period revolves around the positive responses of Scots to the growth of the international economy.

Yet shifts in the economic structure of Scotland were negatively conditioned as challenges from the United States and other primary producers developed. Gradually, competition from new industrial nations also acted as a brake to further economic growth. For world transport and shipping greatly improved their technical efficiency, and lowered land and ocean freight costs heightened competition in agricultural and other produce. Traditional sea-routes were shortened by the opening of the Suez and Panama canals; submarine cables increasingly raised the level of international commercial knowledge and aided the evolution of world-wide commodity markets.

Scotland gained greater benefits than most of Britain from the widening market for capital goods up to 1914, but equally, the problems of adjustment to changing economic situations were likely to be greater for the Scottish economy later. In the staple industries, such as cotton and iron, the increasing prevalence of tariffs abroad, especially in Europe and the United States, accentuated the problems of exporters and industrialists. The lack of protection

201

within the British market before 1915—and the piecemeal adoption of tariffs up to 1931–2—afforded glorious opportunities for the rise of foreign competition. Relative to some of these new competitors, British industry and marketing methods seemed often to be technically backward, but this reflected the settled habits of longstanding industrial production and was, by no means, true of all Scottish industry.

Particular industries in Scotland increased their output in a spectacular fashion in the period 1870–1914—steel, shipbuilding, coal, heavy engineering, distilling, brewing, other food industries, construction, as examples—but already there were signs of stagnation in others, notably in agriculture, cotton (except for thread), and to a lesser extent jute. Thus, the validity of the term 'Great Depression' as applied to this earlier part of our period is subject to question.[1] Little work has been done on the short-term effects of World War I, although it is clear that there was both considerable pressure on resources, particularly on labour, and a tendency for productivity to lag.[2] About the depressed nature of the economy in the inter-war years there has been singular agreement among historians until recently, for most studies have concentrated upon the persistent unemployment which bedevilled most industries.[3]

However, it seems possible that an examination of the principal components of the economy over the whole period may allow a better evaluation of the underlying causes of the difficulties encountered after the end of the boom in 1920 than would be possible with an approach that sees the war and its immediate aftermath as an intermission separating two distinct levels of economic performance. It may be that the circumstances, which favoured rapid growth for the particular industries outlined above, provide part of the explanation for the difficulties post 1920, the war merely accelerating a process already long begun.

Explanations have been forthcoming in great numbers. None is more superficial than to blame the quality of entrepreneurship, as though the competence of individuals is of greater significance than the rate of market growth.[4] Scottish entrepreneurs in retailing, shipbuilding, engineering, steel, banking, insurance and overseas investment took their opportunities before 1914; it seems at least likely that they would have taken them again in the 1920s and

1930s had they been there. For really solid evidence of entrepreneurial failure in the Scottish context is hard to come by;
possibly the only proven cases are the failures to abandon the
Leblanc process of alkali manufacture in favour of the Solvay
process and to develop an adequate chemical industry based on
coal-tar technology.[5] Even for these examples of entrepreneurial
fatigue there are adequate excuses: the Solvay process was best
worked on the salt-fields of Cheshire and South Lancashire; coal-tar
technology demanded an expanding textile sector. Entrepreneurs
operating in the 1880s and 1890s can not be blamed for the
difficulties encountered between the wars; in a free enterprise
economy innovations can only be reasonably applied when they offer
a short-term private gain rather than an expectation of future
economic growth which is long-term. For concern for the future's
public good does not pay current interest charges to the bank!

The period 1873–96 has been regarded as of special significance in
the passing of British economic supremacy, but this view was largely
based on the obvious downward trends in wholesale prices, the tendency for real wages to rise (as opposed to money wages), and for agricultural rents and some profits to fall. Yet wholesale prices had moved
downwards slowly ever since 1814–15, although there was a substantial
recovery in the early 1850s, followed by a plateau of relative stability
for about twenty years. Thus, the period from 1873 to 1896 merely
continued a trend which had been interrupted.[6] In any event, this
process did not continue in the twentieth century. Nor did real
wages rise uninterruptedly for all; there was seasonal, cyclical or
structural unemployment for some, short-time working for many
and increased house rents for most. These problems for labour
continued in the twentieth century: insecurity of employment was
the bane of most working men's lives and an underlying reason for
trade union organisation, militancy and restrictive practices. Despite
unionisation, most employers regarded labour as cheaper than the
capital costs of new machinery. One must also question the apparent
efficacy of trade unionism in improving the lot of workers over this
period. The influence of market forces on wages remained most
important even if more restrained. Had the aspirations of union
leaders been achieved, the state would, no doubt, have intervened
earlier to control industry and economic life—and on a greater scale.

Had national income been more equitably distributed in consequence and the standard of living improved, one result would have been a more prosperous economy based upon a widening of home demand. Thus, entrepreneurial behaviour and the responses of labour were conditioned by the relatively low cost of labour *vis-à-vis* capital. The domestic market grew, but not fast enough, and thus structural changes in the economy—the expansion of 'new' industries—was limited, as was the application of labour-saving machinery.

Because of the emphasis on the rise of real wages before 1900, the structure of the domestic market, as opposed to the growth of aggregate purchasing power, has been neglected. Scotland's population did not grow at the rates prevailing before 1871, but urban development still proceeded. Changes in diet and spending habits occurred in this urban environment; in these rested the opportunities for retailing entrepreneurs and co-operative societies.

Monetary explanations have also been adduced to explain laggardly economic performance. After 1870 most countries adopted the gold standard as the basis of their currencies, and it is argued that the money supply did not keep pace with the rate of increase in international economic activity; therefore, world commodity prices fell. This, if accurate, was less a problem for Scotland's industrial producers than for her farmers, since agricultural prices were likely to be most severely affected. It has been recently argued that strict adherence to the gold standard after 1925 and up to 1931 lowered demand for British exports and reduced investment, contributing substantially to the inter-war slump.[7] There is little evidence that there was ever any shortage of capital in Scotland for any part of this period. Up to 1914 there was extensive foreign investment by Scots, possibly increasing from about £60 million in 1870 to over £500 million at the outbreak of war. In the 1920s and 1930s the banks held great quantities of government stock because industrial and commercial investment had limited attractions. The problem stated briefly was continuous: the domestic market discouraged investment because it was afflicted by under-consumption rather than by over-production.

Businessmen, having found more profitable investment outlets outside the United Kingdom, helped create the competition which later assailed them. The very profitability of capital goods production up to 1914 caused resources to be taken up by this sector; this impeded diversification in the economy and deliberately encouraged the starvation of small firms in new lines of production and these, in any event, had limited market opportunities. Structural difficulties were, therefore, inevitable in the changed world of the 1920s with or without a return to the gold standard. These were compounded by the rapid decline of world trade and the collapse of the world's credit structure, as Wall Street crashed in 1929. Businessmen looked more and more to government for aid in the form of tariff protection and imperial preference, for help in the organised rationalisation of the industrial structure, for subsidies and a managed economy. As *The Economist* (18 March 1939) announced with absolute exaggerated certainty:

> Complete *laisser faire* went by the board decades ago, but until recently the tendency has been, at least among businessmen, to regard State intervention in industry as perhaps necessary, but if so a necessary evil. As a purely abstract proposition that would still doubtless be maintained. But in practice the attitude has changed.... Since 1932 the State has no longer appeared to industry solely in the guise of monitor or policeman; it has favours to dispense.... The result has naturally been to revolutionise the attitude of industry to the State: the policeman has turned Father Christmas.

AGRICULTURE

Agriculture was more vulnerable in the home market to the challenge of international competition than most industries. Hence the period of greatest general prosperity occurred in World War I. The trend was to fewer farms—from 80,716 in 1875 to 74,335 in 1935.[8] This decline cannot be explained in terms of the amalgamation of existing farms, for the number of large farms (over 300 acres of crops and grass) fell from 1895 onwards. There were, however, significant changes in tenure, although the rural social structure was little affected. In 1875 about fifteen per cent of the farmed acreage was owned by its occupiers—Kinross, Fife and Argyll had the highest proportions—but there was a steady decline to 1912. From

1912 to 1933 owner occupation was on the increase, accounting for over thirty per cent of the acreage in the latter year, as small holding and crofting became more widespread, but by 1939 there was a slight decline.[9] The movement to owner occupation was also assisted substantially by the investment of windfall profits accruing from high wartime prices in later years when land values tended to fall.

Over the whole period there can be no doubt that Scottish agriculture adjusted better to changing market circumstances than was true of British experience as a whole. Principally, this was because mixed farming was dominant in most areas of Scotland, and thus, adjustment to short-term market fluctuations and long-term price trends was an easier process than for more specialised regions such as East Anglia.[10] In general, the cereals best grown in Scotland, barley and oats, did not suffer the massive price falls encountered by wheat as Table 25 makes clear. Foreign suppliers developed a greater control over the British wheat market than prevailed in barley or oats.

Table 25: Cereal prices (per cwt.) 1870–1939

Year	Wheat £ s. d.			Barley £ s. d.			Oats £ s. d.		
1870		10	10		9	7		8	2
1880		10	5		9	2		8	2
1890		7	5		8	0		6	10
1900		6	5		7	0		6	5
1910		7	5		6	7		6	2
1920		19	0	1	5	0	1	0	5
1930		8	0		7	10		6	2
1939		5	0		8	10		6	10

Source: *A century of Agricultural Statistics* (HMSO), 82

In Scotland cattle-farming was always relatively more significant than in England, and fat cattle prices held up better than cereal prices after 1870, despite the introduction of chilled and frozen foreign meat, especially from the United States and New Zealand, in the 1880s.[11] Even though foreign meat supplies continued to grow, as Argentina became a significant exporter after 1900, domestic demand for meat increased substantially, partly as a consequence of increases in the population but mainly because of dietary changes allowed by upward movements in real income. During World War I cattle prices shot upwards and then fell until 1937. Relative price changes between cereals and cattle were reflected in the changing areas devoted to arable farming and to permanent grasses. Table 26 indicates this conclusively.

Table 26 : Acreage (thousand acres) of crops and grasses 1870–1939

Year	Total	Arable	Permanent grass
1870	4451	3486	965
1880	4738	3579	1159
1890	4896	3671	1225
1900	4899	3491	1408
1910	4853	3348	1475
1920	4739	3380	1359
1930	4641	3072	1569
1939	4558	2935	1623

Source: *Agricultural Statistics*, 94–6

From the pattern of land utilisation the general picture of a decline in the significance of arable crops emerges. This was true except for the period 1914–20; generally, the numbers of livestock moved upwards, but sheep- and pig-farming was more susceptible to rapid changes.

Table 27 : Arable crop acreages (thousand acres) 1870–1939

Year	Wheat	Barley	Oats	Potatoes	Turnips
1870	126	244	1020	180	499
1880	74	264	1037	187	486
1890	62	216	1014	142	482
1900	49	240	949	131	465
1910	53	192	958	137	442
1920	54	204	1032	162	425
1930	54	107	862	123	373
1939	80	100	777	134	309

Source: *Agricultural Statistics*, 98–103

The linkages between arable crops and animal and poultry feeding stuffs were important in some areas and, for instance, a decline in sheep or pig numbers tended also to affect local arable acreages. Wheat and pig-production increased in the 1930s in response to government protection, but barley and oats were ignored by government policy-makers and thus suffered. Dairy and poultry farming became more important as the period progressed.

Table 28 : Livestock numbers (thousands) 1870–1939

Year	Cattle and Calves	Sheep	Pigs
1870	1041	6751	159
1880	1099	7072	121
1890	1186	7361	160
1900	1198	7315	132
1910	1171	7145	133
1920	1166	6361	129
1930	1236	7650	143
1939	1349	8007	252

Source: *Agricultural Statistics*, 122–6

Before 1880 price movements in agricultural commodities were the subject of concern but not alarm. In the 1880s, however, the price fall, at first most marked in wheat, became generally apparent. Bad seasons were unaccompanied for once by the compensating blessing of high prices, and epidemics of animal diseases, common enough in the late 1870s, could no longer mask the fundamental changes taking place in world trade. Scots cattle-farmers benefited, however, from the cheapening of feeding stuffs, and barley producers from the increasing production of whisky. Thus, regional experience was often widely different. Aberdeenshire saw little change in its pattern of cultivation before 1914, but in other counties, notably in the Lowlands, farmers increased their permanent pasture.[12] The Highlands and Islands suffered greatly. Over-grazing was a common problem which, after 1880, was coupled to declining wool prices, as Australasian competition bit deep into the British market.[13] Hill sheep farming, in consequence, became much less profitable at a time when merchants and industrialists increasingly aped their betters in their demands for trout streams, deer forests, and grouse moors.[14] Sheep numbers declined from 1890 to 1920; the area of deer forest, on the other hand, increased from 1,975,209 acres in 1883 to 3,584,966 acres in 1912.[15]

There were varied local responses to the depression in prices, as marginal land changed its use. In some counties, notably Stirlingshire, the turnip acreage was reduced in favour of cattle- and dairy-farming.[16] Government inquiries, notably the Richmond Commission (1879–82), were weak in their analysis of the nature of the problems besetting British agriculture, and the solutions they proffered were usually variants of the policies of self-help like those that Stirlingshire farmers were already adopting for themselves.[17] Government action before 1914, therefore, ranged from the superfluous to the irrelevant.

Unrest in the crofting counties was general in the late 1870s and early 1880s, and although recent studies have emphasised its political causes, there were major economic and social problems affecting the region, notably arising from rural over-population.[18] Because these problems appeared intractable, the government appointed a royal commission headed by Lord Napier in 1884. The commissioners found that 'the crofter of the present time has through past evictions been confined within narrow limits sometimes on inferior and exhausted soil'; he was without security of tenure and subject to arbitrary rent increases; his living conditions 'imply physical and moral degradation'. They advocated security of tenure, a reduction in the population on the land and increased state aid for land purchase, fishing, education and for emigration. Recognising the force of habit, sentiment and patriotism, they apparently still found it strange 'that Highlanders will be found who would rather be proprietors in the mountains of Skye, or the wastes of Lewis, than on the fertile plains of Manitoba'.[19]

Fortunately, other self-interested motives inspired the legislature. The croft might be uneconomic, but it was an excellent training ground for the army and navy, for the police force—especially of Glasgow—and for some of the professions. The Crofters Holdings (Scotland) Act of 1886 was the beginning of a legislative trend favouring the smallholder. Its promoters believed that it would provide security of tenure and the right to a fair rent; a Crofters'

Commission was appointed to operate the Act and to relieve land congestion. But further legislation was necessary. The Congested Districts (Scotland) Act of 1897 empowered a Board to provide, equip and adapt land for crofts and to assist the development of supplementary occupations such as fishing and weaving.[20]

Intermittent aid for the Highlands and Islands continued to be government policy. From 1888 special road grants were paid, from 1891 west-coast steamers were subsidised, and in 1913 the Highlands and Islands Medical Services Grant Act established a cheap medical service for the region. But these measures merely emphasised the inadequacies of existing policy for by 1939 no region presented a more telling portrait of poverty and unrelieved decay. The young and the competent tended to leave; the remaining population grew older and less able to sustain itself. City commentators referred to the 'tragic predicament of the fishermen and crofters of the Highlands and Islands, many of whom appear under present conditions to be engaged in a losing struggle for existence'.[21] On the eve of war in 1939 the potential of this region, despite brave attempts to exploit hydro-electricity by aluminium producers or to develop forestry or tweed production, was virtually untapped.

Throughout Scotland rural depopulation was general and continuous. Job opportunities in agriculture were declining; in 1881 240,000 people were engaged in agriculture but by 1911 over 40,000 had left the industry, some the country. Between the wars this process continued. One solution was thought to be encouragement of small-holding.[22] Accordingly, the Small Landholders' (Scotland) Act was passed in 1911 and became the model for post-war Acts in 1919 and 1934; in 1912 the Board of Agriculture for Scotland was established and included in its remit the stimulation of land settlement.[23] But officialdom bumbled slowly onwards with inadequate funds and lacking legislation to protect farmers from the blizzards of international competition or to devise regional planning programmes likely to stimulate domestic consumption.

It was not that the operation of international market forces raised the efficiency of agriculture or that of the economy as a whole, as classical economists preferred to believe. Productivity might have been expected to improve with the passing of marginal land to pasture and the shedding of labour to industry. With regard to the former there is little evidence that this was so, at least before 1914; as for the latter, apart from the war years, in no industry was there ever a continuous shortage of labour and thus, there was little apparent gain in industrial productivity, judging from the evidence of the censuses of production. The cause of improved farming methods received an academic fillip from the founding of colleges of agriculture in Glasgow, Edinburgh and Aberdeen following the establishment of the Dairy School for Scotland at Kilmarnock in 1889.[24] Milk production did become more scientific, and new varieties of oats and potato offered the prospect of better yields. Yet farming practice varied widely, and there was no general trend to greater productivity.[25]

With the coming of the war in 1914, prices moved noticeably upward, particularly for cereals. Grain production increased, commonly at the expense of root crops, but only very slowly up to 1916. Government was slow to plan the necessary disposition of resources in order to increase output. From 1916 Lloyd George's administration began to devise more radical policies, in particular the guaranteeing of grain prices in 1917. Labour scarcity became apparent in the winter of 1917–18, and shortages of eggs, milk, meat and potatoes made price control of these commodities necessary. An increasing arable acreage produced a shortage of feed, as temporary and permanent grasslands were ploughed for grain production; this bottleneck affected the numbers of pigs, poultry, sheep and dairy cattle more adversely than those of beef cattle and contributed to the upward movement of prices.[26]

After the war, prices were maintained till 1920 in a period of artificial prosperity which prevailed in most advanced industrial countries. Foreign imports, particularly of grain and dairy products, soared—and prices gradually reflected the reassertion of long term international trends. In the course of 1920–1, as the effects of price decontrol became evident and demand was gradually over-supplied, price falls followed, puncturing the boom. At first farmers did not regard these price changes as catastrophic, because they still reflected an advance on the pre-war situation. However, when price guarantees finally disappeared in 1921, the government found it necessary to make an acreage payment of £4.4 million to compensate Scots farmers for their losses.[27]

Land costs and other capital items, incurred in the period of high wartime prices, bore heavily on farmers in the changed circumstances of the 1920s, but the burden of rates was reduced progressively in 1923, 1926, and 1929. Prices gradually steadied after 1923, as did the costs of seed, fertilisers and equipment. Poultry farming and market gardening—together with the specialised production of seed potatoes —gained in popularity and reinforced the inherent resiliency of the mixed farming economy.

A severe slump affected all farm prices in 1929, and farms at a distance from urban markets suffered most. Dumping agricultural goods on the British market was a macabre international practice, and the temporary fall in domestic food consumption occasioned by industrial depression added weight to the downward price spiral. Land values fell, farm bankruptcies multiplied, and much land passed out of cultivation. For these difficulties it is customary to blame trade policies and deficient government action. Economic policy was certainly inadequate, but the lack of organisation among farmers partly explains why there was no rapid adjustment to price changes. Middlemen, on the other hand, were strongly organised, especially in the sale of perishable food-stuffs; farmers were slow to develop alternative methods of marketing and, therefore, were often under the thumb of merchant combines. Despite the existence of the National Farmers' Union of Scotland since 1913, the farming community looked for salvation not to mutual co-operative action nor to increased efficiency but to the state. They relied on the government to introduce protection and other piecemeal measures such as marketing boards.[28]

The abandonment of free trade, like the introduction of state-backed marketing schemes, is part of the general story of British farming. Yet Scotland's experience of state intervention in agriculture demonstrated the difficulty of devising a common policy to suit all farmers. As with the Beet Sugar Act of 1925, Scots farmers gained little from the Wheat Act of 1932, for oats, barley, turnips and potatoes were more significant crops for them than sugar beet or wheat. Scotland had one-third of British sheep stocks in the 1930s and, therefore, suffered from steep price falls which affected this sector. However, policies designed to stabilise beef prices were particularly favourable to Scotland. Meat imports were restricted from 1932; subsidies on fat cattle, introduced as a temporary expedient in 1934, were incorporated as a significant feature of the Livestock Industry Act of 1937. Of agricultural subsidies totalling £1.4 million paid to Scots farmers in 1938, £950,755 went to cattle farmers. The Agriculture Act (1937) contained provisions for price guarantees for oats and barley and thus redressed the deficiencies of the earlier Wheat Act. Farmers also gained from the implementation of fertiliser subsidies. Of the marketing boards, the most important for many small farmers was the Milk Board (1935); Scots dairy farmers in 1938 received a subsidy of £113,285.[29]

Despite government action, the fall in agricultural prices was redressed only fitfully after 1933 as Table 29 demonstrates.

Table 29 : An index of agricultural prices 1927–39 (1927–9 = 100)

Year	Index
1927	98
1928	106
1929	96
1930	87
1931	86
1932	77
1933	68
1934	72
1935	74
1936	76
1937	92
1938	84
1939	86

Source: *Agricultural Statistics*, 85

High prices in the period 1914–20 clearly represented an unusual interlude during which the pace of change was not being set by the international economy, but for most of the period from 1870 to 1939 Scots farmers were able to exercise little control over their economic fortunes. Yet their adjustment to international competition, measured by the stability of the structure of Scottish agriculture, was better than was true of British farmers as a whole. However, Scotland's share of total British farm production tended to fall in the 1930s.

Table 30: Gross output (£ millions) of British agriculture
1908–39

Year	Scotland	Great Britain	Scotland's percentage share
1908	26.5	153.7	17.2
1925	48.7	282.2	17.2
1930–1	37.7	250.4	15.0
1936–7	38.1	264.0	14.4

Sources: *Reports on Agricultural Output* (HMSO)

South of the Border, more radical adjustments had been made by 1939 than was true of Scotland, principally as a consequence of state intervention.[30]

INDUSTRY

Taking into account the earlier discussion of the decline of the cotton industry, the basic industries after 1870 became increasingly interdependent. There were significant changes in the metallurgical industries, notably the expansion of shipbuilding, heavy engineering, and steel, the latter offset by the relative decline of iron production. Coal output moved sharply upwards, Lanarkshire producing more by 1900 than all the Scottish coalfields together had mined in 1870.[31] Partly the coal industry grew because of its relationship to other heavy industries but partly also because foreign demand for coal was generally buoyant before 1914. There was substantial growth in the food and drink industries, in building and in the clothing trades, an indication of the aggregate increase in disposable income. Textiles remained both a substantial employer of labour and an important producer for the decline of cotton was offset by the rise of woollens and the ability of jute to maintain and slightly improve on its position of 1870.

C. H. Lee recently expressed the view that Scotland's growth-rate in the period 1881–1921 was below the average for the United Kingdom and virtually stationary up to 1939.[32] Taking into account price changes, for the earlier period his conclusion seems most questionable and for the later perhaps too optimistic.

Table 31 : Gross valuation of Scottish output 1907–35

Year of census	Gross valuation of output (£ million)	Percentage share in net output of Britain
1907	208	12.5
1924	366	10.6
1930	325	9.6
1935	300	8.6

Sources: *Censuses of Production,* 1907, 1924, 1930, 1935; J. A. Bowie, *The Future of Scotland* (1939), 172

Before 1870, for instance, very little steel was made in Scotland for iron-masters had too good a market for pig- and cast-iron to bother with expensive alterations in methods of production. The Bessemer process of steel production was tried but was generally inappropriate for it was only applicable to ores containing little phosphorus, and Scottish raw materials had a high phosphoric content.[33] Existing

Table 32 : Scottish steel production 1885–1900

Year	Output (tons)
1885	241,000
1890	485,000
1900	964,000

iron-masters, owning ironstone mines and collieries as well as furnaces and foundries, had too much capital committed to existing methods to launch precipitately into steel production. Markets for pig- and cast-iron became highly competitive in the 1870s and 1880s and, contemporaneously, local ironstone began to run out. An additional and most important factor favouring change was the growth of steel shipbuilding on the Clyde. The Siemens open-hearth process had been well tried and compensated for the apparent defects of the Bessemer method. Thus, haematite ores were brought in from Cumberland, Spain and North Africa, and the difficulties of transferring from iron to steel production apparently overcome. The speed of this transformation can be appreciated by reference to Table 32.

Ten firms in 1885 produced in Scotland twenty per cent of all the steel made in Britain, and by 1900 Scottish open hearths produced nearly thirty-five per cent of total Siemens-type steel.[34]

This success was closely linked to the development of shipbuilding, and yet the relative backwardness of the Scottish steel industry remained a theme of contemporaries. Shipbuilding increasingly became the barometer of the economy. The regional specialisation of Clydeside after 1870, shipbuilding and marine engineering, had been traditionally associated most obviously with the Thames. Aided by the presence of cheap, versatile and highly skilled labour, organised with considerable entrepreneurial skill and financed by a sophisticated banking system. Clydeside replaced London as the main centre of British shipbuilding. As world trade expanded continuously until 1920 and shipping fleets, including many controlled from Glasgow, turned to steam and steel, the yards on the Clyde exerted formidable additional advantages, for the variegated metal industries (including copper and brass working) and marine engine-making were already well established. Naval rearmament based upon dreadnoughts was a special bonus to the region as government orders sped northwards.[35]

Essentially, the West of Scotland derived great prosperity before 1920 from its very dependence on the production of capital goods. However, this prosperity was subject to cyclical and seasonal fluctuations. It had further disadvantages. First, it accentuated the tendency to integration within the basic industries and may have encouraged the process of concentration of economic power which made the economy particularly vulnerable after 1920. Secondly, further growth depended upon diversification of the industrial structure, and this was difficult to achieve when the domestic market was apparently not sufficiently attractive to stimulate continuous investment in consumer goods production compared with the short-term profitability of producing capital goods.[36] In any competition for resources light engineering lost to heavy engineering. War demand for ships and munitions increased the profitability of these integrated industries and thus heightened existing trends in the economy. Relative to profits, labour was cheap; there was, therefore, little incentive to alter existing methods of production.

With hindsight, of course, it is possible to argue that Scotland's very prosperity before 1920 was based on very shallow foundations. Although the *Census of Production* (1907) was not completely accurate, its statistics indicate the very narrowness of the industrial structure and the limitations imposed by the existing level of home demand. Increases in demand were manifest principally in food and drink production, house building (which was losing its impetus after 1904) and the clothing trades but in little else.

Table 33 :   Major categories of production by value and employment
1907

	Value (£ thousands)	Employees
Mines and quarries	22,617	132,096
Iron and steel, engineering and shipbuilding	61,513	230,691
Other metal trades	1,790	5,555
Textiles	29,154	141,184
Clothing trades	8,737	75,899
Chemicals	6,591	9,274
Paper, printing etc.	8,771	44,440
Food and drink	31,064	70,968
Leather and canvas	2,945	6,208
Timber	7,590	34,480
Clay, stone, building	12,831	80,557
Miscellaneous trades	599	3,940
Public utilities	6,609	29,395
Totals	207,840	885,403

(Note: Some items are included in the Scottish totals but given for the United Kingdom only e.g. tobacco processing and rubber production)

Source: *BPP* (1912–13), CIX, *Final Report of Census of Production, 1907*, 19

In recognising that insufficient expansion occured in the electrical engineering and light engineering sectors before 1914, we do not imply that no development occurred. Singer, having opened a factory in Glasgow in 1867, created a great factory complex at Clydebank in the early 1880s, but the firm supplied a wider demand than that afforded by the Scottish market.[37] In any case, the sewing machine (like the Acme wringing machine) was either a consumer good confined to the upper and middle classes or a capital good dominating a number of sweated trades; it rarely penetrated working-class homes as a personal possession.

Neglect of electrical engineering partly reflected the low-costing abundance of coal and miners, partly the efficiency of steam engine production, but mostly the inadequacies of the domestic market which, by its structure, deterred the development of mass production techniques. Many firms were founded for the production of motor cars but few were successful; similarly, cycle production did not flourish so luxuriantly in Scotland as in the English Midlands. Of these new goods net imports were greater than exports.[38] Even though the economy generated an abundance of capital, there existed the paradox that light engineering firms often encountered difficulties in raising finance. Foreign economies and the home capital goods sector competed more effectively for capital.

The post-war world was a totally different place from that in which demand for capital goods had been buoyant and international trade had expanded greatly, largely under British financial management. New York was the new financial capital of the world; world trade was no longer expanding, and industrial production possessed a new international structure, in which countries like Japan and India had taken a place. World demand for British-built ships and capital goods, at first maintained, declined in the 1920s. Home shipping firms carried less of Britain's trade, and economic nationalism encouraged foreign governments to place shipbuilding orders in their own countries. Germany, Japan and Italy discriminated against British shipping lines and shipbuilding firms alike and used subsidies to ensure victory for their own industries. Thus, while world tonnage rose from forty-nine million to sixty-six million between 1914 and 1937, British mercantile tonnage fell from over nineteen million to 17.5 million.[39] Compared with pre-war, Scottish shipbuilding output fell, as Table 34 indicates.

However, east-coast yards, victims of the increasing dominance of Clydeside before 1914, were less subject to international fluctuations because they concentrated on small ships, averaging 2,000 tons gross.[40] Other shipbuilding regions in Britain were worse hit than Clydeside. Scotland tended to improve its share of United Kingdom

*Table 34: Shipbuilding output and Scottish share of UK output
1882–1938*

Year/period	Output (tons)	Share of UK output (per cent)
1882	391,934	28
1902	516,977	35
1909–13	2,673,000	35.1
1919–23	2,685,000	39
1924–28	2,525,000	43.3
1929–33	1,492,000	39
1934–38	1,679,000	44.6

Sources: N. K. Buxton, 'The Scottish Shipbuilding Industry between the Wars: A Comparative Study', *Business History*, X, 2 (1968), 107; *Glasgow Herald Commercial Supplements*; J. Mackinnon, *The Social and Industrial History of Scotland* (1921), 103

output and was responsible before other regions for introducing new methods of ship propulsion. For this comparative advantage over other regions Scotland owed virtually nothing to the efficiency of firms but perhaps a little to the cheapness of its labour. It was more likely that the structure of the shipbuilding industry in Scotland better suited the changed circumstances of world demand. For instance, cargo ships were less important to Clyde shipbuilders than to firms on the Tyne and Wear. Production of passenger liners and, later, warships provided better prospects during a period of declining world trade. Between 1921 and 1938 the Clyde yards produced 60 per cent of total passenger liner tonnage. In terms of ship repair work, Scotland was less well supplied, and this too followed the pre-war pattern for new construction had been more important in total production than was usual elsewhere in Britain. Between 1918 and 1939 repair work was often the most stable element in demand, since shipowners, faced with declining freight rates and profitability, preferred to prolong ship life rather than to order new ships.[41]

Instability in demand for ships led to rationalisation of the ship-building industry. However, in the immediate post-war situation of relatively high demand, shipbuilding firms acquired steel firms in the hope that vertical integrations would ensure supplies of suitable steel and cut costs. The firm of Colvilles was taken over by Harland and Wolff, James Dunlop and Company by Lithgows and the Steel Company of Scotland by a consortium led by Stephen of Linthouse.[42] Thus, the process of interdependence between sectors of heavy industry continued, and in the more difficult circumstances of the later 1920s and early 1930s made the maintenance of output or capital re-equipment more unlikely. There were also horizontal integrations, as shipbuilding firms absorbed their competitors. Most notably, there were attempts on a United Kingdom scale to reduce capacity. The National Shipbuilders' Security Limited (1930) closed down seven firms in Scotland, placed two yards in 'mothballs' and restricted output at three others.[43]

Although this part of the rationalisation process was deliberately fostered by the government and aided by the Bank of England, government policy, in general, did not lead to any sharp recovery. Attempts to stimulate demand for ships were insufficient. The Trade Facility Acts 1921–6 probably brought £5 million of orders to Scotland, the British Shipping (Assistance) Act in 1935 introduced a 'scrap and build' scheme which had little impact but was supplemented by another, slightly more effective Act in 1939. Particular government financial support for the construction of the *Queen Mary* (1934) and increasing naval expenditure connected with re-armament from 1933 onwards were of greater significance.[44]

The experience of the shipbuilding industry was more than matched by that of the coal industry. As Britain's trade contracted, so the demand for bunker coal fell; more efficient methods of propulsion—and in particular, the use of oil in ships—accelerated this process. Foreign markets for coal were already affected by a number of circumstances. Polish and German competition took some markets; hydro-electricity was a competing substitute not only at home but also in Scandinavian markets where, pre-war, Scottish coal had sold well. The slackening of economic activity in capital goods' production vastly reduced home demand; this was also adversely affected by the general fall in money incomes. And so Scottish coal output fell from forty-two million tons in 1913 to thirty-four million in 1929, and further to twenty-nine million by 1933, with only a slight recovery to thirty million tons in 1939.[45]

The main Lanarkshire coalfield, an area of principal expansion from 1870 to 1914, contracted more sharply than the other coalfields. Some seams were exhausted; others required extensive investment before profitable operation was possible. In general, the smaller Scottish collieries were, however, more cost efficient than larger collieries in other British coalfields. Productivity in the larger pits was increased by mechanisation but this led to 'technological unemployment' in mining districts: output per mine in 1936 was roughly the same as in 1913 but employment per mine fell by about one-fifth. By 1937 seventy-nine per cent of Scottish coal was mechanically cut, and fifty-seven per cent was mechanically conveyed. Most of this progress was achieved in the 1920s and certainly by 1933; most other districts in Britain were behind Scotland in technical progress until the mid 1930s. Rationalisation of the industry via large companies was already beginning in the 1870s; by 1930 three-quarters of output was produced by twenty companies, although there were 400 collieries. The major problem of Scottish coal-owners was the relatively low price they obtained for coal; in nine of the years between 1921 and 1938 the industry incurred deficits because effective demand was so low. Any attempt to lower costs—and thereby to increase profits—endangered the miner's living standard or his safety, or both. Labour relations were inevitably embittered.[46]

The iron and steel industry, subject, as we have seen, to transformation in the period after 1870, was already reorganising by 1914. Exhaustion of ore seams led increasingly to the import of foreign ores and reduced the competitiveness of pig-iron production. Cleveland pig-iron was brought into Scotland in greater quantities from the 1890s, but pig-iron output remained the most important element of iron and steel production in terms of value at the census of 1907.[47] Malleable ironworks had begun to buy mild steel billets from Belgium and Germany for re-rolling and finishing, an indication that this sector was sufficiently pressed to reduce its costs by buying abroad; the installation of gas furnaces before 1914 also reflects this drive for efficiency.[48] After four good years malleable iron firms were badly affected by the depression of 1911, and in the following thirteen firms, operating fifteen works with a capacity of over 250,000 tons per annum, amalgamated as the Scottish Iron and Steel Company Limited. Only four firms stayed outside this combine. Tube making was controlled by a similar combine which was headed after 1903 by the amalgamation of Stewarts and Lloyds. Against this firm the Scottish Tube Company was formed in 1912 from eight partnerships.[49]

During the war years iron and steel firms, even faced with declining productivity levels, made considerable profits. After the war pig-iron production declined further, never attaining more than half the output of 1913. International competition was such that steelmakers found it cheaper to import pig-iron and scrap than to buy native pig-iron. Bairds of Gartsherrie, the most important pig-iron producers until the mid-1930s concentrated more and more on producing pig-iron for the foundry rather than for steel-making. Thus, steel-makers became highly dependent on foreign supplies of pig-iron: when about two million tons of steel were produced in 1937, the best year of the 1930s, almost half a million tons of pig-iron was imported.[50] The deficiencies of the industry were thoroughly exposed in the harsh post-war environment. Many of the furnaces were too small, too labour-intensive, poorly organised and badly located; transport costs were compounded by the need to import ore, scrap and pig-iron; supplies of coking coal were not adequate without extensive reinvestment in deeper coalmining.[51] In general, both pig-iron and steel producers possessed non-competitive capacity and faced a highly protectionist world without any tariff defences of their own.

Had the shipbuilding industry been even less prosperous in the 1920s, then the iron and steel industry might have collapsed. As it was, some firms were living precariously on profits made in the war; others sought to diversify. Shipbuilding firms, as we have seen, dominated the steel industry by 1920, but the dumping of steel by Belgian, German and American producers made even this integration uneconomic without considerable rationalisation. An indication that co-operation to restrict competition and to fix prices was an insufficient solution was the early failure in 1922 of the National Federation of Iron and Steel Manufacturers formed in 1920. A number of other schemes were apparently floated with the aim of unifying the United Kingdom industry in one great holding company, but these seem to have been blocked, possibly because the

City of London—and in particular, the Bank of England—lacked confidence in the proposals.[52] An American expert, Henry Brassert was appointed to examine the problems of the industry in Scotland and to make recommendations; he advocated in 1929 abandoning inland production and moving the industry to a coastal site near Renfrew where a fully integrated ore-terminal and steel-works could be built. This scheme, despite its logic, was shelved.[53]

Instead, after Lithgows, the shipbuilders, sold their steel interests to Colvilles, it was this latter firm under John Craig that set the rationalisation of the heavy steel industry in train, beginning the modernisation of the Clyde iron-works in 1936–7 and laying down plans for a new integrated plant inland and not on the coast.[54] The tube-makers were finally brought together by Stewarts and Lloyds in 1932 when they absorbed the Scottish Tube Company. Two years earlier in 1930 this firm began to plan a great new integrated tube-making plant at Corby located directly on the Northampton-shire orefield; this began production in 1934, at the expense of operations at Coatbridge.[55] A final stage in integration was achieved in 1939 when William Baird and Company absorbed the Scottish Iron and Steel Company, the dominant firm, as we have seen, in wrought iron manufacture.[56]

Scottish engineering gained a world-wide reputation in the period after 1870 but was increasingly faced with economic problems after 1920. At the census of 1907, the engineering industries employed 65,092 workers, and output was valued at £15,877,000, excluding ship machinery and marine engines. Two-thirds of this production consisted of steam engines, boilers and a variety of heavy machinery, exactly the products most likely to be displaced or to be in declining demand, as the standards of international technology improved.[57] Locomotive-building firms, for instance, had encountered extensive American competition in foreign markets during the 1890s, and the three leading companies merged in 1903 as the North British Locomotive Company.[58] Within the British market this new company, like its predecessors, faced competition from the railway company workshops. International and domestic markets for heavy machine tools had been buoyant since the 1850s, mainly as a consequence of railway building, but in the twentieth century these markets fluctuated wildly.

The textile sector had mixed experience before 1914. Woollens and jute survived international competition better than cotton. After the war the decline of cotton was very rapid, but there was no depression in jute until after 1929 and the woollen industry showed slight progress principally because of demand for carpets and fancy hosiery. Lace was another industry which grew rapidly from the 1880s and managed to maintain its momentum, largely at the expense of Nottingham, in the 1920s. Everywhere in the world competition intensified after 1920. Dundee's jute industry was at the mercy of Calcutta, but principally because of difficulties in India still maintained itself. Cotton was least successful, mainly because of Indian, Japanese and American competition abroad and the success of Lancashire at home. Woollens, faced with extensive European competition, did well in North America.[59]

Scotland's industrial structure which had brought great prosperity before 1914 was too narrowly based after 1920. Some towns depended almost entirely upon a single industry, for example Dundee and jute or Galashiels and woollens; most regions depended upon a limited range of economic activities, and nowhere was this more apparent than in the west of Scotland. Regional specialisation accentuated this vulnerability, as for instance when soap production and window-glass manufacture left Scotland for Lancashire.

However, no economy would be insulated from the effects of the world slump after 1929. The greatest swings—both downward and upward—in economic activity happened in the capital goods industries. Some industries showed few signs of recovery, for example mining and the drink industries. On the other hand, food, paper and printing, gas, urban transport, water and electricity showed no depression whatsoever.[60] However, these industries were not sufficient in themselves to produce the level of economic activity necessary to avoid massive unemployment. Although service industries—wholesale and retail trade, banking and insurance, entertainment—also prospered relatively, neither was this development adequate compensation for decline elsewhere.

The fate of the building industry perhaps mirrors the outstanding contradictions within the economy over the period 1870–1939. Great expansion occurred in the 1870s and 1890s, but always Scottish housing conditions lagged behind English. Demand pressure was fed by the growth of city centre shopping facilities and commercial development, middle-class suburban housing expansion and speculative building for the working classes. Overcrowding was a constant problem, indicating a high level of ineffective demand. Paisley in 1870 had forty-two per cent of its families living in one room, Dundee thirty-seven per cent, Aberdeen thirty-five per cent, Edinburgh and Glasgow both thirty-four per cent. Public standards rose slowly, but public inquiries such as the Royal Commission on Housing (1917) revealed an apparently intractable problem.[61]

Table 35 : Housebuilding in Scotland
1929–39

Year	No. of houses
1929	18,978
1931	12,693
1935	25,900
1937	21,528
1938	26,473
1939	25,529

Source: *Annual Abstract of Statistics*
(1924–38), 70

During the 1920s and early 1930s the building industry experienced a severe depression, and even in 1935 employment and output hardly exceeded the level of the census of 1907. Local improvement Acts before 1914 had been the principal agencies for demolition and rebuilding; after the 1914–18 war, state grants to local authorities augmented existing financial provisions. Yet high interest rates in the 1920s restricted speculative building, and even with lower rates and the increased pace of urban renewal in the later 1930s overcrowding remained a stubborn problem: only 34,500 families or thirteen per cent of the total had been removed from overcrowded houses by 1938. At that date, of all working-class housing 22.6 per cent was officially recognised as overcrowded compared with 3.8 per cent in England and Wales. In general, demolition moved faster than rebuilding: in the 1930s over 70,000 houses were demolished—the process accelerating from 1934—and 67,524 new houses built.[62]

The pace of new housebuilding can be assessed from Table 35.

Building for the private, rather than for the council market began to pick up in 1927, but in the 1930s fluctuated very widely. During the period 1934–6 when interest rates were at their lowest, private building paradoxically did very badly.[63] Lower interest rates and falling prices for materials and labour certainly aided the development of the building industry in the 1930s, but pressure on resources developed by 1939, in particular, a shortage of skilled workers and of some materials. However, some progress was made as 315,578 people were rehoused between 1930 and 1939.[64]

Expansion of the building industry also was conditioned by an increasing demand for cinemas, ballrooms, and departmental stores as well as by government support for road and electricity schemes. Unfortunately, for the economy as a whole, there was little new factory-building, apart from at Hillington Industrial Estate which contributed little to total employment before 1939. In fact, between 1932 and 1938, 146 factories were opened in Scotland, 150 closed and forty-three extended.[65]

Clearly private enterprise investment was not raising a sufficient level of employment and purchasing power. More and more there were demands for state action. At first agitation aimed at tariff reform—agriculturalists and cotton manufacturers leading the van before 1914. Protection was introduced gradually from 1915 onwards as a wartime piecemeal expedient and became general only in 1931–2. Although tending to favour increases in production and employment, tariff protection at first had only a marginal effect primarily because the main industries were geared to exporting. However, the iron and steel industry gained substantially for imports fell sharply after 1932. Of greater significance were the Ottawa trading agreements—which became known as Imperial Preference—since these liberalised trade between Britain and the Empire and raised a tariff wall against the rest of the world. As a result, the Empire became a better market for Scots goods, notably for machinery and other iron and steel products.[66]

The cry was also raised for regional planning—'aid for development areas'. For Scotland's problems were not entirely structural: regional infrastructures were often poor, especially when compared with the English Midlands or the South-east; mobility of labour was not good within Scotland, probably being retarded by poor housing provision in the 1920s. It was possibly easier for Scots to migrate to England, as the transfer to Corby of labour from the Monklands proved.[67] Legislation designating special areas and authorising expenditure on public works was passed in profusion in the period 1934–7.[68] By December 1938 £4.9 million had been spent by the Commissioner for the Special Areas in Scotland. Yet central planning according to the Scottish Economic Committee still lacked effective teeth; this body in *Scotland's Industrial Future* (1937) stressed:

> the need for the planning of industrial development in the national interest, as opposed to the principle of *laissez faire* which has resulted in undue concentration of modern industries in certain Southern areas, involving dangerous social and strategic consequences.[69]

Rearmament, the ultimate in state policies, had a much greater influence on economic recovery than any other demand factor in the late 1930s. Armaments firms and shipyards generally were in receipt of considerable government support in the form of orders and investment.[70] Ordnance factories were built at Bishopton; Rosyth naval dockyard was reactivated; orders for sandbags bolstered the declining jute industry; expansion of aircraft production heralded the arrival of light engineering. By February 1938 the Clydesdale Bank's *Annual Survey* indicated that 'what building was to English recovery, rearmament has been to Scottish'. Thus, capital goods production was at last boosted; it was a pity that Scotland's basic industries had to depend upon the stimuli of approaching war.[71]

COMMERCE, BANKING AND FOREIGN INVESTMENT

A number of circumstances aided the expansion of domestic commerce. Falling wholesale prices and rising real incomes from the 1870s to the late 1890s encouraged the development of retailing. The expansion of international trade before 1914 underpinned this process, and importers gained as well as retailers. There were also greater opportunities for publicans, tobacconists, confectioners, fruiterers, newsagents and druggists and for those who produced or processed commodities sold by these groups. Demand was initially linked to a relatively few products—food, drink, tobacco and drapery —but the continued expansion of retailing throughout the period under review was only possible because the range of demand was extended. This 'retailing revolution' was accompanied by an expansion in the number of shops, increased efficiency and productivity in distribution, cost reduction, energetic and imaginative advertising together with a variety of sales gimmicks, and improved quality for many products.[72]

It is relatively easy to over-emphasise the speed of this change in retailing. But it should be remembered that urbanisation as a process had relied earlier upon solving victualling problems; thus, the cities, especially, had depended upon the expansion of markets and the development of other retail outlets. However, the occupational structure of the cities was increasingly influenced by the growth of distribution as an industry; Aberdeen, for instance, had nearly nineteen per cent of its population in the wholesale, retail and service trades by 1938. Compared with 1861 the number of shops had more than doubled by 1911, but then began to decline, as Table 36 shows.

Table 36 : Number of shops in Aberdeen 1861–1938

Year	Shops
1861	848
1911	1,816
1921	1,711
1938	1,532

Source: *Third Statistical Account,* Aberdeen, 303

Up to 1914 the typical unit in retailing was the corner shop, and its main strengths were its accessibility and offer of credit.

In general, the main drive for change came from two sources—the co-operative societies and the entrepreneurial teams which produced the multiple stores, often from small beginnings. Led by skilled men in their local communities who were imbued with an idealism which stimulated expansion, the co-operatives grew substantially in significance by 1939, having over three-quarters of a million members at that date. Retail sales at £2.5 m in 1881 had reached £41.5 m by 1919 and £43.8 m by 1939. The Scottish Co-operative Wholesale Society, established in 1868 and owned by the retail societies, sold more than £1 million of goods to them in 1882, £5 million in 1899, £19 million in 1919 and £20 million in 1936. In the 1890s it greatly expanded its activities, under the entrepreneurial guidance of William Maxwell, diversifying extensively into production, and by 1935 the Wholesale owned fifty-six factories or depots in various parts of Scotland as well as plantations, mills and creameries overseas, and produced *inter alia* foodstuffs, tobacco products, drapery, boots and shoes, pharmaceutical products, furniture, bedding and mineral waters. An equally significant feature was the spread of co-operation from the cities and mining areas into the market towns and small burghs of the countryside.[73]

Like the co-operative stores, the multiples had been born in an earlier age but after 1870 there developed a number of substantial retailing empires. Firms like Lipton's (1871), Massey's (1872), Templeton's (*c.* 1875), Cochrane's (1881) and Galbraith's (1884) began in a modest way, often in rented premises with relatively small capital. Their entrepreneurs were commonly young men from the 'shopocracy' or from other social groups but with training as counterhands. All these firms were based on the cities where the volume of business was increasing and, like the co-operative societies, they specialised in supplying a few products at first—only gradually extending their range—and depended upon a rapid turnover at competitive prices, selling only for cash. This emphasis on cash trade and the refusal to give credit reduced the risk of bad debts and the costs of administration while aiding the process of business expansion through internal financing.[74]

Substantial progress was made in Scotland by multiple and departmental stores by 1914, but several of these firms also penetrated the English market. Lipton's, for instance, from their Glasgow base expanded and diversified at home and abroad; by 1939 this firm had 449 branches and a turnover of £6.8 million. Cochrane's began with one shop in 1881, had 110 by 1920 and 119 by 1930; Galbraith's had 159 grocery branches and twelve butchers' shops by 1939 and, following the lead of the SCWS gravitated systematically into food-processing between 1902 and 1918—tea-blending, bakery, ham-curing and sausage-making, jam-making were all logical extensions of the earlier business.[75]

This process of vertical integration was not limited to the food firms, although it was most common among them. Fleming Reid began retailing knitting wools in Greenock in 1881, thereby eliminated middlemen for its factory output, and by 1939 possessed 412 Scotch Wool shops throughout Britain. Singers had begun even earlier retailing sewing machines from a shop in Glasgow in 1856 and by 1877 had 166 such retail outlets which also acted as service centres.[76] From the drapery firms extension into departmental store organisation was relatively common; a few such as Walter Wilson's were conducted with outstanding panache and profitability.[77]

Incomes, purchasing power and buying habits were affected by the economic difficulties of the 1920s and 1930s after a profits bonanza for retailers during the war. Competition among retailers, and especially the squeeze imposed on the independent shopkeeper by both the co-operative societies and the multiples, became more intense. Shop numbers began to fall in the cities, but existing trends in distribution accelerated in their effects. Manufacturers bypassed wholesalers and traded directly with retailers,; retailers were encouraged to beat down the economic barriers to manufacturing; wholesalers began to amalgamate to safeguard themselves, the trading firms in the meat trade, for instance, forming the Union Cold Storage Company in 1923.[78] Co-operative societies began to feel the pinch as competition heightened in the early 1930s, and average annual trade per member declined from £67 7s. 7d. in 1919 to £46 8s. in 1939.[79] Even the larger retail combines began to fall victims: Cochrane's and Massey's were both bought by the Margarine Union in 1929, and so the process of rationalisation we have already noted in industry spread to retailing.[80]

After the war the pressures in difficult times were such that food retailers moved into the bread and milk trades, since demand for these products was remarkably inelastic. Again, this process of integration had been pioneered by the co-operative societies before the war but was taken up most energetically by firms such as Allied Suppliers, the principal firm behind amalgamations and consolidation in the period 1929-34. The main sufferers were the independent retailers, as motor transport made delivery from city centre stores cheaper.[81]

Dynamism in the inter-war period was represented by the creation of Hugh Fraser's business empire and by the development of Isaac Wolfson's Great Universal Stores. Significantly, both these men spread their wings for England, just as great English-based firms such as Lewis, Woolworth, Marks and Spencer, Boots, Montague Burton, and Austin Reed began to move into Scotland.[82] For most Scots these developments represented an uneven but gradual improvement in the standard of life, even though by the standards of today life seemed relatively bleak.

Foreign trade saw a remarkable expansion in the last half of the nineteenth century: in 1850–1 imports were roughly half the value of exports, and together international trade totalled £26 million; by 1900 imports through Scottish ports exceeded exports, and trade had reached £71 million.[83] The story up to 1938 subject to the qualifications below, is summarised in Table 37.

Table 37 : Trade (£ million) through Scottish ports 1900–38

Year	Imports	Exports
1850–1	8.9	17.9
1900	38.7	32.3
1913	56.5	53.5
1920	138.8	125.6
1927	80.8	61.2
1933	39.3	29.6
1938	62.3	44.0

Sources: Appendix IV p. 247; M. W. Flinn, 'Overseas Trade of Scottish ports 1900–1960', *SJPE*, XIII (1966), 223–4

In considering Table 37 it should be borne in mind that some Scottish goods moved through English ports and had done so for a long period of time, and because of the way statistics were collected from the later nineteenth century it is only possible to calculate trade through Scottish ports. On the import side, the story is essentially of the great inflow of food-stuffs and raw materials up to the 1920s, of collapse after 1927 down to 1933 and of recovery from 1933 onwards. Demand for Scottish exports also grew substantially, even allowing for substantial inflation from 1914 to 1920. However, there was a change in the composition of exports. Textiles in 1870 still accounted for about sixty per cent of exports and were less than twenty per cent by 1938; coal was the most important single export by 1900, representing over 18 per cent of the value of all exports and, as we have seen, this trade suffered severely in the 1920s and 1930s.[84]

From 1900 the propensity to import was stronger than the capacity to export. Increasingly, processed flour and food-stuffs were imported rather than raw products, especially into Glasgow, although the growth in the export of food, drink, tobacco and timber products initially depended upon imports. Iron and steel products, mainly in the form of capital goods, became very significant exports by 1900 but increasingly, as we have seen, relied upon the import of raw materials.[85]

The closer integration of the main sectors in the economy was accompanied by a weakening export performance in the twentieth century. For products in growing demand in international trade were often inadequately represented in the industrial structure or subject to competition. Thus, according to the Census of Production (1907), the net import of motor cars and vehicle chassis parts was greater than exports; there was no production of tinplate, very little of wire, cutlery, locks or small arms, and virtually none of electrical goods, watches and clocks. Despite resources of shale oil and skilled manpower, the share of the British oil market controlled by home-based refineries fell consistently. Net imports of oil at 229 million gallons in 1907 were seven and a half times the quantity produced in Britain, and between the censuses of 1924 and 1930 there was a fall of twenty-five per cent in British control of the home market for oil.[86]

The sharp fall in exports after 1927 reflected the developing uncertainty surrounding international trade. Primary producers had reduced purchasing power as world prices fell, and, therefore, found it impossible to maintain their level of demand for the goods of other nations; sterling was overvalued *vis-à-vis* the dollar, and because of Scotland's reliance on North American sales this was a particular disadvantage. Depression in the United States and Canada, war in the Far East between China and Japan, national dumping campaigns by industrialised nations, all tended to dislocate international markets—as did the trend towards increased tariffs. The political uncertainty occasioned by the rise of dictatorships in Europe did not aid long-term capital investment, and thus it was difficult for producers to make their goods competitive abroad.[87] The recovery of Scottish exports after 1933 was slower than prevailed for British exports as a whole, although imports rose in a spectacular fashion.[88] Thus, Scotland's foreign trade was not sufficiently diversified to aid the recovery of the economy, but that was also a broader industrial weakness.

The Scottish banks, as we observed earlier, by 1870 were extending their business into England, but this process was abruptly halted in the 1880s if not entirely reversed. One significant trend was the involvement of banks in foreign investment; another was the drive towards amalgamation. In 1907 the North of Scotland amalgamated with the Town and Country Bank, and the Caledonian was absorbed by the Bank of Scotland.[89] The English banks were readily interested in expanding their business into Scotland, and after the war several of them took over Scottish banks—Lloyds absorbed the National Bank of Scotland (1918), Barclays the British Linen Bank (1919), and Midland the Clydesdale (1920) and the North of Scotland (1924). As far as can be presently judged, the alternative policy open to these English banks was to open branches in Scotland, likely to be a more costly operation than amalgamation. Significantly, the absorbed banks retained their own names and semblance of independence, they became parts of larger banking units with the additional advantages accruing from increased financial size, and their shareholders were offered very attractive terms when the take-overs occurred. That the traffic in amalgamations was not in a single direction can be gathered from the fact that the Royal Bank absorbed three English private banks in the period 1924 to 1939—Drummonds, Williams Deacons, and Glyn Mills.[90] Over the period, the number of bank branches increased two-fold, as Table 38 indicates.

Table 38 : Number of bank branches
in Scotland 1870–1939

Year	Number
1872	912
1895	1,015
1914	1,253
1921	1,343
1938	1,831

Source: M. Gaskin, *The Scottish
Banks: A Modern Survey*
(1965), 33

Thus, there was apparently little correlation between the number of
bank branches and the state of the economy; banks flourished in
most circumstances, and Scots demonstrated their canniness by a
higher rate of savings per capita than the English.

Of course, there were exceptions, the most notable being the
failure of the City of Glasgow Bank (1878) which stimulated the
movement among bankers away from private partnerships to limited
liability.[91] Apart from changes in the legal form of banking, there
were other developments: the use of the bill of exchange declined
at home, for instance, and was replaced by bank advances and
cheques. Before the 1914–18 war banks were heavily committed to
the servicing of trade and industry—and foreign investment—and
very little to government stock; in the 1920s high interest rates on
offer at home led to increases in bank holdings of government
stock, less involvement in foreign investment and trade and a
decided fall in industrial investment save for supporting reorganisation schemes approved by the Bank of England. These switches
within the credit structure reflected the changed economic circumstances of the post-war world but they made industrial diversification less likely, maintenance or recovery of foreign trade more
difficult, and a substantial improvement in aggregate employment
impossible.[92] Some nationalists in the 1930s pressed for both
financial and political independence of England, because they
claimed that the Scottish banks and investment institutions were
controlled from London.[93]

Foreign investment by Britons was a marked feature of the period 1870–1914, although this capital flow had earlier origins.[94] As Table 39 indicates, its pace certainly quickened after 1870.

Table 39 : Estimates of British capital abroad 1870–1914

Year	Amount (£ million)
1870	700
1885	1,500
1900	2,400
1914	4,000

Source: A. Imlah, *Economic Elements in the Pax Britannica* (1958), 72–5

The circumstances favouring this increase in foreign investment were wide-ranging. Capital accumulation in the United Kingdom had been very rapid from the mid-1840s to the early 1870s, and this tended to reduce the long-term domestic rate of interest at a time when interest rates elsewhere in the world, notably in North America, were rising. Thus, businessmen believed—whether it was true or false—that opportunities for short-term gains were more numerous outside Britain than at home. Better commercial information was available to them more quickly about the external possibilities, as world communication and travel facilities improved with the development of the electric telegraph and the advent of ocean-going steamships. There was a general willingness to accept the limited liability company as the legal form most suited to channelling funds abroad. Joint-stock ventures had always been more popular in Scotland than in England from at least the eighteenth century, but the railway 'mania' of the 1840s and legislation of the 1850s and 1860s giving greater scope to limited liability aided the acceptance of the investment company as the best mechanism for Scottish investment overseas.

Apart from railway companies, public utilities and oil companies, Scottish industry, dominated by private unincorporated partnerships, was slow to adopt the limited liability company form. Thus, domestic industry and trade offered few continuous opportunities to would-be investors even if suitable returns on capital had been available. There was little incentive to substitute capital for labour in most Scottish industries because of the prevalence of low wages; in turn, regional purchasing power was restricted and economic pressures for structural changes in the economy were reduced. In consequence, capital flowed out of Scotland in greater quantities while regional economies remained labour-intensive, became increasingly integrated around relatively few industries and showed few signs of diversification.

Table 40 : Estimates of Scottish foreign investment 1870–1914

Year	Amount (£ million)
1870	60
1885	150
1900	300
1914	500

Sources: Unextracted Processes Scottish Record Office; J. C. Logan, 'Scottish Investment in America' (unpublished BA dissertation, University of Strathclyde, 1968); *The Economist* 1870–1914; W. T. Jackson, *The Enterprising Scot* (Edinburgh, 1968)

It is virtually impossible, at present, to measure the volume of Scottish capital exports accurately for funds flowed out via London as well as through Edinburgh, Aberdeen, Dundee and Glasgow. For example, the Emma Silver Mining Company (1871), formed to exploit precious metals in Utah, although London-based, apparently sold half of its nominal capital stock of £1 million to Scots, mostly in the Glasgow area.[95] Possibly as much as one eighth of British foreign investment came from Scotland during the period 1870–1914, the proportion rising most rapidly after 1885.

The direction of capital outflows is more easily charted. Three continents—North America, Australasia and Asia—predominated, with the first probably accounting for forty per cent or £200 million by 1914.[96] Dundee by 1890, according to one estimate, had invested £5 million in the United States, and recent research suggests this is conservative.[97] Aberdeen and Edinburgh took a particular interest in Australasia, and Glasgow and Dundee investors were apparently quick to exploit the agricultural, industrial and railway assets of India, Ceylon and Burma as well as Japanese state bonds.

Investment in foreign railways was most important in the 1870s; in the 1880s American land and cattle companies, mortgage companies and mining ventures attracted considerable capital: 'in the summer of 1882 hardly a train came into Edinburgh from the West or the South which did not bring a Yankee with a cattle ranch [sic] in one pocket, a "timber limit" in another, and perhaps an embryo Erie Railway up his sleeve.' The fashionable period of investment in American land and cattle companies was relatively short—1880–6; investment trusts retained greater favour over a longer period. Mining ventures, in which the West of Scotland took a particular interest, were most popular after 1890, especially after 1895; mortgage companies attracted most capital before 1890.[98]

Commonly, directorates of companies were interlocking. For instance, Sir George Warrender, formerly an officer in a Highland Regiment and a captain in the Coldstream Guards, was a director of seven companies. Yet he was not one of the aristocratic front men, so commonly derided as 'Titled Decoy Ducks' by the financial journals, as frauds and mismanagement in some companies unfolded.[99] Edinburgh insurance companies contributed a number of directors to investment trusts, probably a reflection of the transfer of insurance funds abroad.[100]

The composition of the investing public is by no means clear-cut. Well-established industrial dynasties like the Baxters and Coxes of Dundee, Cowans of Edinburgh and Coats of Paisley were significant investors.[101] Yet the number of small investors was very numerous— shopkeepers, self-employed tradesmen, professional groups and merchants. In the Scottish American Investment Trust there were 385 shareholders: over half invested less than £400, and of those investing more than £3,000, the majority were merchants and manufacturers. Edinburgh had more investors from professional groups than Dundee or Glasgow where merchants and industrialists were most important. There was certainly a rentier mentality among small investors, clearly justified by their number, and this helps to explain the success of some of the fraudulent promoters: 'our canny friends north of the Tweed . . . could not resist the bait'.[102]

Returns on foreign investment were both direct and indirect. Many companies performed well at the beginning of their existence, but initial promise was commonly not maintained. Solid rather than spectacular returns were made as the sample of American land and cattle companies in Table 41 indicates.

Table 41 : Returns on investments in selected American land and cattle companies

Company	Life	No. of annual dividends	Average rate %	Final bonus %
Western Ranches	1883–1911	27	11	17
Hansford	1882–1904	17	4.3	15
Matador	1882–	62	8	
Missouri Land	(?)	24	4	
Prairie	1880–1920	39	8	
Swan	1883–1926	43	6	
Texas	1881		3	

Sources: W. T. Jackson, op. cit., chs 3 and 5; *Journal Economic History*, Suppl. IX (1949)

Even allowing for reinvestment of such profits overseas, foreign investment made a significant addition to Britain's balance of payments. Indirectly, it cheapened the cost of British imports by stimulating primary production overseas, thereby lowering the cost of living and costs of production. By making sterling readily available, foreign investment increased international purchasing power and almost certainly demand for British exports. Yet foreign investment was no long-term substitute for domestic investment, although the extent of domestic capital formation during this period should not be under-played.[103] Scotland almost certainly invested more abroad and not enough at home, but this judgement essentially depends upon hindsight. Foreign competition was assisted and at the same time new industrial development and future employment at home was sacrificed. But at the time investment abroad seemed to possess a comparative advantage!

POPULATION AND SOCIAL CONDITIONS

In the period under review the population increased from 3,360,018 to 5,006,689, but most of this increase was achieved by 1914.[104] For between the wars there was a marked decline in the birth-rate and a tendency for migration to England and for emigration to increase. Better medical care, improved dietary and living standards had produced a slow decline in the death-rate from the late 1870s, but generally, mortality was higher for all age-groups in Scotland than in England as time passed, although infantile mortality was lower till 1910.[105] Urbanisation proceeded, but Glasgow and Clydeside did not increase the dominance they already enjoyed in 1871, mainly because of emigration and migration. However, the development of middle-class suburbs—and in the 1930s working-class housing estates—increased the residential area, and commuting traffic assumed significant proportions with the advent of suburban tram and train services.[106]

Immigration was less significant than outward movements, but by 1931 there were more English-born residents than Irish-born, a marked contrast with nineteenth-century experience.[107] However, in the 1920s migration to the Midlands and South-east England coupled with emigration outstripped the natural increase in the population, and the Census of 1931 showed a decline on the 1921 figure.[108]

Most observers noticed the increased life expectancy—although this lagged behind England—but were particularly struck by the decline in the birth-rate from the late nineteenth century. Total births reached their peak in 1903 and then declined; between the wars the birth-rate was roughly half the level of the 1870s.[109] This change in fertility was even more marked in England, possibly because Scotland possessed a higher proportion of Roman Catholics in its population and of manual workers. The small planned family slowly became the ideal of most married couples, and this significant change was pioneered by the middle-classes.[110] The age at which women married in Britain started to rise probably in the 1860s and continued to do so till 1940. Scotland was only slightly affected by this phenomenon, for the average age at marriage rose only six months between 1860 and 1930.

The principal agent bringing about the small planned family was clearly the spread of family planning methods; birth-control appliances, however, only became widely used during the inter-war period. A range of influences stimulated the widespread belief in smaller families, and not merely the more widely diffused knowledge of contraception. Children were a greater financial and moral responsibility after 1870 in an age of growing international insecurity, of withdrawal of child labour, of compulsory education and of the emancipation of women. Existing standards of comfort were difficult enough to maintain in the period 1919–39 without family ties; there was little real warmth or enjoyment in 'love on the dole'. Thus rates of marriage fell in depressions.[111]

Social and geographic mobility in a period of job insecurity was desirable if not absolutely necessary—'he travels fastest who travels alone'. An indirect consequence of this mobility was the dissemination of social attitudes favouring the small planned family and the spread of birth control methods. As infantile mortality declined, so it became less necessary to have more children in the fatalistic expectation that not all would live to adulthood. People took time to become really aware of the significance of lower infantile mortality, but as parents brought up their children, they were faced increasingly with the choice of improving the lot of their family and themselves or having more children. For those who regarded themselves as free from religious sanctions there was little real choice—and no problem of conscience.

Although the rate of increase in the employed population slowed, it is unlikely that income per capita rose significantly because of the effects of seasonal, cyclical and structural unemployment. In the inter-war years there was virtually no change except after 1937 when real income (i.e. allowing for price changes) rose by about sixteen per cent compared with 1924.[112] Wage-rates in the later nineteenth century tended to catch up with those prevailing in England, although national income did not grow so fast. In 1886 Scottish wages had been lower than the UK average, and much of the evidence presented to the Royal Commissioners investigating the economic conditions of labour in the 1890s corroborated this situation. There is much qualitative evidence that the problems of urban poverty, demonstrated by Charles Booth in London and Seebohm Rowntree in York, existed in profusion in Scotland's towns and cities. Wage rates were highest in Glasgow and Edinburgh and lowest in Dundee and Aberdeen. Equally, agricultural wages tended to be highest in and near the central Lowlands.[113]

Generally, Scotland was one of the most prosperous regions in Britain immediately before 1914. Women's wages in 1906 tended to outstrip those obtaining in England; men's wages were definitely catching up the leeway prevailing in 1886. There were much lower levels of unemployment than for instance, in the Midlands and South-east England.[114] The economy, dominated by heavy industry, suffered from seasonal and cyclical fluctuations, but there was apparently little threat of massive structural unemployment. Between the wars, as we have seen, this situation was transformed: unemployment reached record levels continuously, and advancing industries were hardly represented in the industrial structure. Wage-levels were gravely affected as were social conditions as a whole. In consequence, militancy and trade union membership increased, although there was a long history of growing class consciousness and organisation. According to the Webbs, there were 147,000 trade unionists in Scotland in 1892 (or 3.7 per cent of the population); in 1924 536,000 (or 11 per cent) and in 1947 900,000 (or 17.7 per cent). From 1897 the Scottish Trades Union Congress was a significant component of the British Labour movement.[115]

Although we lack definitive studies of working-class expenditure, there is some evidence that Scots tended to spend more on alcohol and less on rent than the English or the Welsh.[116] Everywhere in urban and rural Britain there were housing problems, but in proportion to population, Scotland had more overcrowded and insanitary slums than any other region. Glasgow had begun the drive for improvement before 1914, and local acts and bye-laws preceded adequate general legislation.[117] Yet the Royal Commission on Housing in Scotland (1918) was unequivocal, referring to[118]

> unsatisfactory sites of houses and villages, insufficient supplies of water, unsatisfactory provision for drainage, grossly in-

adequate provision for the removal of refuse, widespread absence of decent sanitary conveniences, the persistence of the unspeakably filthy privy middens in many of the mining areas, badly constructed, incurably damp labourers' cottages on farms, whole townships unfit for human habitation in the crofting counties and islands . . . .

Despite the state-inspired building after 1919 the problem of housing remained intractable in 1939, a testament to past neglect and contemporary impotence.

Appendices

I   Population of Scotland 1801–1971

II   Population of the principal towns

III   Statistics relating to numbers in Scottish retail and wholesale trade from census of 1851
  (a) Numbers in different occupations 1851
  (b) Numbers in selected occupations in the cities 1851

IV   Trends in official values of imports and exports 1755–1851

V   Statistics relating to production
  (a) Linen 1728–1822
  (b) Spirits 1730–1910
  (c) Malt 1770–1880
  (d) Paper 1737–1861
  (e) Iron ore 1855–1938
  (f) Coal 1854–1945
  (g) Pig-iron 1788–1914
  (h) Pig-iron 1915–38
  (i) Inhabited house duty 1851–1924
  (j) Houses at census 1881–1951

243

Appendix I : Population of Scotland 1801–1971

Year	Males	Females	Total
1801	739,091	869,329	1,608,420
1811	826,296	979,568	1,805,864
1821	982,623	1,108,898	2,091,521
1831	1,114,456	1,249,930	2,364,386
1841	1,241,862	1,378,322	2,620,184
1851	1,375,479	1,513,263	2,888,742
1861	1,449,848	1,612,446	3,062,294
1871	1,603,143	1,756,875	3,360,018
1881	1,799,475	1,936,098	3,735,573
1891	1,942,717	2,082,930	4,025,647
1901	2,173,755	2,298,348	4,472,103
1911	2,308,839	2,452,065	4,760,904
1921	2,347,642	2,534,855	4,882,497
1931	2,325,523	2,517,457	4,842,980
*1939	2,412,244	2,594,445	5,006,689
1951	2,434,358	2,662,057	5,096,415
1961	2,482,734	2,696,610	5,179,344
1971	2,515,140	2,712,566	5,227,706

* Mid-year estimate

Source: *Census 1971 Scotland : Preliminary Report*

Appendix II : Population of the principal towns (thousands)

Year	Aberdeen	Edinburgh and Leith	Dundee	Glasgow	Greenock	Paisley
1801	27	83	26	77	17	25
1811	35	103	30	101	19	29
1821	44	138	31	147	22	38
1831	57	162	45	202	27	46
1841	63	166	63	275	36	48
1851	72	194	79	345	37	48
1861	74	203	90	420	43	47
1871	88	242	119	522	58	48
1881	105	295	140	587	67	56
1891	125	332	154	658	63	66
1901	154	394	161	762	68	79
1911	164	401	165	1,000	75	84
1921	159	420	168	1,034	81	85
1931	170	439	176	1,088	79	86
1951	183	467	177	1,090	76	94
1961	178	449	182	898	69	95
1971	182	453	182	897	69	95

Sources: B. R. Mitchell and P. Deane, *Abstract of British Historical Statistics* (1962), 24–27; *Census 1971 Scotland: Preliminary Report* (1972), 3–8

Appendix III : Statistics relating to numbers in Scottish retail and wholesale trade from census of 1851

(a) Numbers in different occupations 1851

Occupation	Males	Females
Druggists	1,225	44
Innkeepers	1,840	674
Lodginghouse keepers	203	5,459
Hatters	772	1,606
Tailors	18,492	234
Hosiers, haberdashers	416	97
Shoemakers	29,703	2,000
'Others providing dress'	3,479	580
Merchants	1,492	107

Appendix III : (a) Continued

Occupation	Males	Females
Brokers	323	
Agents, factors	432	
Salesmen	222	
Commercial clerks	6,257	
Commercial travellers	1,017	
Pawnbrokers	280	
Shopkeepers	1,338	1,358
Hawkers, pedlars	2,475	1,999
'Other merchants and agents'	1,729	752
Carmen, carriers, carters, draymen	12,283	89
Warehousemen	1,425	271
Horse dealers	98	
Cattle, sheep dealers and salesmen	923	
Booksellers	1,434	52
Cowkeepers and milk sellers	983	1,131
Butchers	4,851	152
Provision curers	88	
Poulterers	88	
Fishmongers	374	455
'Others dealing in animal food'	1,481	1,064
Woollen drapers	299	990
Greengrocers	207	418
Corn merchants	956	
Bakers	9,541	642
Confectioners	1,155	309
'Others dealing in vegetable food'	894	238
Licensed victuallers	2,338	1,082
Wine and spirit merchants	2,937	524
Grocers	9,621	4,042
Tobacconists	530	44
'Others dealing in drinks etc.'	2,403	79
Drapers	4,539	315
Stationers	498	236
Coal merchants	764	
Milliners		28,902
Seamstresses		12,971

Appendix III : (b) Numbers in selected occupations in the cities 1851

Occupation	Aberdeen	Dundee	Edinburgh and Leith	Glasgow
Bakers	301	376	1,198	1,569
Butchers	292	129	731	839
Grocers	471	520	985	1,178
Drapers	140	154	538	920
Wine and spirit merchants	150			951

Source: J. H. Dawson, *The Abridged Statistical History of the Scottish Counties* (1862), 277 ff.

Appendix IV : Trends in official values (£) of imports and exports 1755– 1851

Period	Annual average for imports	Annual average for exports
1755–9	566,145	753,053
1760–4	819,720	1,117,091
1765–9	1,077,753	1,331,052
1770–4	1,225,606	1,626,066
1775–9	866,350	905,541
1780–4	935,343	835,717
1785–9	1,382,699	1,079,314
1790–4	1,653,255	1,174,476
1795–9	1,746,107	1,420,533
1800–4	2,563,102	2,422,317
1805–8	2,796,671	2,694,507
1810–4	3,169,889	6,166,564
1815–9	3,356,605	7,218,577
1820–4	3,891,565	6,004,922
1825–9	3,987,857	5,864,371
1830–4	4,373,957	7,353,802
1835–9	5,331,072	9,154,730
1840–4	6,482,950	13,118,790
1845–9	7,939,021	13,634,687
1850–1	8,938,913	17,894,610

Note: No figures are available for 1809. Where possible these annual averages have been calculated over a five-year period.

Sources: H. Hamilton, *Eighteenth Century*, Appendix VIII, pp. 414–15; R. H. Campbell and J. B. A. Dow, *Source Book of Scottish Economic and Social History* (1968), 114–15; J. H. Dawson, *Abridged Statistical History*, XXXIX

Appendix V : Statistics relating to production

(a) *Quantity and value of linen goods stamped in Scotland 1728–1822*

Period	Average annual yards	Estimated annual value (£)
1728–32	3,488,232	132,588
1733–7	4,750,827	179,451
1738–42	4,673,372	189,844
1743–7	5,645,417	231,056
1748–52	7,786,449	350,772
1753–7	8,954,199	393,344
1758–62	11,300,320	477,970
1763–7	12,798,993	595,191
1768–72	12,961,275	624,805
1773–7	12,535,149	573,166
1778–82	14,013,826	655,788
1783–7	18,082,969	860,410
1788–92	19,679,949	791,029
1793–7	21,032,819	804,608
1798–1802	23,822,765	989,554
1803–7	18,553,901	860,735
1808–12	21,758,639	1,094,422
1813–17	26,575,759	1,150,817
1818–22	30,723,707	1,215,699

Note: (i) Linen stamped for sale is not the same as total
production
     (ii) Calculations are based on five-yearly averages

Source: A. J. Warden, *The Linen Trade, Ancient and Modern*
(1867 edn), 480

Appendix V :
*(b) Spirits charged with duty in Scot-
      land 1730–1910*

Year	Gallons (thousands)
1730	209
1740	261
1750	776
1760	55
1770	70
1780	189
1790	No figures
1800	1,670
1810	1,315
1820	2,125
1830	5,777
1840	6,189
1850	6,935
1860	5,581
1870	5,364
1880	6,086
1890	6,264
1900	8,380
1910	4,559

Note: Much evasion of duty before
       1830

Source: Mitchell and Deane,
         *Abstract of British Historical
         Statistics,* 255–9

Appendix V :
*(c) Malt charged with duty in Scot-
      land 1770–1880*

Year	Imperial bushels (millions)
1770	1.8
1780	2.2
1790	1.5
1800	0.9
1810	0.8
1820	1.2
1830	4.1
1840	4.4
1850	4.6
1860	1.6
1870	2.4
1880	2.6

Notes: (i) High corn prices in 1800
            and 1810 led to govern-
            ment action against
            malting

        (ii) From August 1855 malt
             for distillery purposes
             was not charged with
             duty

Source: Mitchell and Deane,
         *Abstract of British Historical
         Statistics*, 247–9

Appendix V :
(d) Paper charged with duty in Scotland
     1737–1861

Period	Annual average tonnage
1737–41	86
1742–6	73
1747–51	70.2
1752–6	98
1757–61	154
1762–6	263
1767–71	351
1772–6	361
1777–80	297
1781	Figures defective
1782–6	403
1787–91	843
1792–6	1,203
1797–1801	1,217
1802–6	1,312
1807–11	1,559
1812–16	1,723
1817–21	2,039
1822–5	2,709
1826	No figures
1827–31	3,428
1832–6	4,581
1837–41	6,800.2
1842–6	8,754
1847–51	11,407
1852–6	15,700
1857–61	19,798

Note: Much evasion of duty in the period
        before 1782. Averages have been
        calculated using a five-year period
        when possible

Source: Mitchell and Deane, *Abstract of*
          British Historical Statistics, 263–4

Appendix V :
(e) Scottish iron ore output 1855–
      1938

Year	Tons (thousands)
1855	2,400
1860	2,150
1865	1,470
1870	1,980
1875	2,452
1880	2,659
1885	1,838
1890	999
1895	825
1900	849
1905	832
1910	648
1914	538
1923	100
1930	21
1938	17

Source: Mitchell and Deane,
         Abstract of British Historical
         Statistics, 129–30

Appendix V :
(f) Scottish coal output 1854–1945

Year	Tons (millions)
1854	7.4
1860	10.9
1865	12.7
1870	14.9
1875	18.6
1880	18.3
1885	21.3
1890	24.3
1895	28.8
1900	33.1
1905	35.8
1910	41.3
1914	38.8
1920	31.5
1925	33.0
1926	16.8
1930	31.7
1935	31.3
1940	29.7
1945	21.4

Source: Mitchell and Deane,
*Abstract of British Historical
Statistics*, 115–17

Appendix V :
(g) Scottish pig-iron output 1788–1914

Years	Tons (thousands)
1788	7
1796	16
1806	22
1823	24
1830	37
1839	196
1840	241
1843	238
1847	539
1852	775
1854–8	870
1859–63	1,017
1864–8	1,083
1869–73	1,122
1874–8	969
1879–83	1,082
1884–8	978
1889–93	830
1894–8	1,001
1899–1903	1,206
1904–8	1,358
1909–13	1,354
1914	1,126

Note: Annual averages calculated over
       five-year intervals from 1854–1913

Source: Mitchell and Deane, *Abstract of
        British Historical Statistics*, 131–3

Appendix V :
(h) Scottish pig-iron output 1915–38

Year	Tons (thousands)
1915	1,109
1916	1,125
1917	1,157
1918	1,091
1919	903
1920	903
1921	289
1922	361
1923	769
1924	668
1925	430
1926	189
1927	692
1928	550
1929	607
1930	466
1931	154
1932	144
1933	220
1934	392
1935	413
1936	471
1937	497
1938	409

Source: Mitchell and Deane,
*Abstract of British Historical
Statistics,* 133

Appendix V : (i) Inhabited house duty in Scotland 1851–1924

Year	Number of houses (thousands)	Value (£ thousands)	Value of exempt property (£ thousands)
1851	24	1,029	
1861	30	1,297	
1871	40	1,876	
1881	61	2,941	4,057
1891	71	3,300	4,784
1901	97	4,338	6,073
1911	128	5,354	7,357
1921		5,630	
1924		6,680	

Source: Mitchell and Deane, *Abstract of British Historical Statistics*, 236–8

Appendix V :
(j) Houses at censuses in Scotland 1881–1951

Year	Number of houses (thousands)
1881	799
1891	869
1901	986
1911	1,102
1921	1,109
1931	1,197
1951	1,442

Source: Mitchell and Deane, *Abstract of British Historical Statistics*, 239

Further Reading,
Notes and References

CHAPTER I

Further Reading

Virtually nothing has been written on the population of Scotland before the Union of Parliaments. On epidemics the classical work of C. Creighton *A History of Epidemics in Britain* (1894) can now be supplemented by J. F. D. Shrewsbury's *A History of the Bubonic Plague in the British Isles* (1970) which has valuable Scottish sections. Overseas emigration has been more fully explored. The modern starting point is G. Donaldson, *The Scots Overseas* (1966). The various works by T. A. Fischer [e.g. *The Scots in Germany* (1902)], are still valuable, and G. P. Insh, *Scottish Colonial Schemes* (1922) is still the best general account.

Notes and References

1 E. M. Barron, *The Scottish War of Independence* (1914), 43

2 P. H. Brown, *Scotland before 1700 from Contemporary Records* (1895), xv

3 M. Bingham, *Scotland under Mary Stuart* (1971), 21

4 Lady A. Fraser, *Mary Queen of Scots* (1969), 165

5 E.g. P. Deane and W. A. Cole, *British Economic Growth 1688–1959* (1967), 6

6 Lord Cooper, 'The Numbers and Distribution of the Population of Medieval Scotland', *SHR*, XXVI, 1947, 2–6. J. C. Russell, *Britain's Medieval Population* (1948), 362

7 J. Strawhorn, 'Ayrshire's Changing Population', *Ayrshire Archaeological and Natural History Collections*, 8, 1967–9, 12

8 C. Innes, *Sketches of Early Scotch History* (1861), 395

9 G. Donaldson, *The Scots Overseas* (1966), 28

10 All these figures are from the records of the burghs named.

11 E.g. T. C. Smout, 'The Glasgow Merchant Community in the Seventeenth Century', *SHR*, XLVII, 1968, 53–71

12 Quotations from contemporary writers, except where otherwise indicated, are taken either from P. H. Brown, *Early Travellers in Scotland* (1891) or from W. C. Dickinson and G. Donaldson, *A Source Book of Scottish History*, I (1958)

13 P. Ziegler, *The Black Death* (1969) and J. F. D. Shrewsbury, *A History of the Bubonic Plague in the British Isles* (1970)

14 R. Chambers, *Domestic Annals of Scotland* (1858), I, 55

15 W. Mackay (ed.), *Chronicles of the Frasers*, Scot. Hist. Soc. XLVII (1905)

16 R. C. Buist, 'Peter Goldman's Description of the Desolation of Dundee', *British Medical Journal*, March 1927

17 J. F. D. Shrewsbury, *Bubonic Plague*, 430

18 J. Scotland, *The History of Scottish Education*, I (1969), 25

19 G. Donaldson, *Scots Overseas*, 26

20 A. Shearer (ed.), *Extracts from the Burgh Records of Dunfermline* (1951), 39

21 A debatable issue. See especially J. Dow, 'Skotter in Sixteenth-Century Scandia', *SHR*, XLIV, 1965

CHAPTER II

Further Reading

J. A. Symon, *Scottish Farming Past and Present* (1959) is the only approach to a comprehensive account of Scottish agricultural history. There is much medieval material in I. F. Grant, *Social and Economic Development of Scotland before 1603* (1930, reprint 1971) and in T. B. Franklin, *A History of Scottish Farming* (1952), the latter being particularly good on monastic farming. G. W. S. Barrow, *The Kingdom of the Scots* (1973) must be read for an understanding of the complexity of tenurial arrangements in the period *c.* 1100–*c.* 1400. W. C. Mackenzie, *The Highlands and Isles of Scotland* (1937, revised ed. 1950) has some useful material on land tenure and utilisation and so have a number of local and county histories. M. L. Anderson, *A History of Scottish Forestry* (2 vols, 1967), contains a mass of information on both the ecological and legal aspects of forestry and on the timber-using industries. *The Agricultural History Review* has a few articles of specifically Scottish interest.

Notes and References

1 I. F. Grant, *Economic and Social Development of Scotland before 1603* (1930, reprint 1971), 44 and 65

2 G. G. Coulton, *Scottish Abbeys and Social Life* (1933), *passim*; J. Fergusson, *The White Hind* (1963), 57–60; T. B. Franklin, *A History of Scottish Farming* (1952), IV, V and VI

3 Coulton, *op. cit.*, 155

4 *La practica della mercatura*, printed in W. Cunningham, *Growth of English Industry and Commerce*, I (1922 ed.), Appendix D

5 T. C. Smout, *A History of the Scottish People* (1969), 41

6 C. Rogers (ed.), *Rental Book of the Cistercian Abbey of Coupar Angus* (Grampian Club, 1879).

7 G. Neilson, 'The Feuing of Drygrange from the Monastery of Melrose', *SHR*, VII, 1909, 358–9

8 W. Mackay (ed.), *Chronicles of the Frasers*, Scot. Hist. Soc., XLVII, (1905), 485

9 A. C. O'Dell and K. Walton, *The Highlands and Islands of Scotland* (1962), 96

10 W. Robertson, *The History of Scotland*, I (1794), 115

11 C. Innes, *Sketches of Early Scotch History* (1861), 375

12 R. Edward, *A Description of the County of Angus 1678* (reprinted, Forfar and District Hist. Soc. 1967)

13 A great 'tinchel' was witnessed by John Taylor, the 'Water-Poet', and described by him in his *Pennyles Pilgrimage* (1618)

14 Conveniently listed in J. A. Symon, *Scottish Farming Past and Present* (1959), Appendix II

15 Symon, *op. cit.*, 87; on crop yields *c.* 1600 see J. E. L. Murray, 'The Agriculture of Crail, 1550–1600', *Scottish Studies*, 8, 1964, 89–90

16 C. Innes (ed.), *The Black Book of Taymouth* (Bannatyne Club, 1885), 352–6

17 A. Ballard, 'The Theory of the Scottish Burgh', *SHR*, XIII, 1915, 16–29; R. Mitchison, 'The Movement of Scottish Corn Prices in the 17th and 18th centuries', *EcHR*, XVIII, 1965, 281

18 On this period important suggestions are advanced in T. C. Smout and A. Fenton, 'Scottish Agriculture before the Improvers', *Agric. Hist. Rev.*, XIII, 1965, 73–93

CHAPTER III

Further Reading

Stimulating introductions to the history of building in Scotland are provided by W. D. Simpson, *The Ancient Stones of Scotland* (1965) and by J. G. Dunbar, *Historic Architecture of Scotland* (1965). S. Cruden, *The Scottish Castle* (1960) has excellent material especially on the military aspects of building. A good deal has been written about Scottish burgh development: W. M. Mackenzie, *The Scottish Burghs* (1949) and D. Murray, *Early Burgh Organisation in Scotland* (1924) provide useful starting points for more specialised reading. T. Pagan, *The Convention of the Royal Burghs of Scotland* (1926) is the standard work on its theme. Many burgh and guild records, some with scholarly introductions, have been published, and virtually any Scottish public library will have a reasonable sample. Amongst these *Dumbarton Common Good Accounts,* edited by F. Roberts and I. M. M. Macphail (1972) is a good example, containing both administrative and economic material for the early seventeenth century.

Notes and References

1 P. H. Brown, *Scotland before 1700 from Contemporary Records* (1895), XVI, and W. C. Dickinson, *Scotland from the Earliest Times to 1603* (1961), 228

2 W. D. Simpson, *The Ancient Stones of Scotland* (1965), XIV

3 W. C. Dickinson (ed.), *Early Records of the Burgh of Aberdeen* (1957), XXXI

4 T. C. Smout, *A History of the Scottish People* (1969), 31

5 W. B. Cook and D. B. Thomis (eds), *Extracts from the Records of the Merchant Guild of Stirling* (1916), 66 and 90

6 G. S. Pryde (ed.), *The Court Book of the Burghs of Kirkintilloch, 1658–1694* (1963), XXXVIII

7 T. Pagan, *The Convention of the Royal Burgh of Scotland* (1926), 150

8 I. F. Grant, *Social and Economic Development before 1603* (1930, reprint 1971), 368

9 Pryde, *op. cit.*, lxxi

10 The Ayr material is from G. S. Pryde (ed.), *Ayr Burgh Accounts* (1937)

11 This paragraph is based on J. Elder, *History of Early Scottish Education* (1893) and J. Scotland, *The History of Scottish Education* (1969)

12 Summarised in G. Nicholls, *A History of the Scotch Poor Law* (1856)

13 A. Maxwell, *The History of Old Dundee* (1884), 297

14 G. Eyre-Todd, *History of Glasgow,* II (1931), 259

15 P. H. Brown, *Scotland in the Time of Queen Mary* (1904), 160

16 A. J. Warden (ed.), *Burgh Laws of Dundee* (1872), 336

17 S. G. E. Lythe, *The Economy of Scotland 1550–1625* (1960), 113

CHAPTER IV

Further Reading

There is no book devoted specifically to the early history of industry in Scotland. Some material may be found in I. F. Grant, *Social and Economic Development before 1603* (1930, reprint 1971), R. W. Cochran-Patrick, *Mediaeval Scotland* (1892), W. C. Dickinson, *Scotland from the Earliest Times to 1603* (1961), S. G. E. Lythe, *The Economy of Scotland 1550–1625* (1960) and similar general works. Some individual industries have received attention, for example R. W. Cochran-Patrick *Early Records relating to Mining in Scotland* (1878); A. Fleming, *Scotland*

and Jacobite Glass (1938); I. Finlay, *Scottish Gold and Silver Work* (1956); D. Thomson, *The Weaver's Craft* (1903), and there is much Scottish material in J. U. Nef, *The Rise of the British Coal Industry* (1934); A. and N. L. Clow, *The Chemical Revolution* (1952) and W. R. Scott, *The Constitution and Finance of Joint-Stock Companies to 1720* (1910).

Notes and References

1 C. Innes, *Sketches of Early Scotch History* (1861), 131–2

2 Several similar fragments of evidence can be found in J. Bain (ed.), *Calendars of State Papers relating to Scotland* (various dates)

3 I. F. Grant, *Social and Economic Development before 1603* (1930, reprint 1971), 317

4 J. U. Nef, *The Rise of the British Coal Industry* (1932), 19–20

5 R. Douglas, *The Peerage of Scotland,* I (1813), 517; A. I. Bowman, 'Culross Colliery', *Industrial Archaeology,* 7, 4, 1970, 355

6 T. C. Smout, *A History of the Scottish People* (1969), 180

7 W. Brereton, *Travels in Holland . . . Scotland and Ireland, 1634–5* (1844 ed.), 98

8 W. G. Aitken, 'Excavation of Bloomeries in Rannoch and elsewhere', *Proceedings of the Society of Antiquaries of Scotland,* 102, 1973, 188–204

9 W. I. Macadam, 'Notes on the ancient iron industry of Scotland', *Proceedings of the Society of Antiquaries of Scotland,* IX, 1887, 89–131

10 J. Jolliffe (ed.), *Froissart's Chronicles* (1968), 265

11 R. W. Cochran-Patrick, *Early Records relating to Mining in Scotland* (1878), 4–9

12 R. Douglas, *op. cit.,* I, 743

13 *The Diary of Sir John Hope 1646,* Scot. Hist. Soc., L (1958)

14 I. Finlay, *Scottish Gold and Silver Work* (1956), 57

15 A. Fleming, *Scottish and Jacobite Glass* (1938), 100

16 W. C. Dickinson (ed.), *Early Records of the Burgh of Aberdeen* (1957), XCV–XCVIII

17 I. F. Grant, *op. cit.,* 116

18 A summary of S. G. E. Lythe, *The Economy of Scotland 1550–1625* (1960), 38–40 and 93–95

19 W. R. Scott, *The Constitution and Finance of Joint-Stock Companies to 1720* (1910), III, 124–129; W. R. Scott (ed.), *Minute Book of the Managers of the New Mills Cloth Manufactory 1681–1690* (1905)

20 G. Eyre-Todd, *History of Glasgow,* III (1934), 75; W. R. Scott, *Joint-Stock Companies,* III, 187 and 191

21 By A. J. S. Brook, quoted in I. Finlay, *op. cit.,* 41

22 G. E. P. How, quoted in I. Finlay, *op. cit.,* 73

23 W. R. Scott, *Joint-Stock Companies,* III, 180

24 W. Mackay (ed.), *Chronicles of the Frasers,* Scot. Hist. Soc., XLVII (1905), 297

CHAPTER V

Further Reading

On the sea fisheries there is useful material in J. R. Elder, *The Royal Fishery Companies* (1912) and in A. M. Samuel, *The Herring, its Effects on the History of Britain* (1918). Overseas trade between the Restoration and 1707 is fully treated in T. C. Smout, *Scottish Trade on the Eve of the Union* (1963); for earlier periods little has been written on trade generally except in I. F. Grant, *Social and Economic Development before 1603* (1930, reprint 1971) and S. G. E. Lythe, *The Economy of Scotland 1550–1625* (1960).

Some selected topics are well covered. On the staple at Veere there are two classic studies: M. P. Rooseboom, *The Scottish Staple in the Netherlands* (1910)

and J. Davidson and A. Gray, *The Scottish Staple at Veere* (1909). T. Keith, *Commercial Relations of England and Scotland, 1603–1707* (1910) is still useful. Stimulating tastes of original material can be got from *The Ledger of Andrew Halyburton, Conservator of the Privileges of the Scottish Nation in the Netherlands*, ed. C. Innes (1867); 'Shipping Lists of Dundee', in *The Compt Buik of David Wedderburne*, ed. A. H. Millar (1898) and in *Aberdeen Shore Works Accounts 1596–1670*, ed. L. B. Taylor (1972), but Scotland is very short of early commercial records and reliance has to be placed heavily on Scandinavian, Dutch and French sources. The Darien Scheme has been the subject of many studies, the most recent being J. Prebble, *The Darien Disaster* (1968). W. S. Reid's *Skipper from Leith* (Philadelphia, 1962) is an excellent case study of an early sixteenth-century merchant with much valuable material on trade, naval warfare and public finance.

Notes and References

1 *The Calendars of Documents Relating to Scotland* have thirty-seven such references between 1357 and 1509

2 W. Mackay (ed.), *Chronicles of the Frasers*, Scot. Hist. Soc., XLVII (1905), 251

3 I. F. Grant, *Social and Economic Development before 1603* (1930, reprint 1971), 549

4 J. R. Elder, *The Royal Fishery Companies* (1912); W. R. Scott, *The Constitution and Finance of Joint-Stock Companies to 1720* (1910), II

5 'Aberdeen Register of Births', printed in J. Maidment (ed.), *Analecta Scotica* (1832), I, 286

6 G. Eyre-Todd, *History of Glasgow*, II, (1931), 217

7 The primary source is *The Calendars of Documents Relating to Scotland*; see also Grant, *op. cit.*, 113–117

8 E. E. Power and M. M. Postan (eds), *Studies in English Trade in the Fifteenth Century* (1933)

9 Grant, *op. cit.*, 336

10 J. W. Dilley, 'German Merchants in Scotland', *SHR*, XXVII, 1948, 155

11 S. G. E. Lythe, *The Economy of Scotland 1550–1625* (1960), VII

12 T. C. Smout, *Scottish Trade on the Eve of Union* (1963), 26

13 Quoted in T. A. Fischer, *The Scots in Germany* (1902), 3

14 P. Dollinger, *La Hanse, XIIᵉ-XVIIᵉ siècles* (1964), 305

15 Grant, *op. cit.*, 339

16 Dollinger, *op. cit.*, 482

17 S. G. E. Lythe, 'Scottish Trade with the Baltic 1550–1650', in J. K. Eastham (ed.), *Dundee Economic Essays* (1955), 63–84

18 J. Dow, 'Scottish Trade with Sweden 1512–80', *SHR*, XLVIII, 1 (1969) and 'Scottish Trade with Sweden 1580–1622', *SHR*, XLVIII, 2, 1969

19 J. Davidson and A. Gray, *The Scottish Staple at Veere* (1909), 133–140; R. K. Hannay, 'Shipping and the Staple', *Book of the Old Edinburgh Club*, 9 (1916), 49–77

20 Davidson and Gray, *op. cit.*, 211

21 Notably H. J. Smit (ed.), *Bronnen Tot de Geschiedenis van del Handel met Engeland, Schotland en Ierland* (1928)

22 T. C. Smout, *Scottish Trade*, 167

23 M. Mollat, *Le commerce maritime normand à la fin du moyen âge* (1952), 171 and 508

24 E. Trocmé et M. Delafosse, *Le commerce rochelais à la fin du moyen âge* (1952), 84

25 D. Matthew, *Scotland under Charles I* (1955), 109

26 Based on Dundee Shipping lists printed in A. H. Millar (ed.), *The Compt Buik of David Wedderburne*, Scot. Hist. Soc. (1898); M. Wood (ed.), *Extracts from the Records of the Burgh of Edinburgh*, VI (1936), Appendix XV

27 G. S. Pryde (ed.), *Ayr Burgh Accounts 1534–1624*, Scot. Hist. Soc., 1937, 161

28 W. L. Mathieson, *Politics and Religion, A Study in Scottish History* (1902), I, 257

29 R. W. Cochran-Patrick, *Mediaeval Scotland* (1892), 104 and 121

30 E.g. W. A. McNeill, 'Papers of a Dundee Shipping Dispute 1600–1604', in *Miscellany X*, Scot. Hist. Soc. (1965)

31 T. Tucker, 'Report upon the Settlement of the revenues in Scotland AD 1656', *Miscellany of Scottish Burgh Records Society* (1881), 26

32 T. C. Smout 'The Development and

Enterprise of Glasgow', *SJPE*, VII, 1960, 208

33 J. McUre, *The History of Glasgow* (1736), 170–1

34 P. Gouldesbrough, 'An attempted Scottish Voyage to New York in 1669', *SHR*, XL, 1961, 56–62; T. Keith, *Commercial Relations of England and Scotland 1603–1707* (1910), 112–117

35 T. C. Smout, 'The Glasgow Merchant Community in the seventeenth century,

SHR, XLVII, 1968, 56

36 D. Matthew, *Scotland under Charles I* (1955), 100. I am grateful to Mr McFaulds for information on this subject.

37 R. K. Hannay (ed.), *Rentale Dunkeldense: being the Accounts of the Chamberlain of the Bishopric of Dunkeld 1506–17*, Scot. Hist. Soc. (1915)

38 *Extracts from the Records of the Royal Burgh of Lanark* (1893), 251

CHAPTER VI

Further Reading

The relationship between political and economic affairs in Scotland can—with perseverance—be detected in such recent works as W. C. Dickinson, *Scotland from the Earliest Times to 1603* (1961), G. Donaldson, *Scotland, James V to James VII* (1965) and W. Ferguson, *Scotland 1689 to the Present Day* (1968), which largely replace the older general histories, though W. L. Mathieson, *Politics and Religion: a Study of Scottish History from the Reformation to the Revolution* (2 vols, 1902) is still useful. On the Scottish parliament we still rely on R. S. Rait, *The Parliaments of Scotland* (1924) and C. S. Terry, *The Scottish Parliament, its Constitution and Procedure, 1603–1707* (1905).

Scottish public finance awaits its economic historian, but a vast amount of economic material on some aspects is available in R. W. Cochran-Patrick, *Records of the Coinage of Scotland* (2 vols, 1876).

Important recent works on the Reformation (with some attention to its economic and social aspects) are G. Donaldson, *The Scottish Reformation* (1960) and D. McRoberts (ed.) *Essays on the Scottish Reformation* (1962). The economic consequences of the Commonwealth await a modern scholar, but the Union of 1707 has had much attention. The best modern introduction is T. C. Smout, 'The Road to Union', in G. Holmes (ed.), *Britain after the Glorious Revolution 1689–1714* (1969).

Notes and References

1 W. Robertson, *The History of Scotland*, I (1794), 33

2 J. A. Mackie, *A History of Scotland* (1964), 119

3 A. S. Robertson, 'The Renfrew (1963) Coin Hoard', *Glasgow Archaeological Journal* (1969), 72

4 R. W. Cochran-Patrick, *Mediaeval Scotland* (1892), 84–100

5 R. Mitchison, *A History of Scotland* (1970), 134

6 W. Mackay (ed.), *Chronicles of the Frasers*, Scot. Hist. Soc., XLVII (1905), 415, 447

7 G. Donaldson, *Scotland, James V to James*

VII (1965), 133; M. H. B. Sanderson, 'The Feuars of Kirklands', *SHR*, LII, 1973, 117–136

8 W. L. Mathieson, *Politics and Religion: a Study of Scottish History from the Reformation to the Revolution* (1902), 26

9 J. Major, *History of Greater Britain* (Trans. A. Constable, 1892), 136

10 J. Ridley, *John Knox* (1968), 380

11 J. Fergusson, *The White Hart* (1963), 60

12 Donaldson, *op. cit.*, 296–98

13 T. C. Smout, *A History of the Scottish People* (1969), III

14 M. Weber, *The Protestant Ethic and the*

Spirit of Capitalism (1930)

15 M. Lee, 'The Scottish Reformation after 400 years', *SHR*, XLIV, 1965, 141–3; S. A. Burrell, 'Calvinism and the Middle Classes', *Journal of Modern History*, XXXII, 1960, 129–41

16 S. G. E. Lythe, *The Economy of Scotland*

1550–1625 (1960), 202–3

17 On the economic background see especially T. C. Smout, 'The Anglo-Scottish Union of 1707', *EcHR*, XVI, 1964, 455–67

18 T. C. Smout, *Scottish Trade on the Eve of Union 1660–1707* (1963), XII

CHAPTER VII

Further Reading

To put the Scottish story into a wider context consult M. W. Flinn, *British Population Growth 1750–1850* (1970) which also has an excellent bibliography. T. C. Smout, *A History of the Scottish People* (1969) has useful sections relating to population as does R. H. Campbell, *Scotland since 1707: the Rise of an Industrial Society* (1965) and H. Hamilton, *An Economic History of Scotland in the Eighteenth Century* (1963). D. F. Macdonald, *Scotland's Shifting Population 1770–1850* (1937) considers a range of questions but particularly migration. On emigration, the best studies are I. C. C. Graham, *Colonists from Scotland* (New York, 1956) and G. Donaldson, *The Scots Overseas* (1966). On Irish settlement in this period J. E. Handley, *The Irish in Scotland 1798–1845* (1945) is invaluable.

Notes and References

1 T. C. Smout, *Scottish Trade on the Eve of Union* (1963), 246–8; R. Mitchison, 'The Movement of Scottish Corn Prices in the seventeenth and eighteenth centuries', *EcHR*, 2nd series, XVIII, 2, 1965, 287

2 *Vide infra*, p. 3

3 Webster's figures are given in full in J. G. Kyd, *Scottish Population Statistics*, Scot. Hist. Soc., 3rd series, XLIV, 1952, 1–81

4 A. J. Youngson, 'Alexander Webster and his "Account of the Number of People in Scotland in the Year 1755"', *Population Studies*, XV, 1961–2, 198–200; D. F. Macdonald, *Scotland's Shifting Population 1770–1850* (1937), 4

5 Kyd, *op. cit.*, xviii

6 K. Helleiner, 'The Population of Europe from the Black Death to the Eve of the Vital Revolution', *Cambridge Economic History of Europe* (1967), 1; cf. also his 'The Vital Revolution Reconsidered', *Canadian Journal of Economics and Political Science*, XXIII, 1957, reprinted in D. V. Glass and D. C. Eversley (eds), *Population in History* (1965), 79–86

7 Cf. the stimulating discussions in H. J.

Habakkuk, 'The Economic History of Modern Britain', *Journal of Economic History*, XVIII, 1958, 468–501, reprinted in *Population in History*, 147–58 and in M. W. Flinn, *British Population Growth 1700–1850* (1970), *passim*

8 *Census of Scotland*, 1801

9 Macdonald, *op. cit.*, 158–9; *OSA*, xvii, 562; J. E. Handley, *The Irish in Scotland* (1945) *passim*; *BPP*, 1835, XXXII, Report on the Irish Poor in Great Britain, Appendix G, 152–8 *passim*

10 J. M. Houston, 'Village Planning in Scotland 1745–1845', *Advancement of Science*, V, 1948, 129–32; T. C. Smout, 'The Landowner and the Planned Village in Scotland 1730–1830', in N. T. Phillipson and R. Mitchison, *Scotland in the Age of Improvement* (1970), 73–106; J. D. Wood, 'Regulating Settlers and Establishing Industry', *Scottish Studies*, XV, 1971, 39–52

11 J. R. Hume and J. Butt, 'Muirkirk 1786–1802: the creation of a Scottish industrial community', *SHR*, XLV, 1966, 160–83

12 J. Butt, 'Glenbuck Ironworks', *Ayrshire Collections*, 8, 1967–9, 68–75

13 I. Donnachie and J. Butt, 'The 'Wilsons of Wilsontown Ironworks 1779–1813', *Explorations in Entrepreneurial History,* 2nd series, IV, 1967, 150–68

14 J. R. Hume, 'The Industrial Archaeology of New Lanark', J. Butt (ed.), *Robert Owen, Prince of Cotton Spinners* (1971), 215–53; *OSA,* xv, 34 ff.

15 *NSA,* X, Perthshire, 1844, 1233–9

16 J. H. G. Lebon, 'The Beginnings of the Agrarian and Industrial Revolution in Ayrshire', reprinted in J. Strawhorn (ed.), *Ayrshire at the time of Burns* (1959), 170; *OSA,* xx, 175 ff.

17 *NSA,* X, 435 and 440

18 Smout, *Scottish Trade,* 90–5

19 Cf. V. Morgan, 'Agricultural Wage Rates in late Eighteenth-Century Scotland', *EcHR,* 2nd series, XXIV, 1971, 181–201

20 *Census,* 1801 and 1811

21 Cf. A Sabbath School Teacher [William Logan], *The Moral Statistics of Glasgow in 1863 practically applied* (1864), 77

22 Cf. A. G. Macpherson, 'An Old Highland Parish Register, Survivals of Clanship and Social Change in Laggan, Inverness-shire 1775–1869', *Scottish Studies,* XI, 2, 1967, 149–62 and XII, 2, 1968, 102 ff. especially; *OSA, passim*

23 Mitchison, 'Corn Prices', 282–3

24 Ibid., 278–91; J. R. McCulloch, *A Statistical Account of the British Empire* (1837), i, 424n.; *BPP,* 1846, Accounts and Papers, XXVII, 502, Report on Distress in Scotland 1783; *OSA,* xiv, 419; xvi, 193; S. G. E. Lythe, 'The Tayside meal mobs 1772–3', *SHR,* XLVI, 1967, 26–36

25 M. Gray, *The Highland Economy* (1957), *passim*

26 E. R. Cregeen (ed.), *Argyll Estate Instructions 1771–1805,* Scot. Hist. Soc. (1964), i, xxviii–xix

27 Kyd, *op. cit.,* 80–1

28 T. H. Hollingsworth, 'A Demographic Study of British Ducal Families', *Population Studies,* XI, 1957, 4–26; and cf. also his *The Demography of the British Peerage,* supplement to *Population Studies,* XVIII, 1964

29 Flinn, *op. cit.,* 38–9n. Swedish experience in the eighteenth century was essentially of a fall in death-rate.

30 Directed by Professor Flinn

31 T. C. Smout, *A History of the Scottish People* (1969), 271 ff; R. H. Campbell, *Scotland since 1707: the Rise of an Industrial Society* (1965), 16; P. E. Razzell, 'Population Growth and Economic Change in England', reprinted in E. L. Jones and G. E. Mingay (eds), *Land, Labour and Population in the Industrial Revolution* (1967), 263

32 Flinn, *op. cit.,* 44; J. Cleland, *Abridgment of the Annals of Glasgow* (1817), 510n.

33 Cf. Cleland, 508 ff.

34 H. G. Graham, *The Social Life of Scotland in the eighteenth century* (1899), ii, 207 ff.

35 Improvements by Burgh regulations, local Acts or Police Acts. Cf. J. H. F. Brotherston, *The Early Public Health Movement in Scotland* (1952), *passim*; N Longmate, *King Cholera: the biography of a disease* (1966), 56–7

36 H. Hamilton, *An Economic History of Scotland in the Eighteenth Century,* (1963), 380 ff.

37 Ibid., 377–9; cf. R. N. Salaman, *The History and Social Influence of the Potato* (1949); C. Creighton, *History of Epidemics in Britain* (reprint ed. 1965)

38 Hamilton, *op. cit.,* 378 ff.; there is frequent comment in *OSA* about the acquisition of luxuries, e.g. V, 403–4; cf. also John Galt, *Annals of the Parish* (1919 ed.), 15, 70, 185 and John Mitchell, *Memories of Ayrshire about 1780* (1939), 262–6

39 *Census,* 1871

40 Cf. William Mackenzie, *A History of the Highland Clearances* (1883); I. Grimble, *The Trial of Patrick Sellar* (1962); J. Prebble, *The Highland Clearances* (1963)

41 *Census,* 1871

42 L. J. Saunders, *Scottish Democracy 1815–40* (1950), 130; *Census,* 1871

43 Saunders, *op. cit.,* 137; *Census,* 1871

44 *Census,* 1851 and 1871

45 *Census,* 1851; J. B. Russell, *Public Health Administration in Glasgow* (1905), 303

46 *Census,* 1851

47 *James Beattie's London Diary 1773* (1946), *passim*; J. G. Fyfe (ed.), *Scottish Diaries and Memoirs 1746–1843* (1942), 129–30

48 *SRO,* Abercromby of Forglen Muniments, Letterbook of Douglas and Shaw

49 *Census*, 1851, Pt II, i, Rept cii; G. Best, *Mid-Victorian Britain* (1971), 15

50 Cf. J. Morley, *Life of Gladstone* (1903), i, 7–9; S. G. Checkland, *The Gladstones* (1971), 3 ff.

51 T. A. Fischer, *The Scots in Sweden* (1907), *passim*; his *The Scots in Germany* (1902) 51 ff., 118 ff.; A. F. Steuart, *Scottish Influences on Russian History* (1913), 124 ff.

52 G. Donaldson, *The Scots Overseas* (1966), 31

53 J. Walker, *Economical History of the Hebrides and Highlands of Scotland* (1808), ii, 400

54 SRO, GD 103, Society of Antiquaries Papers; Irvine Robertson Muniments, 73–4; Donaldson, *op. cit.*, 57

55 I. C. C. Graham, *Colonists from Scotland* (New York, 1956), 25 ff.

56 J. Knox, *A Tour through the Highlands and Islands of Scotland* (1787), 2; I. C. C. Graham, *op. cit.*, 185–9; J. D. Wood, 'Scottish Migration Overseas', *SGM*, LXXX, 1964, 164–177

57 *BPP*, 1803, VIII, Pt II, A Survey of the Coasts and Central Highlands of Scotland, p. 15

58 SRO, Broughton and Cally Muniments, GD 10/489 and 1421–46

59 T. D. Selkirk, *Observations on the Present State of the Highlands of Scotland with a view to emigration* (1805) 48, 54 and 83; M. I. Adam, 'The Highland Emigration of 1770', *SHR*, XVI, 1919, 280–93; and 'The Causes of the Highland Emigrations 1783–1803', *SHR*, XVII, 1920, 73–89

60 E.g. SRO, Airlie Muniments, GD 16/35/68, copy letter from James Robison, 17 Jan 1830; Barclay Allardyce Muniments, GD 3/520, Account of the family of John Barclay; Breadalbane Muniments, Box H/63; Lindsay Muniments, Box 21; John MacGregor Collection, 186/125

61 A. Irvine, *An Inquiry into the Causes and Effects of Emigration from the Highlands and Islands of Scotland* (1804), 66; I. C. C. Graham, *op. cit.*, 23

62 SRO, Ailsa Muniments, GD 25/9/Box 27; Clerk of Penicuik Muniments, GD 18/5360, Letters of Patrick Houston 1727–48; Cunningham of Lainshaw Muniments, GD 247, Letterbooks give

much local data; I. C. C. Graham, *op. cit.*, 34 ff.

63 I. C. C. Graham, *op. cit.*, 29 ff.

64 R. H. Campbell and J. B. A. Dow, *Source Book of Scottish Economic and Social History* (1968), 2–3

65 43, Geo. III, *c.* 56

66 Cregreen, *op. cit.*, 201n.; *BPP*, 1827, V, Reports on Emigration, 500 ff.

67 SRO, Breadalbane Muniments, Box H/63

68 SRO, Records of the Church of Scotland

69 James Taylor, 'Journal of Local Events or Annals of Fenwick', *Ayrshire Collections*, 9, 1970, 8

70 J. M. Gray, *Lord Selkirk of Red River* (1963), *passim*

71 James Taylor, 'The Emigrant's Salute to America', *Ayrshire Collections*, 9, 1970, 19

72 This view by Dr Charlotte Erickson, who is working on emigration from Britain to North America, is based on the evidence of emigrant shipping lists *inter alia*.

73 Donaldson, *op. cit.*, 114 ff. and 152 ff.

74 *Census*, 1871

75 J. E. Handley, *The Irish in Scotland 1798–1845* (1945), *passim*

76 Ibid., 89–90; *Census*, 1841, preface 13; *Census*, 1871

77 J. Stark, 'Vital Statistics of Scotland', *Statistical Journal*, XIV, 1851, 73–4

78 B. R. Mitchell and P. Deane, *Abstract of British Historical Statistics* (1962), 31 ff.

79 Longmate, *op. cit.*, 50–63, 167–8, 180, 222

80 R. Cowan, *Vital Statistics of Glasgow* (1838); *Vital Statistics, illustrating the sanitary condition of the population* (1840); J. Strang, *Economic and Social Statistics of Glasgow* (1862)

81 Longmate, *op. cit.*, 222

82 For stimulating discussions of this topic cf. M. Drake (ed.), *Population in Industrialization* (1969); M. W. Flinn, *The Origins of the Industrial Revolution* (1966), 19–36; R. M. Hartwell (ed.), *The Causes of the Industrial Revolution* (1967); D. V. Glass and D. C. Eversley (eds), *op. cit.*

83 A. R. B. Haldane, *The Drove Roads of Scotland* (1952, reprint 1968, 1973), *passim*; Hamilton, *op. cit.*, 90 ff.; J. Butt, *The Industrial Archaeology of Scotland* (1967), 15

84 Mitchison, 'Corn Prices', 282 ff.; Hamilton, *op. cit.*, 351–7

85 Morgan, 'Agricultural Wage rates', 181–201

86 Hamilton, *op. cit.*, 377 ff.; W. Aiton, *Agricultural Report, Ayrshire* (1811), 534

87 Campbell and Dow, *op. cit.*, 3–4

88 Hamilton, *op. cit.*, 377 ff.; A. Smith, *Wealth of Nations* (1904 ed.), I, 200

89 Hamilton, *op. cit.*, 351 ff.

90 R. H. Campbell (ed.), *States of the Annual Progress of the Linen Manufacture 1727–54* (1964)

91 Hamilton, *op. cit.*, Appendix IV, 404–5

92 *Vide infra*, p. 193

93 J. H. F. Brotherston, *op. cit., passim*

94 Cf. S. Kuznets, *Economic Growth and Structure* (1966), 13 and 57

95 Best, *op. cit.*, 220

96 Sources for this table: Kyd, *op. cit.*, 81–1; *Census*, 1871. I am grateful to Mrs A. M. C. MacEwan who assisted with the calculations upon which the table is based.

97 Best, *op. cit.*, 79

98 Saunders, *op. cit.*, 388

99 Best, *op. cit.*, 86 and 98

100 Ibid., 100 and 108–9

CHAPTER VIII

Further Reading

There is excellent information in the *Statistical Accounts,* the *General Views of Agriculture* and the accounts of tours by Pennant and Cobbett. Useful sections appear in the books by Hamilton, Smout, and Campbell cited in Chapter VII. Specialist studies worth consulting are T. Bedford Franklin, *A History of Scottish Farming* (1952), J. E. Handley, *Scottish Farming in the Eighteenth Century* (1953), M. Gray, *The Highland Economy* (1957), J. A. Symon, *Scottish Farming, Past and Present* (1959). A. R. Haldane, *The Drove Roads of Scotland* (1952, reprint 1968, 1973) is a classic account of the cattle trade.

Notes and References

1 Anon. [William Mackintosh], *An Essay on Ways and Means of Inclosing, Fallowing, Planting etc in Scotland; and that in Sixteen Years at farthest* (1729), 257

2 Daniel Defoe, *A Tour thro' the whole Island of Great Britain* (1727)

3 T. Pennant, *Tour in Scotland and voyage to the Hebrides 1772* (1774)

4 S. Johnson, *A Journey to the Western Islands of Scotland* (1775)

5 W. Cobbett, *A Tour in Scotland and in the Four Northern Counties of England* (1833)

6 G. East, 'Land Utilisation in Lanarkshire at the end of the eighteenth century', *SGM*, LIII, 1937, 91–2

7 The Scottish land market requires a great deal more investigation. Cf. T. M. Devine, 'Glasgow Colonial Merchants and Land 1770–1815', in J. T. Ward and R. G. Wilson (eds), *Land and Industry* (1971), 205–44

8 *Acts of Parliament of Scotland*, VII, 263

9 Ibid., 576

10 Ibid., VIII, 488

11 Ibid., IX, 421

12 Ibid., IX, 462

13 R. H. Campbell, *Scotland since 1707: the Rise of an Industrial Society* (1965), 18–23; A. Birnie, 'Ridge cultivation in Scotland', *SHR*, XXIV, 1927, 194–201; J. H. Romanes, 'An Enclosure Proceeding in Melrose in 1742', *SHR*, XIII, 1916, 101; Sir John Sinclair, *Analysis of the Statistical Account of Scotland* (1831 ed.), I, 229 ff.; G. Whittington, 'The problem of runrig', *SGM*, LXXXVI, 1970, 69–73

14 J. Headrick, General View of the Agriculture of Bute (1807), 307

15 J. B. Caird, 'The Making of the Scottish Rural Landscape', *SGM*, LXXX, 1964, 72–80

16 G. Robertson, *Rural Recollections* (1829), 20

17 Cf. D. Turnock, 'North Morar—the Improving Movement on a west Highland estate', *SGM*, LXXXV, 1969, 17–30

18 I. F. Grant, 'The Highland Openfield System', *Geographical Teacher*, Autumn 1926; *NSA*, v, 30; viii, 28, 55, 654; xiv, 110; H. Hamilton, *The Industrial Revolution in Scotland* (1932), 13, 14, 18; W. P. L. Thomson, 'Funzie, Fetlar: a Shetland runrig township in the nineteenth century', *SGM*, LXXXVI, 1970, 170–85; H. A. Moisley, 'North Uist in 1799', *SGM*, LXXVII, 1961, 89–92; M. Gray, *The Highland Economy* (1957), 6, 19–20, 82, 84, 233

19 R. H. Campbell, *op. cit.*, 24–34; G. Kay, 'The Landscape of Improvement', *SGM*, LXXVIII, 1962, 100–11; A. Fell, *The Early Iron Industry of Furness and District* (1908), 347 ff.; I. Donnachie, *The Industrial Archaeology of Galloway* (1971), 59; Lady Strachey (ed.), *Memoirs of a Highland Lady* (1899), 171–2, 196; T. Dick Lauder, *The Moray Floods* (1873 ed.), 158; W. H. Marwick, *Scotland in Modern Times* (1964), 29

20 Robertson, *op. cit.*, 352 ff.; R. H. Campbell, *op. cit.*, 34–37

21 F. V. Emery, 'A "Geographical Description" of Scotland prior to the Statistical Accounts', *Scottish Studies*, III, 1959, 12; W. A. J. Prevost, 'Letters reporting the rising of the Levellers in 1724', *Trans. Dumfries and Galloway Arch. Soc.*, 44, 1967, 196–207; cf. also his 'Sir John Clerk's journey into Galloway in 1735', ibid., 42, 1965, 133–9; R. Forsyth, *The Beauties of Scotland* (1806), II, 369

22 E. Cregreen, 'The changing role of the House of Argyll in the Scottish Highlands', in N. T. Phillipson and R. Mitchison (eds), *Scotland in the Age of Improvement* (1970), 10 ff.

23 E. Cregreen, 'The Tacksmen and their Successors. A study in Tenurial reorganisation in Mull, Morven and Tiree in the early eighteenth century', *Scottish Studies*, XIII, 1969, 114 ff.

24 W. Hector, *Selections from the Judicial Records of Renfrewshire* (1878), 296; R. H. Campbell (ed.), *States of the Annual Progress of the Linen Manufacture 1727–1754* (SRO, 1964), 23–64

25 A. R. B. Haldane, *The Drove Roads of Scotland* (1952, reprint 1968, 1973), *passim*; Donnachie, *op. cit.*, 20; J. M. Corrie, *The Droving Days in the southwest district of Scotland* (1915)

26 Haldane, *op. cit.*, 57–8, 70–1, 76–7, 107 ff., 136 ff., 162 ff., 205; *OSA*, I, 43; M. Postlethwaite, *Britain's Commercial Interest Explained and Improved* (1757), I, 57

27 Cf. Thomas Telford's remarks on the effects of the black cattle trade in *BPP*, 1802–3, IV, Survey and Reports of the Coast and Central Highlands of Scotland in the autumn of 1802, 15–17

28 Gray, *op. cit.*, 86 ff.; E. Richards, 'The prospect of economic growth in Sutherland at the time of the clearances 1809–13', *SHR*, XLIX, 1970, 154–71; T. C. Smout, *A History of the Scottish People* (1969), 343–60; T. Sellar, *The Sutherland Evictions of 1814* (1883); N. MacLeod, *Reminiscences of a Highland Parish* (1867), 142 ff.

29 Haldane, *op. cit.*, 187 ff., 201; J. Mitchell, *Reminiscences of my Life in the Highlands* (1969 ed.), I, 336 ff.

30 P. Deane and W. A. Cole, *British Economic Growth 1688–1959* (1969 ed.), 195, and E. H. Whetham, 'Prices and Production in Scottish Agriculture 1850–1870', *SJPE*, IX, 1962, 233–43

31 This progress can be traced in *OSA* and the *General Views of Agriculture*, prepared for the Board of Agriculture between 1793 and 1816. Travellers' accounts, such as those of R. Heron, T. Pennant and James Boswell, also contain interesting comments.

32 Hamilton, *Industrial Revolution*, 66

33 D. F. Macdonald, *Scotland's Shifting Population* (1937), 27–36

34 A. Fergusson (ed.), *Letters and Journals of Mrs. Calderwood of Polton* (1884), 20–1; T. Bedford Franklin, *A History of Scottish Farming* (1952), 117; R. Forsyth, *op. cit.*, ii, 41; T. C. Smout and A. Fenton, 'Scottish Agriculture before the Improvers', *Agric. Hist. Rev.*, XIII, 1963, 73–93

35 Franklin, *op. cit.*, 118

36 J. H. Romanes, *SHR*, XIII, 1906, 101 ff.

37 E. L. Jones (ed.), *Agriculture and Economic Growth in England 1650–1815* (1967), 15

38 T. Donnelly, Arthur Clephane, Edinburgh merchant and seedsman, 1706–30', *Agric. Hist. Rev.*, XVIII, 1970, 151–60; M. Anderson, *History of Scottish Forestry* (1967), I, 599; cf. also R. Forsyth,

op. cit., II, 88, for Dicksons, the Border seedsmen.

39 R. Forsyth, *op. cit.*, I, 431

40 A. Geddes, 'The changing landscape of the Lothians 1600–1800', *SGM*, LIV, 1938, 129–30

41 Franklin, *op. cit.*, 143, 150–1, 156–7

42 A. H. Millar (ed.), *Forfeited Estates Papers* (1907), *passim*; J. Mason, 'Conditions in the Highlands after the "Forty-five"', *SHR*, XXVI, 1947–8, 134–46

43 A. McKerral, 'The Tacksman and his holding in the South-west Highlands', *SHR*, XXVI, 1947–8, 10–25; A. Geddes, 'Conjoint Tenants and Tacksmen in the Isle of Lewis', *EcHR*, 2nd series, I, 1948, 57 ff.

44 J. A. Symon, *Scottish Farming, Past and Present* (1959), 271 ff.; SRO, Campbell of Jura Muniments, GD 64/1/315

45 Gray, *op. cit.*, 66 ff.

46 Ibid., 75 ff.

47 Ibid., 181 ff.

48 J. Anderson, *General View of Agriculture in Aberdeenshire* (1794), 74; A. Birnie, 'Some Aberdeenshire leases in the eighteenth century', *EcHR*, IV, 4, 1933, 464

49 R. A. Gailey, 'Agrarian Improvement and the development of Enclosure in the south-west Highlands of Scotland', *SHR*, XLII, 1963; 108 ff. and his 'Mobility of Tenants on a Highland Estate in the early nineteenth century', *SHR*, XL, 1961, 136–45

50 Gailey, 'Agrarian Improvement', 112–15; cf. also his 'Settlement and Population in Kintyre 1750–1800', *SGM*, LXXVI, 1960

51 M. C. Storrie, 'Landholdings and Population in Arran from the late eighteenth century', *Scottish Studies*, XI, 1967, 49 ff.

52 A. Geddes, 'The Changing Landscape of the Lothians', *SGM*, LIV, 1938, 137

53 Cf. B. M. W. Third, 'Changing Landscape and Social Structure in the Scottish Lowlands', *SGM*, LXXI, 1955, 83–93

54 B. M. W. Third, 'Estate Plans and Associated Documents', *Scottish Studies*, I, 1957, 39–64

55 Cf. S. G. E. Lythe, 'The Tayside meal mobs 1772–3', *SHR*, XLVI, 1967, 28–31

56 Ibid., 31 ff.

57 Examples of government action likely to lead to inflation, apart from war expenditure, include higher direct and indirect taxation and suspension of gold payments in 1797.

58 J. E. Handley, *Scottish Farming in the Eighteenth Century* (1953), 117–43; C. Rogers, *A Century of Scottish Life* (1872), *passim*; Symon, *op. cit.*, 308 ff.

59 A. Smith, *The Wealth of Nations*, I, (1776), xi

60 I. H. Adams, 'The Land Surveyor and his Influence on the Scottish Rural Landscape', *SGM*, LXXXIV, 1968, 248–55; and his excellent pamphlet, *The Mapping of a Scottish Estate* (1971), *passim*

61 Cf. Hamilton, *Industrial Revolution*, 13, 14, 16, 18. For the late survival of runrig see note 18. There is very much less comment in *NSA* about primitive methods than in *OSA*. Local studies, using both sources, could be very informative.

62 R. Forsyth, *op. cit.*, I, 251 ff.

63 Ibid., 422 ff.

64 Ibid., 519–23

65 Ibid., II, 83 and 86

66 Ibid., 438 ff.; J. H. G. Lebon, 'The process of enclosure in the Western Lowlands', *SGM*, LXII, 1946, 100–10; H. Bone, 'The Ayrshire Breed of Cattle', *Ayrshire Collections*, I, 1947–9; cf. also *Ayrshire at the time of Burns* (1959), *passim*

67 Forsyth, *op. cit.*, III, 73 ff.; SRO Closeburn Writs, GD 19/405–9

68 Forsyth, *op. cit.*, III, 338 ff.

69 Ibid., 399 ff.

70 Ibid., 493 ff.

71 G. Whittington, 'Land utilisation in Fife at the close of the eighteenth century', *SGM*, LXXXII, 1966, 184–93

72 Forsyth, *op. cit.*, IV, 65 ff.

73 Ibid., V, 2 ff.; R. Mitchison, *Agricultural Sir John* (1962), 101 ff.

74 Forsyth, *op. cit.*, V, 46 ff.; W. R. Scott, 'The trade of Orkney at the end of the eighteenth century', *SHR*, X, 1913, 362

75 Forsyth, *op. cit.*, V, 126 ff.

76 J. Small, *A Treatise on Ploughs and Wheel Carriages* (1784); Lord Kames, *The Gentleman Farmer* (1776), 57–8; A. Fenton, 'The Chilcarroch Plough', *Scottish Studies*, VIII, 1964, 80–4

77 I. Whitaker, 'The Harrow in Scotland',

Scottish Studies, II, 1958, 149–63

78 J. Butt, *The Industrial Archaeology of Scotland* (1967), 29 ff.; British Patents, 896, 14 March 1768 and 1645, 9 April 1788; N. Cartwright, 'The Meikle Threshing Mill at Beltondod', *Trans. East Lothian Antiq. Soc.,* XI, 1968, 71 ff.; J. E. Handley, *op. cit.,* 217–19; I Donnachie, *op. cit.,* 41–5

79 A. J. Warden, *The Linen Trade, Ancient and Modern* (1867 ed.), 449; Hamilton, *Industrial Revolution,* 54

80 Cf. T. Davidson, 'Animal Treatment in eighteenth century Scotland', *Scottish Studies,* IV, 1960, 134–49

81 Cf. F. M. L. Thompson, 'The Second Agricultural Revolution 1815–80', *EcHR* 2nd series, XXI, 1, April 1968, 62–77

82 Campbell, *op. cit.,* 152 ff.; Select Committee on Depressed State of Agriculture in UK, *BPP,* 1821, IX; Report of Select Committee on present state of Agriculture, *BPP,* 1833, V; Select Committee on Agricultural Distress, *BPP,* 1836, VIII; Symon, *op. cit.,* 169 ff.

83 Derived from E. H. Whetham, 'Prices and Production in Scottish Farming 1850–70', *SJPE,* IX, 1962, 233–43, and Sinclair, *op. cit.*

84 Campbell, *op. cit.,* 204 ff.

85 Anon., *The Present Conduct of the Chieftains and Proprietors in the Highlands* (1773), 14

86 A. Mackenzie, *The History of the Highland Clearances* (1946 ed.), *passim*; E. Richards, 'The Mind of Patrick Sellar', *Scottish Studies,* XV, 1–20; I. Grimble, *The Trial of Patrick Sellar* (1962), *passim*

87 Symon, *op. cit.,* 169; 'Prices of Wool since 1818', *Trans. Highland Agric. Soc.,* 1922, 289 ff.; P. Finlayson, *The Observing Farmer's Travels through Scotland* (1834), 5–9

88 P. Finlayson, *op. cit.,* 67–9; J. A. S. Watson and M. E. Hobbs, *Great Farmers* (1951), 140 ff.; Symon, *op. cit.,* 325 ff.

89 *NSA,* IX, 271; X, 153, 185, 205; XI, 633; Thompson, 'Second Agricultural Revolution', 68

90 Symon, *op. cit.,* 178, 327–8; W. McCombie, *Cattle and Cattle Breeders* (1866), *passim*; Donnachie, *op. cit.,* 20–1; *NSA,* IV, 217; XIV, 48

91 Haldane, *op. cit.,* 131–2; Donnachie,

op. cit., 21

92 W. Cobbett, *A Tour in Scotland* (1833), 89 ff. and 104–7; R. H. Greg, *Scotch Farming in the Lothians* (1842), *passim*; A. G. Bradley, *When Squires and Farmers Thrived* (1927), 68 ff.

93 Symon, *op. cit.,* 312; B. C. Skinner, *The Lime Industry of the Lothians* (1969), *passim*

94 Greg, *op. cit.,* II, 42; Symon, *op. cit.,* 172; James Smith, *Remarks on Thorough Drainage and Deep Ploughing* (1831); Watson and Hobbs, *op. cit.,* 14–23

95 According to Campbell, *op. cit.,* 160, £4 million was spent on grants in the 1840s. Cf. also F. M. L. Thompson, *English Landed Society in the Nineteenth Century* (1963), 253 n. remarks that, under an Act of 1864, Scottish landowners borrowed nearly half the loans made for drainage.

86 Symon, *op. cit.,* 179, 386–7; Watson and Hobbs, *op. cit.,* 47 ff.

97 Symon, *op. cit.,* 393

98 Thompson, 'Second Agricultural Revolution', 69; Symon, *op. cit.,* 311; Watson and Hobbs, *op. cit.,* 71 ff.; J. Butt, 'James Young, Scottish Industrialist and Philanthropist' (Unpublished PhD thesis, University of Glasgow, 1964), 301 ff.

99 Hamilton, *Industrial Revolution,* 74

100 J. H. Clapham, *An Economic History of Modern Britain* (1964), I, 452

101 Aliquis, *Landlords, Land Laws and Land Leagues in Scotland* (1881), *passim*; Marwick, *op. cit.,* 67; J. Mitchell, *Reminiscences of my life in the Highlands* (1971 ed.), 116–7

102 *A Century of Agricultural Statistics* (1968), 22

103 T. C. Smout, 'Scottish Landowners and Economic Growth', *SJPE,* XI, 1964, 218–34; W. H. Marwick, *Economic Developments in Victorian Scotland* (1936), 29–45

104 Brotherton Library, Leeds, MS. 200, Tour Book of John Marshall, 26 Sept. 1800

105 Smout and Fenton, 'Scottish Agriculture', 77

106 H. Hamilton, *An Economic History of Scotland in the Eighteenth Century* (1963); 108; I. A. Glen, 'An Economic History of the Distilling Industry in

Scotland 1750–1914' (Unpublished PhD thesis, University of Strathclyde, 1969), 730

107 London Guildhall Library, Sun Fire Insurance Policy Registers, GH 11937/10, Policy 641751

108 Ibid., GH 11937/12, Policy 649507, and GH 11937/17, Policy 664617

109 Ibid., GH 11937/33, Policy 707682, 6 Sept 1800

110 Ibid., GH 11937/2, Policy 622172

111 Ibid., GH 11937/37, Policy 714523, 26 Jan 1801

112 Ibid., GH 11937/7, Policy 635456, 26 Nov 1794

113 Ibid., GH 11937/32, Policy 699565, 1 March 1800

114 Ibid., GH 11937/17, Policy 664411, 9 Feb 1797

115 SRO, UP G31/11, Glendronach Distillery Co. v. Neilson et al., 1833

116 Glen, 'Distilling Industry', 165–6

117 R. H. Campbell (ed.), States of the Annual Progress of the Linen Manufacture 1727–54, 8, passim

118 N. McClain, 'Aspects of the Scottish Economy during the American War of Independence' (Unpublished MLitt thesis, University of Strathclyde, 1969), 79

119 BPP, 1841, XXIV, Accounts and Papers, 78

120 Smout, 'Scottish Landowners', 218–34

121 Guildhall Library, GH 11937/38, 22 Jan 1801

122 OSA, ii, 279

123 J. Butt (ed.), Robert Owen, Prince of Cotton Spinners (1971), 173 ff.

124 B. F. Duckham, A History of the Scottish Coal Industry, Vol. I, 1700–1815 (1970), 141 ff.

125 Donnachie, op. cit., 116 ff.; T. C. Smout, 'The Lead Mines at Wanlockhead',

Trans. Dumfries and Galloway Arch. Soc., XXXIX, 1960–1, 144–58; cf. also his 'Leadmining in Scotland, 1650–1850', in P. L. Payne (ed.), Studies in Scottish Business History (1967), 103–35

126 Only the Dundee and Newtyle Railway, of all railways built before 1836, was not built to exploit coal deposits.

127 C. F. Dendy Marshall, A History of British Railways before 1830 (1938), 114, 117, 122, 130–2

128 Cf. J. Butt and J. T. Ward, 'The Promotion of the Caledonian Railway', Transport History, III, 1970, 164–92 and 225–54; J. T. Ward, 'Scottish Landowners and the Railways: A Preliminary Note', Scottish Railway Preservation Soc., II, 1967, 3–14

129 W. Vamplew, 'Sources of Scottish Railway Share Capital before 1860', SJPE, XVII, 1970, 425–39; British Transport Commission Archives, Prospectus of Glasgow, Paisley, Kilmarnock & Ayr Railway

130 R. S. Rait, History of Union Bank (1930), 60 ff.; Hamilton, Industrial Revolution, 254 ff.; N. Munro, History of the Royal Bank of Scotland (1928), passim; A. Keith, The North of Scotland Bank Limited (1936), passim; C. A. Malcolm, The British Linen Bank (1950), passim; J. L. Anderson, The Story of the Commercial Bank of Scotland (1910), 89 ff.

131 SRO, B/18/18/14, Minute Book of the directors of East Lothian Bank 1809–14

132 R. H. Campbell and J. B. A. Dow, Source Book of Scottish Economic and Social History (1968), 136

133 Hamilton, Eighteenth Century, 351 ff.

134 L. J. Saunders, Scottish Democracy 1815–1840 (1950), 7 ff.

135 Clapham, op. cit., II, 278

CHAPTER IX

Further Reading

A number of books already cited—the works of Campbell, Hamilton and Smout —have useful sections. Much information can be derived from the Old and New Statistical Accounts. Of general interest are W. H. Marwick's *Economic Developments in Victorian Scotland* (1936) and his *Scotland in Modern Times* (1964). There is no specialist book on foreign trade nor is retailing satisfactorily covered except for the general development of co-operation. On this subject the best book, although now dated, is William Maxwell's *History of Co-operation in Scotland* (1910). More work has been done on banking. R. Cameron discusses the relationship between banking and the onset of economic change in his comparative study, *Banking in the Early Stages of Industrialization* (1967); a number of official histories are readily available—R. S. Rait's *The History of the Union Bank of Scotland* (1930), N. Munro's *History of the Royal Bank* (1928), C. A. Malcolm's *History of the British Linen Bank* (1950) and A. Keith's *North of Scotland Bank Limited* (1937) are the best. A. W. Kerr's *History of Banking in Scotland* (4th ed., 1926) is currently the only good general history but is likely to be replaced by the forthcoming *Scottish Banking : A History 1695–1973* by S. G. and E. O. A. Checkland. H. O. Horne's *A History of Savings Banks* (1947) is the standard work on that subject.

Notes and References

1 D. Macpherson, *Annals of Commerce* (1805), iii, 340

2 R. Davis, 'The Rise of Protection in England, 1689–1786', *EcHR*, 2nd series, XIX, 2, 1966, 306–17; R. H. Campbell (ed.), *States of the Annual Progress of the Linen Manufacture 1727–54* (SRO, 1964), vi; R. H. Campbell, *Scotland since 1707 : the Rise of an Industrial Society* (1965), 38 ff., 54 ff; A. J. Durie, 'The markets for Scottish linen, 1730–1775', *SHR*, LII, 1, 1973, 30–2

3 Controversy rages around the question of the standard of living during the period 1800–50. For an optimist's view cf. R. M. Hartwell, 'The rising standard of living in England, 1800–1850', *EcHR*, 2nd series, XIII, 3, 1961, 397–416; for the opposite cf. E. J. Hobsbawm, 'The British standard of living, 1790–1850', *EcHR*, X, 1, 1957, 46–61. Scottish studies are as yet rare: cf. T. C. Smout, *A History of the Scottish People* (1969), 397–403, and T. R. Gourvish, 'The Cost of Living in Glasgow in the early Nineteenth Century', *EcHR*, 2nd series, XXV, 1, 1972, 65–80. For demand changes in common articles in the eighteenth century cf. M. Plant, *The Domestic Life of Scotland in the eighteenth century* (1952), 19 ff., 43 ff., 76 ff., 111 ff.

4 *BPP*, 1831–2, XIX, Select Committee on the Silk Trade, Q 10578 ff.

5 Campbell, *Linen Manufacture*, 61

6 Ibid., 53

7 J. Gibson, *The History of Glasgow* (1777), 115

8 R. Forsyth, *The Beauties of Scotland*, (1806), III, 207

9 Ibid., I, 33

10 J. Sinclair, *Analysis of the Statistical Account of Scotland* (1825), 219–20

11 *NSA*, Wigtownshire, 193

12 Cf. Cleland, *The Rise and Progress of Glasgow* (1820), 193 ff.; D. Keir (ed.), *Third Statistical Account : Edinburgh* (1966), 657 ff.

13 This characteristic is very apparent from details given in fire insurance policies.

14 *OSA*, vi, 583

15 J. Butt (ed.), *Life of Robert Owen by himself* (1971), 12 ff.

16 Cleland, *op. cit.,* 29

17 Ibid., 93–4

18 W. M. Gilbert (ed.), *Edinburgh in the Nineteenth Century* (1901), 215 ff.

19 SRO, RH 15/318, Copy Sederunt Book of John Buchanan & Co., 1794

20 Senex [Robert Reid], *Glasgow Past and Present* (1884), III, 459

21 SRO, RH 15/138, Sederunt Book of Connell and Company, 1834

22 These figures are based on a search of Sun Fire Insurance Company policy registers deposited in the London Guildhall Library [MS. 11937 CD series]. Policies for less than £200 were excluded from these calculations.

23 *Vide infra*, pp. 245–7

24 Cf. G. Stewart, *Curiosities of Glasgow Citizenship* (1881), 188

25 SRO, RH 15/132, Sederunt Book of Thomas Baird, 1815–16

26 H. C. and L. Mui, 'Andrew Melrose, tea-dealer and grocer of Edinburgh, 1812–33', *Business History*, IX, 1, 1967, 30–48; cf. also their 'The Commutation Act and the British Tea Trade', *EcHR*, 2nd series, XVI, 1963

27 London Guildhall Library, GH 11937/8,

Policy 714813

28 SRO, RH 15/190/2, Sederunt Book of Hugh Walker & Co., 1817

29 SRO, RH 15/137, Sederunt Book of John Craig, 1826

30 *The Scotch Reformers' Gazette,* 14 September 1844

31 This paragraph is based on the first chapter of the forthcoming official history of SCWS, written by James Kinloch, from whose work and conversation I have gained greatly over the past four years. Cf. also W. Maxwell, *History of Co-operation in Scotland* (1910), *passim*

32 *BPP,* 1871, XXIII, Royal Commission on Truck, Report, p. 130

33 *The North British Advertiser,* 10 May 1856

34 W. H. Marwick, *Economic Developments in Victorian Scotland* (1936), 98; J. B. Jefferys, *Retail Trading in Britain* (1954), Ch. 1, *passim*; P. Mathias, *Retailing Revolution* (1967), 40 ff.

35 H. Hamilton, *An Economic History of Scotland in the Eighteenth Century* (1963), 286, and D. Bremner, *The Industries of Scotland: Their Rise, Progress and Present Condition* (1869, reprint 1969), 79; cf. also *BPP,* 1847, XXXII, Accounts and Papers, 654 ff.

36 Hamilton, *op. cit.,* 286 ff.

37 Ibid., 132; Durie, 'Scottish Linen', 30 ff.

38 Hamilton, *op. cit.,* 132

39 Campbell, *Linen Manufacture,* 47; cf. Durie, 'Scottish Linen', 37

40 Campbell, *Linen Manufacture,* 51

41 This information was kindly provided by N. B. Harte of University College, London, who is studying the English linen industry

42 Durie, 'Scottish Linen', 46–7

43 Hamilton, *op. cit.,* 142

44 Ibid., 214 ff.; M. Gray, *The Highland Economy* (1957), 9–10; J. Butt, *The Industrial Archaeology of Scotland* (1967), 14–15; for the Scottish ports and grain trade cf. *BPP,* 1828, XVIII, Accounts and Papers

45 W. Forsyth, *In the Shadow of Cairngorm* (1900), 303–4; G. Jackson, *Hull in the Eighteenth Century* (1972), 184–5

46 Hamilton, *op. cit.,* 262–3

47 G. Jackson, *op. cit.,* 77, 78–80 and 83

48 Hamilton, *op. cit.,* 238

49 For William Stirling cf. GCA, B10/15/5805, and Stewart, *op. cit.,* 126–7; R. H. Campbell, *Carron Company* (1961), 106 ff.; J. C. Logan, *The Dumbarton Glass Work Company* (Unpublished MLitt thesis, University of Strathclyde, 1969)

50 *BPP,* 1849, LIV, 83–4, Accounts and Papers; H. Hamilton, *The Industrial Revolution in Scotland* (1966), 190–1

51 Campbell, *Scotland since 1707,* 127

52 G. Unwin, *Samuel Oldknow and the Arkwrights* (1968), 97; Stewart, *op. cit.,* 113; A. J. Warden, *The Linen Trade, Ancient and Modern* (1867 ed.), 80; C. Gulvin, *The Tweedmakers: A History of the Scottish Fancy Woollen Industry 1600–1914* (1973), 71 ff.

53 Campbell, *Scotland since 1707,* 38 ff.; W. Vamplew, 'Railways and the Transformation of the Scottish Economy', *EcHR,* 2nd series, XXIV, 1971, 43–4; Birmingham Reference Library, Boulton and Watt Collection, Letterbooks give details of many Scottish owners for engines before 1800.

54 Campbell, *Scotland since 1707,* 39

55 Hamilton, *Eighteenth Century,* 249 ff.; T. C. Smout, *Scottish Trade on the Eve of the Union*

56 Hamilton, *Eighteenth Century,* 416; see also Appendix IV

57 Hamilton, *Eighteenth Century,* 255–6; J. M. Price, 'The Rise of Glasgow in the Chesapeake Tobacco Trade 1707–1755', in P. L. Payne (ed.), *Studies in Scottish Business History* (1967), 299 ff.; [James Gourlay], *A Glasgow Miscellany: the Tobacco Period in Glasgow 1707–1775* (privately printed, n.d.), *passim*; J. H. Soltow, 'Scottish Traders in Virginia, 1750–75', *EcHR,* 2nd series, XII, 1959, 83–98

58 The ensuing discussion owes much to discussion with Dr T. M. Devine and to his 'Glasgow Merchants in Colonial Trade 1770–1815' (Unpublished PhD thesis, University of Strathclyde, 1971)

59 T. M. Devine, 'Glasgow merchants and the collapse of the tobacco trade 1775–1783', *SHR,* LII, 1973, 50–74; Campbell, *Scotland since 1707,* 45

60 W. R. Scott, 'Economic Resiliency', *EcHR,* II, 1930, 291–9; H. Hamilton, 'The Founding of the Glasgow Chamber of Commerce in 1783', *SJPE,* 1954,

33–48; Hamilton, *Eighteenth Century*, 270 ff. and 279 ff.; Campbell, *Scotland since 1707*, 77–8

61 T. M. Devine, 'Glasgow Colonial Merchants and Land, 1770–1815', in J. T. Ward and R. G. Wilson (eds), *Land and Industry* (1971), 205–235.

62 M. L. Robertson, 'Scottish Commerce and the American War of Independence', *EcHR*, 2nd series, IX, 1956, 123–31; Campbell, *Scotland since 1707*, 46

63 Cf. T. S. Ashton, *Economic Fluctuation in England 1700–1800* (1959), 65 ff.

64 Hamilton, *Eighteenth Century*, 260–5

65 Ibid., 269–71

66 Campbell, *Scotland since 1707*, 79 ff.; W. H. Marwick, *Scotland in Modern Times* (1964), 94, 114 ff.; Gulvin, *op. cit.*, 110 ff.

67 Hamilton, *Eighteenth Century*, 291 ff.

68 R. S. Rait, *The History of the Union Bank of Scotland* (1930), 2 ff.

69 N. Munro, *The History of the Royal Bank of Scotland, 1727–1927* (1928), 32–5

70 A. W. Kerr, *History of Banking in Scotland* (4th ed., 1926), 23

71 Hamilton, *Eighteenth Century*, 299–300

72 Rait, *op. cit.*, 12

73 C. A. Malcolm, *The History of the British Linen Bank* (1950), 6, 9–11, 50 ff.

74 Cf. *Senex* [Reid], *op. cit.*, I, 463 ff.; Glasguensis [J. Buchanan], *Banking in the Olden Time* (2nd ed., 1884), *passim*

75 Kerr, *op. cit.*, 51–2; Sir William Forbes, *Memoirs of a Banking House* (1860), *passim*

76 Rait, *op. cit.*, 73 and 77

77 Ibid., 16–17

78 A. Keith, *The North of Scotland Bank Limited, 1836–1936* (1937), 1–2

79 Glasguensis [Buchanan], *op. cit.*, 20–1; Rait, *op. cit.*, 23 ff.

80 *GCA*, B10/15/6748, Burgh Deeds; Rait, *op. cit.*, 121 ff.; [J. Buchanan], *op. cit.*, 21–2

81 Munro, *op. cit.*, 113–14 and 117–19

82 Rait, *op. cit.*, 27, 29 ff.

83 On this point cf. the stimulating review article by Professor S. G. Checkland, 'Banking History and Economic Development', *SJPE*, XV, 1968, 152

84 Munro, *op. cit.*, 68–9

85 *BPP*, 1826–7, VI, Report of House of Lords Committee on Circulation of Promissory Notes, 248

86 Cf. H. Hamilton, 'The Failure of the Ayr Bank 1772', *EcHR*, 2nd series, VIII, 1955–6, 405–17

87 Hamilton, *Eighteenth Century*, 311–12, 314

88 R. Cameron, *Banking in the Early Stages of Industrialization* (1967), 66, 70–1

89 *BPP*, 1826, III, Report on State of Commercial Credit, 1793 (reprinted), 124 and 129; cf. also Campbell, *Scotland since 1707*, 136 ff.

90 L. S. Pressnell, *Country Banking in the Industrial Revolution* (1956), 226 ff.; Kerr, *op. cit.*, 134; SRO, GD 113/283, Innes of Stow Muniments, Quarterly stock and profits of the Royal Bank; Hamilton, *Eighteenth Century*, 330 ff.

91 *BPP*, 1812–13, XIII, Account of Country Banks in Scotland licensed to issue notes, 41

92 *BPP*, 1845, Return of Banks of Issue, Scotland, 215

93 *BPP*, 1865, Return of Scots Banks (1864), 144

94 Cameron, *op. cit.*, 66

95 Rait, *op. cit.*, chart facing p. vi; Campbell, *Scotland since 1707*, 148

96 Kerr, *op. cit.*, 235 ff.

97 Cf. P. L. Payne, 'The Savings Bank of Glasgow, 1836–1914', in Payne, *op. cit.*, 157 ff; for the general picture cf. H. O. Horne, *A History of Savings Banks* (1947)

98 Cameron, *op. cit.*, 72–3

99 *TSA*: Edinburgh 578; *Report on the Friendly or Benefit Societies of the Highland Society* (1824), 6 ff.

100 Cf. J. H. Clapham, *An Economic History of Modern Britain, Vol. I: Early Railway Age, 1820–50* (1967 ed.), 471 ff.

101 Cf. Marwick, *op. cit.*, 86 ff.; this paragraph is also based on joint research into the history of the Scottish insurance industry with Dr J. H. Treble, whose comments have been particularly helpful.

102 J. H. Clapham, *An Economic History of Modern Britain, Vol. II: Free Trade and Steel, 1850–86* (1967 ed.), 342–3

103 W. Bagehot, *Lombard Street: A Description of the money market* (1873), 31

104 Clapham, *op. cit.*, II, 343–4

CHAPTER X

Further Reading

There are a number of readily available texts on British economic development against which Scotland's industrial development should be set—M. W. Flinn's *The Origins of the Industrial Revolution* (1966), P. Deane's *The First Industrial Revolution* (1965), E. J. Hobsbawm's *Industry and Empire* (1968) and P. Mathias's *The First Industrial Nation* (1969). Works already cited—by Hamilton, Marwick, Campbell, and Smout—have valuable sections relating to a number of themes discussed in this chapter. D. Bremner's pioneering study, *The Industries of Scotland : Their Rise and Progress,* originally published in 1869 and available as a reprint, is the best contemporary account.

There is no modern general book on the linen industry, although a reprint (1967) of A. J. Warden's *The Linen Trade, Ancient and Modern* (1867 ed.) is readily available. B. P. Lenman has a book forthcoming on the jute industry. On textiles generally, there is much information in the Statistical Accounts. See also C. Gulvin's impressive *The Tweedmakers : A History of the Scottish Fancy Woollen Industry 1600–1914* (1973).

Heavy industry is better served. A. Fell's *The Early Iron Industry of Furness and District* (1908, reprint 1965) contains much interesting information on the charcoal phase of iron-working in Scotland, and P. Caddell's *The Iron Mills at Cramond* (1973) is a careful case-study. A Birch's *The Economic History of the British Iron and Steel Industry 1784–1879* (1967) discusses Scotland's contribution in general terms and a specialist study is R. H. Campbell's *Carron Company* (1961). B. F. Duckham's *History of the Scottish Coal Industry, Vol. I* is an impressive study of this important sector during the period 1700–1815, and a further volume is promised. The best treatment of the rise of the chemical industry is *The Chemical Revolution* (1952) by A. and N. L. Clow, although L. F. Haber's *The Chemical Industry during the Nineteenth Century* (1958) presents a wider setting.

On transport refer to A. R. B. Haldane's *The Drove Roads of Scotland* (1952, reprint 1968, 1973) and his *New Ways Through the Glens* (1961); J. Lindsay's *The Canals of Scotland* (1968) and J. Thomas's *History of the Railways of Great Britain, Vol. 6, Scotland* (1971). A number of histories of railway companies have been written but rarely with the economic historian in mind. On the construction aspect of public works consult J. E. Handley's *The Navvy in Scotland* (1970), so far the best study of the social implications of the development of transport.

Notes and References

1 Cf. W. W. Rostow, *The Stages of Economic Growth* (1960); S. Kuznets, *Economic Growth and Structure* (1966); R. M. Hartwell, *The Causes of the Industrial Revolution in England* (1967); T. S. Ashton, *The Industrial Revolution 1760–1830* (1948); E. J. Hobsbawm, *Industry and Empire* (1968); M. W. Flinn, *The Origins of the Industrial Revolution* (1966); P. Deane and W. A. Cole, *British Economic Growth* (1967 ed.); P. Mathias, *The First Industrial Nation* (1969); P. Deane, *The First Industrial Revolution* (1965).

2 H. Hamilton, *The Industrial Revolution in Scotland* (1932), 1

3 H. Hamilton, *An Economic History of Scotland in the Eighteenth Century* (1963), *passim*; cf. R. H. Campbell, 'An Economic history of Scotland in the eighteenth century', *SJPE*, 1964

4 *Vide infra*, p. 108

5 R. H. Campbell, *Scotland since 1707 : the Rise of an Industrial Society* (1965), especially Pts 1 and 2

6 T. C. Smout, *A History of the Scottish People* (1969), Pt 2

7 J. Butt, *The Industrial Archaeology of Scotland* (1967), 83–90; B. F. Duckham, *A History of the Scottish Coal Industry 1700–1815*, I (1970), 14–17

8 Ibid., 17–18

9 Ibid., 23–30

10 Ibid., 34

11 J. Butt, *op. cit.*, 90

12 *Vide infra*, pp. 129 ff.

13 GCA, Burgh Deeds, B/10/15/5698; 5599; 5967; 6070; 7040; 7048; 7049; 7118

14 T. C. Smout, 'The Early Scottish Sugar Houses, 1660–1720', *EcHR*, 2nd series, XIV, 1961, 240–53

15 The various interests of the Fall family are examined by D. S. Alexander, 'The Falls of Dunbar—An Eighteenth Century Mercantile Family of Scotland' (Unpublished BLitt thesis, University of Glasgow, 1969)

16 London Guildhall Library, GH 11936/84, 10 January 1748

17 Signet Library, Session Papers, 180; 8

18 J. Gibson, *The History of Glasgow* (1777), 242; G. Stewart, *Curiosities of Glasgow Citizenship* (1881), 144 ff.

19 GCA, B/10/15/6361; J. Gourlay (ed.), *The Provosts of Glasgow 1609–1832* (1942), 61–2

20 GCA, B/10/15/6015; cf. also C. Gulvin, *The Tweedmakers: A History of the Scottish Fancy Woollen Industry 1600–1914* (1973), 33

21 GCA, B/10/15/5644

22 Guildhall Library, GH 11936/98, 5 October, 1752; A. Brown, *History of Glasgow* (1795), iii, 209; J. Cleland, *Rise and Progress of Glasgow* (1820), 93

23 Gourlay, *op. cit.*, 66

24 Ibid., 79

25 SRO, Bill Chamber Processes, II, 38634; GCA, B/10/5/8132; SRO, Register of Deeds, Vol. 216 fo. 802 Dal

26 T. M. Devine, 'Glasgow Merchants in Colonial Trade 1770–1815' (Unpublished PhD thesis, University of Strathclyde, 1971), ii, 316–61

27 J. C. Logan, 'The Dumbarton Glass Works Company: A study in entrepreneurship', *Business History*, XIV, 1972, 67 ff.

28 J. R. Hume and J. Butt, 'Muirkirk 1786–1802: the creation of a Scottish industrial community', *SHR*, XLV, 1966, 166 ff.

29 I. L. Donnachie and J. Butt, 'The Wilsons of Wilsontown Ironworks, (1779–1813): A study in entrepreneurial failure', *Explorations in Entrepreneurial History*, 2nd series, IV, 1967, 151

30 Gourlay, *op. cit.*, 80; *Senex* [Robert Reid], *Glasgow Past and Present* (1884), I, 460; J. Gourlay, *A Glasgow Miscellany* (n.d.), 97; Cleland, *op. cit.*, 89; Devine, *op. cit.*, 322.

31 Cf. K. Berrill, 'International Trade and the Rate of Economic Growth', *EcHR*, 2nd series, XII, 1960, 351–59; M. L. Robertson, 'Scottish Commerce and the American War of Independence', *EcHR*, 2nd series, IX, 1956, 123–31

32 SRO, RH 15/814, Sederunt Book of John Renfrew, 1798

33 This is apparent from insurance valuations; cf. also Devine, *op. cit.*, ii, 362–3.

34 SRO, UP Adams Mack, 01/40, Oliphant *v.* William Fleming & Co.

35 SRO, UP Currie Dal Seq R1/34, Rothesay Spinning Company, 1812

36 Hamilton, *Eighteenth Century*, 172; *OSA*, VIII, 383

37 Signet Library, Session Papers, 368; 21 Petition of R. Dunmore; *OSA*, XVI, 117 ff.; SRO, Deeds, Vol. 249 f834

38 SRO, GD 237/134, Minute of partners' meeting, A. Houston & Co., 23 Sept 1806; UP 1 Currie Dal, B11/20, Burns *v.* Houston, Burns & Co., 1811

39 SRO, Cunninghame Graham Muniments, GD 22/1/219, Contract of Copartnery, 26 July and 4 August 1792

40 Anon., *James Finlay and Company Limited 1750–1950* (1951), 7; Devine, *op. cit.*, ii, 386 ff.

41 J. Butt, 'Robert Owen as a Businessman', *Robert Owen, Prince of Cotton Spinners* (1971), 174 ff.

42 Mitchell Library, MS. 79/10 Papers relating to the trust of Alexander Campbell of Hallyards

43 SRO, RH 15/2224, Settlement of G. Yuille and Minutes of his trustees, 1817–19

44 SRO, RH 15/1297, Sederunt Book of

Sharp and Mackenzie, 1799–1800

45 SRO, Particular Register of Sasines, Renfrewshire, Vol. 48, fo 229; Vol. 42, fo 217. I am grateful to Dr T. M. Devine for these references.

46 Cf. D. C. Coleman, *The Domestic System in Industry* (Historical Association pamphlet, 1960) for a resumé of the main features, described in an English context, however.

47 Cf. S. Pollard, *The Genesis of Modern Management* (1968 ed.), 42–50: Hamilton, *Eighteenth Century*, 147–8, 150, 157, 167–8, 172, 178

48 *Vide supra*, pp. 47–8

49 Guildhall Library, GH 11936/54, 1 Nov 1759

50 This generalisation is founded on the examination of nearly two thousand relevant insurance policies.

51 Guildhall Library, GH 11936/75, 19 March 1745

52 Ibid., GH 11936/80, 31 Dec 1747

53 Ibid., 17 Dec 1747

54 Ibid., GH 11936/85, 19 Oct 1748

55 Ibid., GH 11936/106, 22 Sept 1754

56 Ibid., GH 11936/87–131

57 B. C. Skinner, *The Cramond Iron Works* (1965), 3–7

58 Ibid., 17–19; R. H. Campbell, *Carron Company* (1961), 79–81

59 GCA, B10/15/7081

60 A. Brown, *op. cit.*, iii, 305–6

61 Cf. J. P. P. Higgins and S. Pollard (eds), *Aspects of Capital Investment in Great Britain 1750–1850* (1971), particularly S. D. Chapman, 'Fixed Capital Formation in the British Cotton Manufacturing Industry', 57–107, and the ensuing discussion, 108–19.

62 Cf. N. E. McClain, 'Scottish Lintmills, 1729–70', *Textile History*, I, 3, Dec 1970, 293–308

63 For a good discussion of the introduction of improvements to linen bleaching cf. Enid Gauldie, 'Mechanical Aids to Linen Bleaching in Scotland', ibid., I, 2, Dec 1969, 129–57

64 Hamilton, *Eighteenth Century*, 187–8 and 165–6; Brown, *op. cit.*, 275–6

65 A. H. Shorter, *Paper Making in the British Isles* (1971), 192–3; Hamilton, *Eighteenth Century*, 137; Brown, *op. cit.*, 211–12

66 Duckham, *op. cit.*, I, 46, 81 ff.

67 A. Fell, *The Early Iron Industry of Furness and District*; (1908, reprint 1968), 343 ff.; Campbell, *Carron Company*, 4–6

68 *Vide supra*, p. 170; A. Bannatyne, *Memoir of Dugald Bannatyne* (1896), 11; W. T. Peacock, 'Early Stocking-makers and their Industry', *Trans. Hawick Arch. Soc.* (1960), 22–35; Butt, *Industrial Archaeology*, 77

69 A. and N. L. Clow, 'Vitriol in the Industrial Revolution', *EcHR*, XV, 1945, 45–55, reprinted in A. E. Musson (ed.), *Science, Technology and Economic Growth in the Eighteenth Century* (1972), 148–67

70 Butt, *Industrial Archaeology*, 144

71 A. and N. L. Clow, *The Chemical Revolution* (1952), *passim*; J. C. Logan, 'The Operations of a Glassworks in the Industrial Revolution', *Ind. Arch.*, 9, 1972, 179 ff.

72 Butt, *Industrial Archaeology*, 175 ff.

73 Their reports were reprinted by order of the Clyde Trust, cf. *Reports on the Improvement and Management of the River Clyde and the Harbour of Glasgow* (1854), 1–8 and 11–13

74 J. Lindsay, *The Canals of Scotland* (1968), 16 ff.

75 Cf. the excellent collection of essays on this theme by A. E. Musson and E. Robinson, *Science and Technology in the Industrial Revolution* (1969). Professor Musson has also edited *Science, Technology and Economic Growth in the Eighteenth Century* (1972), which contains a thorough-going discussion of the social and economic implications of technical change.

76 Musson and Robinson, *op. cit.*, 63, quoting John Farey

77 Butt, *Industrial Archaeology*, 18–19

78 This is apparent from the records of the Board of Trustees and from the papers of the Glasgow Chamber of Commerce.

79 Cf. A. J. Warden, *The Linen Trade, Ancient and Modern* (1867 ed.), 444 ff.

80 Hamilton, *Eighteenth Century*, 142–3

81 R. H. Campbell (ed.), *States of the Annual Progress of the Linen Manufacture 1727–54* (SRO, 1964), v–vii

82 Hamilton, *Industrial Revolution*, 77–83; *Eighteenth Century*, 134 ff.

83 C. A. Malcolm, *The History of the British*

Linen Bank (1950), 1 ff.

84 Campbell, *Linen Manufacture*, vi; Warden, *op. cit.*, 465–74, 663–70

85 W. H. K. Turner, 'Osnabrück and Osnaburg', *Osnabrücker Mitteilungen* (1966), 53–70; Warden, *op. cit.*, 452. Glasgow and Paisley made 'Bengals', which were striped ginghams

86 Hamilton, *Industrial Revolution*, 92–3, 98–9; *Eighteenth Century*, 147 ff.

87 Hamilton, *Industrial Revolution*, 99

88 *BPP*, 1803, III, Report from Select Committee relating to state of linen trade, 1773

89 E. Gauldie (ed.), *The Dundee Textile Industry 1790–1885* (1969), xvii

90 W. Hector (ed.), *Selections from the Judicial Records of Renfrewshire* (1878), 196–204

91 Hamilton, *Eighteenth Century*, 347–8

92 British Patent No. 1613, 19 June 1787; Gauldie, *op. cit.*, 9

93 Signet Library Session Papers, 224:7; 448:43; 454:56

94 Butt, *Industrial Archaeology*, 59–60

95 Gauldie, *op. cit.*, 9

96 Hamilton, *Industrial Revolution*, 106 ff.; Warden, *op. cit.*, 481 ff.; W. H. K. Turner, 'The Textile Industry of Perth and District', *Trans. Inst. Br Geog.*, 1957, 123–40; 'Some Eighteenth Century Developments in the Textile Region of East Central Scotland', *SGM*, 69, 1, 10–21; 'The Textile Industry of Arbroath', *Abertay Hist. Soc. Trans.*, 1954; P. K. Livingstone, *Flax and Linen in Fife through the Centuries* (1952). There are also a number of references in *OSA* and in the policy registers of the Sun Fire Insurance Company, particularly to mills at Kirkland, Dunbar and Kinghorn.

97 Hamilton, *Industrial Revolution*, 106–7

98 Ibid., 115; Gauldie, *op. cit.*, 74

99 Hamilton, *Industrial Revolution*, 116; Gauldie, *op. cit.*, 20 ff., 52

100 Warden, *op. cit.*, 554–8

101 *BPP*, 1819, XVI, Accounts and Papers, 167; Warden, *op. cit.*, 633

102 Gauldie, *op. cit.*, XV, xxxv–vi, 149 ff.; D. C. Carrie, 'Dundee and the American Civil War, 1861–65', *Abertay Hist. Soc. Pub.*, 1953

103 Gauldie, *op. cit.*, xxviii–xxix; D. Chapman, 'The Jute Industry', *Review of Economic Studies*, 1938; *British Association Handbook*, 1939

104 Warden, *op. cit.*, 589 ff.

105 *BPP*, 1836, XLV, Accounts and Papers; *BPP*, 1871, LXII, Return of Factories and Workshops, 160

106 Gauldie, *op. cit.*, xxxiii

107 National Library of Scotland, Foreign letterbooks of A. G. Houston & Co., 1776–81

108 G. M. Mitchell, 'The English and Scottish Cotton Industries', *SHR*, XXI, 1924, 101–14; W. Pole (ed.), *The Life of Sir William Fairbairn* (1877, reprinted 1970), 121

109 SRO, N91/1/22, Minutes of the Board of Trustees, 27 Jan 1779 and 9 Feb 1780

110 J. E. Reid, *History of the County of Bute and the Families connected therewith* (1864), 103

111 SRO, UP Currie Dal B11/20, Burns v. Houston, Burns & Co., 1811; Signet Library, 264:2, Burns v. Houston, Burns & Co., 1812

112 J. O. Mitchell, *Old Glasgow Essays* (1905), 37, 380, 381 n.; Stewart, *op. cit.*, 182; *James Finlay and Company*, 12

113 Butt, 'Robert Owen', 188 ff.; SRO, RH15/1304, Wage Book of Douglas, Dale and McCall.

114 *OSA*, VIII, 383. My understanding of this venture has been greatly aided by the researches of S. B. Calder who is currently working on 'The Industrial Archaeology of Sutherland'.

115 J. Butt, 'The Industrial Archaeology of Gatehouse-of-Fleet', *Ind. Arch.*, 3, 1960, 127–37; I. Donnachie, *The Industrial Archaeology of Galloway* (1971), 98; A. Keith, *A Thousand Years of Aberdeen* (1972), 309–10; *The North of Scotland Bank* (1936), 70

116 This is apparent from comparisons between *OSA*, *NSA* and the returns made to government inquiries

117 These conclusions emerged during my study of cotton firms (1780–1840) sponsored by the Social Science Research Council. I am extremely grateful to the Council for their support.

118 D. Bremner, *The Industries of Scotland* (1869, reprint 1969), 287

119 Ibid.

120 Factory Returns, 1860–1910

121 A. J. Robertson, 'The Decline of the

Scottish Cotton Industry 1860–1914', *Business History*, XIII, 2, 1970, 116–28; for older views cf. Hamilton, *Industrial Revolution*, 149 and W. H. Marwick, 'The Cotton Industry and the Industrial Revolution in Scotland', *SHR*, xxi, 1924, 207–18; W. O. Henderson, 'The Cotton Famine in Scotland and the Relief of Distress, 1862–4', *SHR*, xxx, 1951, 154–64

122 Campbell, *Scotland since 1707*, 110; The North of Scotland Bank lost £160,000 as a consequence of the failure of cotton and linen firms in 1847 (Keith, *North of Scotland Bank*, 56)

123 Campbell, *Scotland since 1707*, 111

124 *BPP*, 1833, VI, Select Committee on Manufactures, Commerce and Shipping, 37 ff., Evidence of Kirkman Finlay and pp. 321, Evidence of W. Graham; Hamilton, *Industrial Revolution*, 148; A. Slaven, 'A Glasgow Firm in the Indian Market: John Lean and Sons, Muslin Weavers', *Business History Review*, 43, 1969, 496–522

125 Campbell, *Scotland since 1707*, 236; Robertson, *op. cit.*, 122

126 Campbell, *Scotland since 1707*, 109

127 Hamilton, *Industrial Revolution*, 149; W. S. Murphy, *Captains of Industry* (1901), 278–304; Robertson, *op. cit.*, 125–6

128 P. L. Payne, 'The Emergence of the Large-Scale Company in Great Britain, 1870–1914', *EcHR*, XX, 3, 1967, 527 ff.

129 C. K. Hyde, 'The Adoption of Coke-Smelting by the British Iron Industry 1709–1790', *Explorations in Economic History*, X, 4, 1973, 397–418

130 A. Fell, *The Early Iron Industry of Furness and District* (1908), 343–414; Hamilton, *Eighteenth Century*, 189–93; Butt, *Industrial Archaeology*, 104–8; D. Murray, *The York Buildings Company*, (reprint 1973), 63–5 and 64 n.

131 Hyde, *op. cit.*, 403

132 J. Butt, 'The Scottish Iron and Steel Industry before the Hot-Blast', *Journal of the West of Scotland Iron and Steel Institute*, 73, 1965–6, 193–206

133 Hyde, *op. cit.*, 413–4

134 Campbell, *Carron Company*, 7 ff.; H. Hamilton, 'The Founding of Carron Ironworks', *SHR*, XXV, 1928, 185

135 Campbell, *Carron Company*, 36 and 50–2

136 Ibid., 72–122

137 Ibid., 78–82

138 This and succeeding paragraphs are heavily based upon the results of research undertaken into firms in the Scottish iron industry 1780–1840 which was conducted under the auspices of the Social Science Research Council. I am most grateful to the Council for their support. Cf. also Hume and Butt, 'Muirkirk', 160–83; J. Butt, 'Glenbuck Ironworks', *Ayrshire Collections*, 8, 1967–9, 68–75; Donnachie and Butt, 'Wilsontown Ironworks', 150–68

139 Hamilton, *Industrial Revolution*, 179; Campbell, *Scotland since 1707*, 118–9

140 C. K. Hyde, 'The adoption of the Hot Blast by the British Iron Industry: a Reinterpretation', *Explorations in Economic History*, X, 3, 1973, 282–3

141 Hyde, 'Hot Blast', 285

142 R. H. Campbell, 'Statistics of the Scottish Pig Iron Trade', *Journal of the West of Scotland Iron and Steel Institute*, 64, 1956–7, 283–9

143 Campbell, *Scotland since 1707*, 121 ff.; A. Millar, *The Rise and Progress of Coatbridge* (1864), 116 ff.; Anon. [A. B. MacGeorge], *The Bairds of Gartsherrie* (1875), *passim*

144 A. Birch, *The Economic History of the British Iron and Steel Industry* (1967), 128 ff.

145 R. H. Campbell, 'The Iron Industry in Ayrshire', *Ayrshire Collections*, 7, 1961–6, 90–102

146 D. Bremner, *The Industries of Scotland: Their Rise and Progress* (1869), 36

147 A. Millar, *op. cit.*, 117; R. H. Campbell, 'Early Malleable Iron Production in Scotland', *Business History*, IV, 1961

148 Hamilton, *Industrial Revolution*, 187

149 Bremner, *op. cit.*, 35–6

150 B. Baxter, *Stone Blocks and Iron Rails* (1966), 226–32; C. F. Dendy Marshall, *A History of British Railways down to the year 1830* (1938, reprint 1971), 112–35; G. Dott, *Scottish Colliery Wagonways* (1947), *passim*

151 J. Thomas, *A Regional History of the Railways of Great Britain, Vol. 6: Scotland, the Lowlands and the Borders* (1971), 19–20

152 Bremner, *op. cit.*, 86 ff.; Thomas *op. cit.*, 20

153 Hamilton, *Industrial Revolution*, 245 ff.
154 For the general UK picture and Scotland's place in it cf. G. R. Hawke and M. C. Reed, 'Railway Capital in the United Kingdom in the Nineteenth Century', *EcHR*, XXII, 1969, 269–86
155 Cf. O. S. Nock, *Scottish Railways* (1950), *passim*
156 Thomas, *op. cit.*, 25
157 W. Vamplew, 'Sources of Scottish Railway Share Capital before 1860', *SJPE*, 17, 1970, 426
158 J. Butt and J. T. Ward, 'The Promotion of the Caledonian Railway Company: Part Two', *Transport History*, III, 1970, 247; J. Thomas, *The North British Railway*, I (1969), 13 f.; Vamplew, 'Railway Share Capital', 427
159 Bremner, *op. cit.*, 91
160 Cf. Butt and Ward, 'Caledonian Railway', 164–92 and 225–57; Thomas, *North British Railway*, 14–27; H. P. Vallance, *Great North of Scotland Railway*; Bremner, *op. cit.*, 92–6
161 O. S. Nock, *The Highland Railway* (1965); C. Highet, *The Glasgow and South Western Railway* (1965); Thomas, *North British Railway*, 82 ff.
162 D. Bremner, *op. cit.*, 92 ff.
163 W. Vamplew, 'Banks and Railway Finance: A note on the Scottish Experience', *Transport History*, IV, 1971, 166–82; Anon., 'Early Scottish Railways', *Three Banks Review*, June 1967, 29–39; W. H. Marwick, *Economic Developments in Victorian Scotland* (1936), 77
164 Vamplew, 'Railway Share Capital', 425–40

165 T. R. Gourvish and M. C. Reed, 'The Financing of Scottish Railways before 1860—a comment', *SJPE*, 18 (1971), 209–19 and W. Vamplew, 'The Financing of Scottish Railways before 1860—a reply', ibid., 221–3
166 Butt and Ward, 'Caledonian Railway', 241 ff. and 255; Thomas, *North British Railway*, 17–21
167 T. R. Gourvish, 'The Railways and Steamboat Competition in early Victorian Britain', *Transport History*, IV, 1971, 1–13; J. Thomas, *Regional History*, IV, 156 ff.
168 W. Vamplew, 'Railways and the Scottish Transport System in the Nineteenth Century', *Journal of Transport History*, NS, I, 1972, 133–45
169 Ibid., 135–7; Butt and Ward, 'Caledonian Railway', 239–41
170 J. Lindsay, *The Canals of Scotland* (1968), 42 ff. and 59 ff.
171 Vamplew, 'Scottish Transport System', 140–1; G. Channon, 'The Aberdeenshire Beef Trade with London: a study in Steamship and Railway Competition 1850–69', *Transport History*, II, 1969, 1–24
172 Gulvin, *op. cit.*, 117
173 W. Vamplew, 'Railways and the Transformation of the Scottish Economy', *EcHR*, XXIV, 1971, 37–54; 'The Railways and the Iron Industry: a Study of their Relationship in Scotland', in M. C. Reed (ed.), Railways in the *Victorian Economy* (1969)
174 J. E. Handley, *The Navvy in Scotland* (1970), 91–125 and 268 ff.

CHAPTER XI

Further Reading

Three short, stimulating and modestly priced pamphlets (all with excellent bibliographies) provide the best introduction to the literature relating to the British economy in this period—S. B. Saul's *The Myth of the Great Depression 1873–1896* (1969), A. S. Milward's *The Economic Effects of the World War on Britain* (1970) and B. W. E. Alford's *Depression and Recovery? British Economic Growth 1918–1939* (1972). Useful collections of articles similarly orientated include S. Pollard (ed.) *The Gold Standard and Employment Policies between the Wars* (1970) and P. J. Perry (ed.) *British Agriculture 1875–1914* (1973). P. L. Payne's *British Entrepreneurship in the Nineteenth Century* (1974), a thought-provoking short pamphlet, is the best critical summary of existing views on a thorny topic and also has the merit of an excellent bibliography.

Sections of books already cited—Hamilton's *The Industrial Revolution in Scotland* (1932), Campbell's *Scotland since 1707 : the Rise of an Industrial Society* (1965), and Marwick's two works—discuss some of the themes sketched in this chapter, but there is no specialist work on the Scottish economy during this period. There are a number of valuable works dealing with agriculture, especially J. A. Symon's *Scottish Farming, Past and Present* (1959); A. C. O'Dell and K. Walton present the historical geographers' approach in their *Highlands and Islands of Scotland* (1962). D. J. Jones *et al., Rural Scotland during the War* (1926) is a good assessment of the developments in agriculture during the period 1914–20. On the Highlands consult J. P. Day's *Public Administration in the Highlands and Islands* (1918).

On industrial developments, there are very significant gaps in the literature. For instance, apart from official papers, there is no good book on the history of coal-mining in this period. Consult A. Slaven's essay in *Studies in Scottish Business History* (1967), edited by P. L. Payne, and R. Page Arnot's *History of the Scottish Miners* (1955). On developments in the West of Scotland refer to *The Glasgow Region* (1958) edited by R. Miller and J. Tivy, T. R. Miller's *The Monkland Tradition* (1958), J. Strawhorn's *Cumnock* (1966) and J. Thomas's *Springburn Story* (1964).

On the inter-war years, J. Gollan in his *Scottish Prospect* (1948) presents an interesting and provocative account. C. A. Oakley's *Scottish Industry Today* (1937) is a descriptive statement about the main components of the industrial structure. *The Scottish Economy* (1954), edited by A. K. Cairncross, is mainly concerned with the post–1945 situation but contains interesting insights into the earlier period. The mood of the 1930s is best captured from J. A. Bowie's *The Future of Scotland* (1939) and A. M. Thomson's more polemical *Scotland, That Distressed Area* (1933).

On retailing, there is much relevant material in *The Retailing Revolution* (1967) by P. Mathias and in *Retail Trading in Britain 1850–1950* (1954) by J. B. Jefferys. Co-operation attracted many local historians, and there are many histories of retail societies listed by W. H. Marwick in *Studies in Scottish Business History* edited by P. L. Payne. These can be supplemented from J. S. Flanagan's *Wholesale Co-operation in Scotland 1868–1918* (1920) and from the forthcoming official history of SCWS by J. A. Kinloch.

References to works on banking have been given on p. 271; to these should be added M. Gaskin's *The Scottish Banks : A Modern Survey* (1965). Foreign investment is discussed in its British context by S. G. E. Lythe in *Britain Pre-eminent* (1969) edited by C. J. Bartlett, and there is a good collection of authoritative articles in A. R. Hall's edition, *The Export of Capital 1870–1914* (1968). Scottish involvement receives attention from A. K. Cairncross in *Home and Foreign Investment 1870–1913* (1953) and from W. T. Jackson in *The Enterprising Scot* (1968).

Labour and social conditions is the special province of the Scottish Labour History Society, and its *Bulletin* is a valuable source. *A short history of Labour in Scotland* (1967) by W. H. Marwick and the older and less reliable *History of the Working Classes in Scotland* (1920) by T. Johnston are currently the best available books. Volumes of the *Third Statistical Account,* where available, have much useful information, both of a social and of an economic nature. *The Dawn of Scottish Social Welfare* (1948) and *Scottish Social Welfare 1864–1914* (1958), both by

T. Ferguson, set a more general framework. On housing, a particularly severe problem in Scotland, refer to S. D. Chapman's edition, *The History of Working Class Housing* (1971) and E. Gauldie's *Cruel Habitations : A History of Working-Class Housing 1780–1918* (1974).

Notes and References

1 Cf. the excellent short summary contained in S. B. Saul, *The Myth of the Great Depression 1873–1896* (1969); H. W. Richardson, 'Retardation in Britain's Industrial Growth 1870–1913', *SJPE*, XII, 1965, 125–49

2 Cf. A. S. Milward, *The Economic Effects of the World Wars on Britain* (1970)

3 Cf. B. W. E. Alford, *Depression and Recovery? British Economic Growth 1918–1939* (1972); D. H. Aldcroft, 'Economic Growth in Britain in the Inter-War Years: A Reassessment', *EcHR*, 2nd series, XX, 1967, 311–26

4 D. H. Aldcroft, 'The Entrepreneur and the British Economy 1870–1914', *EcHR*, 2nd series, XVII, 1964, 113–34; T. J. Byres, 'Entrepreneurship in the Scottish Heavy Industries 1870–1900', in P. L. Payne (ed.), *Studies in Scottish Business History* (1967), 250–96; J. Butt, 'The Role of Scottish Business History', *The Journal of Economic Studies*, III, 1968, 78–80; P. L. Payne, *British Entrepreneurship in the Nineteenth Century* (1974), 45–56

5 P. H. Lindert and K. Trace, 'Yardsticks for Victorian Entrepreneurs', in D. N. McCloskey (ed.), *Essays on a Mature Economy: Britain after 1840* (1971), 248 ff.

6 D. S. Landes, *The Unbound Prometheus* (1969), 233–4

7 Cf. S. Pollard, *The Gold Standard and Employment Policies between the Wars* (1970), 1–26

8 Min. of Agric., Fish and Food, *A Century of Agricultural Statistics: Great Britain 1866–1966* (1968), 21–2; cf. G. F. B. Houston, 'Agriculture', in A. K. Cairncross (ed.), *The Scottish Economy* (1954), 84–108, for many refreshing insights into the development of modern Scottish agriculture.

9 *Agricultural Statistics*, 28

10 J. A. Symon, *Scottish Farming, Past and Present* (1959), 194

11 *Agricultural Statistics*, 84; R. Perren, 'The North American Beef and Cattle Trade with Great Britain 1870–1914, *EcHR*, 2nd series, XXIV, 1971, 430–44

12 Symon, *op. cit.*, 193 ff.

13 James MacDonald, 'On the Agriculture of the County of Caithness', *Trans. Highland Agric. Soc.*, VII, 1875; *Report of the Royal Commission on the Highlands and Islands*, 1895, Cmd 7681; Symon, *op. cit.*, 192–3

14 Symon, *op. cit.*, 199

15 Ibid., 200; *Report of Departmental Committee on land in Scotland used as Deer Forests*, 1922, Cmd 1636, *passim;* J. Hunter, 'Sheep and Deer: Highland sheep farming 1850–1900', *Northern Scotland*, I, 1973, 199–222

16 Symon, *op. cit.*, 197

17 *BPP*, 1881, XVI, *Royal Commission on the Depressed Conditions of the Agricultural Interests, Reports of Assistant Commissioners on Scotland*; 1895, XVII, *Royal Commission on Agriculture*, 523 ff.

18 A. Collier, *The Crofting Problem* (1953); J. A. Kellas, 'The Liberal Party in Scotland 1876–1895', *SHR*, XLIV, 1965, 5 and his 'The Crofters' War 1882–8', *History Today*, xii, 281–8; D. W. Crowley, 'The Crofters' Party, 1885–92', *SHR*, XXXV, 1965, 110–26; H. J. Hanham, 'The Problem of Highland Discontent 1880–1885', *Trans. Roy. Hist. Soc.*, 1969, 21–67; E. Richards, 'How Tame were the Highlanders during the Clearances', *Scottish Studies*, XVII, 1973, 36, 44 ff.

19 *BPP*, 1884, XXXII–XXXVI, *Royal Commission on the Condition of Crofters and Cottars in the Highlands and Islands of Scotland* (Napier Commission), but especially XXXII, 7, 16, 41

20 J. P. Day, *Public Administration in the Highlands and Islands* (1918), *passim*

21 J. Gollan, *Scottish Prospect* (1948), 167; *Clydesdale Bank Survey*, 1938; Scottish Economic Committee, *Review of the*

Economic Conditions of the Highlands and Islands of Scotland (1938), *passim*

22 Symon, *op. cit.*, 292 ff.; J. Brown, 'Scottish and English Land Legislation 1905–11', *SHR*, XLVII, 1968, 72–85

23 Board of Agriculture for Scotland, *Reports*, 1913–29

24 Symon, *op. cit.*, 312 ff.; J. Kirkwood, 'In the beginning: the West of Scotland College of Agriculture', *Agricultural Progress*, XXV, 1950, 69 ff.; J. A. Hanley, 'Agricultural Education', *Agriculture in the Twentieth Century* (1939), 91 ff.

25 Symon, *op. cit.*, 205–6

26 Symon, *op. cit.*, 209–21; D. J. Jones *et al.*, *Rural Scotland during the War* (1926), *passim*; C. Douglas, 'Scottish agriculture during the war', *Trans. Highland Agric. Soc.*, 1919, 5 ff.

27 Symon, *op. cit.*, 222–6

28 Ibid., 422–34; Horace Plunkett Foundation, *Agricultural Co-operation in Scotland and Wales* (1932)

29 *Clydesdale Bank Surveys* (1932–9)

30 Houston, 'Agriculture', 90 ff.

31 R. W. Dron, *The Coalfields of Scotland* (1902); J. MacKinnon, *The Social and Industrial History of Scotland* (1921), 82–3; A. Slaven, 'Earnings and Productivity in the Scottish Coal-mining Industry', in Payne, *Scottish Business History*, 217–49; A. S. Cunningham, *Mining in the Kingdom of Fife* (1913) and his *Mining in Mid and East Lothian* (1925)

32 C. H. Lee, *Regional Economic Growth in the United Kingdom since the 1880's* (1971), 31

33 I. F. Gibson, 'The Establishment of the Scottish Steel Industry', *SJPE*, V, 1958, 22–39; T. R. Miller, *The Monkland Tradition* (1958), 44 ff.

34 For the general context cf. P. L. Payne, 'Iron and Steel Manufactures', in D. H. Aldcroft (ed.), *The Development of British Industry and Foreign Competition 1875–1914* (1968), 71–99; M. W. Flinn, 'British Steel and Spanish Ore 1871–1914', *EcHR*, 2nd series, VIII, 1955–6, 84–90; Byres, 'Entrepreneurship', 259

35 Byres, 'Entrepreneurship', 259 ff.; R. H. Campbell, 'Scottish Shipbuilding, its Rise and Progress', *SGM*, 80, 2, 107–13; J. Shields, *Clyde Built* (1949), *passim*

36 On this point cf. the stimulating work

of S. B. Saul, 'The Market and the Development of the Mechanical Engineering Industries in Britain 1860–1914', *EcHR*, 2nd series, XX, 1967, 111–30, and his 'The Engineering Industry', in *The Development of British Industry and Foreign Competition 1875–1914* (1968), 186–237; J. Thomas, *The Springburn Story* (1964); R. Miller and J. Tivy, *The Glasgow Region* (1958), *passim*

37 Anon., *The Great Industries of Great Britain* (1883), III, 226 ff.

38 *BPP*, 1912–13, CIX, *Final Report of Census of Production 1907*, 130; A. C. Macdonald and A. S. E. Browning, 'History of the Motor Industry in Scotland', *Institute of Mechanical Engineers, Proceedings of the Automobile Division* (1960–1); S. B. Saul, 'The Motor Industry in Britain', *Business History*, V, 1962, 22–44

39 N. K. Buxton, 'The Scottish Shipbuilding Industry between the Wars: A Comparative Study', *Business History*, X, 2, 1968, 101–20; Lord Aberconway, *The Basic Industries of Great Britain* (1927), 226 ff.

40 S. G. E. Lythe, 'Shipbuilding at Dundee down to 1914', *SJPE*, IX, 1962, 219–32; Buxton, 'Scottish Shipbuilding', 105

41 Buxton, 'Scottish Shipbuilding', 109 ff.

42 C. A. Oakley, *Scottish Industry Today* (1937), 251, 261–2; J. L. Carvel, *Stephen of Linthouse 1750–1950* (1950), 116

43 Gollan, *op. cit.*, 53 ff.; Buxton, 'Scottish Shipbuilding', 114

44 L. Jones, *Shipbuilding in Britain* (1957), 144

45 C. E. V. Leser, 'Coal-mining', in Cairncross, *op. cit.*, 109 ff.; Gollan, *op. cit.*, 25 ff.

46 N. K. Buxton, 'Entrepreneurial Efficiency in the British Coal Industry between the Wars', *EcHR*, 2nd series, XXIII, 1970, 476–97; *Scottish Coalfields Report*, 1944, Cmd 6575, *passim*; Aberconway, *op. cit.*, 203 ff.

47 *Final Report Census of Production 1907*, 171–2; Aberconway, *op. cit.*, 217 ff.

48 Miller, *op. cit.*, 49

49 Ibid., 56–61 and 78–9; H. W. Macrosty, *The Trust Movement in British Industry* (1907), 46 ff.

50 Gollan, *op. cit.*, 38; Oakley, *op. cit.*, 248–9

51 British Iron and Steel Federation and Joint Iron Council, *White Paper on Iron and Steel Industry*, 1946, Cmd 6811; T. H. Burnham and G. O. Hoskins, *Iron and Steel in Britain 1870–1939* (1943), 319

52 J. C. Carr and W. Taplin, *History of the British Steel Industry* (1962), 445 ff.

53 Gollan, *op. cit.,* 40

54 Miller, *op. cit.,* 64 ff.; Carr and Taplin, *op. cit.,* 326–7, 386–7 and 539; Oakley, *op. cit.,* 251

55 Miller, *op. cit.,* 79–80

56 *The Economist,* 18 March 1939

57 *Final Report, Census of Production 1907*, 190; C. E. V. Leser and A. H. Silvey, 'Scottish Industries during the Inter-War Period', *The Manchester School of Economics and Social Studies*, XVIII, 1951, 163 ff.

58 S. B. Saul, 'The Engineering Industry', in *The Development of British Industry and Foreign Competition 1875–1914* (1968), 197 ff.; W. Vamplew, 'Scottish Railways and the Development of Scottish Locomotive Building in the Nineteenth Century', *Business History Review*, XLVI, 1972, 320–38

59 These conclusions are based principally upon the Censuses of Production of 1924, 1930 and 1935. Cf. also H. W. Richardson, *Economic Recovery in Britain, 1932–9* (1967), 70 ff. and Oakley, *op. cit.,* 60 ff., 112 ff., 185 ff.

60 G. M. Thomson, *Scotland, That Distressed Area* (1933), 46 ff.; Richardson, *op. cit.,* 70–1; C. H. Lee, *Regional Economic Growth in the United Kingdom since the 1880s* (1971), 19

61 J. Butt, 'Working-class Housing in Glasgow, 1851–1914', in S. D. Chapman (ed.), *The History of Working-Class Housing* (1971), 55–92; A. K. Chalmers (ed.), *Public Health Administration in Glasgow* (1905), *passim*; B. Lenman et al., *Dundee and its Textile Industry* (Abertay Hist. Soc. Pub. 14, 1969), 77–104; *Report of the Royal Commission on Housing in Scotland 1917–18*, XIV, *passim*; T. Ferguson, *Scottish Social Welfare 1864–1914* (1958), 85 ff.

62 H. W. Richardson and D. H. Aldcroft, *Building in the British Economy between the Wars* (1968), 106–7, 186–7

63 Richardson and Aldcroft, *op. cit.,* 202–3

64 *Report of the Committee on Scottish Building Costs*, 1939, Cmd 5977; *Report of the Department of Health for Scotland*, 1938, Cmd 5969, p. 28

65 Richardson and Aldcroft, *op. cit.,* 114; Richardson, *Economic Recovery*, 236 ff.

66 Leser and Silvey, 'Scottish Industries', 169; G. R. Denton, 'Investment and Location in the Steel Industry—Corby', *Oxford Economic Papers* (1955); J. A. Bowie, *The Future of Scotland* (1939), 150 ff.

67 S. R. Dennison, *The Location of Industry and the Depressed Areas* (1939), *passim*; P.E.P., *Report on the Location of Industry in Great Britain* (1939), *passim*

68 *Clydesdale Bank Survey*, 1939

69 Cf. *The Economist*, 26 Nov. and 3 Dec. 1938; Oakley, *op. cit.,* 180; Gollan, *op. cit.,* 112

70 *Clydesdale Bank Survey*, 1939

71 Cf. P. Mathias, *The Retailing Revolution* (1967), 3–29; J. B. Jefferys, *Retail Trading in Britain 1850–1950* (1954), *passim*; *Stratton's Glasgow and its Environs* (1891), 47–9, 52, 55, 57 ff., 60–2 and 84; Anon., *Men of the Period* (1896), 143; W. H. Marwick, *Scotland in Modern Times* (1964), 98–103; C. Wilson, *History of Unilever*, II (1970 ed.), 40–1

72 J. S. Flanagan, *Wholesale Co-operation in Scotland 1868–1918* (1920), *passim*; W. H. Maxwell, *History of Co-operation in Scotland* (1910), *passim*; A. M. Carr Saunders et al., *Consumers' Co-operation in Great Britain* (1938), *passim*; cf. also the many histories of local co-operative societies

73 Mathias, *op. cit.,* 55–72

74 Ibid., 66–8, 96–124 and 358

75 Alison Adburgham, *Shops and Shopping* (1964), 114 and 191–2

76 A. Wilson, *Walter Wilson, Merchant 1849–1917* (1920), *passim*

77 Jefferys, *op. cit.,* 41 ff., 47, 59, 64; Marwick, *op. cit.,* 160–1

78 A. Bonner, *British Co-operation* (1961), 162

79 Mathias, *op. cit.,* 237 ff.

80 Ibid., 258 ff.

81 Marwick, *op. cit.,* 163–4

82 M. W. Flinn, 'Overseas Trade of Scottish Ports 1900–60', *SJPE*, XIII, 1966, 220–37

83 Ibid., 234–6; W. M. L. Murray, 'Trade' in Cairncross, *op. cit.,* 139

84 J. Nicol, *Vital, Social and Economic Statistics of Glasgow* (1891), 318; *Clydesdale Bank Surveys*, 1932–9; M. W. Flinn, 'British Steel and Spanish Ore 1871–1914', *EcHR*, 2nd series, VIII, 1955–6, 84–90

85 *BPP*, 1912–13, CIX, Census of Production 1907, 50, 130, 141, 177, 181, 209 and 233; Census of Production 1930, 237

86 *Clydesdale Bank Survey*, 1939

87 Thomson, *op. cit.*, 58; Murray, 'Trade', 138–9

88 A. Keith, *The North of Scotland Bank Limited, 1836–1936* (1936), 100 n. and 127

89 C. A. Malcolm, *The History of the British Linen Bank* (1950), 146 ff.; Keith, *op. cit.*, 153 and 155–7; N. Munro, *The History of the Royal Bank of Scotland* (1928), 251–342; R. S. Tait, *The History of the Union Bank of Scotland* (1930), 316 ff.

90 Keith, *op. cit.*, 101; Rait, *op. cit.*, 321 ff.; Munro, *op. cit.*, 271–87

91 W. F. Crick and J. E. Wadsworth, *A Hundred Years of Joint Stock Banking* (1936), 366–407; Bowie, *op. cit.*, 192 ff.; M. Gaskin, *The Scottish Banks: A Modern Survey* (1965), *passim*

92 Thomson, *op. cit.*, 89 and 94

93 S. G. E. Lythe, 'Britain, the Financial Capital of the World', in C. J. Bartlett (ed.), *Britain Pre-eminent* (1969), 31 ff.; A. R. Hall (ed.), *The Export of Capital, 1870–1914* (1968), *passim*; L. H. Jenks, *The Migration of British Capital to 1875* (1963 ed.), *passim*; C. K. Hobson, *The Export of Capital* (1914); A. K. Cairncross, *Home and Foreign Investment 1870–1913* (1953), *passim*

94 C. C. Spence, *British Investments and the American Mining Frontier 1860–1901* (New York, 1958), 146, 163–5

95 W. H. Marwick, *Economic Developments in Victorian Scotland* (1936), 81 ff.; W. T. Jackson, *The Enterprising Scot* (1968), *passim*; A. W. Paton and A. H. Millar (eds), *British Association Handbook, Dundee 1912* (1912), 118–20, 349–56; J. C. Gilbert, *A History of Investment Trusts in Dundee* (1939), *passim*; J. D. Bailey, 'Australian Borrowing in Scotland in the Nineteenth Century', *EcHR*, XII, 1959, 268–79; N. G. Butlin, *Investment in Australian Economic Development 1861–1900* (1964), *passim*

96 Jackson, *op. cit.*, 315; B. P. Lenman and K. Donaldson, 'Partners' Incomes, Investment and Diversification in the Scottish Linen Area 1850–1921', *Business History*, XIII, 1971, 3 ff.

97 D. R. Adler, *British Investment in American Railways 1834–1898* (Virginia, 1970), 92–3, 116 n., 147 n., 148 n., 192 n., 195 n., 209; Jackson, *op. cit.*, *passim*; C. C. Spence, *op. cit.*, *passim*; W. G. Kerr, 'Scottish Investment and Enterprise in Texas', in Payne, *Scottish Business History*, 367–86; R. E. Tyson, 'Scottish Investment in American Railways: the Case of the City of Glasgow Bank, 1856–1881', ibid., 387–416; W. M. Pearce, *The Matador Land and Cattle Company* (1964), *passim*; *The Statist*, 10 Jan 1885

98 Jackson, *op. cit.*, 14, 16, 17, 39, 152, 167, 171–2, 216, 218, 221, 223 and 229; Marwick, *Victorian Scotland*, 40 and 82; C. C. Spence, *op. cit.*, 52–3

99 D. R. Adler, *op. cit.*, 92 n.; *The Scottish Banking and Insurance Magazine*, 1 February 1879; on this subject and on Scottish investment in Canada, I have gained greatly from the unpublished work of P. D. Holcombe who is currently researching at the University of Strathclyde.

100 Jackson, *op. cit.*, 21, 24, 192, 236, 238, 242, 307; Lenman and Donaldson, 'Partners' incomes', 1–18

101 Jackson, *op. cit.*, 14 ff.; Spence, *op. cit.*, 164

102 Lythe, 'Britain', 47 ff.; S. B. Saul, *Studies in British Overseas Trade, 1870–1914* (1960), 202; A. K. Cairncross, 'Did Foreign Investments Pay?', *Review of Economic Studies* (1935), 67–78

103 *Census of Scotland*, 1871 and mid-year estimate for 1939

104 D. J. Robertson, 'Population Growth and Movement', in Cairncross, *Scottish Economy*, 9–20, and C. V. Leser, 'Births and Deaths', ibid., 21–34; Bowie, *op. cit.*, 11–56

105 H. J. Dyos and D. H. Aldcroft, *British Transport* (1969), 350–1; J. Butt, *The Industrial Archaeology of Scotland* (1967), 184–7; W. H. Bett and J. C. Gilham, *Great British Tramway Networks* (1962), *passim*; D. L. Thomson and D. E. Sinclair, *The Glasgow Subway* (1964), *passim*

106 *Census of Scotland*, 1931

107 *Census of Scotland*, 1921 and 1931

108 B. R. Mitchell and P. Deane, *Abstract of British Historical Statistics* (1962), 31–2

109 Cf. H. J. Habakkuk, *Population Growth and Economic Development since 1750* (1968), 53 ff.; Bowie, *op. cit.,* 47 ff.

110 Cf. J. A. Banks, *Parenthood and Prosperity* (1954), *passim*; Bowie, *op. cit.,* 47–8; *Report of Committee on Scottish Health Services*, 1936, *passim*

111 A. D. Campbell, 'Income', in Cairncross, *Scottish Economy*, 50; cf. also his 'Changes in Scottish Incomes 1924–49', *Economic Journal*, LXV, 1955, 225–40

112 D. J. Robertson, 'Wages' in Cairncross, *Scottish Economy*, 149 ff.; BPP, 1887, LXXIX, *Return relating to wages*, 273; BPP, 1892, XXXIV, *Royal Commission on Labour*

113 Board of Trade Earnings Enquiry, 1906; W. Beveridge, *Full Employment in a Free Society* (1944), 74

114 J. D. M. Bell, 'Trade Unionism', in Cairncross, *Scottish Economy*, 280 ff.; S. and B. Webb, *The History of Trade Unionism* (1894), 415; W. H. Marwick, *A Short History of Labour in Scotland* (1967), *passim*; T. Johnston, *History of the Working Classes in Scotland* (1920), 302 ff.; K. C. Buckley, *Trade Unionism in Aberdeen, 1878–1900* (1955), *passim*; W. H. Fraser, *Trade Unions and Society : The Struggle for Acceptance, 1850–1880* (1974), *passim*; R. K. Middlemas, *The Clydesiders : a left-wing struggle for Parliamentary Power* (1965), *passim*

115 D. J. Robertson, 'Consumption', in Cairncross, *Scottish Economy*, 170 ff. and R. Baird, 'Housing', ibid., 193 ff.

116 Butt, 'Working-class Housing', 55–92; A. K. Chalmers (ed.), *Public Health Administration in Glasgow* (1905), *passim;* BPP, 1884–5, XXXI, *Royal Commission on Housing of the Working Classes,* 60 ff.

117 *Report of the Royal Commission on Housing in Scotland,* 1918, Cmd 8731, 346

118 Bowie, *op. cit.,* 74 ff.; Department of Health for Scotland, *Planning our New Homes* (1944), para. 2

Index

Abbeys, *see* Monasteries
Aberdeen, 5, 6, 9, 10, 11–12, 14, 30, 31, 37, 45, 51, 52, 54, 58, 60, 63, 67, 68, 69, 88, 96, 138, 153, 155, 182, 225; *see* Appendices II and III(b)
Aberdeenshire, 88, 93, 94, 111, 124, 157, 158, 187, 208
Abernethy, 27, 145, 189
Acts of the Scots Parliament, 18, 23, 24, 30–1, 32, 36, 40, 41, 46, 47, 48, 49, 53, 67, 78, 80, 109, 150
Acts of the Union Parliament, 37, 155, 156, 157, 177, 180, 209, 210, 211, 212, 213, 220, 227
Agriculture, 15–26, 85, 89, 91, 102, 106, 108–35, 162, 163, 202, 205–14; improvement of, 94, 104, 109, 111–13, 115–16, 121–2, 123, 175; value of output of, 214; *see* Cattle, Enclosure, Harvests, Runrig, Sheep, Tenure
Alexander I, 17, 64, 71; II, 17, 68, 71, 79; III, 15, 17, 71, 74, 79
Amalgamations, 156, 159, 197, 219–20, 221–2, 230, 233
America, 11, 13–14, 55, 64, 98, 100, 146–149, 164, 165, 184, 201, 206; South, 149
American War of Independence, 89, 147–8, 149, 163–4, 166, 181, 184
American Civil War, 183, 188
Anglo-Normans and their influence, 5, 15, 27, 29
Angus, 23, 45, 88, 90, 94, 96, 145, 157, 182, 183
Argyll, 43, 88, 92, 95, 112, 114, 120, 205
Aristocracy, 109, 115, 116, 117, 118, 131, 132, 133; *see* Landowners
Assembly, General, of the Church of Scotland, 36, 71
Australasia, 99, 100, 149
Ayala, Pedro de, 7, 52
Ayr, 10, 33, 34, 47, 57, 64

Ayr Bank, 109, 133, 155
Ayrshire, 4, 25, 26, 41–2, 87, 88, 94, 95, 96, 108, 119, 124, 167, 174, 175, 187

Baltic, 9, 48, 50, 51, 57–9, 117, 149
Banks, 79, 109, 127, 132–3, 147, 150–8, 159–60, 163, 165, 188, 191, 202, 204, 233–4; English, 154, 159–60, 233; Savings, 133, 157–8
Bank of England, 154, 159–60
Bank of Scotland, 79, 132, 150–1, 153, 154, 157
Bank, Royal, 132, 151, 152, 153, 154, 155, 157, 233
Barley, 92, 111, 119, 122, 123, 128, 206, 207, 208
Berwick-on-Tweed, 5, 29, 30, 31, 55
Berwickshire, 87, 96, 119, 122
Biscay, 12, 58, 62–3, 64
Black Death, *see* Plague
Bleaching, 130, 148, 172, 174, 179
Boece, Hector, 11, 22, 39, 43, 45
Borders, 3, 6, 7, 8, 10, 15, 16–17, 21, 73, 87, 97, 108, 112, 114, 115, 175
Brechin, 6, 27, 182
Brewing, 121, 129, 134, 165, 175, 202
Bruce, Robert the, 3, 72
Bruges, 60, 61
Buchanan, John & Co., 139–40
Building industry, 27, 28, 39, 60, 68, 130, 163, 172, 173, 177, 178, 224–6; *see* Appendices V(i) and (j)
Burghs, 27, 29, 30–8, 40, 45–6, 53, 130, 152; charters, 29, 30, 46; conflicts between, 31; courts, 33; expenditures, 34–5; and royal policy, 29, 31; revenues, 34; social policies, 34–6; taxation, 30, 34, 36

Caithness, 96, 121, 124
Canada, 13, 64–5, 98, 99, 201

Canals, 114, 132, 137, 146, 198

Capital, 40, 47, 50, 64, 65, 66, 110, 126, 131, 132, 133, 140, 142, 143, 147, 150, 151, 154, 155, 158, 159, 163–5, 168, 169, 172, 176, 178, 186, 187, 190, 191–192, 196, 204, 218; formation, 102, 104–5, 133, 148–9, 161, 164–5, 176, 182–3, 186, 196–7, 229; investment, 102, 103, 105, 109, 129, 132, 148, 150, 159, 164–74, 187, 193, 195, 204, 226, 233, 234, 238; overhead, 149

Capital equipment, 19, 169, 170, 171, 174–5, 188

Capital goods industries, 39, 102, 146, 199, 204–5, 216, 217, 220, 226, 227

Carron Company, 146, 171, 190, 191

Castles, 5, 27, 28

Cattle, 19, 22, 23, 112, 114, 120, 121, 122, 124, 206, 208; trade, 25, 56, 83, 85, 91, 112–13, 116, 124, 127, 198

Charcoal, 39, 42, 59, 111–12, 130, 174, 189, 190

Charles I, 67, 77; II, 78

Chemicals, 148, 164, 165, 173, 203

Church(es), 5, 16–17, 27, 76, 77, 80–2; collegiate, 28; post-Reformation, 35, 36, 41, 49, 64

Clackmannanshire, 87, 95, 175

Classes, managerial, 185–6; middle, 106, 136, 138; professional, 97, 106; working, 106, 107, 136, 137, 143, 157; see Aristocracy, Landowners, Society, Trade Unionism

Clyde, River, 29, 31, 54, 59, 65, 175–6, 216, 218, 219

Coal, industry, 39, 41, 55, 131, 162–3, 165–6, 177, 199, 202, 214, 218, 220–1; trade, 40, 41, 56, 57, 61, 145, 146, 149, 174, 175, 220; see Appendix V(f)

Coinage, 73, 74, 150

Colonies, 13–14, 65–6, 98–9

Commerce, see Trade

Commonwealth, 56, 77, 82–3; see Cromwell and War

Companies, joint-stock, 47, 48, 54, 65–6, 143, 150–2, 159, 164, 165, 199–200, 221, 222, 223, 235

Competition, 53, 65, 179, 180, 188, 191, 193, 201, 206, 211, 212, 213, 218, 220, 222, 223, 224

Consumer goods, 102–4, 137–8, 146

Convention of Royal Burghs, 9, 31, 32, 46, 53, 71, 179

Co-operative Societies, 143, 158–9, 228–229

Corn Laws, 85, 117, 127

Cotton, 137, 161, 167–8, 172–4, 177, 178, 181, 184–9, 202, 224

Coupar Angus, 16, 17, 20, 45

Coutts, John & Co., bankers, 133, 152

Craftsmen, 28, 30–1, 134–5, 157, 175; Flemish, 46, 47; French, 51, 175; guilds of, 30–1, 36, 46; Italian, 44, 45; in metal, 39, 42, 97; in mining, 40, 97; in textiles, 46, 97, 170; in precious metals, 49

Credit, 52, 103, 125, 131, 133, 147, 150, 152, 153, 154–5, 159, 165, 178, 179–80, 184, 205

Cromwell, Oliver, 14, 62

Cunninghame, Robert, 40, 42

Customs duties (and Excise), 85, 137, 201–2, 212, 226; foreign, 201

Cycles, business/trade, 112, 115, 127, 137, 155, 156, 169, 170, 190, 191, 196, 216, 221, 224

Dairying, 25; 119, 120, 121, 124, 211

Dale, David, 131, 155, 167, 169

Danzig, 12, 57, 58, 59

Darien Scheme, 14, 66, 83, 85, 150

David I, 15, 28, 29, 71, 74; II, 30, 74

Debt, National, 85, 133

Demand, domestic, 55, 67, 102, 103, 104, 105, 119, 136, 137, 179, 180, 181, 182, 189, 199, 216, 217, 219; foreign, see Exports and Trade

Depopulation, 95–6, 210

Diet, 94, 206–7

Disease, 89, 93, 101; see Plague

Distilling, 91, 92, 121, 129, 134, 172, 173, 202; see Appendix V(b)

Doctors, 25, 93

Domestic service, 106, 107, 157

Domestic 'System', 48–9, 166–7, 168–171, 172, 180, 181, 182–3, 184

Dumbarton, 6, 31, 65, 146, 166

Dumfries, burgh, 8; county, 93, 95, 157

Dunbar, 58, 97, 157, 164, 182

Dunbartonshire, 87, 95, 96, 119–20, 166, 167

Dundee, 6, 23, 31, 34, 35, 36, 38, 47, 52, 55, 58, 59, 60, 63, 67, 77, 87, 88, 95, 96, 138, 155, 182, 183, 224, 225, 236, 237; see Appendices II and III(b)

Dunfermline, 6, 17, 88, 93, 182–3

Dunlop, James (of Garnkirk), 166, 167

Dyestuffs, 62, 63, 79, 120, 129, 130, 164, 165, 175, 184

East Anglia, 25, 113, 115

East Lothian, 26, 41, 87, 95, 96, 115, 125, 133, 170, 175, 187

Edinburgh, 5, 6, 7, 8, 9, 10, 25, 31, 35, 37, 38, 39, 47, 48, 58, 64, 67, 73, 87, 88, 93, 96, 97, 101, 115, 119, 120, 124, 128, 133, 138, 139, 152, 153, 155, 156, 157, 159, 162, 170, 172, 180, 225, 236, 237, 238; see Appendices II and III(b)

Education, 34, 35, 176–7

Edward I, 7; III, 79

Elphinstone, 11, 40, 68

Emigration, 11–14, 57, 88, 90, 92, 97, 98–100, 113, 239

Employment, 113, 121, 123, 125, 183, 187–8, 189, 240–1; structure of, 106–7, 108, 137, 200

Enclosure, 24, 109–10, 111–12, 115, 116–18, 119, 120, 121, 125–6

Engineers, civil, 97; mechanical, 184, 185; marine, 216

Engineering industry, 193, 199, 202, 216, 217–18, 223, 227

England, 4, 11, 13, 16, 40, 46, 52, 55, 60, 66, 89, 97–8, 105, 106, 107, 110, 111, 144–6, 175–6, 179, 184, 185, 225; north of, 19, 175, 179

English, 5, 15, 22, 28, 29, 39, 42, 46, 55, 66, 72, 73, 78, 79, 96, 97

Entrepreneurs, 97, 102, 128, 129, 145, 162, 164–71, 176, 178, 181–2, 186, 189, 190, 191, 193, 194, 202–3, 204, 229

Equivalent, 85, 151; arising, 85

Europe, 9, 11–12, 17, 23, 25, 29, 37, 44, 45, 54–69, 70, 89, 98, 102, 148, 149, 201

Excise, see Customs

Exports, 22, 40, 41, 43, 49, 52–3, 55, 56, 57, 58–9, 60, 61, 67, 105, 127, 128, 136, 148–50, 218, 220, 231–3; composition of, 148, 149, 232; value of, 149–50, 231; see Appendix IV

Factories, 167, 168, 169, 170–2, 177, 178, 181, 182, 183, 185

Fairs, 32, 62, 138

Falkirk, 113, 155, 165

Famine, 7, 8, 9, 10, 36, 89, 94

Farming, see Agriculture

Feudalism, see Tenure

Fife, 21, 31, 39, 41, 88, 94, 95, 110, 120–1, 145, 157, 182–3, 187, 205

Fish, 41, 52, 53, 55, 56, 57, 58, 61, 64, 94, 148

Fishing, 52, 91, 106, 121; boats and tackle, 53, 54; capital, 53–4; credit, 52;

conflicts with Dutch, 53; organisation, 54; prices, 53; protection, 53

Flanders, 12, 17, 25, 32, 42, 43, 60, 62; Flemish language, 29; see Holland

Flax, 48, 59, 110, 122, 123, 128, 130, 174, 179, 180–1, 182, 183

Forbes, Duncan (of Inverness), 52

Forestry, 15, 20–2, 25, 111–12, 145

Forfar, 6, 73; see Angus

Forth, River, 9, 40, 41, 67

France, 11, 12, 25, 60, 62–4, 79, 136, 148, 179

Friendly Societies, 135, 158

Galloway, 96, 97–8, 112, 113, 124, 131, 145, 186, 187

Germany, 64, 149, 179; see Hanse

Glasgow, 6, 10, 31, 32, 36, 39, 48, 50, 51, 54, 57, 58, 65–6, 67, 68, 87, 88, 89, 93, 96–7, 101, 119, 124, 128, 138, 139, 140, 146–8, 152, 153, 155, 156, 157, 162, 164, 165, 166, 167, 168, 171, 172, 173, 181, 184, 185, 186, 187, 199; Diocese of, 18; see Appendices II and III(b)

Glasgow Thistle Bank, 133, 153; Ship Bank, 153

Glass, 44–5, 130, 162, 164, 166, 175, 224

Goats, 21, 22, 23

Gold, mining, 43–4; ware, 49

Government, 70–3, 117, 148, 204, 205, 208, 209, 210, 211, 212, 213, 216, 220, 226–7; see Acts, Scottish Privy Council, Parliament

Grain, production, 116, 117, 118, 120, 121, 122, 123, 125, 126, 206, 207, 211; trade, 55, 57, 59, 60, 62, 91, 117, 127, 128, 152

Grant, Dr I. F., 16, 22, 53

Greenock, 150, 155, 164; see Appendix II

Gross National Product, 89, 101, 177, 178, 200

Hanse League, 57, 58

Harvests, 87, 91, 110, 111, 127, 181

Hay, Sir George, 42, 44

Health, public, 23, 93, 105, 194–5

Heriot, George, 28, 35

Herring, see Fish

Hides, see Skins

Highlands, 4, 10, 15, 19, 22–3, 24, 29, 53, 87, 91–2, 94, 95, 98, 99, 101, 112, 113, 114, 116, 178, 181, 189, 208, 209, 210

Hilderstone, see Linlithgow
Holland, 43, 50, 51, 53, 54, 60–1, 62, 122, 138, 148, 174, 175, 179
Hope, Sir John, 43, 44
Horses, 22, 23, 25, 68, 112, 114, 115, 119
Horticulture, 25, 115
Hosiery, knitted, 56, 121, 148; thread, 137, 170, 175
Housing, 93, 101, 105, 177, 195, 224–6, 241–2; see Appendices V(i) and (j)

Immigrants, 46, 47, 50, 51, 53, 90, 96–7, 100, 200, 239
Imports, 23, 25, 42, 48, 49, 51, 54, 56, 57, 59, 61, 62, 63, 67, 79, 127, 136, 147, 171, 177, 179, 180–1, 183, 189, 206, 215, 218, 231–2; see Appendix IV
Income, local, 134, 179; per capita, 137; national, 101, 103, 105, 106–7, 108, 162, 203–4
Industrialists, 109, 164–8, 170–1, 182, 183, 185; see Entrepreneurs
Industrial output, 192, 194, 215, 217, 219, 220, 222, 223; see individual industries
Industry, rationalisation of, 219–20, 221, 222, 223; see Amalgamations
Inflation, 75, 76
Insurance, companies, 152, 159, 202; valuations, 140, 164, 170–1, 172–4, 187
Interest, rates of, 34, 127, 148, 154–5, 157, 225, 234, 235
Inventions, 122, 125, 174–7, 184, 185, 192, 215
Inventors, 176, 177, 181, 182, 184, 185, 189, 192
Inverness, burgh, 13, 21, 23, 37, 50, 52, 64, 77, 88, 89; county, 21, 65, 88, 94, 95, 96, 111
Investment, domestic, see Capital; foreign, 160, 202, 204, 233, 235–9
Ireland, 25, 56–7, 79, 101, 105, 107, 174, 178, 179
Irish, 96, 97, 100, 193, 200; Northern, see Ulster
Iron, industry, 132, 189–95, 199, 215, 221–3; cast, 190; exports, 150; firms, 143, 164, 166, 171–2, 189–91; furnaces, 189, 192, 193, 194; goods, 41, 105, 164; imports, 59, 221–2; mining, 42, 43, 131–2, 162, 165, 192; output, 192, 194; pig, 59, 146, 177; smelting, 39, 42, 175; see Appendices V(e), (g) and (h)
Irvine, 13, 57, 146
Islands, 23, 43, 53, 72–3, 111, 113, 116, 117, 208, 209, 210; see Orkney and Shetland

James I, 28, 53; II, 74; III, 73, 74, 76, 80; IV, 21, 44, 51, 62, 72, 73, 76; V, 43, 44, 49, 74, 76, 81; VI, 12, 14, 35, 43, 44, 47, 53, 72, 73, 77, 81, 82
Justice, feudal, 72; royal, 73
Jute, 183, 224

Kelp, 44, 91, 92
Kelso, 16, 19, 68
Kennedy, Bishop, 50–1
Kilmarnock, 170–1
Kincardineshire, 157, 182
Kirkcudbright, 97, 167
Kirkcaldy, 9, 31, 34, 41
Kirkwall, 27, 28
Knox, John, 6, 36

Labour, 16, 28, 40–1, 42, 43, 44, 45, 46, 50, 90, 102, 103, 104, 125, 134–5, 161, 169, 176; 179, 183, 184, 185, 186, 187–8, 193, 202, 216, 221; mobility of, 90, 94, 102, 127, 178, 200; see Classes, Craftsmen and Trade Unionism
Lanark, 5, 10, 31, 68
Lanarkshire, 67, 87, 88, 90, 94, 95, 96, 108, 117, 119, 157, 186, 187, 214, 221
Lancashire, 97, 98, 124, 145, 184, 185, 188, 197, 224
Land, arable, 15, 20, 113, 120, 121, 207; cultivable, 108, 110; pastoral, 20, 22, 112–13, 114, 120, 121, 123, 207; market, 109, 166; see Agriculture, Cattle, Monasteries, Sheep, Tenure
Landowners, 16, 17, 40, 41, 42, 43, 53, 99, 108–9, 110, 112, 115, 116, 117, 118, 119, 120, 121, 123, 124, 125, 126, 131–133, 135, 152, 159, 179, 197, 205–6, 212, 213
Lead, 42–3, 131
Leadhills, 43–4, 67, 131
Leather, 42, 130
Leith, 31, 45, 49, 50, 52, 58, 59, 63, 88, 96, 128, 145, 155, 171, 199; Water of, 50; see Appendices II and III(b)
Lesley, Bishop, 23, 52
Letterewe (Wester Ross), 42, 44
Lewis, 53, 54
Lime, production of, 162, 166
Linen, 48–9, 56, 64, 83, 85, 105, 129, 130, 136, 137, 144, 145, 152, 164, 166–167, 170, 171, 177, 178–83; see Appendix V(a)

Linen Company, British, 131, 132, 152, 179–80, 233
Linlithgow, 28, 31, 44
London, 21, 44, 52, 56, 66, 97, 98, 115, 145, 150, 151, 159, 160, 197, 216
Lovat, Lord, 24, 52
Low Countries, *see* Flanders
Lowlands, 4, 19, 29, 94, 208

Machinery, 122, 125, 150, 174, 175, 177, 182, 183, 184, 185, 188
Malcolm Canmore, 15, 71
Malt, 128, 129, 130, 131; *see* Appendix V(c)
Marketing, 25, 36–7, 48, 49, 78, 91, 102, 103, 104, 105, 113, 117, 178
Markets, 138, 162, 178, 190, 191, 204; *see* Demand and Trade
Mary, Queen of Scots, 37, 63, 67
Masons, 27, 28, 177
Materials, Raw, 54, 59, 113, 130, 149, 176
Meat, 123, 124, 198, 206–7
Medicine, state of, *see* Doctors
Meikle, Andrew and James, 122
Melrose, 16, 17, 20, 23, 111, 115
Mercantilism, 43, 46–7, 53, 55, 78–9, 85, 136, 146, 179, 180
Merchants, 21, 35, 46, 48, 52, 58, 97, 109, 117, 131, 152, 172, 184, 191–2, 197; German, 55; guilds, 30, 31, 36; in colonial trade, 65–6, 146–8; in foreign trade, 54–5, 60, 61, 64, 163–8
Middleburgh, 60, 61
Midlothian, 87, 88, 94, 95, 96, 97, 115, 175, 187
Mills, corn, 128, 130, 131; cotton, 131, 186, 187; flax, 182–3; fulling, 4–5; jute, 183; lint, 174; thread, 175; *see* Factories
Mining, 105, 106, 130, 131–2, 162–3, 178, *see* Coal, Iron, Appendices V(e) and (f)
Monarchy, expenditure, 75–7; royal council, 71, 73; sources of income, 75–7, 80–1; *see individual monarchs*
Monasteries, 5, 16–17, 18, 20, 22, 23, 25, 27, 36, 39, 41, 45, 68, 81; *see* Church(es)
Montrose, 14, 52, 171
Moray, 4, 5, 9, 15, 111
Munro, Donald, 22, 43

Navigation Act (1660), 65, 85, 146
Newbattle, 17, 39

New Zealand, 99, 206
Norway, 51, 59–60
Nova Scotia, 13–14, 65

Oats, 24, 37, 92, 94, 111, 120, 121, 122, 123, 125, 206, 207, 208
Orkney, 5, 27, 73, 96, 121, 171
Owen, Robert, 131, 139, 167

Paisley, 6, 16, 88, 89, 93, 145, 155, 168, 170, 181, 185, 186, 187, 189, 225; *see* Appendix II
Paper industry, 50, 129, 173, 177; *see* Appendix V(d)
Parliament of Scotland, 18, 46, 53, 66, 71, 74, 77, 78, 80, 82, 83–4; *see* Acts
Peebles, 10, 35
Perth, 5, 6, 9, 10, 23, 31, 34, 35, 47, 67, 88, 93, 128, 138, 155, 181
Perthshire, 21, 42, 88, 94, 96, 99, 110, 145, 157, 168, 174, 183
Pestilence, *see* Plague
Pigs, 23, 114, 207, 208
Plague, 7, 8–11, 17, 18, 36
Poor, 46, 186; relief of, 36; law, 103, 123; *see* Poverty
Population, 3–14, 15, 87–102, 137, 150, 204, 239–40; birth rate of, 7, 90, 92, 100, 239; death rate of, 70, 92, 93, 100–1, 239; migration of, 5, 13, 89–90, 92, 96–8, 100, 103, 134; rate of growth of, 3–6, 87–9, 94–5, 97, 239; *see* Appendices I and II, Immigrants and Urbanisation
Ports, 31, 34, 65, 144, 145, 150, 180
Potato, 25, 91, 92, 94, 111, 115, 116, 119, 120, 207
Pottery industry, 165, 175
Poverty, 7, 10, 12, 13, 35–6, 92, 123, 136
Power, 122, 123, 125, 174, 175, 182, 185, 186, 210
Prestonpans, 41, 44–5, 165, 175
Price movements, 36, 37, 52, 74–5, 91, 102, 103, 104, 110, 112, 113, 117, 118, 122, 123–4, 127, 134, 137, 163, 181, 190, 203, 204, 206, 208, 211, 212, 213, 227; controls on, 37–8
Printing, 50, 62, 172, 173
Publishing, 50, 107

Railways, 114, 124, 132, 134, 177, 193, 194, 195–200, 201
Reformation, 11, 25, 28, 34, 35, 60, 79, 80–2

Regions, development in, 128–9; specialisation in, 178, 180–1, 224; planning of, 226–7

Renfrewshire, 26, 87, 90, 94, 95, 97, 112, 157, 168, 185

Rents, 24, 73–4, 99, 103, 112, 113, 118, 119, 121, 122, 123, 203

Retailing, 97, 138, 139–41, 142, 143, 202, 227–31; see Appendix III

Roads, 67–8, 198; drove, 23; turnpike, 132

Rope-making, 51, 164, 173

Ross and Cromarty, 42, 88, 95, 96

Roxburgh, 29, 31, 96, 119, 157

Runrig, 19, 20, 48, 102, 110–11, 115, 116, 118, 121, 126; see Tenure

Russia, 12, 98, 171

St Andrews, 8, 27, 31, 49, 51

Salmon, see Fish

Salt, production, 41–2, 63, 162; trade, 42, 55, 58, 61, 62–3, 79

Saltcoats, 41–2, 63, 131

Scandinavia, 12; see Norway and Sweden

Scottish Co-operative Wholesale Society, 143, 239

Scottish Privy Council, 48, 56, 63, 66, 71, 74

Selkirk, 5, 8, 157

Sheep, farming, 17, 22–3, 113, 114, 119, 120, 121, 122, 123, 124, 130, 207, 208, 209

Shetland, 5, 73, 121

Shipbuilding, 50–1, 64, 145, 150, 173, 202, 215, 216, 218–20

Shipowning, 50, 65, 150, 218

Shipping, 50, 51, 54, 55, 58, 59, 65, 144, 198, 201, 218

Shops, 138–41, 170, 228, 229

Silk, 137, 145

Silver, mining, 43; ware, 49; trade in, 57

Skins (and Hides), 22, 23, 55, 56, 57, 61, 64, 112, 120

Smuggling, 56, 57, 63, 146, 180

Soap-making, 49–50, 152, 224

Society, Industrial, 40–1, 90, 105, 137, 176–7, 203, 239–42; rural, 15–16, 17–18, 19, 20, 29, 42, 90, 91, 95–6, 123, 134–5, 205; serfdom in, 40–1; urban, 28–9, 30, 31, 33, 100–1, 150; see Appendix II

Spain, 64, 66, 98, 215

Spirits, 127, 130, 177; see Appendix V(b)

Standard of living, 102, 103, 104, 137, 178, 203–4

Staple, Scottish, 32, 60

Steel industry, 199, 202, 215–16

Stirling, 5, 6, 10, 31, 38, 61, 128, 155

Stirlingshire, 87, 94, 95, 96, 120, 167, 187, 209

Sugar, refining, 50, 152, 164, 165, 178; trade, 56, 66, 145

Sutherland, 24, 96, 113, 114, 123, 124, 167, 186, 187

Sweden, 12, 58, 59, 98, 171

Tanning, 129, 130, 152, 165, 173; see Skins (and Hides)

Taxation, 5, 16, 18, 28, 77, 78, 85, 133

Tay, River, 31, 67, 68, 87

Tenure, 15, 18, 19, 109, 205–6; Celtic, 5; feudal, 15–16, 29; steelbow, 19

Textiles, 45–9, 56, 61, 62, 65, 67, 149, 150, 164, 168–71, 210, 224, 232; see Cotton, Linen, Silk, Wool and Appendix V(a)

Timber, 21, 39, 59–60, 67, 111–12, 115, 145

Tobacco, processing, 148; trade, 56, 65, 85, 145, 146–9, 152, 153

Towns, 5–6, 7, 8, 9, 10, 12, 15, 23, 28–9, 60, 87–8, 89–90, 96–7, 101, 107, 161, 181; relationship with rural hinterland, 32–3, 88; see Appendices II and III(b)

Trade, 31, 50, 55, 67, 110, 133, 138, 139; balance, 58–9, 62, 84, 127–8; coastal, 15, 21, 40, 52, 55–6, 102, 117, 141, 144–5, 163, 193, 198–9; colonial, 64–6, 94, 102, 145–9; domestic, 9, 24, 30, 36–7, 55, 102–3, 128, 136–44, 198, 199, 227–31; foreign, 8–9, 12, 21, 22, 31, 32, 40, 41, 42, 52–3, 54–69, 79, 136, 137, 146, 148, 149–50, 163, 193, 218, 222, 223, 224, 227, 231–2

Trade Unionism, 203, 241

Transport, 15, 21, 40, 67–9, 89, 102, 103, 104, 106, 114, 124, 130, 132, 134, 137, 162, 163, 175–6, 178, 189, 193, 195–200, 224

Truck, payment in, 143, 185

Trustees, Board of, 137–8, 175, 179, 185

Ulster, 11, 13, 57, 98

Union of the Crowns (1603), 13, 49, 56, 79, 82–3

Union of Parliaments (1707), 65, 79, 83–4, 85, 87

Union, Treaty of, 84, 85, 127, 136, 137
Universities, 11–12, 28, 35, 48, 49
Urbanisation, 29, 87–8, 89–90, 96–7, 102, 103, 106, 239; *see* Appendix II

Veere, 60, 61
Villages, industrial, 90, 185, 186; planned, 90

Wages, 40–1, 99, 102, 103, 104, 134, 137, 143, 169, 170, 181, 200, 203, 204, 240–1
Wales, 3, 16, 89, 97, 106, 107, 191, 193, 199, 225
War, 3, 22, 62, 75–6, 112, 122, 133, 207, 211, 222; effects on population, 7, 17–18; mercenaries, 12; civil, 7, 10, 13, 56, 77
Wars of Independence, 17–8, 27–8, 39, 72, 79

Weavers, 46, 48, 119, 158, 166, 169, 170, 171, 173, 181, 182–3, 187
West Indies, 65, 98, 148, 149, 164, 166, 167, 168, 184
West Lothian, 87, 95, 115, 117, 120, 187
Wheat, 119, 120, 122, 123, 129, 206, 207
Whisky, 57, 208; *see* Appendix V(b)
Wholesalers, 139, 140–3; *see* Appendix III
Wigtown, 25, 87, 96
Wilsontown, 166, 190, 191
Wine, 62, 63, 64, 67, 79
Wool, manufacture, 45–8, 113, 133, 149, 170; 171, 224; production, 17, 22, 129, 164; trade, 17, 56, 61, 64, 113, 123–4, 127, 129

Yarn, 57, 144, 145, 169
York Buildings Company, 112, 175, 189
Yorkshire, 17, 113, 126, 145